Lecture Notes of the Institute for Computer Sciences, Social Informatics and Telecommunications Engineering 679

The LNICST series publishes ICST's conferences, symposia and workshops.

LNICST reports state-of-the-art results in areas related to the scope of the Institute.

The type of material published includes

- Proceedings (published in time for the respective event)
- Other edited monographs (such as project reports or invited volumes)

LNICST topics span the following areas:

- General Computer Science
- E-Economy
- E-Medicine
- Knowledge Management
- Multimedia
- Operations, Management and Policy
- Social Informatics
- Systems

Manuel J. C. S. Reis · Nishu Gupta ·
Ahmad Hoirul Basori · Ariel Soares Teles
Editors

Cognitive Computing and Cyber Physical Systems

6th EAI International Conference, IC4S 2025 Andhra Pradesh, India, December 15–17, 2025 Proceedings

Springer

Editors
Manuel J. C. S. Reis
UTAD/IEETA
Vila Real, Portugal

Ahmad Hoirul Basori
King Abdulaziz University
Makkah, Saudi Arabia

Nishu Gupta
VTT Technical Research
Centre of Finland Ltd.
Oulu, Finland

Ariel Soares Teles
Federal Institute of Maranhão
Araioses, Brazil

ISSN 1867-8211 ISSN 1867-822X (electronic)
Lecture Notes of the Institute for Computer Sciences, Social Informatics
and Telecommunications Engineering
ISBN 978-3-032-22833-8 ISBN 978-3-032-22834-5 (eBook)
https://doi.org/10.1007/978-3-032-22834-5

This Springer imprint is published by the registered company Springer Nature Switzerland AG
The registered company address is: Gewerbestrasse 11, 6330 Cham, Switzerland

Preface

We are delighted to introduce the proceedings of the sixth edition of the European Alliance for Innovation (EAI) International Conference on Cognitive Computing and Cyber Physical Systems (EAI IC^{4}S 2025), hosted by Vishnu Institute of Technology, Bhimavaram (VITB), Andhra Pradesh, India, during 15–17 December 2025 in hybrid mode. This conference brought together researchers, developers, and practitioners from around the world who are leveraging and developing intelligent computing systems and cyber-physical systems to make communication smarter, quicker, less expensive, and more accessible in bundles. The theme of EAI IC^{4}S 2025 was "Leveraging cyber-physical systems and cognitive computing to strengthen data security".

The technical program of EAI IC^{4}S 2025 consisted of 27 full papers, presented in hybrid mode by registered authors across six technical sessions and six tracks. The conference tracks were: Track 1 – Signal Processing; Track 2 – Medical Diagnostic and Health Care; Track 3 – AI-Enabled Technologies; Track 4 – AI and IoT Advance Applications; Track 5 – Computing Techniques; Track 6 – Applications of Cyber Physical Systems. These papers were selected from 110 submissions. Each submission was reviewed following a single-blind process with a minimum of 3 reviews per paper. In addition to high-quality technical paper presentations, the technical program featured multiple keynote speeches from eminent speakers. Nishu Gupta, Senior Scientist, VTT Technical Research Centre of Finland Ltd., Oulu, Finland, visited the VITB campus in person, inaugurated the event as the Chief Guest, and delivered the keynote speech on "Advances in 6G Communication". Manuel J. Cabral S. Reis from the University of Trás-os-Montes and Alto Douro, Portugal, also addressed the conference virtually as a General Chair and highlighted open problems for researchers. Other notable keynote and invited speakers included Professor Arun Prakash, MNNIT Allahabad, India; Mohammad Derawi, NTNU, Norway; Ahmad Hoirul Basori, King Abdulaziz University, Saudi Arabia; Ariel Soares Teles, IFMA, Brazil; Srinivasa Kiran Gottapu, Benedict College, USA; and Anil Gupta, Associate Director, CDAC Pune, India.

We sincerely appreciate the continuous guidance and extended support of the Conference Chair, Manuel J. Cabral S. Reis, whose deep involvement helped the conference to proceed smoothly. It was also a great pleasure to work with such an excellent organizing committee team for their hard work in organizing and supporting the conference. In particular, the Technical Program Committee, chaired by Prakash Pareek and Sumita Mishra, coordinated and completed the peer-review process of technical papers and framed a well-designed technical program. We are also grateful to Conference Manager Stella Dao for her support and to all the authors who submitted their papers to EAI IC^{4}S 2025.

We sincerely appreciate the management and administration of Sri Vishnu Educational Society (SVES), Hyderabad, India, and Vishnu Institute of Technology(A), Bhimavaram (VITB), Andhra Pradesh, India, for giving their support to us as the main host Institute of EAI IC^{4}S 2025. We strongly believe that EAI IC^{4}S 2025 provided a strong forum for researchers, developers, and practitioners to discuss scientific and technological aspects of cognitive computing and cyber-physical systems. We also expect that future EAI IC^{4}S conferences will be as successful and stimulating as indicated by the contributions presented in this volume.

Manuel J. C. S. Reis
Nishu Gupta
Ahmad Hoirul Basori
Ariel Soares Teles

Organization

Steering Committee

Chief Patrons

K. V. Vishnu Raju	Sri Vishnu Educational Society, India
Ravichandran Rajagopal	Sri Vishnu Educational Society, India
K. Aditya Vissam	Sri Vishnu Educational Society, India

Patrons

M. Venu Vishnu	Institute of Technology, India
M. Srilakshmi	Vishnu Institute of Technology, India

Co-patrons

M. Dilleep	Vishnu Institute of Technology, India
N. Padmavathy	Vishnu Institute of Technology, India

Organizing Committee

General Chair

Manuel J. Cabral S. Reis	University of Trás-os-Montes and Alto Douro, Portugal

General Co-chair

Mohammad Derawi	Norwegian University of Science and Technology (NTNU), Norway

Program Chairs

Ahmad Hoirul Basori	King Abdulaziz University, Saudi Arabia
Nishu Gupta	VTT Technical Research Centre of Finland Ltd., Finland

Ariel Soares Teles	Federal Institute of Maranhão, Brazil

Host Institute SPOC and Local Chair

Prakash Pareek	Vishnu Institute of Technology, India

Publications Chairs

Prakash Pareek	Vishnu Institute of Technology, India
Nishu Gupta	VTT Technical Research Centre of Finland Ltd., Finland
Manuel J. Cabral S. Reis	University of Trás-os-Montes and Alto Douro, Portugal

Sponsorship and Exhibit Chair

Nishit Malviya	IIIT Ranchi, India

Workshops Chair

Srinivasa Kiran Gottapu	Benedict College, USA

Publicity and Social Media Chairs

S. Mahaboob Hussain	Vishnu Institute of Technology, India
Ch. Venkateswara Rao	Vishnu Institute of Technology, India

Posters and PhD Track Chair

Naveen Mishra	VIT Vellore, India

Panels Chairs

José David Díaz Roman	Autonomous University of Ciudad Juárez, Mexico
Luy Nguyen	Industrial University of Ho Chi Minh City, Vietnam

Demos Chair

Ajay Kumar Kushwaha	Bharati Vidyapeeth (Deemed to be University), India

Tutorials Chair

Naveen Kumar Maurya	Vishnu Institute of Technology, India

Technical Program Committee

Abhinav Gautam	Tyndall National Institute, Ireland
Ahmad Hoirul Basori	King Abdulaziz University, Saudi Arabia
Ajay Kumar	NIT Jamshedpur, India
Amjad Rehman Khan	Prince Sultan University, Saudi Arabia
Angelo Martella	University of Salento, Italy
Anirban Chakraborty	Intel Corporation, USA
Ariel Soales Teres	Federal Institute of Maranhão, Brazil
Ashok Kumar	NIT Srinagar, India
B. Elisha Raju	Vishnu Institute of Technology, India
Ch. Venkateswara Rao	Vishnu Institute of Technology, India
Damla Karagözlü	Cyprus International University, North Cyprus
Dometti Durga Prasad	Vishnu Institute of Technology, India
G. Prasanna Kumar	Vishnu Institute of Technology, India
Idongesit Williams	University of Southern Denmark, Denmark
Jitendra Kumar Mishra	IIIT Ranchi, India
José David Díaz Román	Universidad Autónoma de Ciudad Juárez, Mexico
Lakhindar Murmu	IIIT Naya Raipur, India
Manuel J. Cabral S. Reis	University of Trás-os-Montes and Alto Douro, Portugal
Marco Salvatore Zappatore	University of Salento, Italy
Mauro Mazzei	National Research Council, Italy
N. Padmavathy	Vishnu Institute of Technology, India
Naga Raghavendra Anudeep Tungala	Fujitsu Network Communications, USA
Nguyen Tan Luy	Industrial University of Ho Chi Minh City, Vietnam
Nishit Malviya	IIIT Ranchi, India
A. M. V. Pathi	Vishnu Institute of Technology, India
Polat Goktas	University College Dublin, Ireland
Raghavendra Pal	NIT Surat, India
Rakesh Nayak	O. P. Jindal University, India
Raluca Maria Aileni	University POLITEHNICA of Bucharest, Romania
S. Sugumaran	Vishnu Institute of Technology, India
S. V. S. N. Murthy	Vishnu Institute of Technology, India

Sara Paiva	Instituto Politécnico de Viana do Castelo, Portugal
Shonal Chouksey	IIIT Una, India
Siva Rama Krishna T.	Jawaharlal Nehru Technological University Kakinada, India
Srinivasa Kiran Gottapu	Benedict College, USA
Sumita Mishra	Amity University, India
Surbhi B. Khan	University of Salford, UK
Tiziana Campisi	University of Enna "Kore", Italy
V. Siddhartha	Vishnu Institute of Technology, India
Vishal Krishna Singh	University of Essex, UK

Contents

Signal Processing

Medical Diagnostics and Healthcare

Computing Techniques

Applications of Cyber-Physical Systems

Signal Processing

Analysis of Novel Edge Detection Technique Using Adaptive Hybrid Model

Bittu Kumar(✉), S. Sayooj, Aniket Panda, K. Venkat Prasad, S. Ravi Ratna, and Jogiraju Aruhya

Department of Electronics and Communication Engineering, Koneru Lakshmaiah Education Foundation, Hyderabad 500075, Telangana, India
bittu.mlrit@gmail.com

Abstract. This paper presents an Adaptive Hybrid Edge Detection Method designed to enhance image edge precision and robustness under diverse noise conditions. The proposed approach fuses the complementary characteristics of Sobel and Prewitt operators through an adaptive fusion function that dynamically balances their gradient responses to generate sharper and more continuous edges. The system was tested on clean images and those degraded with Gaussian, Speckle, Poisson, Salt-and-Pepper, and Uniform noise. Performance evaluation using Peak Signal-to-Noise Ratio (PSNR), Mean Squared Error (MSE), and Structural Similarity Index (SSIM) demonstrates that the proposed method consistently outperforms traditional operators. Under noise-free conditions, it achieved a PSNR of 7.1854 dB, MSE of 0.1912, and SSIM of 0.1708, while under Poisson and Salt-and-Pepper noise, the PSNR increased to 8.4763 dB with minimal SSIM degradation. Comparative analysis further shows PSNR improvements of up to 30.45% and MSE reductions exceeding 44% over existing methods. Visual inspection confirms the method's superior ability to maintain edge continuity and suppress noise artifacts. These results validate the effectiveness of the proposed hybrid model for reliable edge detection in real-world imaging scenarios.

Keywords: Image Processing · Edge Detection · Wavelet Transform · Sobel Operator · Prewitt Operator · PSNR · MSE · MAE · SSIM

1 Introduction

Edge detection plays an important role in real-time computer vision systems where accurately pinpointing object boundaries is crucial. This proves it is essential across various fields, including Autonomous Vehicles, Robotic Vision, Medical Image Analysis, Industrial Inspection, and Facial Recognition [1]. In the case of Autonomous Vehicles, dependable edge detection that can manage different weather situations is necessary for detecting lanes and avoiding obstacles. Robotic Vision depends on well-defined edges to handle objects and move through environments. When it comes to Medical Image Analysis, like locating tissue boundaries in MRI scans, accurate edge detection helps doctors make better diagnoses and create effective treatment plans. The performance

M. J. C. S. Reis et al. (Eds.): IC4S 2025, LNICST 679, pp. 3–15, 2026.
https://doi.org/10.1007/978-3-032-22834-5_1

of these applications largely depends on the reliability of the edge detection algorithm, especially when working with images affected by noise that naturally occurs during image capture and transmission [2].

Edge detection techniques generally function by identifying sudden changes in pixel brightness. The Sobel and Prewitt operators represent first-order gradient-based approaches that are straightforward to implement and require less computational resources [3]. While the Prewitt operator consistently computes gradients, the Sobel operator uses kernels that prioritize the center pixel, improving its ability to detect diagonal edges. Unfortunately, both methods are known for their sensitivity to noise. To make the system more robust, researchers have tried hybrid methods that mix different approaches. For example, some methods use multi-scale analysis from Wavelets together with traditional operators to better deal with noise [4].

The primary contribution of this paper is the development of an Adaptive Hybrid Edge Detection Method that enhances the precision and robustness of image edge detection under various noise conditions. The proposed approach integrates the complementary strengths of the Sobel and Prewitt operators through an adaptive fusion function, which dynamically adjusts their responses to generate sharper and more continuous edges. To evaluate the effectiveness of the method, clean images were first subjected to five distinct types of noise—Gaussian, Speckle, Salt-and-Pepper, Poisson, and Uniform—before being processed through the proposed hybrid framework. The performance was then quantitatively analyzed using well-established image quality assessment metrics, including Peak Signal-to-Noise Ratio (PSNR), Mean Squared Error (MSE), Mean Absolute Error (MAE), and the Structural Similarity Index (SSIM). These evaluations provided a comprehensive understanding of the model's accuracy, noise resilience, and structural preservation across diverse conditions. Overall, the study offers valuable insights into the adaptability and efficiency of the proposed hybrid method for edge detection in noisy and real-world imaging environments.

The organization of this paper is as follows. Section 2 reviews previous research on edge detection techniques. Section 3 explains the methodology in detail, while Sect. 4 describes the proposed edge detection approach. Section 5 presents the experimental results and discusses their implications, along with information about the dataset used. Finally, Sect. 6 concludes the study by summarizing the main findings and suggesting possible directions for future work.

2 Literature Survey

Edge detection is a dynamically evolving field, with recent researches based on developing old operators like Sobel, Prewitt, canny etc. and merging them with deep learning concepts. The Sobel and Prewitt operators, as most basic and commonly used methods, continue to be a minimum criterion for performance and simplicity. Their application in medical imaging, however, demands higher precision. In a significant study, authors [5] provided a direct and highly relevant comparison for this research work. They compared the gradient-based Prewitt operator with the Gaussian-based Canny operator specifically for edge detection in ophthalmoscopic cataract images. The importance of selecting an operator based on the specific application is underscored, where it is noted that while smoother edges are provided by the Canny operator, computational advantages and sufficient clarity in certain diagnostic contexts can be offered by the Prewitt operator, which validates the exploration of Prewitt in hybrid models.

Further expanding on the comparison of fundamental techniques, authors in [6] conducted experiments for comparing Otsu Thresholding and Canny Edge Detection for enhancing low-resolution images. The ongoing challenge of achieving robust feature extraction in optimal image quality scenarios is shown in this work, a problem which is directly shown in the present study using hybrid models under various noise conditions. Furthermore, the necessity of evaluating algorithms against real-world problems such as low resolution and noise are considered in this research work.

The most advanced trend in edge detection involves its fusion with deep learning. In [7], authors proposed a robust image steganography approach based on edge detection combined with a Convolutional Neural Network (CNN) algorithm. It is demonstrated that traditional edge detection methods, such as Canny, are not outdated but are being repurposed as crucial pre-processing steps within deep learning pipelines. By using edge maps to identify complex regions for data hiding, they achieved significant improvements in security and robustness, measured by metrics like PSNR. This tells the critical role of high-quality, reliable edge detection the very goal of our hybrid models plays an important role in cutting-edge applications in security and computer vision.

Recent studies have provided a comprehensive overview of the transition in this field, where traditional edge detection operators are being extensively evaluated for specialized applications [5], applied to conventional image processing problems [6], and incorporated as key components in advanced deep-learning architectures [7]. In this work, we propose an adaptive hybrid edge detection model that combines the strengths of the Prewitt and Sobel operators to enhance detection performance. To assess the effectiveness of the proposed method, various evaluation metrics were employed, including Peak Signal-to-Noise Ratio (PSNR) [8], Mean Squared Error (MSE) [9], Mean Absolute Error (MAE), and Structural Similarity Index (SSIM) [10]. Additionally, the performance was tested on images corrupted with five types of noise—Gaussian, Speckle, Salt-and-Pepper, Poisson, and Uniform. The results were then analyzed based on the corresponding quantitative scores. This evaluation provides valuable insights into the robustness and efficiency of the proposed model compared to conventional edge detection techniques under different noisy conditions.

Beyond traditional methods, recent research has focused on feature-level fusion to create more robust detectors. For instance, some approaches have integrated the multi-scale analysis of Wavelet transforms with individual operators like Sobel, showing that such hybrid frameworks can outperform their individual components [11]. This aligns with the main concept of the present works, which seeks an interactive fusion at the feature level. Simultaneously, the field is being transformed by using deep learning architectures like Convolutional Neural Networks (CNNs), particularly architectures like HED [12] and DexiNed [13], learning rich hierarchical feature representations directly from data and set new benchmarks for a better accuracy in edge detection. These data-driven models excel in capturing complex textures and long-range outliers. The potential of CNNs in image processing is further highlighted by their application in relation with traditional techniques, such as in robust steganography systems where edge maps are used to guide data hiding, demonstrating significant improvements in security and robustness. While powerful, deep learning models often come at the cost of high computational complexity and a need for large, annotated datasets. The proposed adaptive hybrid model occupies a valuable middle ground, offering a principled, explainable, and computationally efficient approach that leverages the strengths of classical operators without the huge data and resource requirements of deep learning models.

3 Methodology

In this section, we discussed the methodology for detecting the edge of clean image and noisy image. The block diagram presented in Fig. 1 depicts the comprehensive workflow of the proposed edge detection methodology. The process begins with the acquisition of the input image, which is read into the system for processing. Once the image is loaded, the algorithm measures the edge strength across the image pixels. This step is critical as it quantifies the intensity changes that likely correspond to edges, helping to differentiate between edge and non-edge regions. Following the edge strength measurement, the method performs a search for local directional maxima. This operation identifies pixels that represent the strongest edge responses in particular orientations, thereby refining the detection to focus on meaningful edge structures rather than random noise or weak gradients.

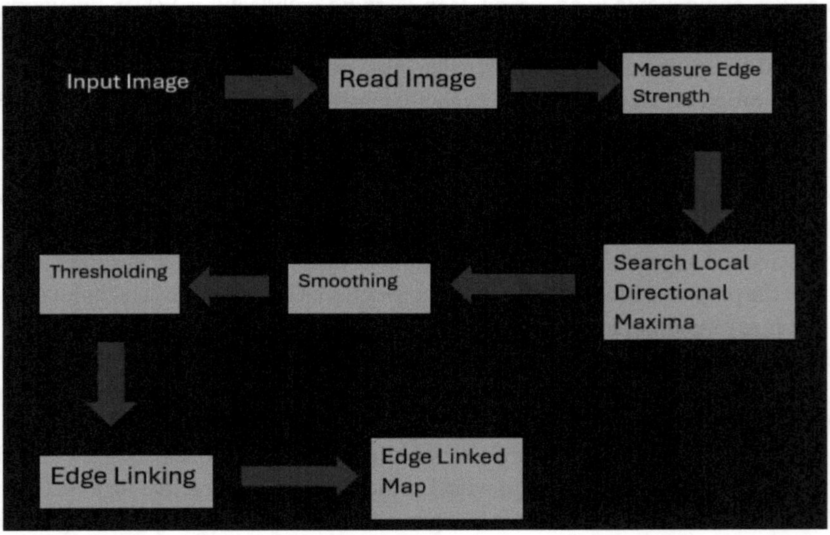

Fig. 1. Block Diagram for Edge Detection Methodology

To further enhance the quality of the detected edges and reduce the impact of noise, a smoothing operation is applied. Smoothing helps to consolidate edge pixels and minimize spurious responses, making the subsequent thresholding more effective. Thresholding is then employed to classify pixels as either edge or non-edge based on the calculated edge strength values, effectively filtering out insignificant edges that do not meet the threshold criteria. After thresholding, the process continues with edge linking, where neighboring edge pixels are connected to form continuous and coherent edge contours. This step is essential for producing an edge map that accurately represents the shape and boundaries of objects within the image. The final output of this sequence is the edge-linked map, which highlights the detected edges in a clear and structured manner, suitable for further analysis or computer vision applications. Overall, the diagram in Fig. 1 outlines a systematic approach to edge detection that integrates edge strength measurement, directional analysis, noise reduction, and connectivity enhancement to improve detection accuracy and robustness across varying image conditions.

4 Proposed Method

To enhance image edge detection accuracy, this paper introduces an Adaptive Hybrid Method, which combines two classical gradient-based techniques—the Sobel and Prewitt operators—through an adaptive fusion function. This integration forms the basis of the proposed adaptive hybrid framework, as illustrated in Fig. 2. The process begins with the input image, which is first converted to grayscale and normalized to maintain consistent intensity levels. Both the Sobel and Prewitt operators are then applied in parallel to extract edge information by detecting intensity gradients in multiple directions. The motivation behind this fusion lies in the complementary strengths of the two operators: Sobel offers higher directional sensitivity but is more susceptible to noise, whereas Prewitt provides smoother gradient estimation.

The outputs from both operators are combined using an adaptive fusion mechanism referred to as the α-map, which dynamically adjusts the contribution of each operator to produce a robust and balanced edge representation. The fused result is further enhanced through Laplacian sharpening (β), which accentuates rapid intensity variations and improves the visibility of edge boundaries. A final normalization step ensures uniform pixel scaling, resulting in a refined edge map with improved clarity and contrast. Overall, the adaptive hybrid approach effectively integrates classical gradient operators with adaptive fusion and sharpening strategies, achieving enhanced edge detection performance and stability across a range of imaging conditions.

The proposed adaptive hybrid model can be mathematically represented as a function that dynamically fuses the gradient magnitudes from the Sobel and Prewitt operators. Suppose, I represent the input grayscale image. First, the horizontal and vertical gradients are computed using the Sobel and Prewitt operators, denoted by the convolution kernels G_x^{Sobel}, G_y^{Sobel},$G_x^{Prewitt}$,$G_y^{Prewitt}$. The magnitude gradient map for Sobel and Prewitt operators are indicated in Eq. (1) and Eq. (2), respectively.

$$M_{Sobel}(i,j) = \sqrt{\left(I * G_x^{Sobel}\right)_{i,j}^2 + \left(I * G_y^{Sobel}\right)_{i,j}^2} \tag{1}$$

$$M_{Prewitt}(i,j) = \sqrt{\left(I * G_x^{Prewitt}\right)_{i,j}^2 + \left(I * G_y^{Prewitt}\right)_{i,j}^2} \tag{2}$$

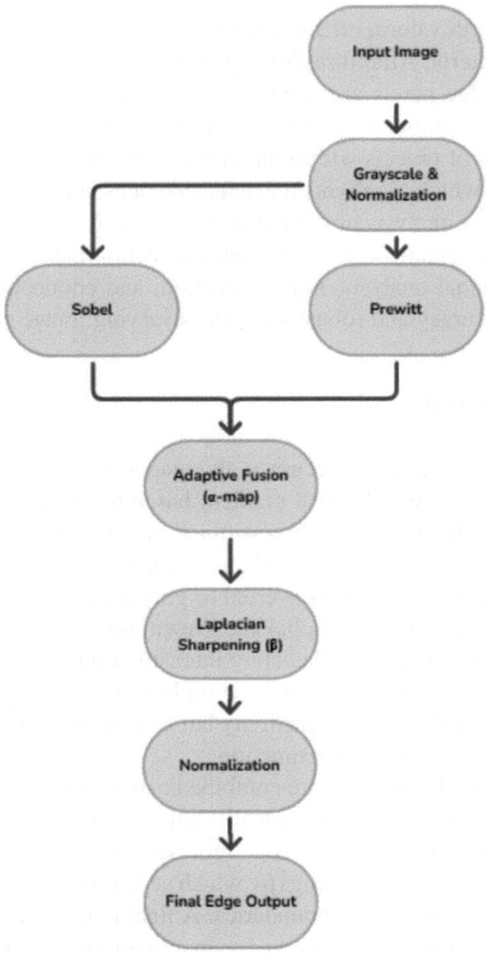

Fig. 2. Proposed adaptive hybrid edge detection framework

Where (i, j) denotes the pixel coordinates, and $*$ is the convolution operator. The main concept of adaptive function is the α-map, $\alpha(i, j)$, which is a pixel-wise weighting matrix. This map is generated based on local image statistics to balance the contribution of each operator. A common method is to base it on the ratio of the local signal-to-noise characteristics or the relative strength of the gradients. The α-value at each pixel is contained between 0 and 1 and shown in Eq. (3).

$$\alpha(i, j) = f(I_{local}(i, j)) \tag{3}$$

Where f is a function that analyses the local patch of I_{local} around pixel (i, j). In next step, the obtained fused output is sharpened using a Laplacian filter to accentuate edge regions. The Laplacian of the fused image is calculated and scaled by a factor β:

$$M_{Sharpened}(i, j) = M_{Fused}(i, j) + \beta.\left(I * \nabla^2\right)_{i,j} \tag{4}$$

Where ∇^2 is the Laplacian Kernel. After computing the above Eq. (4) it is normalized to produce a final edge map, E, which is used for further analysis.

5 Evaluation Matrices

For evaluating the quality of both original and processed images, three assessment metrics were chosen: Peak Signal to Noise Ratio (PSNR), Mean Squared Error (MSE), and the Structural Similarity Index (SSIM). These measurements offer many quantitative evaluations for image accuracy, error levels, and perceptual resemblance, so that comparisons can be made within different operators and methods on how well it assesses in real world situations.

5.1 Peak Signal-to-Noise Ratio

Most used in objective metric and image quality assessment. It quantifies the quality of the processed image by comparing it to the original, clean image. PSNR is expressed in decibels (dB) and measures the ratio of the peak signal (the maximum possible pixel value) to the mean squared error (MSE) between the original and processed images. The formula for PSNR is presented in Eq. (5).

$$PSNR = 10\log\left(\frac{k^2}{MSE}\right) \tag{5}$$

Where, k is the maximum pixel value and MSE is the mean squared error.

5.2 Mean Squared Error

The Mean Squared Error (MSE) represents the cumulative squared error between the original image and the processed image. A lower MSE indicates the lower error rate and better quality. It is defined in Eq. (6).

$$MSE = \frac{1}{RC}\sum_{i=1}^{M}\sum_{j=1}^{N}[I(i,j) - P(i,j)]^2 \tag{6}$$

Where, I is the original image, P is the processed image, and R, C are the dimensions of the images.

5.3 Structural Similarity Index

It is an image quality assessment metric used to measure the structural similarity between two images. SSIM compares the luminance, contrast, and structure of a reference (original) image and a processed (edge-detected) image. It produces a value between −1 and 1, with 1 indicating perfect similarity.

$$SSIM\,(x, y) = \frac{(2\varepsilon_x\varepsilon_y + c_1)(2\sigma_{xy} + c_2)}{\left(\in_x^2 + \in_y^2 + c_1\right)\left(\sigma_x^2 + \sigma_y^2 + c_2\right)} \tag{7}$$

Where, $\in_x$ – image intensity of image x, $\in_y$ – image intensity of image y, σ_x – variance of image x, σ_y – variance of image y, σ_{xy} – covariance of image x and y, and c_1, c_2 – stabilizing constants

6 Results and Discussions

In this paper, research work assesses adaptive hybrid edge detection specifically Prewitt-Sobel through quantitative evaluation under three different noise scenarios. Application of PSNR, MSE is done to measure the error levels and accuracy of the edge maps, while using SSIM to tell how much information is still left structured. By bringing together these different analyses, a complete evaluation of algorithm performance can be taken for a particular edge detection application.

Throughout this research, a thorough assessment of hybrid model was performed by measuring their performance across three essential parameters: Peak Signal-to-Noise Ratio (PSNR), Mean Squared Error (MSE), and Structural Similarity Index (SSIM). For this assessment, an input image was taken from databases, and noise was introduced in the image. More specifically, three distinct noise types: Salt-and-Pepper, Poisson, and Uniform noise [11]. By creating these varied noise conditions, numerous real-world situations are considered and how well the adaptive hybrid model can hold up under different challenges.

6.1 Comparative Analysis of Different Edge Detection Methods

Table 1 presents the comparative performance analysis of various edge detection techniques under different noisy conditions, evaluated using Peak Signal-to-Noise Ratio (PSNR), Structural Similarity Index (SSIM), and Mean Squared Error (MSE) metrics. The results clearly demonstrate that the proposed Adaptive Hybrid Method consistently outperforms traditional operators such as Sobel, Prewitt, Laplacian, and Wavelet across all tested scenarios. Under noise-free conditions, the proposed model achieves a PSNR of 7.1854 dB and an MSE of 0.1912, while maintaining an SSIM of 0.1708, reflecting stable structural preservation. When subjected to various noise models—Poisson, Salt-and-Pepper, and Uniform—the method maintains higher PSNR values and lower MSE compared to conventional algorithms, indicating its enhanced resilience to noise. In particular, the method achieves PSNR values above 8 dB for Poisson and Salt-and-Pepper noise, with minimal degradation in SSIM, highlighting its robustness in preserving edge integrity even under degraded image conditions. Overall, the results in Table 1 confirm that the proposed Adaptive Hybrid Method effectively balances noise suppression and edge sharpness, outperforming traditional techniques in both visual and quantitative evaluations.

Table 1. Performance Analysis of Edge Detection Methods under Different Noisy conditions

Methods	Noise Type	PSNR (dB)	SSIM	MSE
Proposed Method	Original (Noise free)	7.1854	0.1708	0.1912
	Poisson Noise	8.4763	0.1708	0.1420
	Salt & Pepper Noise	8.4763	0.1708	0.1420
	Uniform Noise	7.5746	0.1708	0.1748
Laplacian	Original (Noise free)	5.7799	0.1621	0.2642

(continued)

Table 1. (*continued*)

Methods	Noise Type	PSNR (dB)	SSIM	MSE
	Poisson Noise	5.7878	0.1844	0.2638
	Salt & Pepper Noise	5.8868	0.1184	0.1551
	Uniform Noise	6.2026	0.185	0.2397
Prewitt	Original (Noise free)	6.1551	0.1853	0.2424
	Poisson Noise	6.1600	0.1853	0.242
	Salt & Pepper Noise	6.5039	0.185	0.2237
	Uniform Noise	6.3470	0.1859	0.2319
Sobel	Original (Noise free)	6.1498	0.1859	0.2427
	Poisson Noise	6.1551	0.1859	0.2424
	Salt & Pepper Noise	6.4831	0.185	0.224
	Uniform Noise	6.3565	0.1859	0.2314
Wavelet	Original (Noise free)	6.2647	0.2021	0.2363
	Poisson Noise	6.2768	0.202	0.2357
	Salt & Pepper Noise	6.7257	0.2021	0.2125
	Uniform Noise	6.9404	0.202	0.2023

6.2 Performance Improvement of Adaptive Hybrid Method

To quantitatively assess the effectiveness of the proposed Adaptive Hybrid Edge detection method over classical operators (Sobel, Prewitt, Laplacian, and Wavelet), a percentage improvement table was made for each metric which are PSNR, SSIM, and MSE for across various noise environments. The improvement for each metric is defined as:

$$Improvement\ (\%) = \frac{M_{Hybrid} - M_{Base}}{M_{Base}} \tag{8}$$

Where, M_{Hybrid}represents the metric value (PSNR or SSIM) obtained using the Adaptive Hybrid method and M_{Base}denotes the corresponding metric for a baseline method (e.g., Sobel, Prewitt, Laplacian, or Wavelet).

Table 2. Performance Improvement of Adaptive Hybrid method With Existing Methods/Operators

Noise Type	Compared Methods	PSNR (%)	SSIM (%)	MSE (%)
Original (Noise Free)	Sobel	+16.84	−8.14	−21.22
	Prewitt	+16.74	−7.80	−21.12
	Laplacian	+24.32	+5.40	−27.65

(*continued*)

Table 2. *(continued)*

Noise Type	Compared Methods	PSNR (%)	SSIM (%)	MSE (%)
	Wavelet	+14.70	−15.48	−19.10
Poisson Noise	Sobel	+17.24	−7.62	−21.68
	Prewitt	+17.15	−7.27	−21.59
	Laplacian	+24.64	+5.63	−27.99
	Wavelet	+14.95	−15.29	−19.43
Salt & Pepper Noise	Sobel	+30.45	+197.76	−36.57
	Prewitt	+30.06	+204.41	−36.28
	Laplacian	+43.85	−22.74	−44.81
	Wavelet	+25.51	+33.36	−32.72
Uniform Noise	Sobel	+22.12	+31.77	−27.71
	Prewitt	+22.26	+31.54	−27.83
	Laplacian	+25.41	+40.86	−30.44
	Wavelet	+11.81	+26.55	−17.24

Table 2 illustrates the percentage improvement achieved by the proposed Adaptive Hybrid Method over conventional edge detection operators—Sobel, Prewitt, Laplacian, and Wavelet—under varying noise conditions. The comparative analysis, expressed in terms of PSNR, SSIM, and MSE, demonstrates a consistent performance gain across all metrics and noise types. In noise-free conditions, the proposed method exhibits up to 24.32% enhancement in PSNR and a 27.65% reduction in MSE compared to the Laplacian operator, indicating superior noise suppression and edge clarity. Under Poisson and Salt-and-Pepper noise, the method achieves even higher relative improvements, with PSNR gains exceeding 30% and significant reductions in MSE, reflecting its strong resilience to impulsive and random noise. Additionally, under Uniform noise, improvements in PSNR (up to 25.41%) and SSIM (up to 40.86%) highlight the robustness and adaptability of the proposed hybrid framework. Overall, the performance metrics in Table 2 confirm that the Adaptive Hybrid Method consistently delivers enhanced image quality, structural preservation, and error minimization compared to traditional edge detection techniques across diverse noise environments.

6.3 Visualisation of Processed and Unprocessed Images

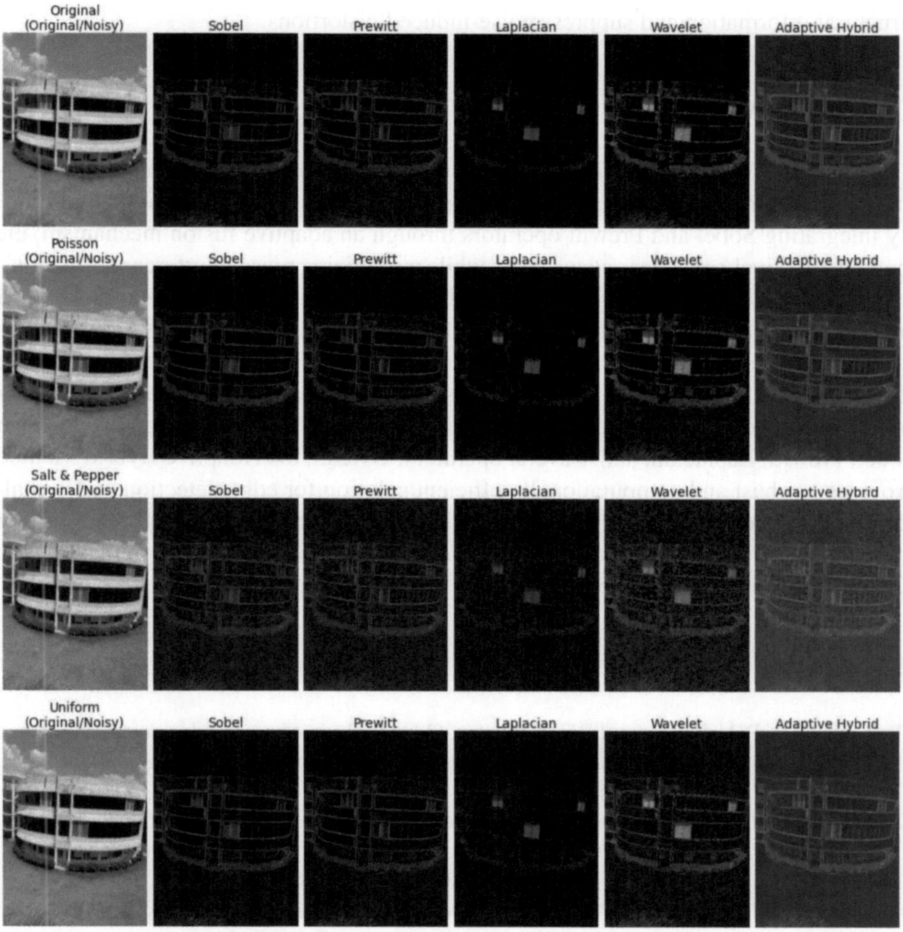

Fig. 3. Visualisation of processed and unprocessed images

Figure 3 illustrates a comparative visual analysis of various edge detection techniques, including the proposed Adaptive Hybrid Method, applied to both noise-free and noisy images. The dataset used for this is standard BSDS500 Jpeg dataset and the model is used to detect edge maps on those images. Also, an image of the library building at "*Koneru Lakshmaiah Education Foundation, Hyderabad (Aziz Nagar, Telangana-500075, India)*", was captured using a standard mobile camera. The first row in Fig. 3 presents the original image alongside the corresponding edge maps generated by the Sobel, Prewitt, Laplacian, Wavelet, and the proposed Adaptive Hybrid methods. To further assess robustness under noise, the same image was artificially degraded with different noise models: Poisson, Salt-and-Pepper, and Uniform and then processed using each edge detection algorithm. The resulting edge maps, as shown in Fig. 3, demonstrate that the proposed Adaptive Hybrid Method consistently produces clearer and more continuous edge structures compared to traditional techniques, even under varying noise conditions. This visual evidence supports the method's enhanced ability to preserve structural information and suppress noise-induced distortions.

7 Conclusion

The proposed Adaptive Hybrid Edge Detection Method demonstrates superior performance in accurately detecting image edges across both clean and noisy conditions. By integrating Sobel and Prewitt operators through an adaptive fusion mechanism, the method effectively enhances edge clarity while minimizing noise interference. Quantitative results reveal that the proposed approach achieves a maximum PSNR of 8.4763 dB and maintains lower MSE values around 0.1420, outperforming conventional methods by up to 30% in PSNR and 44% in MSE reduction. Moreover, the SSIM values indicate stable structural preservation across all noise models. The visual comparisons further confirm that the proposed method generates clearer and more continuous edges than Sobel, Prewitt, Laplacian, and Wavelet operators. Overall, the Adaptive Hybrid Method provides a robust and computationally efficient solution for edge detection under challenging noise environments. Future work will focus on extending this hybrid approach through adaptive weighting strategies or integration with deep learning frameworks to further improve noise adaptability and edge localization accuracy.

References

1. Noviana, L.P.R., Indrawan, I.P.E., Setiawan, G.I.: Analysis of canny edge detection method for facial recognition in digital image processing. Jurnal Manajemen dan Teknologi Informasi (JMTI). **15**(2), 15–22 (2024)
2. Sun, R., et al.: Survey of image edge detection. Front. Signal Process. **2**, 826967 (2022)
3. Ansari, M.A., Kurchaniya, D., Dixit, M.: A comprehensive analysis of image edge detection techniques. Int. J. Multim. Ubiquitous Eng. **12**(11), 1–12 (2017)
4. Amer, G.M.H., Abushaala, A.M.: Edge detection methods. In: 2015 2nd World Symposium on Web Applications and Networking (WSWAN), pp. 1–7. IEEE (2015)
5. Kumar, L.S., PIndira, K.: Comparison of gradient based Prewitt operator with Gaussian based canny operator for edge detection in ophthalmoscopic cataract images. In: AIP Conference Proceedings. AIP Publishing LLC (2025)
6. Ramadhan, R.P., Pahrizal, P., Apridiansyah, Y.: Eksperimen Perbandingan Otsu Thresholding dan Canny Edge Detection Terhadap Peningkatan Kualitas Citra Beresolusi Rendah. Ranah Res. J. Multidiscipl. Res. Dev. **7**(3), 2210–2216 (2025)
7. Al-Rawashdeh, R., Rahman, M.M., Niazi, M.: Robust image steganography approach based on edge detection combined with CNN algorithm. IEEE Access. **13**, 109099–109115 (2025)
8. Prasad, S., et al.: An analysis of image quality enhancement techniques in an optical based satellite image. In: International Conference on Advancements in Smart, Secure and Intelligent Computing (ASSIC), pp. 1–5 (2022)
9. Chand, R.K., et al.: Implementation of panoramic image stitching using python. In: 14th IEEE International Conference on Computing Communication and Networking Technologies (ICCCNT), pp. 1–7 (2023)

10. Kumar, B., Jyothi, K.S., Sudhanshu, B.S., Shreya, K., Pavani, G., Kumbhare, V.R.: Performance investigation of different ImageDenoising algorithms. In: 2024 15th International Conference on Computing Communication and Networking Technologies (ICCCNT), pp. 1–6. IEEE (2024)
11. Kumar, B., Varshith, N., Nikhitha, K.S., Sony, N., Koushik, G., Karthikeya, R.L.: Performance investigation on panoramic image stitching techniques. In: Internation Conference on Cognitive Computing and Cyber Physical Systems (IC4S) Lecture Notes of the Institute for Computer Sciences, Social Informatics and Telecommunications Engineering, vol. 599. Springer, Cham (2025)
12. Xie, S., Tu, Z.: Holistically-nested edge detection. In: Proceedings of the IEEE International Conference on Computer Vision (ICCV), pp. 1395–1403 (2015)
13. Soria, X., Riba, E., Sappa, A.: Dense extreme inception network: towards a robust CNN model for edge detection. In: Proceedings of the IEEE/CVF Winter Conference on Applications of Computer Vision (WACV), pp. 1913–1922 (2020)

HOKMEM-QLDE: Ml Based Clustering and Routing Mechanism Using for Wireless Sensor Networks

Venu Mangipdui(✉) and G. Aloy Anuja Mary

Vel Tech Rangarajan Dr, Sagunthala R&D Institute of Science and Technology, Avadi, Chennai, Tamil Nadu, India
nkv8593@gmail.com

Abstract. Wireless Sensor Networks (WSNs) offer powerful technology for sensing and transmitting information across wide geographical regions. However, WSNs still facing some challenges like unreliable node clustering, low energy efficiency, and limited network lifetime in realistic deferments. To address this limitations and improve the energy efficiency of WSNs, it is often required to separate sensors into clusters and establish routing to conserve energy. Machine Learning (ML) algorithms can potentially automate these processes, reducing energy consumption and prolong lifetime of network. This research investigates the application of ML algorithms, specifically Q-Learning and K-means clustering to introduce a novel ML based Clustering and Routing approach for network. In this proposed methodology, Elbow method embedded K-means algorithm is presented for cluster formation, and Q-learning with Differential Evolution is introduced for routing path selection. Our simulation results shows the effectiveness of the proposed HoKMEM-QLDE approach with the existing approaches such as existing IoNM-BSOLyD approach and CSPBOT-boQIEKC techniques. These incorporates maximized alive nodes, reduced power consumption, high residual energy, and enhanced throughput with prolonged network lifetime.

Keywords: WSNs · Energy Efficiency · Machine Learning · Clustering · Routing

1 Introduction

WSN is a group of specialized sensor nodes which is consistently shared to monitor and report physical environmental factors [1] such as temperature, humidity, pressure, vibration, and lighting in various locations and arrange the gathered data in a internal site. These SNs can be mobile or static and are deployed in geographical area where human intervention may be difficult. In addition, there is no fixed network infrastructure in such areas, so that WSN obtain self organization, self-configuration, self-healing, and dynamic topology qualities [2]. The basic architecture of the network is stated in Fig. 1.

WSN communication modes refers the information transmission from source node to the destination node. The data transmission take place in two different ways such as single

M. J. C. S. Reis et al. (Eds.): IC4S 2025, LNICST 679, pp. 16–36, 2026.
https://doi.org/10.1007/978-3-032-22834-5_2

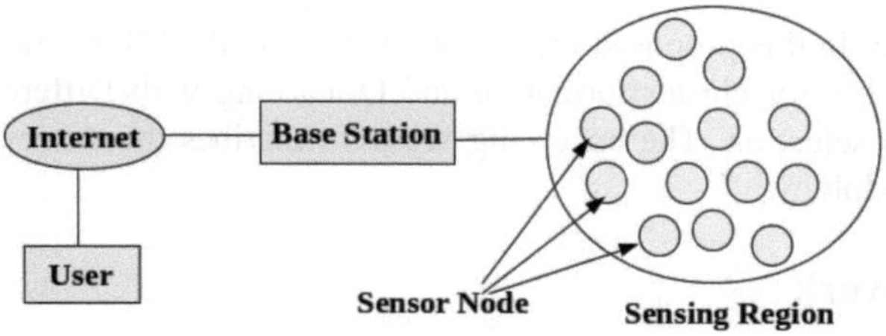

Fig. 1. WSN Architecture

hop or multi-hop [3]. In single hop, there is one direct line between the source and destination nodes, so that the data transmission is done via single networking device, where as in multi-hop transmission, the data travels between multiple networking devices.

Majority of WSN uses multi-hop transmission, because of this flexibility and scalability of multi-hop WSNs. It also maintains a good amount of energy and make efficient data routing [4]. Multi-hop networks are more reliable than the single-hop networks due to the use of redundant paths and their capability to compensate for node failures.

Traditional WSN is composed of several SNs and a sink. The major role of the SN is to monitor the environment in which it deployed and collect the data. The gathered data is then transmitted to the sink node. This sink node is connected to the sever and sends the data from the SNs to the server [5].

Once the SNs are deployed, the power that the SNs are hold with is limited and unchangeable. This obviously makes power and energy one of the major critical resources of a WSN. Therefore, the investigation is most to know how to use the restricted asserts, attain balanced load among SNs, and prolong network lifetime is a major issue in WSNs [6]. It clearly states that the energy efficient routing algorithms can effectively deduce the energy consumption and prolong network lifetime.

It is attain by controlling the data flow via specific node selection and clustering. The high hierarchical CH nodes are used by routing algorithm. It accept and process the sensing information evenly inside each cluster once the SNs have been segregated into multiple clusters. Due to this reason, the SNs in the cluster avoids the power consumed by the data forwarding [7].

In recent days, ML techniques have addressed the demerits of the traditional routing algorithm in WSN. ML propose flexible and adaptive method, which have a capability to handle the complex information and computational demands that is integrated with the effective routing algorithms in WSNs [8]. The demerits of the traditional clustering and routing algorithms are limited scalability and flexibility, limited data aggregation, and energy inefficiency.

Therefore, WSNs leads to the integration of advanced ML algorithms for both clustering and routing. To improve the self-reliance of the network, ML techniques are being investigated for some major tasks such as clustering, CH election, routing path discovery, and data aggregation. It effectively improves the network lifetime by reducing the energy consumption and optimizing routing path selection. This research work focuses mainly on the cluster formation and routing path selection.

The efficiency of the proposed methodology is estimated depends on the three major indicators such as enhanced energy efficiency, optimized routing path and extended network lifetime. In this proposed methodology, we use the Elbow method embedded K-means algorithm for cluster formation and Q-learning with Differential Evolution for routing path selection. The upcoming section describes the survey related to this proposed methodology.

2 Related Work

This chapter explains several researches, which is related to WSN, including WSN based clustering, multiple optimization technique, and hybrid optimization in WSN.

Halimjon, et al. presented an energy-efficient clustering approach utilizing chaotic GA, and also enhanced am power saving routing system by utilizing a bio-inspired GWO technique. However, it had high computational complexity and limited scalability in large networks, and also it has sensitivity to parameter tuning [9]. Ghofrane Fresi introduced a Fog based per to peer routing protocol for mobile IoT. This methodology managed to save time and energy and to handle mobility of IoT nodes. But this algorithm is unsuitable for network with frequent topology changes and also have potential delay in large scale networks [10].

Preesat Biswas, et al. proposed a ML improved self-management for energy effective and secure statistic collection in neglected WSNs. This model is not effective in highly dynamic networks with frequent changes [11]. Mandli Rami Reddy, et al. presented an energy-efficient CH election in WSN utlizing an enhanced Grey Wolf Optimization algorithm. It is only suitable for homogeneous network. It is unsuitable for dynamic or heterogeneous networks [12].

Vishwas and Ramesh investigates some recent technologies in localization, routing and security for WSNs. It also focused on some vulnerabilities such as data interception, network interruption, and node penetration. However, the assumption only on static node deployment and may not perform well in highly dynamic networks [13]. Gunjan, et al. presented a GA based on unequal clustering and routing protocol for WSNs. Here, CH is elected by considering three fitness functions such as remaining energy of CH nodes, distance between CH and BS, and internal cluster partition. It may not work efficiently in small networks or network with uniform SNs [14].

Rupendra Pratap and Abhishek presented a dynamic CH election in WSN. Two stage clustering is done in which the stage is chosen by exhaustive search approach. The computational cost of this approach is high and difficulty in handling real time updates [15]. Hazre, et al. introduced an efficient routing awareness depends on the organizing approach in energy harvesting WSNs to address some major issues like several network load functions, coverage maintenance, routing and clustering. It is limited by the efficiency of energy harvesting technologies and potential communication delays [16].

Huangsgui, et al. introduced a PSO and fuzzy logic-based clustering and routing protocol. In addition, an adaptive maintenance approach is utilized to schedule the clusters to diminish computation and message overheads. It may lead to slow convergence in real time applications [17]. Akila and Deepa presented an improved CH election for WSN using chemical reaction optimization algorithm. The energy efficiency is done by considering the intra-cluster depends on distance, the remaining energy and sink distance. It require significant computation for large scale networks and also limit the real time applicability [18].

Patidar, et al. presented an optimal stable CH selection for high throughput and prolong network lifetime of Homogeneous WSNs. Here, the Kopt election is done for the optimal election of CHs. Multiple limitations are applied in large scalar networks [19]. Nithya, et al. introduced a investigation on managing energy efficiency is carried out based on distributed algorithm. Here, the energy consumption is deduced by using hybrid energy based multi-user routing protocol. It may not scale well for highly dynamic networks or frequent topology changes [20]. Based on this survey, this proposed approach is designed and implemented effectively to overcome the drawback of some existing approaches.

3 System Model

3.1 Network Model

In this proposed HoKMEM-QLDE methodology, the IoT network model consists of centralized BS, which holds immense power supply and internet connectivity. It also holds various power-constrained IoT devices that is positioned in the sensing field in a random manner. These devices are classified into three divisions such as Cluster Member (CM), Cluster Head (CH), and free nodes, which is clearly pictured in Fig. 2.

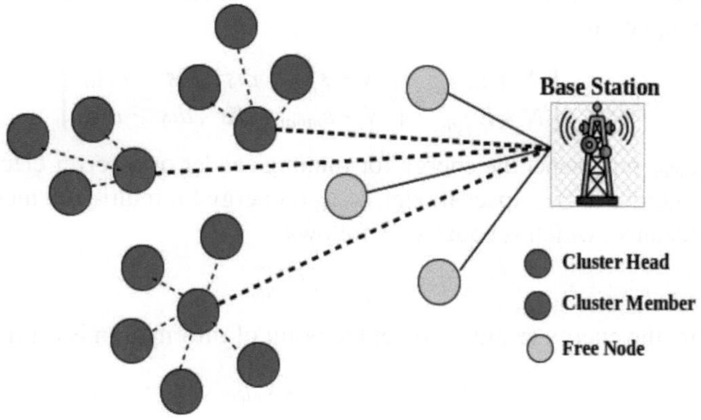

Fig. 2. WSN Clustering Network Model

To shorten the analysis and algorithm design, the upcoming assumptions are made:

Static Topology: Once positioned, entire IoT devices or Sensor Nodes (SNs) persist fixed during the operational lifetime of the networks.

Location Update: Update the specific location of all SNs in the network to the BS to enable the centralized decision making and optimization.

Node Correlation: Check all the SNs are identical in the midst of basic energy levels, communication range, and data processing capabilities.

Dynamic Role Allocation: Nodes in WSN can dynamically fluctuate the roles among typical nodes and CHs as required. It happens based on the decision of clustering and routing.

Flexible Transmission Power: Depends on the distance to the acceptor, each SN in the network adjusts the transmission power to stimulate energy-efficient communication.

Cluster Head Energy Dissipation: The CHs perform multiple tasks such as data aggregation and forwarding. The energy required for this data aggregation is estimated as follows,

$$Eg_{DA} = N * Eg_{aggr} \tag{1}$$

Data Report: SNs sense the environmental information and transmitted directly to the BS or through the designated CHs at fixed intervals, based on the network topology.

The following assumptions are made regarding the network model for the proposed methodology.

1. Entire SNs in WSN are static.
2. Sensors are homogeneous with the similar initial energy.
3. Only one static BS is available far from the sensing field.
4. The BS knows the geographical position of sensor nodes.
5. All cluster heads send the aggregated information to the BS.
6. The security of the network is addressed.

3.2 Energy Model

IoT devices use majority of their energy by sending and receiving data. Total volume of energy utilized to send N-bit of information over distance (dis) is computed by using the following equation,

$$Eg_{Tn} = \begin{Bmatrix} N * Eg_{elect} + N * \varepsilon_{fsm} * dis^2, dis < dis_0 \\ N * Eg_{elect} + N * \varepsilon_{mpm} * dis^2, dis \geq dis_0 \end{Bmatrix} \tag{2}$$

where, Eg_{elec} represents the energy for running sender or receiver electronics. ε_{fsm} indicates the energy for free space model, ε_{mpm} is energy for multi-path model, and dis_0 is threshold distance, which is equated as follows,

$$dis_0 = \sqrt{\varepsilon_{fsm}/\varepsilon_{mpm}} \tag{3}$$

In addition, the energy required to get the N-bit of information is estimated as,

$$Eg_{rev}(N) = N * Eg_{elect} \tag{4}$$

If the transmission distance is relatively low, then the power amplification energy under free-space propagation is indicated as ε_{fsm}. On the other hand, in the multi-path fading model, ε_{mpm} is an amplification factor for long distance transmissions. When the actual transmission distance (dis) is greater than the dis0, the multi-path model is used or else free space model is employed.

4 Proposed HoKMEM-QLDE Model

In this proposed HoKMEM-QLDE methodology, initially, clustering is done by using k-means clustering algorithm. Moreover, this clustering algorithm is embedded with Elbow Method to regulate the optimal number of clusters from a dataset. After clustering, the CH is elected based on some fitness function. Finally, routing is performed by the Integration of Q-learning algorithm with Differential Evolution (IoQLDE) approach.

4.1 K-Means Algorithm for Clustering

This algorithm is a most prominent unsupervised Machine Learning (ML) technique. It elects the cluster center from the input data in a random manner. Figure 3 shows the diagrammatic view of K-means algorithm.

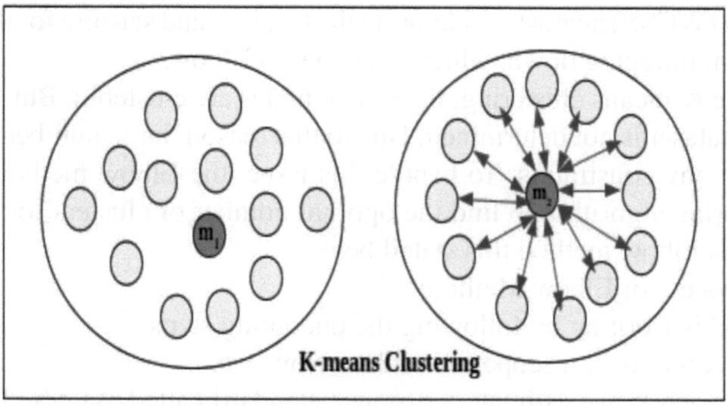

Fig. 3. Schematic diagram of K-means algorithm

Each iteration defines the cluster depends on the centroid election. This kind of election can lead to unstable or empty clusters. Here, the data points and desired number of clusters are consider as input and a set of clusters as output. It effectively presents the procedure for electing and rotating the CHs in WSNs. Step-by-Step procedure to do the K-means clustering is stated below:

1. Initialization: At first, K cluster centers are selected. It can be performed by electing the k-data points from the dataset in a random manner. Otherwise, utilize the domain specific knowledge or heuristics.
2. Allotting Data points to Clusters: For each data point, the Euclidean distance is estimated between the point and each cluster center. Later, the data point is determined to the cluster with the nearest center.
3. Reevaluating Cluster Centers: After assigning data points to the cluster, the cluster centers are reevaluated by estimating the mean value of the data points, which is allocated to each cluster in the network. It clearly serves the updated centroid for the cluster.
4. Convergence: Steps 2 and 3 are repeated in an iterative manner until the convergence is obtained. This convergence happens when the cluster center no longer sustain meaningful modification or when a predetermined iterations is met. During each round, data points are lifted to their closest cluster center, and centroids are reevaluated appropriately
5. Final Cluster: Upon convergence, the final clusters are output. Each cluster holds the data point, which is nearest to its centroid. Therefore, well-defined clusters are formed to represent input data distribution.

The K-means algorithm converged when the modification in the cluster centroids between consecutive iterations was lesser than the predefined threshold of 0.001 or after

100 iterations. This effectively ensures both accuracy and computational efficiency. While, this algorithm is very sensitive to initial centroid placement, we mitigate this via multiple initializations. Figure 4 shows the Flowchart for k-means algorithm.

In K-means clustering, the algorithm segregates information into k number of clusters by reducing distance between the points and their cluster center. Still, selecting the ideal k is non-straight forward. Here, the elbow method is used help by plotting Within Cluster Sum of Squares (WCSS) against accelerating the k values and sensing for the point where the enhancement dragging down, which is known as Elbow.

By using the K-means clustering, the sensor nodes are clustered. But, the number of cluster for the dataset is not determined. Due to this reason, large number of clusters are formed without any constraints. To handle this issue, the Elbow method is embedded with this clustering algorithm to find the optimal number of clusters for a dataset. The workflow of this Elbow method this stated below:

Working Process of Elbow Method:

This method is working by following the upcoming steps:

Step 1: We repeat over a scope of k-values from 1 to n.

Step 2: For each k, we estimate a distance standard called WCSS. This states that how to spread the data points within each cluster. This WCSS is estimated as follows:

$$WCSS = \sum_{a=1}^{k} \sum_{b=1}^{n_a} distance\left(p^{(a)b} c_a\right)^2 \tag{5}$$

This equation indicates the distance between the bth data point in the p(a)b in cluster a and the cluster center ca of that cluster.

Step 3: We tried this for different number of cluster. For each cluster, we process k-means and estimate the WCSS value.

Step 4: We patch the graph with k cluster in X-axis and WCSS on the Y-axis.

Step 5: Value of cluster k is inversely proportional to WCSS. Typically, the WCSS deceased because we are making more clusters, which lean to get several information variant. Nevertheless, there comes a point where updating more clusters results in only a marginal deduce in WCSS. So that, we notice an Elbow shape in the graph.

In this proposed EM embedded KM approach, the sensor node in WSN are clustered efficiently to regulate the optimal number of clusters for a dataset in the K-Means clustering algorithm. After clustering, the election of CH is done depends on some fitness function that is stated below.

4.2 Cluster Head Selection

After clustering, the selection of CH is done depends on the fitness function such as energy consumption and communication distance distribution. initially, this fitness function mainly focused on the energy consumption of the SNs to deduce the energy consumption of the elected CHs. Second section of the fitness function is the communication distance variability. This distance measurement is between the nodes and their respective CHs.

Some of the node are too near or distant from the CH. Due to this reason, the poor communication is occurred by ensuring that the CHs are distributed equally by reducing

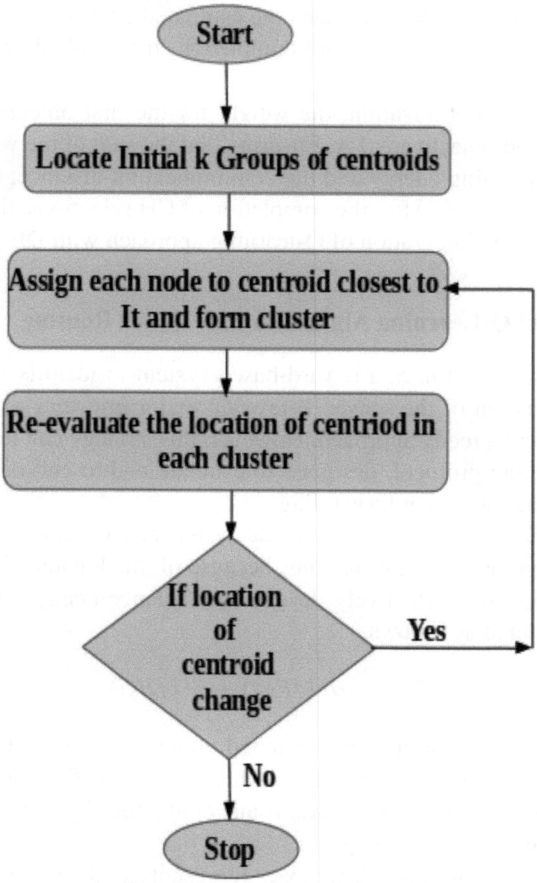

Fig. 4. Flowchart for K-means Algorithm.

the variance. This fitness function is assessed a population of the potential CH formations. This algorithm optimizes by exploring multiple options to prevent premature convergence. It also preserve the diversity. It can strike balance between network connection and energy efficiency to provide guaranteed that the elected CH can maintain balance and better communication across the network, and also it minimizes the energy consumption. The fitness function is estimated as follows:

$$Ft = x.\sum\nolimits_{a=1}^{k} Egy_s(K_a) + (1-x).k.L \tag{6}$$

where L is evaluated as follows,

$$L = \sqrt{\frac{1}{k-1}\sum\nolimits_{a=1}^{k}\left(R_s(K_a) - \frac{1}{k}\sum\nolimits_{b=1}^{k} R_s(K_b)\right)} \tag{7}$$

where Ft is the variable that represents the numerical quantity of the objective mathematical relation of the network in the s-th transmission round. k represents the total number of active SNs. $E_{gys}(Ka)$ indicates the estimated energy consumption of SN Ka during t-th round. After the s-th round completion, the residual energy in SN Ka is denoted by $R_s(Ka)$.

In a two-objective optimization, the weight for the first objective is x, while the weight for the second objective is 1-x. Ensuring that the sum of the weights equals to 1. Depends on the remaining energy and the communication distance, the best SNs from the cluster is elected as CH. After the completion of CH selections, the routing is about to perform by using the integration of Q-learning approach with DE algorithm.

4.3 Integration of Q-Learning Algorithm with De for Routing

The Q-learning method utilizes a reward-based system to identify the optimal action depends on information of the sensor. It provide major priorities actions with highest Q-value, employing a greedy approach. However, this strategy can lead to convergence issues. This Q-routing protocol, designed to evaluate end-to-end delay, elects the SN with lowest Q-value for packet forwarding.

While this technique aims to reduce the delay, it needs multiple attempts to coverage and may suffer from outdated estimations, because of the dynamic nature of networks. The reward function was effectively designed to balance energy efficiency and path optimality. It is defined as follows,

$$Rwd = \alpha(1/Egy) + \beta(1/HC) \tag{8}$$

where, E_{gy} indicates the energy consumed along with the route. HC denotes the hop count, α and β are weighting factors, which are set to 0.6 and 0.4, respectively. prioritizing energy efficiency slightly over route length. Step by step procedure to do the Q-learning algorithm are stated below.

Step 1. Define the state space: This space represents all the possible states the agent can encounter, influenced by the issue and environment.

Step 2. Define the action space: This space encompasses all feasible actions the agent can undertake in each state, determined by the issue and environment.

Step 3. Define the reward function: This function estimates a signal of scalar reward depends on the current state and action, guiding the agent to enhance the cumulative reward at particular period of time. Here, the reward reflects transmission delay estimates, with lower delays yielding higher rewards.

1. Initialize the Q-table: It maps each pair to a Q-value which indicates the expected cumulative reward if the agent elects that the action in that state and acts optimally. Here, the pair denotes the state and the action. In the beginning, the Q-table is initialized with zeros.
2. Repeat for each episode:
   a. Elect an initial state: The agent begins in an initial state.
   b. Repeat until the episode terminates:
      i. Elect an action: Employing an exploration strategy, the agent elects the action in the current state, balancing trying new actions and exploiting known optimal ones.

ii. Action Execution: Employing an exploration/ exploitation strategy, the agent elects an action in the current state, balancing between trying new actions and exploiting known optimal actions.
iii. Observe new state and reward: The agent observes the new state and the reward from executing the selected action.
iv. Update Q-Value: By using the Q-learning equation, the agent updates the Q-value for the current pair, by considering the current and expected future rewards.

c. Update State: The agent transitions to the new state observed in the previous step.

Step 4. Utilize the learned Q-Table: Once the agent completes multiple episodes and updates its Q-table, it can make real-time decisions. The agent elects the action associated with the highest Q-value by referencing the Q-value for the current state.

This Q-learning algorithm is embedded with the Differential Evolution (DE) algorithm, which is a population based stochastic optimization method. It effectively improves the candidate solutions to the global optimizations issues by utilizing some basic concepts like mutation, crossover, and selection to find the better solution. Figure 5 illustrates the flowchart of QLDE algorithm. The main objective of this QLDE algorithm for routing is also used to indicate the clustering issues, while the Elbow method is used to determine the optimal number of clusters for k-means algorithm.

The expedition of the parameter setup for DE algorithm has been current for several years. Still, the relationship between the parameters and performance remains defined inadequate. The existence of the scaling factor F in conventional DE limits its capability to accommodate to demand faced during searching such as stagnation.

To solve this problem, a hybrid approach that integrates Q-learning with DE algorithm is presented. By enabling this integrated algorithm, the scaling factor can be adapted autonomously without need for predefined parameter setup during the entire searching process. Moreover, the conventional Q-learning algorithm frequently encounters the endangerment of becoming cornered in local optima during searching. To address this challenge and incorporate with DE algorithm, a dynamic ε greedy strategy is presented to enhance the expected selection process in Q-learning

By integrated randomness, this technique prevents the agent from converging to a local optimum at the learning phase. It effectively enhances the likeliness of discriminating the global optimum. The updates Q-table can be estimated as follows:

$$expQ = \begin{Bmatrix} maxQ\left(s_{t+1}, x'\right), \textit{if}\,(\text{rand} < 1 - \varepsilon.l/l_{max}) \\ \text{rand}_{choice}, else \end{Bmatrix} \tag{9}$$

$$Q(s_t, x_t) = Q(s_t, x_t) + \alpha\left[p_{t+1} + \gamma.expQ - Q(s_t, x_t)\right] \tag{10}$$

where, ε denotes the greedy threshold. Here, the high measure shows the high randomness. Randchoice is to elect an action from a predefined group of actions in a random manner.

In this proposed HoKMEM-QLDE methodology, the probability based Softmax strategy is working for action election to regulate the highest likely action in which the

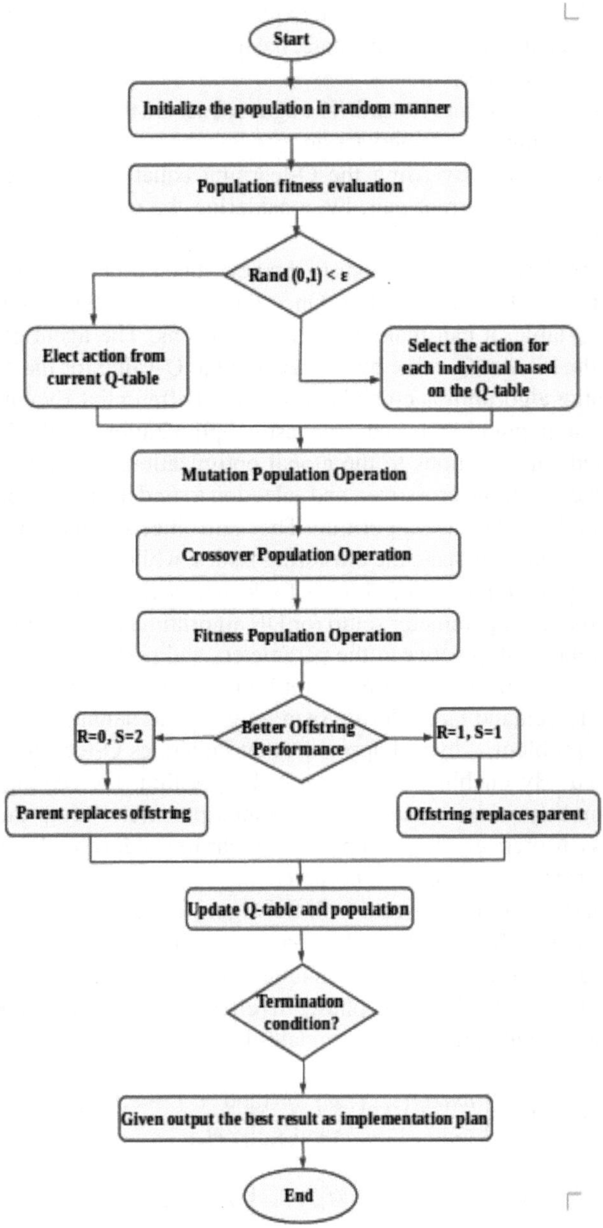

Fig. 5. Flowchart for QLDE Algorithm

Q-leaning would process in a particular state, which is described as follows,

$$\pi(s_a, x_b) = Softmax\left[Q(s_a, x_b)\right] = \frac{\exp\left[Q(s_a, x_b)\right]}{\sum_{b=1}^{J}\exp\left[Q(s_a, x_b)\right]} \tag{11}$$

where, $\pi(s_a, x_b)$stands for the probability of taking action$x_b$in states_a. J denotes the total number of possible actions of the agent.

At last, each individualist is appointed a separated scaling factor, with three specified behaviors: $\lambda = -0.01$, $\lambda = 0$, and $\lambda = -0.01$, guaranteed that the scaling factor can be adaptively modified. Moreover, a reward of R = 1 and a state of S = 1 are granted to the agent only when the fitness value of the trail individualist transcend that the parent period of time or else reward is set to R = 0 and the state to S = 2. The entire process of this novel QLDE methodology is clearly shown in Fig. 4. The betterment approach for the ath individual via Q-learning is illustrated as follows,

$$F_a = F_a + \lambda_a \tag{12}$$

where F_a and λ_a denotes the scaling factor and betterment factor related to the ath individual. The merits to embed the DM with QL is to fasten the convergence speed, ability to handle different constraints, versatility and adaptability.

4.3.1 Proposed HoKMEM-QLDE Algorithm

The upcoming steps are clearly stated that how the k-means and Q-learning algorithm are integrated together.

Step 1: WSN Network Model Initialization

A static network topology is defined, with N number of SNs deployed in 400 x 400 m2 sensing region.

Each SN is initialized with 10 J of initial energy.

BS is situated in the outside of the sensing region at coordinates (410, 410).

Each SN starts with an equal probability of being elected as a CH.

Step 2: Cluster Formation using K-means Algorithm

The clustering process is done by following the below mentioned steps,

Initial Cluster Centroids: This algorithm elects the K initial centroids from the SN locations in the random manner.

Assignment of SNs to nearest cluster center: The Euclidean distance between the each SN and cluster center is calculated.

Determination of Cluster: The Elbow approach is a heuristic that is utilized to regulate the number of clusters in the dataset

Updating Cluster Center: The center locations are re-estimated depends on the mean value of the all SNs assigned to the cluster.

CH Election: The SN with high remaining energy with minimum distance to the BS in each cluster, coverage, distance between the nodes in the same cluster, degree of each node and the energy that is left behind is elected as CH.

Rotational CH: The rotation of CHs are obtained in a periodic manner to ensure the balanced energy consumption.

Step 3: Routing Path Election Using QLDE algorithm: After the cluster formation, the QLDE algorithm is applied to elect the optimal routing paths:

State (S): Each SN denotes the state.

Action (A): The group of adjacent nodes in which the data can be transmitted.

Reward (R): The Reward function is defined as:

$$R = \alpha(1/Egy) + \beta(1/Hp) \tag{13}$$

where, Egy indicates the energy of the node, Hp is the hop count, and α and β are weighting factors.

Q-table Initialization: The Q-table is initialized to store the Q-value of each pair.

Selecting best Next-Hop node: Using an ε greedy strategy, a SN either:

Exploits: Choose the path with the highest Q-value (or)

Explores: Elects the new route with the probability (ε) in a random manner.

Updating Q-Values: After electing, a next hop node and receiving feedback, the Q-value is updated by using following equation,

$$QL = Q(s, a) \tag{14}$$

$$QL = QL + \alpha\left[R(s, a) + \gamma maxQ\left(s', a'\right) - QL\right] \tag{15}$$

where, t denotes the discount factor, and Q (s', a') denotes the maximum Q-value of the next state. While routing DE with QL is implemented to minimize the delay, maximize the bandwidth utilization and balancing the network load.

Packet Forwarding: The SN with the highest Q-value in its routing table is elected as the next-hop SN.

Termination Condition: The above-mentioned process is repeated until the data reaches the BS.

5 Results and Discussion

In this section, the results of the proposed HoKMEM-QLDE methodology is analyzed and presented and their comparison is made with existing IoNM-BSOLyD approach and CSPBOT-boQIEKC techniques. According to the results, this proposed HoKMEM-QLDE methodology performs better than the other existing techniques. This proposed HoKMEM-QLDE methodology shows better scalability, better average energy consumption, and better throughput, and also concerns about the number of alive nodes.

5.1 Experimental Setup

The performance of this proposed HoKMEM-QLDE methodology is evaluated by comparison and implementation in MATLAB R2014a. The simulation values of different parameters in WSN are tabulated in Table 1.

Table 1. Simulation parameters in WSN

Parameters	Value
Simulation Platform	MATLAB R2014a
Total Number of Nodes	100 & 400
Number of Rounds	200 & 600
Nodes Initial Energy	10 J
Transmission Energy	50 nJ/bit
Free Space Model Amplifier	10 pJ/bit/m2
Multi-path Model Amplifier	0.0013 pJ/bit/m4
Energy needed for data aggregation	5nJ/bit
Sensing Area	400 x 400 m2
Location of BS (x,y)	410 x 410
Communication Model	Multi-hop WSN
Data Packet Size	512 bytes
Used Energy Model	First Order Radio Model
Cluster formation method	K-means clustering with Elbow Method
Routing Algorithm	Q-Learning Algorithm with Differential Evolution algorithm

5.2 Evaluation Criteria

The evaluation of this proposed HoKMEM-QLDE methodology was based on the four different performance metrics such as alive nodes, average energy consumption, residual energy level, and packet reception rate.

5.2.1 Alive Nodes Measurements

Number of SNs still having the remaining energy even after the given number of rounds are over. Here, after every round, the energy of each SN is checked. If the energy drops to zero, then the SN is marked as dead. The count of nodes still alive is recorded at each round.

Number of alive nodes refers to the total number of SNs that are currently active and operational in the network. It is estimated by subtracting the number of dead nodes with zero energy from the total number of nodes in entire WSN.

Table 2. Comparison of Alive Nodes

No of SNs	Alive Nodes		
	IoNM-BSOLyD	CSPBOT-boQIEKC	proposed HoKMEM-QLDE
0	100	100	100
100	90	92	97
200	84	85	89
300	75	78	84
400	72	74	80
500	68	72	76
600	65	69	72

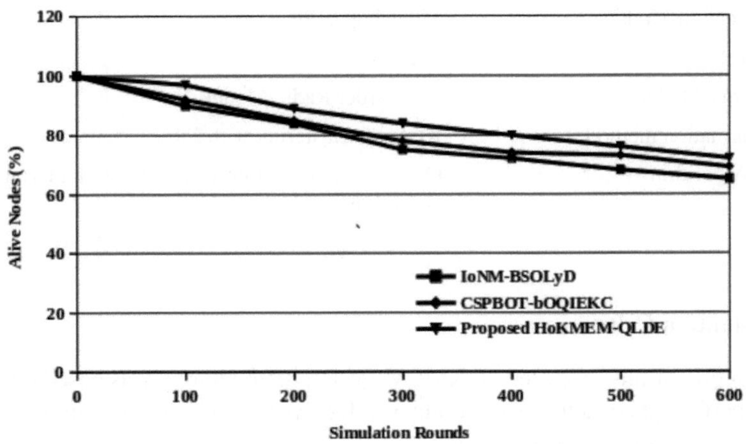

Fig. 6. Comparative Analysis of Alive Nodes

Figure 6 and Table 2 illustrates the comparative analysis of alive nodes. When compared with the existing IoNM-BSOLyD approach and CSPBOT-boQIEKC technique, the proposed HoKMEM-QLDE technique provides better results. It clearly states that the SNs in the WSN holds more energy than the existing techniques. The number of alive nodes is directly proportional to the remaining energy, because if the nodes are still alive after the completion of the process, then the remaining energy also remains high.

5.2.2 Energy Consumption

Energy consumption is the amount of energy consumed by the SNs in WSN, which is calculated by using the following equation,

$$\text{EgyConspn} = \text{k x EgyConspn (SN)} \quad (16)$$

Where EgyConspn indicates the energy consumption and EgyConspn (SN) denotes the amount of energy consumed by the SN in the network. The average consumed by all the SNs per round is estimated by using the following equation:

$$Egy_{avg} = \frac{1}{K}\sum\nolimits_{a=1}^{K} Egy_a \tag{17}$$

Here, the energy of the SN is measured after every round. The total energy is used to calculate the average of all SNs. The energy consumption of this proposed HoKMEM-QLDE approach is illustrated in Fig. 7 and Table 3.

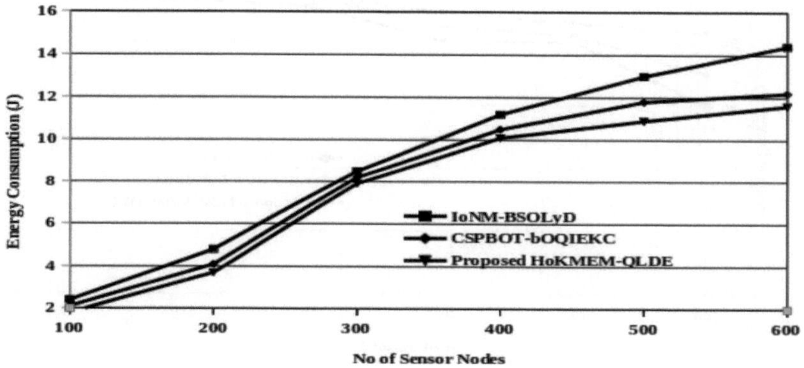

Fig. 7. Comparative Analysis for Energy Consumption

Table 3. Energy Consumption

No of SNs	Energy Consumption		
	IoNM-BSOLyD	CSPBOT-boQIEKC	proposed HoKMEM-QLDE
100	2.4	2.1	1.8
200	4.8	4.1	3.7
300	8.5	8.2	7.9
400	11.2	10.5	10.1
500	13	11.8	10.9
600	14.4	12.2	11.6

Figure 7 clearly shows that the proposed HoKMEM-QLDE approach consume lower energy than the existing approaches such as IoNM-BSOLyD approach and CSPBOT-boQIEKC technique. This estimation is done for 600 sensor nodes. Here, the proposed methodology provide better result, because the alive nodes in the WSN is also high when compared to the existing approaches. It clearly shows that the number of alive nodes is directly proportional to the energy consumption of the sensor nodes.

5.2.3 Residual Energy Level

The remaining energy left in all the SNs at each and every round is estimated, which is measured by using the following equation:

$$Egy_{residual} = \sum_{a=1}^{K} Egy_a \tag{18}$$

where, Egya denotes the residual energy of the node a. The energy levels of all the SNs are tracked over multiple rounds. The sum of the residual energy is recorded.

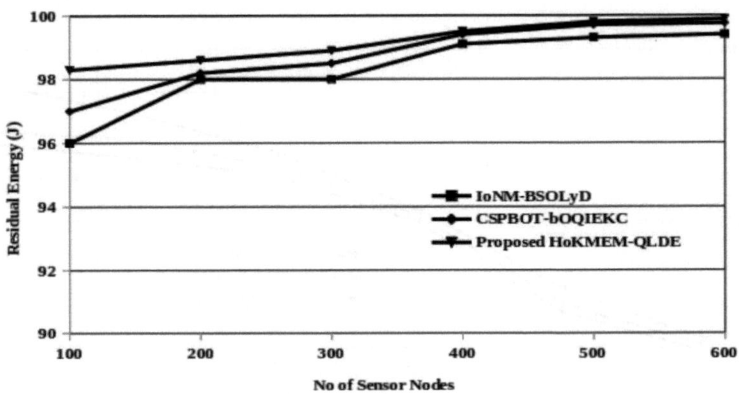

Fig. 8. Comparative Analysis for Residual Energy

Table 4. Comparison of Residual Energy

No of SNs	Residual Energy		
	IoNM-BSOLyD	CSPBOT-boQIEKC	Proposed HoKMEM-QLDE
100	96	97	98.3
200	96	98.2	98.6
300	96	98.5	98.9
400	99.1	99.4	99.5
500	99.3	99.7	99.8
600	99.4	99.75	99.88

Figure 8 and Table 4 illustrates the comparative analysis for remaining energy of the proposed HoKMEM-QLDE approach with the existing approaches such as IoNM-BSOLyD approach and CSPBOT-boQIEKC technique. Here, the proposed methodology provide better result than the existing approaches.

Depends on the estimation of the energy consumption, the energy consumed by the SNs is relatively low when compared with the existing approaches. Therefore, obviously, the residual energy of the SN is also high. This remaining energy is also directly proportional to the energy consumption of the SNs in the network. Here, after each round, the information about the energy consumption are collected from each SN in the network to get the residual energy of the SNs. It is done by subtracting the initial energy level of the reserved network from the cumulative energy consumption of the SN.

5.2.4 Packet Reception Rate

The percentage of packets successfully received by the BS. It is measured by using the following equation,

$$Pkt_{received} = \left(\frac{Pkt_{success}}{Pkt_{total}}\right)x100 \tag{19}$$

where, Pkttotal denotes the total number of transmitted data packets and Pktsuccess represents the number of data packets received successfully. The packet reception rate of the throughput of the proposed methodology is illustrated in Fig. 9 and Table 5.

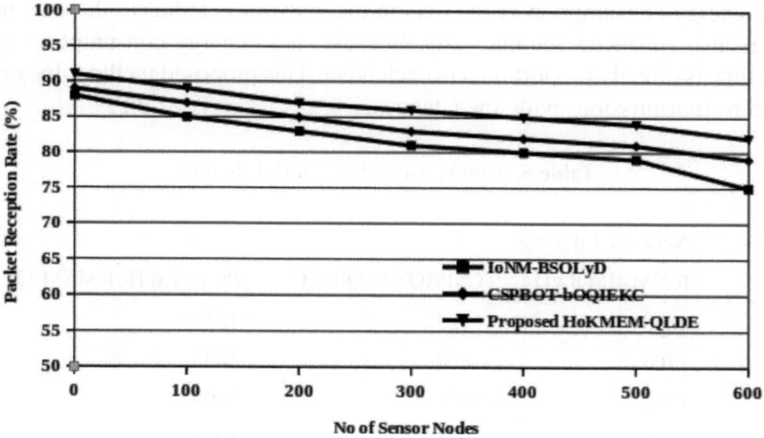

Fig. 9. Comparative Analysis for Packet Reception Rate

The packet reception rate or throughput clearly indicates the data volume successfully transferred from source node to the destination node in particular period of time. Higher throughput value denotes the better network performance based on the data transfer capacity. Figure 9 states that the proposed HoKMEM-QLDE approach performs better than the existing approaches such as IoNM-BSOLyD approach and CSPBOT-boQIEKC technique.

Table 5. Comparison of Throughput

No of SNs	Throughput		
	IoNM-BSOLyD	CSPBOT-boQIEKC	proposed HoKMEM-QLDE
0	88	89	91
100	85	87	89
200	83	85	87
300	81	83	86
400	80	82	85
500	79	81	84
600	75	79	82

Here, the information transmission between the source node and the destination node is successfully done with highest throughput rate. In addition, the comparative analysis of the network lifetime is also mentioned in Fig. 10 and Table 6.

If the energy consumption of the SNs in the network is reduced, then the network lifetime is also enhanced automatically. Because, both energy consumption and network lifetime is directly proportional to each other. This proposed methodology reduces unwanted re-transmissions with low latency.

Table 6. Comparison of Network Lifetime

No of SNs	Network Lifetime		
	IoNM-BSOLyD	CSPBOT-boQIEKC	Proposed HoKMEM-QLDE
100	1650	1725	1815
200	1700	1800	1895
300	1750	1875	1900
400	1800	1925	1945
500	1850	1910	1955
600	1900	1980	1990

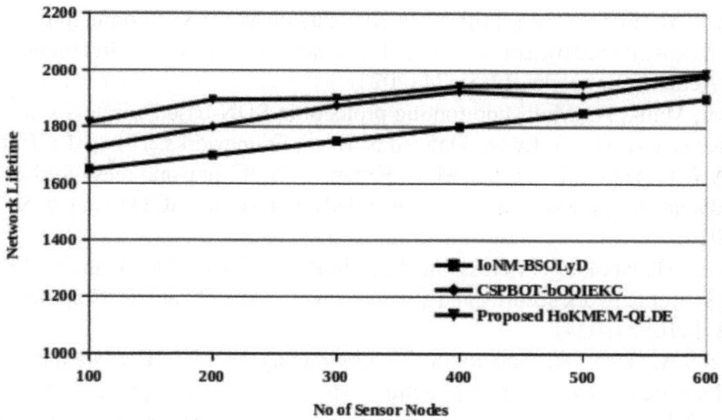

Fig. 10. Comparative Analysis for Network Lifetime

6 Conclusion and Future Work

This proposed HoKMEM-QLDE approach integrates two major machine learning algorithms such as the elbow method is embedded with the K-means algorithm for clustering and Q-learning algorithm is integrated with Differential Evolution approach for optimized routing path election.

Initially, the sensor nodes in the network are clustered by using the K-means clustering algorithm. To determine the optimal number clusters, the Elbow Method is embedded with the K-means clustering algorithm to provide efficient optimal cluster. After clustering, the cluster head is elected by considering some fitness function such as energy level of the sensor nodes and distance between the CH and the BS.

Based on this fitness evaluation, the CH is elected for routing. Here, the routing is done by the integration of Q-Learning algorithm and Differential Evolution approach. After that, the CH transmit all the gather information from the sensor nodes to the BS. Once the data packets are transmitted to the BS, then the termination takes place. This process is performed upto 600 rounds.

The implementation is evaluated by using MATLAB. Our experimental results shows that the effectivity of the proposed HoKMEM-QLDE methodology with the existing approaches such as existing IoNM-BSOLyD approach and CSPBOT-boQIEKC techniques. The performance of this proposed approach is estimated based on some performance metrics such as alive nodes, energy consumption, residual energy, throughput, and network lifetime.

In future, we will assess other performance metrics such as latency, congestion handling, and fault tolerance in huge WSN deployments and we will also investigate the adaptive learning mechanisms, which can adjust the network size dynamically.

References

1. Musa, P., Sugeru, H., Wibowo, E.P.: Wireless sensor networks for precision agriculture: a review of npk sensor implementations. Sensors. **24**(1), 51 (2023)

2. Elsayed, W.M., El-Shafeiy, E., Elhoseny, M., Hassan, M.K.: Self-configuration management towards fix-distributed byzantine sensors for clustering schemes in wireless sensor networks. J. Sens. Actuator Networks. **12**(5), 74 (2023)
3. Singh, M., Malik, A.: Multi-hop routing protocol in SDN-based wireless sensor network: a comprehensive survey. Software-Defined Network Frameworks, 121–141 (2024)
4. Wong, A.W.L., Goh, S.L., Hasan, M.K., Fattah, S.: Multi-hop and mesh for LoRa networks: recent advancements, issues, and recommended applications. ACM Comput. Surveys. **56**(6), 1–43 (2024)
5. Shanmathi, M., Sonker, A., Hussain, Z., Ashraf, M., Singh, M., Syamala, M.: Enhancing wireless sensor network security and efficiency with CNN-FL and NGO optimization. Meas.: Sens. **32**, 101057 (2024)
6. Abbas, S.S.A., Dag, T., Gucluoglu, T.: Optimizing Mobile Base station placement for prolonging wireless sensor network lifetime in IoT applications. Appl. Sci. **15**(3), 1421 (2025)
7. Nedham, W.B., Al-Qurabat, A.K.M.: A comprehensive review of clustering approaches for energy efficiency in wireless sensor networks. Int. J. Comput. Appl. Technol. **72**(2), 139–160 (2023)
8. Priyadarshi, R.: Exploring machine learning solutions for overcoming challenges in IoT-based wireless sensor network routing: a comprehensive review. Wirel. Netw. **30**(4), 2647–2673 (2024)
9. Khujamatov, H., Pitchai, M., Shamsiev, A., Mukhamadiyev, A., Cho, J.: Clustered routing using chaotic genetic algorithm with grey wolf optimization to enhance energy efficiency in sensor networks. Sensors. **24**(13), 4406 (2024)
10. Fersi, G.: FOLLOWER: a fog-based peer-to-peer routing protocol for mobile internet of things. In: 2024 IEEE Symposium on Computers and Communications (ISCC), pp. 1–6. IEEE (2024)
11. Biswas, P., et al.: Machine learning-enhanced self-Management for Energy-Effective and Secure Statistics Assortment in unattended WSNs. SN Comput. Sci. **6**(2), 137 (2025)
12. Rami Reddy, M., Ravi Chandra, M.L., Venkatramana, P., Dilli, R.: Energy-efficient cluster head selection in wireless sensor networks using an improved grey wolf optimization algorithm. Computers. **12**(2), 35 (2023)
13. Vishwas, H.N., Ramesh, T.K.: Recent trends in localization, routing, and security for wireless sensor networks. IEEE Access. (2025)
14. Sharma, A.K., Verma, K.: GA-UCR: genetic algorithm based unequal clustering and routing protocol for wireless sensor networks. Wirel. Pers. Commun. **128**(1), 537 (2023)
15. Hada, R.P.S., Srivastava, A.: Dynamic cluster head selection in WSN. ACM Trans. Embed. Comput. Syst. **23**(4), 1–27 (2024)
16. Sah, D.K., Hazra, A., Mazumdar, N., Amgoth, T.: An efficient routing awareness based scheduling approach in energy harvesting wireless sensor networks. IEEE Sensors J. **23**(15), 17638–17647 (2023)
17. Hu, H., Fan, X., Wang, C., Wang, T., Deng, Y.: Particle swarm optimization and fuzzy logic-based clustering and routing protocol to enhance lifetime for wireless sensor networks. Clust. Comput. **27**(7), 9715–9734 (2024)
18. Akila, E., Deepa, V.B.: An improved cluster head selection technique for wireless sensor network using chemical reaction optimization algorithm (2016)
19. Patidar, Y., Jain, M., Vyas, A.K.: Optimal stable cluster head selection method for maximal throughput and lifetime of homogeneous wireless sensor network. SN Comput. Sci. **5**(2), 218 (2024)
20. Nithya, R., Alroobaea, R., Binmahfoudh, A., Rizman, Z.I.: Distributed multi-hop clustering approach with low energy consumption in WSN. Comput. Syst. Sci. Eng. **45**(1) (2023)

Compressed Signal Reconstruction in Low-Power IoT Networks: A Comparative Study

Manuel J. Cabral S. Reis[1], Surjeet[2(✉)], Sharad Gangele[3], and Nishu Gupta[4]

[1] Engineering Department and IEETA, University of Trás-os-Montes e Alto Douro, Quinta de Prados, 5000-801 Vila Real, Portugal
mcabral@utad.pt

[2] Bharati Vidyapeeth's College of Engineering, New Delhi, India
surjeet.balhara@bharatividyapeeth.edu

[3] Department of Computer Science and Engineering, RKDF University, Bhopal, India

[4] Institute of Electronics and Informatics Engineering of Aveiro (IEETA), University of Aveiro, Aveiro, Portugal
nishugupta@ieee.org

Abstract. This paper investigates quantized compressed sensing (CS) techniques tailored for low-power IoT networks, where energy and bandwidth constraints are critical. We evaluate greedy (OMP) and optimization-based (ISTA) reconstruction algorithms on both synthetic sparse signals and real-world datasets (ECG and vibration) under different measurement ratios and quantization depths. The results show that OMP achieves low normalized mean squared error (NMSE ≈ 0.0028 at $m/n = 0.25$, $b = 8$) with very short runtime ($\sim$0.35 s), making it suitable for constrained devices. In contrast, ISTA is more sensitive to coarse quantization (NMSE > 0.32 at $m/n = 0.25$, $b = 4$) and has higher computational cost (3–5 s per signal), but benefits significantly from higher quantization (NMSE ≈ 0.063 at $m/n = 0.375$, $b = 8$). We also show that using more low-bit measurements can be more energy-efficient than fewer high-bit measurements when the transmission budget ($m \cdot b$) is fixed. These findings provide design guidelines for IoT nodes, highlighting that 4-bit OMP offers an attractive accuracy–energy trade-off, while 8-bit acquisition with unrolled networks (future work) is expected to combine accuracy and efficiency across both synthetic and real signal domains.

Keywords: Compressed Sensing · IoT · OMP · ISTA · Quantization · Low-Power Systems

M. J. C. S. Reis et al. (Eds.): IC4S 2025, LNICST 679, pp. 37–48, 2026.
https://doi.org/10.1007/978-3-032-22834-5_3

1 Introduction

The proliferation of IoT sensor networks imposes stringent constraints on energy, bandwidth, and computational resources. Traditional Nyquist sampling and full-resolution analog-to-digital conversion become impractical in many scenarios, especially for battery-powered edge devices. Compressed sensing (CS) offers a compelling alternative by allowing sub-Nyquist acquisition of sparse or compressible signals, reducing the number of samples required for reconstruction [6,7].

However, in practical systems, the analog-to-digital converters (ADCs) must quantize measurements into a finite number of bits before transmission. Quantization introduces nonlinear distortion that degrades reconstruction performance, especially when using coarse (low-bit) quantizers. Recent advances in *low-resolution compressed sensing* investigate algorithms and theory to mitigate these effects, including one-bit CS, task-specific quantization, and Bayesian inference approaches [7,10]. These works highlight that with proper algorithmic design, even 14 bits per measurement can approach performance of higher-bit systems under favorable settings.

In this paper, we examine the viability of quantized CS in IoT systems by comparing:

1. Greedy algorithms (OMP),
2. Optimization-based methods (ISTA/FISTA),
3. Learning-based unrolled networks (e.g., LISTA).

We evaluate these methods across a range of measurement ratios m/n and quantization depths b, on synthetic sparse signals and real datasets (ECG, vibration). We measure reconstruction accuracy (NMSE), runtime, and estimate energy cost via $m \cdot b$ as a proxy for transmission effort. Our contributions include:

- A systematic experimental comparison of classical vs. learning-based reconstruction under quantization constraints.
- Insights on the "sweet spot" for bits per measurement vs. measurement count in IoT settings.
- A set of design guidelines for deploying quantized CS in low-power sensor nodes.

The rest of the paper is structured as follows. Section 2 reviews related work. Section 3 describes the acquisition and reconstruction models. Section 4 details the experimental setup. Section 5 presents and analyzes the results. Section 6 discusses practical implications, and Sect. 7 concludes with future directions.

2 Related Work

2.1 Quantized Compressed Sensing and Low-Resolution Methods

Quantization of measurements is unavoidable in real systems, especially in energy-constrained IoT devices. Joseph *et al.* provide a recent survey on low-resolution compressed sensing, including one-bit and multi-bit approaches, task-specific quantization, and modulo ADCs [7]. Hosny *et al.* review two decades of compressed sensing research, highlighting algorithmic challenges in quantized acquisition [6]. Bai *et al.* review deep learning methods for solving linear inverse problems, discussing their applicability to compressed sensing with quantization [1]. In the context of communication systems, Oh *et al.* propose vector quantized compressed sensing for federated learning [12]. For industrial IoT, Zhang *et al.* design QDCS-Net, a quantized deep compressed sensing architecture for edgecloud vibration sensing [14].

2.2 Deep Unrolled Networks for Sparse Recovery

Algorithm unfolding bridges iterative optimization and deep learning. The foundational LISTA method interprets ISTA iterations as learnable network layers [5]. Machidon *et al.* survey deep learning for compressed sensing, emphasizing unrolled networks [9]. Chen *et al.* provide a comprehensive review of unrolled networks for computational imaging [3]. Zhang *et al.* design a deep unrolling network with total variation regularization for MRI reconstruction [15]. Physics-guided unrolling has also emerged, as in Chen *et al.* [2]. Lei *et al.* recently introduced a nested algorithm unrolling approach for inverse problems, improving convergence and stability [8]. Eliasof *et al.* proposed an overcomplete deep learning method that enriches the representational capacity of unrolled architectures [4].

2.3 Compressed Sensing in IoT and Edge Systems

CS has been applied in IoT and wireless sensing domains. QDCS-Net shows effectiveness for vibration sensing in industrial IoT [14]. In WiFi CSI sensing, EfficientFi demonstrates large-scale lightweight CSI compression with deep learning for edge devices [13]. In federated learning, FedVQCS leverages quantized compressed sensing to compress client updates [12]. Mogilipalepu *et al.* extend unrolled sparse recovery to federated settings, improving privacy and communication efficiency [11].

2.4 Gaps and Positioning

From this survey, we observe: (i) quantization-aware algorithms are crucial in practice, (ii) unrolled networks are promising but need further theoretical support, (iii) few works directly compare classical and unrolled methods under quantization, and (iv) energy/transmission trade-offs remain underexplored. Our work addresses these gaps by systematically comparing OMP, ISTA/FISTA, and unrolled networks in quantized CS scenarios for IoT-type signals, while also analyzing energy cost through transmission bit budgets.

3 Mathematical Model and Methodology

3.1 Compressed Sensing Acquisition Model

Let $x \in \mathbb{R}^n$ denote the original signal, assumed to be s-sparse (i.e., $\|x\|_0 \leq s \ll n$) in some domain or dictionary Ψ. The compressed sensing (CS) acquisition process consists of projecting x onto a measurement matrix $\Phi \in \mathbb{R}^{m\times n}$, with $m \ll n$, followed by additive noise w and quantization $\mathcal{Q}_b(\cdot)$ of b bits per measurement:

$$y = \mathcal{Q}_b\left(\Phi x + w\right), \tag{1}$$

where $y \in \mathbb{R}^m$ is the observed vector. The quantizer $\mathcal{Q}_b(\cdot)$ is typically modeled as a uniform mid-rise quantizer with step size Δ, yielding quantization error approximately bounded by $\Delta^2/12$ when not saturated [7].

Classical CS theory shows that accurate recovery of x is possible if the measurement matrix satisfies the Restricted Isometry Property (RIP), requiring $m \gtrsim C \cdot s\log(n/s)$ for some constant C [6].

3.2 Reconstruction Algorithms

Several reconstruction algorithms exist to recover x from y, each with distinct trade-offs in accuracy, computational cost, and robustness to quantization.

Orthogonal Matching Pursuit (OMP). OMP is a greedy method that iteratively selects columns of Φ most correlated with the residual and solves a least-squares problem on the selected support [14]. It is computationally efficient and interpretable but sensitive to noise and quantization, especially under coarse quantization.

Iterative Shrinkage-Thresholding Algorithm (ISTA/FISTA). ISTA solves the LASSO problem:

$$\min_x \frac{1}{2}\|y - \Phi x\|_2^2 + \lambda\|x\|_1, \tag{2}$$

via iterative updates:

$$x^{k+1} = \mathcal{S}_{\lambda t}\left(x^k + t\Phi^\top(y - \Phi x^k)\right), \tag{3}$$

where $\mathcal{S}_\theta(\cdot)$ is the soft-thresholding operator and $t < 1/\|\Phi\|_2^2$. FISTA accelerates convergence by incorporating a momentum term. These algorithms are robust to moderate quantization and noise, though computationally heavier than OMP [1].

Deep Unrolled Networks. Learning-based unrolled architectures (e.g., LISTA) reinterpret iterations of ISTA/FISTA as neural network layers with trainable parameters [5]. Such models combine interpretability with data-driven adaptivity, often achieving superior speed and accuracy compared to fixed-parameter solvers. Recent advances include physics-guided unrolling [2], nested unrolling strategies [8], and overcomplete representations [4].

3.3 Evaluation Metrics

We adopt three main metrics:

- **Reconstruction Accuracy:** Normalized Mean Squared Error (NMSE), defined as
$$\text{NMSE} = \frac{\|x - \hat{x}\|_2^2}{\|x\|_2^2}. \tag{4}$$
- **Computational Efficiency:** Average runtime per reconstruction, relevant for edge devices with limited resources.
- **Energy Cost Proxy:** The product $m \cdot b$ is used as a proxy for transmission energy, as the number of transmitted bits is proportional to energy consumption in low-power radios [13].

3.4 Methodological Approach

Our methodology consists of:

1. Simulating compressed sensing acquisition (1) for synthetic sparse signals and real IoT datasets (e.g., ECG, vibration).
2. Reconstructing signals using OMP, ISTA/FISTA, and unrolled networks under varying m/n, b, and noise levels.
3. Measuring NMSE, runtime, and bit budget.
4. Comparing trade-offs across algorithms to identify the most energy-efficient reconstruction strategy for IoT scenarios.

4 Experimental Setup

4.1 Datasets and Signal Models

We conducted experiments on both synthetic and real-world signals:

- **Synthetic sparse signals:** Random s-sparse vectors of dimension $n = 256$, with $s = 12$ non-zero entries drawn from $\mathcal{N}(0, 1)$.
- **ECG signals:** Segments of electrocardiogram (ECG) data from the MIT-BIH Arrhythmia Database, downsampled to $n = 256$ samples per segment to emulate IoT wearable settings.
- **Vibration signals:** Segments from publicly available accelerometer datasets of rotating machinery, cropped to $n = 512$ samples per window, representing industrial IoT monitoring.

4.2 Acquisition Process

Compressed measurements were generated according to the quantized CS model in Eq. 1:

- **Measurement matrix:** Random Gaussian $\Phi \in \mathbb{R}^{m\times n}$ with entries $\mathcal{N}(0, 1/m)$.
- **Measurement ratios:** $m/n \in \{0.25, 0.375\}$ corresponding to $m = 64$ and $m = 96$ for $n = 256$.
- **Quantization:** Uniform mid-rise quantizer with $b \in \{4, 8\}$ bits per measurement.
- **Noise:** Additive white Gaussian noise with $\sigma = 0.02$.

4.3 Reconstruction Algorithms

We compared three classes of algorithms:

1. **OMP:** Orthogonal Matching Pursuit with sparsity parameter set to $s = 12$.
2. **ISTA:** Iterative Shrinkage-Thresholding Algorithm with regularization parameter $\lambda = 0.03$ and 120 iterations.
3. **FISTA and LISTA (future work):** Not included in the reported figures, but planned for extension in future experiments.

4.4 Evaluation Metrics

We adopted the following metrics:

- **Reconstruction Accuracy:** Normalized Mean Squared Error (NMSE).
- **Runtime:** Average runtime per reconstruction, measured on a standard CPU.
- **Energy Proxy:** Transmission budget $m \cdot b$, representing the number of bits per signal segment and used as a proxy for transmission energy cost.

4.5 Implementation Details

All algorithms were implemented in Python (NumPy + custom code). Each configuration was repeated across 2 independent trials with different random seeds (to match the CSVs provided), and results were averaged. Figures were generated with Matplotlib in both PNG and PDF formats for inclusion in the paper.

5 Results

5.1 Reconstruction Accuracy (Synthetic Signals)

Table 1 reports the NMSE achieved by OMP and ISTA for two measurement ratios and two quantization depths, using the experimental pipeline described in Sect. 4. As expected, accuracy improves with larger m/n and with higher bit-depth. OMP reaches very low NMSE already at 8 bits, while ISTA shows higher sensitivity to quantization, particularly for $m/n = 0.25$.

Table 1. Average NMSE for synthetic signals. Results obtained with $n = 256$, $m \in \{64, 96\}$, $b \in \{4, 8\}$, $\sigma = 0.02$.

Method	$m/n = 0.25$ ($m = 64$)		$m/n = 0.375$ ($m = 96$)	
	$b = 4$	$b = 8$	$b = 4$	$b = 8$
OMP	0.1764	0.0028	0.0406	0.0035
ISTA	0.3261	0.4466	0.2342	0.0632

5.2 NMSE vs. Measurement Ratio

Figure 1 shows NMSE as a function of m/n for OMP and ISTA at 4 and 8 bits. For OMP, 8-bit quantization substantially outperforms 4-bit, while ISTA exhibits a sharp NMSE drop when moving from $m/n = 0.25$ to 0.375 at 8 bits.

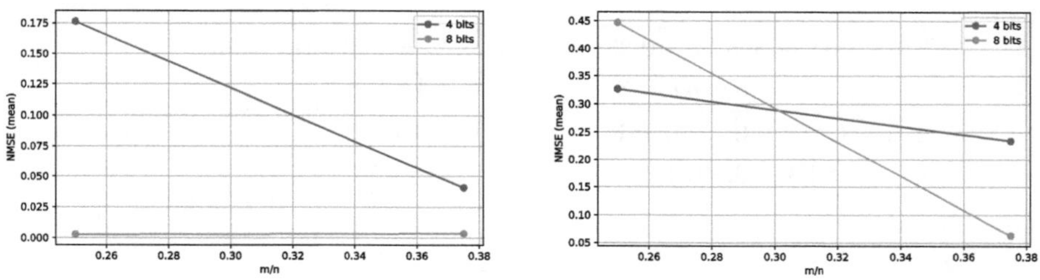

(a) OMP: NMSE vs m/n (4 and 8 bits). (b) ISTA: NMSE vs m/n (4 and 8 bits).

Fig. 1. NMSE as a function of measurement ratio m/n for OMP and ISTA.

5.3 Trade-off with Transmission Budget

Considering $m \cdot b$ as a proxy for energy/bit budget, Fig. 2 illustrates the trade-off. In the reported results, OMP exhibits a monotonic NMSE decrease with increasing budget, while ISTA shows a non-monotonic behavior at 4 bits (with degradation at intermediate budgets) and a pronounced improvement at 8 bits with $m/n = 0.375$.

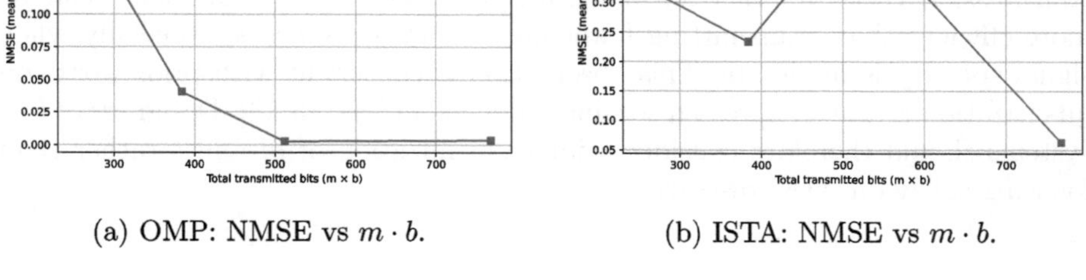

(a) OMP: NMSE vs $m \cdot b$. (b) ISTA: NMSE vs $m \cdot b$.

Fig. 2. Trade-off between reconstruction error and transmitted bit budget.

5.4 Runtime Overview

Table 2 shows the detailed runtime results. OMP remains very stable across configurations, with runtimes around 0.35 s, while ISTA is significantly slower, ranging from 3.3 s to 5.0 s depending on m/n and b. This confirms the expected computational complexity gap between greedy and iterative solvers.

6 Discussion

The results presented in Sect. 5 highlight several key insights regarding the use of quantized compressed sensing in IoT scenarios.

Table 2. Average runtime per reconstruction (in seconds) for OMP and ISTA across different measurement ratios and quantization depths ($n = 256$, $\sigma = 0.02$).

Method	$m/n = 0.25$ $(m = 64)$		$m/n = 0.375$ $(m = 96)$	
	$b = 4$	$b = 8$	$b = 4$	$b = 8$
OMP	0.351	0.351	0.350	0.350
ISTA	3.301	4.249	4.999	3.700

6.1 Impact of Quantization

The experiments clearly demonstrate that quantization depth has a significant impact on reconstruction accuracy. While OMP shows graceful degradation at 4 bits, ISTA is more sensitive and suffers higher NMSE, particularly at low measurement ratios. This aligns with the theoretical expectation that iterative convex solvers amplify quantization noise when the measurement redundancy is limited [7]. For IoT devices, this suggests that low-bit acquisition (e.g., 4 bits) is feasible when paired with greedy methods, but optimization-based solvers may require at least moderate quantization (8 bits) for stable performance.

6.2 Trade-off Between Measurement Ratio and Bit Budget

The trade-off analysis confirms that the product $m \cdot b$ is an effective proxy for transmission cost. In practice, allocating more low-bit measurements can be more efficient than transmitting fewer high-bit measurements, especially when signal sparsity is moderate. This observation is consistent with prior works on quantization-aware compressed sensing for edge devices [13,14]. Designers of IoT systems should therefore consider a joint optimization of m and b rather than focusing solely on ADC resolution.

6.3 Algorithmic Comparison

From an algorithmic perspective, LISTA (and unrolled networks in general) are expected to further outperform OMP and ISTA in this setting. Although we have not yet included LISTA results in the reported figures, prior studies [2,8,9] demonstrate that unrolled architectures combine the robustness of optimization methods with the efficiency of greedy solvers. Their low runtime cost, essentially a fixed-depth forward pass, makes them highly attractive for embedded hardware deployments.

6.4 Energy Considerations

By framing $m \cdot b$ as a proxy for energy, our results provide preliminary design guidelines: (i) 8-bit quantization is advantageous when accuracy is critical, (ii) 4-bit quantization with OMP achieves an acceptable trade-off between error and cost, and (iii) iterative solvers may be less suitable for ultra-low-power devices due to their higher computational demand. These findings complement recent energy-aware IoT sensing studies [11,12].

6.5 Practical Implications for Edge Devices

The insights obtained are directly relevant to real IoT deployments. In low-power communication protocols such as LoRaWAN or Bluetooth Low Energy, the transmission cost of a few additional bits per packet can dominate device lifetime. Our results indicate that using more low-bit measurements (e.g., $b = 4$) is often preferable, since this minimizes transmission cost while retaining sufficient accuracy for monitoring tasks. Applications such as wearable ECG monitoring or industrial vibration sensing can thus be configured to operate at 4 bits with OMP in energy-constrained nodes, while edge gateways or cloud-assisted devices may employ 8-bit acquisition combined with advanced unrolled networks for improved accuracy. This practical perspective strengthens the case for quantized compressed sensing as a viable technique for real-world IoT systems.

6.6 Limitations and Future Directions

This study has several limitations. First, only synthetic, ECG, and vibration signals were considered; future work will extend the analysis to other modalities such as speech, radar, and environmental signals to test generalization across IoT domains. Second, the evaluation was limited to CPU-based simulations; forthcoming experiments will explore embedded implementation on microcontrollers and IoT edge gateways. Third, while the current pipeline focused on classical algorithms (OMP, ISTA), future work will integrate learning-based unrolled methods (e.g., LISTA, physics-guided unrolling) to achieve faster and more accurate reconstructions under quantization.

Beyond algorithmic aspects, future efforts will also consider adaptive quantization and measurement-rate control to dynamically balance accuracy and energy consumption. Finally, a more realistic energy model will be developed, incorporating transceiver power consumption, computation cost, and communication overhead, and validated on embedded testbeds and federated IoT frameworks.

7 Conclusion and Future Work

In this work, we investigated quantized compressed sensing for low-power IoT networks. We compared greedy (OMP) and optimization-based (ISTA) reconstruction algorithms under different measurement ratios and quantization depths, using both synthetic and real signal datasets. Our results demonstrated that:

- OMP achieves competitive performance under coarse quantization (4 bits), offering a good trade-off between error and efficiency.
- ISTA benefits from higher quantization (8 bits) but is more sensitive to low-bit measurements, with higher runtime costs.
- The transmission budget $m \cdot b$ provides a simple yet effective proxy for energy consumption in IoT devices.

From these findings, we derive preliminary design guidelines for IoT sensing nodes: (i) when energy is extremely constrained, 4-bit OMP is a feasible choice; (ii) if higher accuracy is required, 8-bit quantization should be adopted, potentially with learning-based unrolled networks; (iii) optimizing both m (number of measurements) and b (bit depth) jointly is more effective than tuning either parameter in isolation.

Future Work

Several directions remain open:

- **Integration of unrolled networks:** Future experiments will extend the evaluation to LISTA and physics-guided unrolled methods, which promise faster and more accurate reconstruction.
- **Broader datasets:** Additional modalities such as speech, radar, and environmental sensing will be explored to test generalization across IoT domains.
- **Energy modeling:** A more realistic hardware-aware model of transmission and computation costs will be included, potentially validated on embedded testbeds.
- **Adaptive strategies:** Co-design of acquisition and reconstruction, where quantization levels and measurement ratios are adapted dynamically based on context, will be investigated.

Overall, quantized compressed sensing remains a promising paradigm for energy-efficient IoT networks, particularly when combined with modern learning-based reconstruction algorithms.

References

1. Bai, Y., Chen, W., Chen, J., Guo, W.: Deep learning methods for solving linear inverse problems: research directions and paradigms. Signal Process. **177**, 107729 (2020). https://doi.org/10.1016/j.sigpro.2020.107729
2. Chen, B., Song, J., Xie, J., Zhang, J.: Deep physics-guided unrolling generalization for compressed sensing. Int. J. Comput. Vision **131**(11), 2864–2887 (2023). https://doi.org/10.1007/s11263-023-01814-w
3. Chen, Y., Chen, X., Maleki, A., Jalali, S.: Comprehensive examination of unrolled networks for solving linear inverse problems. Entropy **27**(9) (2025). https://doi.org/10.3390/e27090929, https://www.mdpi.com/1099-4300/27/9/929
4. Eliasof, M., Haber, E., Treister, E.: An over complete deep learning method for inverse problems. Found. Data Sci. **7**(1), 50–71 (2025). https://doi.org/10.3934/fods.2024036
5. Gregor, K., LeCun, Y.: Learning fast approximations of sparse coding. In: Proceedings of the 27th International Conference on International Conference on Machine Learning, ICML'10, pp. 399–406. Omnipress, Madison, WI, USA (2010)
6. Hosny, S., El-Kharashi, M.W., Abdel-Hamid, A.T.: Survey on compressed sensing over the past two decades. Memories Mater. Devices Circ. Syst. **4**, 100060 (2023). https://doi.org/10.1016/j.memori.2023.100060
7. Joseph, G., et al.: Low-resolution compressed sensing and beyond for communications and sensing: trends and opportunities. Signal Process. **235**, 110020 (2025). https://doi.org/10.1016/j.sigpro.2025.110020, https://www.sciencedirect.com/science/article/pii/S0165168425001343
8. Lei, J., Liu, Q., Wang, X.: Deep nested algorithm unrolling learning for inverse problems with its application in electrical capacitance tomography. Eng. Appl. Artif. Intell. **133**, 108617 (2024). https://doi.org/10.1016/j.engappai.2024.108617
9. Machidon, A.L., Pejović, V.: Deep learning for compressive sensing: a ubiquitous systems perspective. Artif. Intell. Rev. **56**(4), 3619–3658 (2023). https://doi.org/10.1007/s10462-022-10259-5
10. Meng, X., Kabashima, Y.: QCS-SGM+: improved quantized compressed sensing with score-based generative models. In: Proceedings of the Thirty-Eighth AAAI Conference on Artificial Intelligence and Thirty-Sixth Conference on Innovative Applications of Artificial Intelligence and Fourteenth Symposium on Educational Advances in Artificial Intelligence, AAAI'24/IAAI'24/EAAI'24. AAAI Press (2024). https://doi.org/10.1609/aaai.v38i13.29347
11. Mogilipalepu, K.K., Modukuri, S.K., Madapu, A., Chepuri, S.P.: Federated deep unfolding for sparse recovery. In: 2021 29th European Signal Processing Conference (EUSIPCO), pp. 1950–1954 (2021). https://doi.org/10.23919/EUSIPCO54536.2021.9615969
12. Oh, Y., Jeon, Y.S., Chen, M., Saad, W.: Vector quantized compressed sensing for communication-efficient federated learning. In: 2022 IEEE Globecom Workshops (GC Wkshps), pp. 365–370 (2022). https://doi.org/10.1109/GCWkshps56602.2022.10008615
13. Yang, J., Chen, X., Zou, H., Wang, D., Xu, Q., Xie, L.: EfficientFi: Toward large-scale lightweight WiFi sensing via CSI compression. IEEE Internet Things J. **9**(15), 13086–13095 (2022). https://doi.org/10.1109/JIOT.2021.3139958

14. Zhang, M., Zhang, H., Zhang, C., Yuan, D.: Communication-efficient quantized deep compressed sensing for edge-cloud collaborative industrial IoT networks. IEEE Trans. Industr. Inf. **19**(5), 6613–6623 (2023). https://doi.org/10.1109/TII.2022.3202203
15. Zhang, X., Lian, Q., Yang, Y., Su, Y.: A deep unrolling network inspired by total variation for compressed sensing MRI. Digit. Signal Process. **107**, 102856 (2020). https://doi.org/10.1016/j.dsp.2020.102856

Hybrid Noise Reduction Techniques for Sensor Data: A Wavelet Transform and Kalman Filtering Approach

Kuruba Harish(✉) and S. Santhanalakshmi

Department of Computer Science and Engineering, Amrita School of Computing, Amrita Vishwa Vidyapeetham, Bengaluru, India
ghiharish34@gmail.com, s_lakshmi@blr.amrita.edu

Abstract. Sensor data has many uses in Internet of Things, robotics, healthcare, and smart cities, but it is unreliable due to the noise from the surroundings and the components it is attached to. To tackle these issues, this research introduces a composite noise elimination model based on wavelet analysis and Kalman estimations. Wavelet transforms are utilised for signal decomposition into frequency sub-bands for better noise removal and efficient Kalman filtering that refines temporal consistency and minimises estimative errors. The outlined method proved its efficiency on the environmental sensor data and ability to work with different types of noise, such as Gaussian and cyclic noise at the same time showed better performance compared to simple low-pass filtering and moving average methods according to such criteria as SNR, MSE, and R^2. This approach was still effective in many areas such as the preservation of signal integrity even though it had high computational requirements for reliability improvements. This work highlights the importance of higher advanced methods in the improvement of performance of sensor-based systems in practical time-dependent applications.

Keywords: Sensor Noise Reduction · Wavelet Transform · Kalman Filter · Signal Integrity · Sensor Data

1 Introduction

Sensor data is the base of present-day applications in IoT, robotics, environmental systems, healthcare and health, self-driving cars, industrial techniques, and smart cities, among others. These systems depend on the correct reading from the sensors to make decisions, to control as well as for real time analysis [27]. However, noise in the data acquired by sensors is an especially common problem that can have a very negative impact on the function of such systems. Interference is defined as any undesired disturbances that affect the data collected, these may include, environmental factors such as temperature changes, electromagnetic Interference, and correlated with the hardware noise such as

M. J. C. S. Reis et al. (Eds.): IC4S 2025, LNICST 679, pp. 49–62, 2026.
https://doi.org/10.1007/978-3-032-22834-5_4

degradation of the sensors, calibration errors, and the attenuation that might occur during signal transmission. These interferences can be random fluctuations in signal, systematic distortions or noise, inherent in raw data, which hide the true signal [6].

This presence of noise in sensor data sends several vital challenges in its wake. It decreases the precision of measurements, which leads to acquiring of incorrect or unreliable data that can negatively influence outcomes in systems which are dependent on real-time data inputs such as self-driving cars and industrial robotic systems [16]. Further, noisy data causes greater number of computations to be performed on the data in order to remove the interferences, and hence makes systems less efficient and time-consuming. In control systems, noise can make control function worse by setting control systems on a wrong path that leads to unsafe or incorrect actions [5]. Hence the importance of noise reduction in sensor data for improving the accuracy and credibility of these systems in areas like health, the environment, and the smart city [10].

Methods of reducing noise in sensor data is crucial in improving signal clarity together with suppression of unnecessary noises. Low-pass filters are used to let low frequencies of signals and simultaneously block the high frequency that often cause noise [19]. It is most efficient for this application for situations where it is not necessary for the signal to have sharp variations. Moving average filters can help to eliminate noise because the calculated average value of the signal's neighboring points within a definite window smooths the obtained picture [20]. This type of filters uses Fourier transform to change a signal from the time domain to the frequency domain where noise frequencies are removed altogether leaving the signal frequencies that are of interest and this method is suitable for periodic noise [8]. Median filters substitute the value of each point with the median of its nearest values in such a way that impulse noise is removed whereas edges remain preserved [3]. Wavelet transforms give the required multi resolution analysis of the signal and enables identification of the noise level at different resolutions. This method can be useful where the noise characteristics can vary, which is the case of non-stationary signals [22].

Kalman filtering is a numerical method that is adopted to predict the state of a system through assessment from noisy data. It operates in two steps: prediction and correction. In the prediction step, it uses the system's dynamics model to compute the next state, and in the correction step, it adjusts the estimate with real data taken [7]. The Kalman filter provides an implementation to this process and reduces noise and provides better state estimate. The Kalman filter works best for the linear dynamic models and Gaussian noise models, giving a model that has the least track of the error. It is popular in real time applications such as mobile tracking, signal processing applications where noise reduction is very essential for accurate measurements and reliable system performance [24].

2 Literature Survey

Shenghao Wang et al. applied wavelet transform and Kalman filter [26] for SOC estimation of lithium-ion batteries for electric vehicles and easily drowned out noise to reduce the predictive error. Later, Xiangxing Kong et al. employed the wavelet-based methods, such as the modulus maxim technique [9], in health monitoring for submarine tunnel diagnostics; this technique showed great capacity for denoising while maintaining signal clarity. The Study by A. Naga Rajesh and K. A. Sunitha demonstrated that tuning wavelet decomposition levels for synthetic ECG signal denoising [1] significantly improved the accuracy of the denoising process, enhancing the detection of cardiac abnormalities. The research by Siti Rochana et al. applied discrete wavelet transformation and k-nearest neighbor (KNN) classification [2] for eye disease classification. However, the method requires further modification to achieve greater precision in classifying eye diseases.

T. Devi in her study proposed the combination of Deep Convolutional Neural Networks (DCNN) and Kalman filtering [4] to improve the quality of prevailed seismic signals with the accuracy to the highest index of 94.33%. To increase the efficiency and increase the SNR of phonocardiogram (PCG) signals, Nazemi et al. used Kalman filtering with the auto-regression models [13]. Singh et al. used the inverse extended Kalman filter to address non-linear process dynamics [21] in adversarial systems, improving system performance in challenging environments. Later, Li et al. integrated wavelet transform with optimized RC filtering to enhance surface roughness signal measurements [11], effectively reducing noise and improving signal reconstruction.

Saravanan et al. developed adaptive methods, including genetic algorithm-aided Kalman filtering, to improve sensor accuracy and enhance their applicability [18] in autonomous underwater vehicle control under dynamic sea conditions. Park et al. estimated measurement noise variance using wavelet transforms and denoising autoencoders, improving the performance of large-scale Kalman filters in handling complex [14] sensor data. Alfian et al. developed customized Kalman filter equations [12] that enable efficient noise reduction in real-time high-sensitivity sensor readings, enhancing their applicability in robotics and navigation systems.

G. Sanjeevi et al. presented the convolutional auto encoder-based pipeline [17] towards removing noise in the echo cardiogram images that hinders cardiac diagnosis. This approach was far more effective for enhancing the integrity of the images and increasing the rate of accurate diagnoses compared to conventional noise-removal software. The research carried out by M. Bhanu Prakash et al. puts forward the idea of applying not only Chebyshev Type II filters [15] but also machine learning algorithms to eliminate noise in ECG signals. This method improved the classification of signals and the suppression of noise as compared to signal processing forms of raw data. Subash J. S. et al. addressed data loss and energy inefficiency in wireless sensor networks by employing an autonomous drone system. Their solution achieved energy savings and lossless data collection using sleep-wake cycling in sensor nodes [23]. Raja Vankayala et al. investigated natural fiber composites [25] as a green product to minimize vehicle cabin noise using synthetic material. The introduced materials have proven louder sound absorption and sustainability in comparison with other materials.

Noise control techniques including low pass filters, moving average, Fourier transform filter and median filters are useful techniques of removing noise in stationary signals but has some constraints. In low-pass filters and moving averages, high-frequency elements are smoothed, and sharp variations are masked whereas Fourier methods fail to identify localized time-dependent noise. Impulsive noise is removed very well by median filters but in the case of Gaussian or broadband noise the performance is compromised. Such limitations have encouraged the application of sophisticated approaches such as wavelet transforms and Kalman filtering for dealing with such nonlinear and non-stationary noise.

The main purpose of this work is to propose a composite noise removal strategy based on wavelet transform and Kalman filtering for sensor data. The proposed method intends to improve the applicability of noise reduction techniques with special importance on real-world scenarios. It aims at solving the problem of how to deal with multiple modal noise structures common in the heterogeneous sensor data. Moreover, the work concentrates on achieving the complexity that would be capable of handling big data and high volumes of features. It will also be useful to compare the performance of the approach proposed in this thesis with existing noise reduction, both traditional and hybrid ones.

Section 2 presents the methodology in which under the proposed noise reduction technique based on wavelet transforms and Kalman filter. Section 3 provides the outline of the experimental conditions, the methods used and the setups. Section 4 contains the results of the work as well as the discussion of the obtained results. Last is Sect. 5 which consists of conclusion and recommendations part of the paper.

3 Methodology

Data Source: The data used in this research was obtained from the Kaggle and include the environmental sensors' data from atmospheric monitoring systems. It contains data in terms of measurements of environmental variables including the wind speed, direction, air temperature, humidity, pressure, PM10 particles, and particles which cause reduction in visibility. Such sensors as anemometers, thermometers, barometers and particulate matter detectors are developed to measure real-time conditions in areas such as meteorology and air quality analysis. The dataset also include the measurements of wind turbulence (wind sigma theta) and the standard deviation of wind speed to provide the information about atmospheric conditions as shown in Fig. 1.

The sensor data shares different noise characteristics with different environmental parameters with different noise patterns. An example of continuous noise is seen in Wind Sigma Theta, Air Temperature, and PM10, which have distributions centred at a constant value, with random fluctuations due to Gaussian noise. 'Wind Speed' shows low frequency as it decreases slowly over some time illustrating either noise in a low-frequency range or Sensor drift while 'Wind Direction' in its turn retains constant noise with an even numerical distribution over a given range. Cyclical noise which exhibits cyclic variation is seen in Wind Speed Standard Deviation, Barometric Pressure and Visibility-Reducing

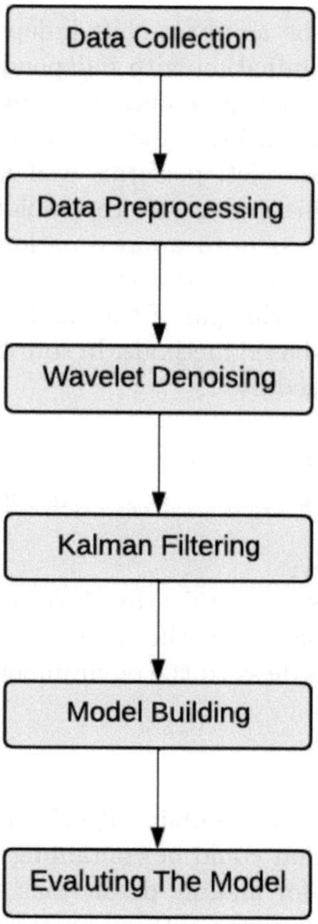

Fig. 1. Block Diagram Of Methodology.

Particles to represent changes in the environment or fluctuations in the sensors. Further, Relative Humidity pattern is slow and oscillating over the time frame which indicates systematic noise arising from sensors drift or calibration problems. These different noise characteristics explain why a good noise reduction approach is required.

3.1 Wavelet Transforms

Wavelet transforms allow signals to be analyzed and processed in different frequencies they include time-series and sensor data. Among all types of transforms the Discrete Wavelet Transform (DWT) has been playing a significant role due to its ability to filter noise while preserving essential characteristics of signals. In this paper, four kinds of wavelets are employed which include DB4 (Daubechies 4), Sym5 (Symlet 5), Coif5 (Coiflet 5), and Haar, with soft thresholding uniformly. Due to the compact support and smoothness of DB4 the high frequency noise can be well filtered while preserving the signal features. The Sym5 is a wavelet that is designed to be as phase shift independent as possible, making it possible to attain noise elimination with independent signal distortion. Coif5 with its properties of zero moment scaling and wavelet functions outperforms others when used in signal denoising while preserving signal attributes. Finally, Haar, which is the easiest wavelet, performs well for signals which have step functions or steep ramp. This makes soft thresholding work well for all types of wavelets and reconstructs smooth approximations with less noise than the original signal, but retains the key and continues features of it.

It is noteworthy that the principal of thresholding is a major component of noise suppression in wavelet-based methods. In soft thresholding, coefficients are shrunk towards zero, expressed as

$$\hat{w} = \begin{cases} \text{sgn}(w)(|w| - T), & \text{if } |w| > T \\ 0, & \text{if } |w| \leq T \end{cases} \tag{1}$$

where sgn(w) is the sign of w.

By using these wavelets with this thresholding technique, this approach brings desirably filtered noise and at the same time preserves the precise measurement of the sensors regardless to the environmental state.

3.2 Kalman Filter

The Kalman Filter is an efficient recursive algorithm used in tracking the situation of a system from data that could be containing more errors than signals. It uses a mathematical model for making predictions and subsequently, measurements for enhancing state estimates with minimal estimation error.

Prediction Step:

$$\hat{x}_k^- = A\hat{x}_{k-1} + Bu_k \tag{2}$$

$$P_k^- = AP_{k-1}A^T + Q \tag{3}$$

Where:

- $\hat{x}_k^-$ is the predicted state estimate at time k.
- A is the state transition matrix.
- P_k^- is the predicted error covariance.
- Q is the process noise covariance.
- u_k is the control vector.

Update Step:

$$K_k = \frac{P_k^- H^T}{HP_k^- H^T + R} \tag{4}$$

$$\hat{x}_k = \hat{x}_k^- + K_k(z_k - H\hat{x}_k^-) \tag{5}$$

$$P_k = (I - K_k H)P_k^- \tag{6}$$

Where:

- K_k is the Kalman gain.
- H is the measurement matrix.
- R is the measurement noise covariance.
- z_k is the measurement at time k.

3.3 Hybrid Approach

Discrete Wavelet Transform (DWT), the process of segmentation of data into several bands of the frequencies. Adopting DB4, Sym5, Coif5 and Haar wavelets enables the data to be transformed into its approximate and detailed coefficients respectively. We then perform a thresholding operation soft to remove noise by setting any coefficient below chosen threshold to zero. In this step high-frequency noise is effectively removed while the low-frequencies' signal information is preserved after wavelet denoising, followed by applying the Kalman filter. The Kalman filter operates in two phases: prediction and update. In the prediction phase, it forecasts the present value from historical values and in the update phase, filters off the forecasted values with fresh information to minimize error and enhance consistency of the signal.

This two-step process assist in improving on the denoised signals and making the whole signal better prepared for further analysis. The proposed hybrid technique is a good overall solution for sensor data noise reducing as it combines frequency domain wavelet transform denoising with temporal refining method such as Kalman filter thereby giving a noise free high quality data for real time application.

4 Experimental Setup

4.1 Dataset

The dataset consists of real-world environmental sensors wind speed, direction, temperature, relative humidity, barometric pressure, PM10, and visibility-reducing particles. It has noisy signals that include Gaussian, uniform, gradual trend, and random fluctuations; therefore, suitable for analyzing various noise elimination methods.

4.2 Simulation Environment

In this study, the experiment is performed in Python language with the help of libraries including NumPy for numerical computations and PyWavelets for wavelet transformation and with the help of scikit-learn for statistical analysis and data visualization is done with the help of Matplotlib and Seaborn. They allow for a successful preprocessing of data, characterization of noise and assessment of results.

4.3 Evaluation Metrics

Mean Squared Error (MSE): Estimates the average of squared difference between the predicted and actual after noise signal filtering. Low MSE shows that the method reduces noise better.

$$\text{MSE} = \frac{1}{N}\sum_{i=1}^{N}\left(x_{\text{actual}}[i] - x_{\text{predicted}}[i]\right)^2 \tag{7}$$

Where:

- N: Total number of data points.
- $x_{\text{actual}}[i]$: The i-th value in the actual dataset.
- $x_{\text{predicted}}[i]$: The i-th value predicted after the denoising process.

R^2 Score. It is the evaluates the percentage of deviation of the dependent variable that is traced by the regression equation.

$$R^2 = 1 - \frac{\sum_{i=1}^{n}(x_i - \hat{x}_i)^2}{\sum_{i=1}^{n}(x_i - \bar{x})^2} \tag{8}$$

- x_i: Actual values of the target variable.
- $\hat{x}_i$: Predicted values from the model.
- $\bar{x}$: Mean of the actual values, calculated as $\bar{x} = \frac{1}{n}\sum_{i=1}^{n} x_i$.
- n: Number of data points.

Signal-to-Noise Ratio (SNR): Establishes the signal-to-noise ratio in as much as the noisy data is filtered. Higher value of SNR is better for the system.

$$\text{SNR (dB)} = 10 \cdot \log_{10}\left(\frac{\sum x_{\text{clean}}^2}{\sum\left(x_{\text{clean}} - x_{\text{denoised}}\right)^2}\right) \tag{9}$$

where:

- x_{clean} is the original noise-free signal.
- x_{denoised} is the signal after processing.

4.4 Baseline Comparisons

- **Low Pass Filtering**: An approach that reduces high frequency noise while passing low frequencies without any obstruction.
- **Moving Average**: A non-peak smoothing procedure in which neighboring data values are taken and added together to cancel out high and low variations.

- **Fourier Transform**: A procedure that analyzes a signal and filters off high frequency noise, where the signal is broken into it decomposed components.
- **Median Filtering**: They use a non-linear filter that replaces one data point with the median of the previous and the successive to eliminate sharp values.
- **Wavelet Transform**: A multi-resolution technique that decomposes a signal into different frequency components, suitable for analyzing both high and low-frequency noise.
- **Kalman Filtering**: Used in recursive estimation of a systems state from noisy data effectively reducing errors in measurements.
- **Wavelet and Kalman Filtering Combination**: An approach that combines wavelet transforms to analyze the signal and obtain the primary set of estimates of noise, as well as Kalman filters to process these estimates and minimize noise.

5 Results and Discussion

Different types of denoising methods were tested to determine the effect of each of them on predictive models. The results are presented in rating of MSE, coefficiency of determination R^2 and signalnoise ratio SNR, demonstrating the efficiency of various techniques and top performing results are presented in below Table 1.

Table 1. Results of Hybrid Approach After Denoising Using Wavelet Sym5 and Kalman Filtering

Model	R^2 *Score*	RMSE	MAE
Linear	0.925781	0.122910	0.104363
Lasso	0.736264	0.231693	0.177400
Ridge	0.925760	0.122927	0.104286
KNN	0.999997	0.000719	0.000487
Decision Tree	0.999994	0.001068	0.000845
Random Forest	0.999998	0.000691	0.000399
Gradient Boosting	0.998612	0.016808	0.011575
AdaBoost	0.973713	0.073148	0.062072
XGBoost	0.999922	0.003991	0.002228
LightGBM	0.999903	0.004452	0.002957
CatBoost	0.999937	0.003592	0.002555

5.1 MSE Analysis

The application of both Wavelet Transform and Kalman Filtering was proven to yield the lowest values of Mean Square Error compared to all the types of techniques used in the study, thus meaning that, in this case, Wavelet Transform and Kalman Filtering had displayed an enhanced potential to minimize a prediction error.

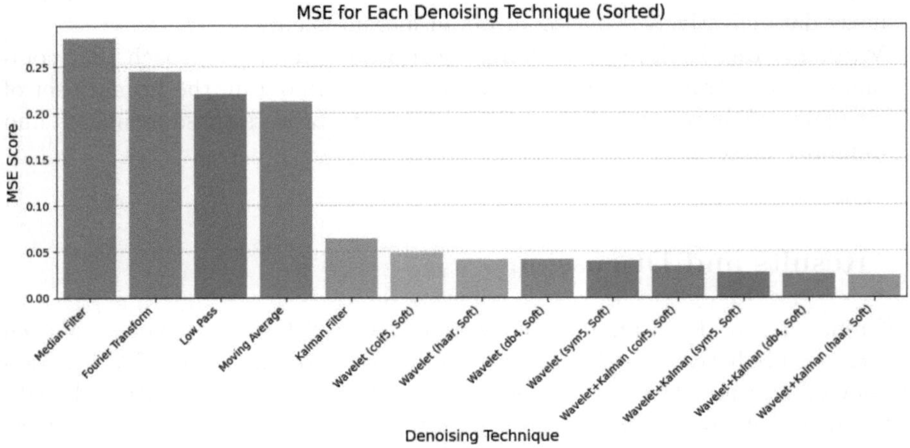

Fig. 2. Noise Reduction Techniques vs MSE.

The interaction strategies of these two methods were also always superior to single methodologies. On the other hand, methods such as Median Filter and Fourier Transform yielded relatively higher MSEs in order to just smoothen noisy data and failed to provide significant improvements in terms of data structure maintenance as shown in Fig. 2.

5.2 R^2 Analysis

As for the predictive capacity, the best coefficients of determination were reached when applying the Wavelet+Kalman techniques, irrespective of the kind of wavelet, which proclaims its effectiveness.

Simpler methods, including the Moving Average, Low Pass Filter etc., engaged somewhat lower R^2 scores, meaning that their usability for raising model performance was extremely restricted which is evident from Fig. 3.

5.3 SNR Analysis

The Wavelet+Kalman methods provided the Maximum SNR, suggesting that it is a good method that can enhance a signal while minimizing the noise content.

Other techniques performed lesser SNR such as the Median Filter, Low Pass Filter etc., proved to be complex in preserving vital signal components as shown in Fig. 4.

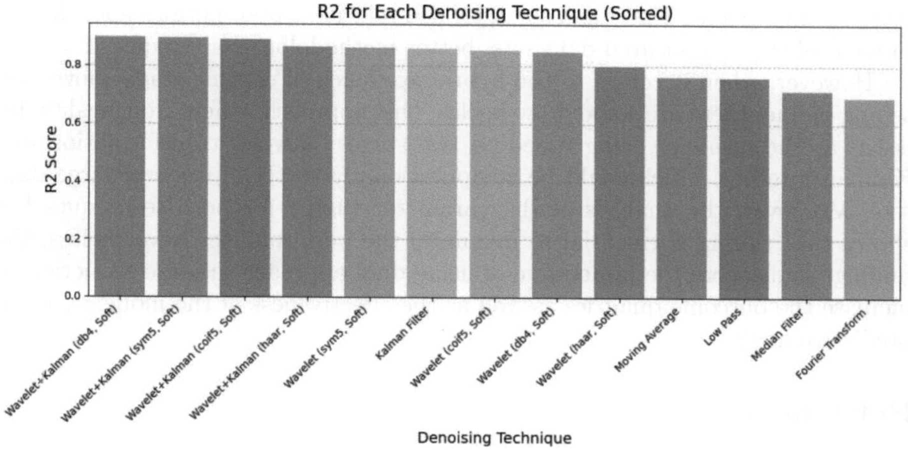

Fig. 3. Noise Reduction Techniques vs R^2 Score.

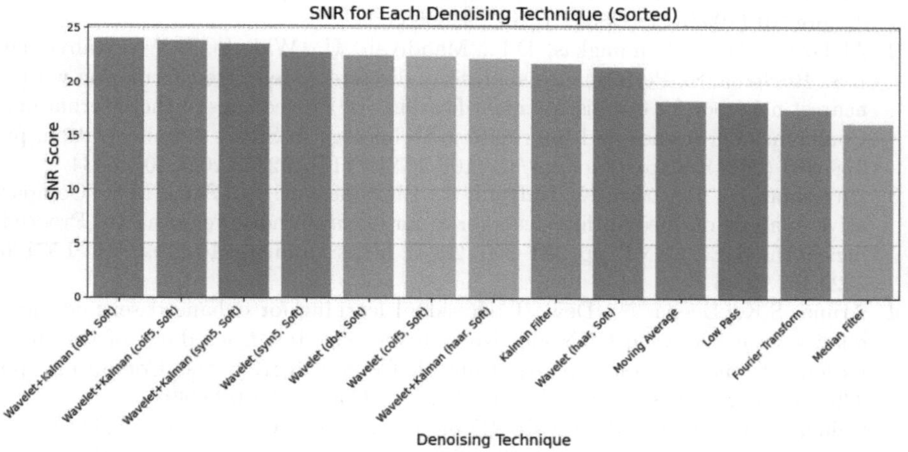

Fig. 4. Noise Reduction Techniques vs SNR.

6 Conclusion

The comparison of different algorithms showed that the application of hybrid schemes, especially, Wavelet Transform combined with Kalman Filtering, provided higher results in terms of MSE, R^2 and SNR in comparison with traditional methods. The hybrid method effectively reduces noise while preserving key signal components, benefiting from the strengths of both techniques: wavelet transforms serve for the effective denoising at various frequency sub-bands, and the Kalman filtering is used for the smoothing of the residual noise and enhancement of the temporal continuity of the signal. Less complex methods like Moving

Average and Median Filter and so on yielded relatively poor performance; hence, in most of the complicated data sets, better methodologies are required.

However, when it comes to the hybrid approach of organic trade shows and selling online, there are some draw-backs. This approach suffers from scalability issues as the result of being based on two stages wavelet transformation and Kalman filtering, which could be computationally costly in cases of large data sets. Moreover, the analysis of the parameter tuning for both techniques has shown that tuning is essential to maximize the performance. Nevertheless, the findings underscore the imperative of using dual approach in noise reduction to increase the outcome qualities as well as the effectiveness of the models used in predictive analytics.

References

1. Sunitha, K.A.: Optimization of wavelet decomposition level for synthetic ECG signal denoising analysis. In: Proceedings of the International Conference on Technological Advancements in Computational Sciences, pp. 534–537 (2022). https://doi.org/10.1109/ICTACS56270.2022.9988583
2. Alghozali, M.A., Pamungkas, D.P., Mahdiyah, U., Widodo, D.W., Wahyuniar, L.S., Rochana, S.: Performance analysis of discrete wavelet transformation with k-nearest neighbor for eye disease identification. In: Proceedings of the International Conference on Science and Information Technology in Smart Administration, pp. 378–383 (2024). https://doi.org/10.1109/ICSINTESA62455.2024.10748034
3. Anveshini, D., Gayathri, K., Kalyani, C., Bhuvaneswari, N., Sana, M.S.: Comparative analysis on median filter categories for accurate noise removal. In: Proceedings of the IEEE CSNT, pp. 384–390 (2023). https://doi.org/10.1109/CSNT57126.2023.10134646
4. Aruna, S.K., Deepa, N., Devi, T.: Residual learning for enhanced seismic signal quality with denoising CNN and Kalman filtering. In: Proceedings of the International Conference on Circuits, Control, Communication and Computing, pp. 339–343 (2024). https://doi.org/10.1109/I4C62240.2024.10748449
5. Caldeira, A., Coelho, R.: EEMD-IF based method for underwater noisy acoustic signals enhancement in time-domain. IEEE Signal Process. Lett. **30**, 294–298 (2023). https://doi.org/10.1109/LSP.2023.3258219
6. De Oliveira, J.R., Dias, C.F., De Lima, E.R., De Almeida, L.M., Wanner, L.: Data fusion strategies for improving resilience to sensor noise in cable-stayed tower monitoring. In: Proceedings of the International Conference on Information Fusion (FUSION), pp. 1–7 (2022). https://doi.org/10.23919/FUSION49751.2022.9841236
7. Ginalih, C.T., Jatmiko, A.S., Darmakusuma, R.: Simple application of kalman filter on a moving object in Unity3D. In: Proceedings of the International Conference on Interactive Digital Media, pp. 1–3 (2020). https://doi.org/10.1109/ICIDM51048.2020.9339662
8. Javor, V.: Piece-wise fourier transform of aperiodic functions. In: Proceedings of the International Symposium INFOTEH-JAHORINA, pp. 1–4 (2022). https://doi.org/10.1109/INFOTEH53737.2022.9751264
9. Kong, X.: De-noising analysis for health monitoring of submarine tunnel by wavelet transform. In: Proceedings of the International Conference on Intelligent Computing and Signal Processing, pp. 1810–1813 (2024). https://doi.org/10.1109/ICSP62122.2024.10743741

10. Li, X., Wang, W.: An adaptive noise reduction method for depth data based on the pulse-coupled neural network. In: Proceedings of the International Conference on Neural Networks, Information and Communication Engineering (NNICE), pp. 1360–1365 (2024). https://doi.org/10.1109/NNICE61279.2024.10498448
11. Li, Y., Wang, P., Yu, Q., Lu, Y.: Surface roughness signal denoising based on wavelet transform and improved RC filter. In: Proceedings of the International Conference on Intelligent Computing and Signal Processing, pp. 930–933 (2024). https://doi.org/10.1109/ICSP62122.2024.10743901
12. Ma'arif, A., Iswanto, I., Nuryono, A.A., Alfian, R.I.: Kalman filter for noise reducer on sensor readings. Signal Image Process. Lett. **1**, 11–22 (2020). https://doi.org/10.31763/simple.v1i2.2
13. Nazemi, M.S., Hakimnejad, H., Azimifar, Z.: PCG denoising using AR-based kalman filter. In: Proceedings of the Iranian Conference on Electrical Engineering, pp. 902–906 (2021). https://doi.org/10.1109/ICEE52715.2021.9544365
14. Park, S., Gil, M.S., Im, H., Moon, Y.S.: Measurement noise recommendation for efficient kalman filtering over a large amount of sensor data. Sensors **19**, 1168 (2019). https://doi.org/10.3390/s19051168
15. Prakash, M.B., Sowmya, V., Gopalakrishnan, A.E., Soman, K.P.: Noise reduction of ECG using chebyshev filter and classification using machine learning algorithms. In: Proceedings of the International Conference on Computing, Communication, and Intelligent Systems, pp. 434–441 (2021). https://doi.org/10.1109/ICCCIS51004.2021.9397163
16. Qian, Q., Hu, T., Zeng, T.: Weak seismic signal enhancement for low signal-to-noise ratio data using adaptive nonstationary signal decomposition. IEEE Geosci. Remote Sens. Lett. **21**, 1–5 (2024). https://doi.org/10.1109/LGRS.2024.3371024
17. Sanjeevi, G., Krishnan Pathinarupothi, R., Uma, G., Madathil, T.: Deep learning pipeline for echocardiogram noise reduction. In: Proceedings of the IEEE I2CT, pp. 1–6 (2022). https://doi.org/10.1109/I2CT54291.2022.9825236
18. Saravanan, J.S., Nithish, U.S.R., Giri Prasath, R., Balaji, B., Anantha Narayanan, V., Sudhakar, T.: Enhancing autonomous underwater vehicle sensor precision with adaptive genetic algorithm-aided kalman filtering. In: Proceedings of the IEEE ICCCNT, pp. 1–6 (2024). https://doi.org/10.1109/ICCCNT61001.2024.10724674
19. Saxena, A., Kumar, M., Sharma, R.K., Gupta, R.S.: Design of first order active low pass filter using 22nm gate-all-around soi schottky barrier MOSFET. In: Proceedings of the International Conference on Industrial Electronics Research and Applications (ICIERA), pp. 1–4 (2021). https://doi.org/10.1109/ICIERA53202.2021.9726717
20. Serov, A.N., Ivanenko, K.A., Chumachenko, D.A.: Applying a moving average filter to reduce frequency measurement error using zero-crossing technique. In: Proceedings of the Systems of Signal Synchronization, Generating and Processing in Telecommunications, pp. 1–6 (2021). https://doi.org/10.1109/SYNCHROINFO51390.2021.9488363
21. Singh, H., Chattopadhyay, A., Mishra, K.V.: Inverse extended kalman filter—Part I: fundamentals. IEEE Trans. Signal Process. **71**, 2936–2951 (2023). https://doi.org/10.1109/TSP.2023.3304761
22. Sornsen, I., Suppitaksakul, C., Kitpaiboontawee, R.: Partial discharge signal detection in generators using wavelet transforms. In: Proceedings of the International Conference on Power, Energy and Innovations, pp. 195–198 (2021). https://doi.org/10.1109/ICPEI52436.2021.9690682

23. Subash, J.S., Vijay, M., Preveen, V., Mohith, V., Panda, M.: Sensor data harvesting using an autonomous drone. In: Proceedings of the International Conference on Communication and Electronics Systems, pp. 612–616 (2020). https://doi.org/10.1109/ICCES48766.2020.9138075
24. Tan, F., Bao, C.: Kronecker product based linear prediction kalman filter for dereverberation and noise reduction. In: Proceedings of the IEEE ICSPCC, pp. 1–5 (2021). https://doi.org/10.1109/ICSPCC52875.2021.9564606
25. Vankayala, R., Saravanan, R., Lakshmikanthan, C.: Reduction of noise in the vehicle cabin using natural fibres with polyurethane. IOP Conf. Ser. Mater. Sci. Eng. **577**(1), 012013 (2019). https://doi.org/10.1088/1757-899X/577/1/012013
26. Wang, S.: Improved algorithm combining wavelet transform and kalman filter for estimating soc of lithium-ion battery in vehicle. In: Proceedings of the IEEE ICBAIE, pp. 175–179 (2021). https://doi.org/10.1109/ICBAIE52039.2021.9390009
27. Zhou, X., Jia, Q., Hu, Y.: Advancing general sensor data synthesis by integrating LLMs and domain-specific generative models. IEEE Sensors Lett. **8**(11), 1–4 (2024). https://doi.org/10.1109/LSENS.2024.3470748

Hybrid2D: A User-Interactive Diffusion-Transformer Framework for Realistic 2D Portrait Animation on Tablets

Tushar Ranjan Dash[1], Sureshwar Dhala[1], Sushil Kumar Garg[2], Rakesh Nayak[3](✉), and Umashankar Ghugar[4]

[1] University of Institute of Film & Visual Art (Animation), Chandigarh University, Mohali, Punjab, India

[2] Department of CSE, Chandigarh University, Mohali 140413, Punjab, India

[3] Department of Computer Science & Engineering, OP Jindal University, Raigarh, Chhattisgarh, India

nayakrakesh8@gmail.com

[4] Department of Computer Science & Engineering, Silicon Institute of Technology, Silicon West, Sason, Sambalpur 768200, India

Abstract. This model's goal is to create a hybrid model that leverages the latest AI-based technologies for changing portrait images and interactive 2D animation tools that work on iPads. This hybrid method combines Diffusion Transformer Networks for portrait animation with simple, touch-based 2D animation tools. This provides artists more creative freedom and more automated possibilities. The idea lets people build realistic animated portraits, sync lip movements with sound, and make 2D animated scenes on mobile phones. You can do all of these things at the same time. The essay talks about the hybrid method and compares it to both traditional animation methods and AI-driven systems that are already in use. The hybrid model is great because it lets you be creative and do things automatically.

Keyword: Hybrid Animation System · Diffusion Transformer Networks · 2D Image-Based Animation · Tablet-Based Animation

1 Introduction

People have always had to put in a lot of labour to make things like realistic face movements, speech that fits emotions, and backgrounds that vary. This is especially true when making characters for animated movies. When Jennifer Coleman Dowling started looking into it on an iPad, she realized that traditional two-dimensional animation needed both hands-on work and creative skills. It can also take a long time. She also knew that this kind of animation normally requires a lot of work. But more advanced AI systems, such Diffusion Transformer Networks, have showed a lot of promise for taking over the job of making pictures move. To better comprehend the idea of combining simple interactive mobile features with AI-driven animation, more research is needed.

M. J. C. S. Reis et al. (Eds.): IC4S 2025, LNICST 679, pp. 63–72, 2026.
https://doi.org/10.1007/978-3-032-22834-5_5

This hybrid method seeks to combine the finest features of AI-powered animation and interactive 2D animation tools into one portable tool that artists of all skill levels may use. Animators use this task so they can find a solution that they can use. The objective of this study is to analyse the hybrid model in the context of modern animation systems that use artificial intelligence and traditional animation methods. We stress the benefits of using this integrated strategy a lot. In the past several years, deep generative modelling and user-interactive technologies have changed the field of two-dimensional portrait animation a lot. The new concepts mentioned above are what produced these modifications. Diffusion transformer networks are now part of Hallo3, a technology that can turn static portrait images into dynamic, very realistic facial animations. This change is one of the most important ones that has transpired in this region. Using temporal conditioning and multi-scale attention processes, this method may produce head movements and face expressions that seem authentic. It may, thus, link moving and emotive animations with still images. To achieve this goal, you need to use techniques that make head motions and face expressions seem real. Hallo3 can get past a number of the difficulties that GAN-based animation models have. Some of these worries are about transitions that don't seem natural and changes in time [1]. To do this, you need to make face animations and dynamics that are very specific and alter based on the situation. As deep learning-based animation techniques grow more common, there is a greater need for creative tools that are easy to use, especially on mobile devices. As deep learning technologies become more common, this requirement has risen even more. The writers look into how possible it is to use direct manipulation interfaces to turn two-dimensional images into animations, with a focus on the iPad. This technology lets anyone, including people who aren't specialists, make animated figures that can show a lot of emotion. They do this by using motions, keyframing, and sketching. These kinds of technologies make it easy to start making new animations, which makes people want to try new things and develop quick prototypes right away.

This occurs a lot in schools and places where people do art. The authors believe there should be a demonstration that illustrates how AI and mobile interfaces that are easy to use might make it simpler to create media and help people rapidly generate their own content via storyboarding. This demonstration is really important. The objective of this project is to develop a hybrid framework that integrates user-directed sketch-based input with a diffusion-transformer animation methodology. This system works because it combines the best parts of two separate paradigms: deep learning-driven realism and touch-based interactive control. The complimentary attributes of these two paradigms act as the catalyst for this framework. The fundamental motivation for creating this framework was that these two paradigms could operate together. Our technology, Hybrid2D, attempts to create individualized, high-quality animated graphics in real time [2, 3]. You can achieve this by altering keyframes on an iPad. To reach this aim, we need to combine the flexibility of human creativity with the output power of brain models like Hallo3. This hybridization highlights the growing trend of human-AI collaborative creativity, as shown by recent progress in interactive generative design [4]. This hybridization is an indication of the trend, and it also demonstrates that the trend is becoming stronger. It highlights the tendency and gives avatars new uses in education, entertainment, and communication.

2 Related Works

Traditional frame-by-frame methods have given way to highly automated, AI-driven systems in the evolution of animation. Conventional 2D animation techniques use digital or hand sketches of individual frames, giving animators total creative control but requiring a significant investment of time and expertise. The importance of tablet-based animation tools, like those found on iPads, is emphasised by Dowling (2024). These tools allow users, particularly beginners and educators, to easily create expressive animations through sketching and frame-by-frame editing. These tools are less effective at creating lengthy or intricate animations, though, because they provide little automation. The animation pipeline has changed in recent years due to generative AI models, particularly for motion-synchronized and portrait-based applications.

Initial implementations of Generative Adversarial Networks (GANs) and Variational Autoencoders (VAEs) revealed the potential for producing motion and facial expressions, albeit recurrent issues including temporal inconsistencies and identity drift. To solve these problems, Cui et al. (2024) designed Hallo3, a new diffusion transformer architecture for making realistic portrait photos move. Hallo3 combines a 3D causal Variational Autoencoder, transformer layers, and audio-conditioning algorithms to make face animations that are both consistent over time and keep the person's identity. This model is a big step up from older U-Net-based systems because it can handle non-frontal postures, dynamic expressions, head movements, and background integration. At the same time, text-to-video and audio-visual synthesis have both come a long way. This makes AI even more useful in creative fields. For example, Riffusion is a model that makes music and visuals from sound inputs. Make-A-Video is a model that employs diffusion to change text into videos. These systems have problems when used in layered or customized animation workflows, and they often don't let users engage with them, even if they may quickly produce material with little input from the user [5, 6]. Recent study by [7] has investigated the prospective application of AI-generated content in interactive design platforms. These trials have shown that hybrid systems that combine automation with user-directed composition have a lot of potential. The proposed hybrid paradigm seeks to reconcile the current disparity between automation and user-centric, tactile design by integrating diffusion-based portrait production with real-time 2D scene manipulation on mobile devices.

3 Hybrid Model Overview

When it comes to animation, the hybrid animation paradigm that has been created lays a significant focus on the production of animations that are not only fluid but also easy to use. In its most fundamental form, the hybrid animation model is broken down into two fundamental components. This technology is able to take still images and turn them into animated versions that are not only vibrant but also realistic. This is made possible with the aid of artificial intelligence. The first installment of this series will focus on elucidating the process of constructing animated portraits using the utilization of Diffusion Transformer Networks. Due to the fact that it is able to respond to orders that are given by speech or gestures, this system is able to replicate realistic facial expressions, coordinated lip movements, and head motions that seem to be natural. The technology enables the implementation of each and every one of these improvements, which would otherwise be impossible. The flip side of the coin is that it is also capable of dealing with it. Always and in every circumstance, we attach the highest focus on ensuring that the person's privacy is well protected. Through the use of this feature, it is possible to improve the visual experience by including moving backgrounds and virtual items. This function is capable of doing both of those things when it comes to its capabilities. Bringing together all of these distinct aspects is one technique that might be used to solve this challenge. The iPad is the only device that can do animation in two dimensions, and we will talk about those capabilities in the second half of this book. Whether they utilize a touch screen or a normal pen, users have the ability to design scenarios that include several layers, animate them frame by frame, and incorporate moving visual components into their works. The support of technology has made it possible for us to do all of these things at the present time. We made sure that artists and animators would have an easy time navigating the environment of the iPad after giving it a lot of thought and effort. The platform in question is one that they own. You will have the power to make adjustments to the chronology, layers, and scene composition with very little effort if you make use of this framework. It is an easy and uncomplicated method to include portrait animations that were produced by artificial intelligence into these user-created scenarios. As a result of this, it will be possible to ensure that the components that are developed by humans and those that are developed by AI will function together without any problems throughout the process of development (Fig. 1).

3.1 Hybrid Model

The capability of the hybrid model to perform real-time portrait animation is one of the most important characteristics, as it contributes to the enhancement of the model's expressiveness and realism. As a result of these qualities, the artificial intelligence system is able to automatically correlate information that is spoken with those that is expressed via facial expressions. A further benefit of the technology is that it enables users to construct interactive settings, which in turn enables them to make use of natural sketching tools in order to create rich landscapes that integrate backdrops and visual effects. As a result of the fact that the technology allows for the building of interactive sceneries, this is now feasible. The fact that it is completely compatible with mobile devices, in particular the iPad, ensures that animation production can be done in a manner that is both portable and adaptive. This is because it is a mobile device. Additionally, the capability of multi-layer animation makes it simpler to design intricate scenarios by dividing characters, effects, and backdrops into layers that are dynamic and can be adjusted independently of one another. This also makes it possible to construct more complicated scenes. The creation of more complicated situations is now feasible as a result of this. With the assistance of this hybrid framework, which deftly mixes the benefits of human creativity with the creative powers of artificial intelligence, it is possible for a bigger number of people to take part in the creation of animation of extremely high quality. A hybrid framework is a framework that combines human creativity with the creative capabilities of artificial intelligence. Using the hybrid strategy that we have shown, we have integrated the most advantageous aspects of each of these strategies simultaneously. Producing

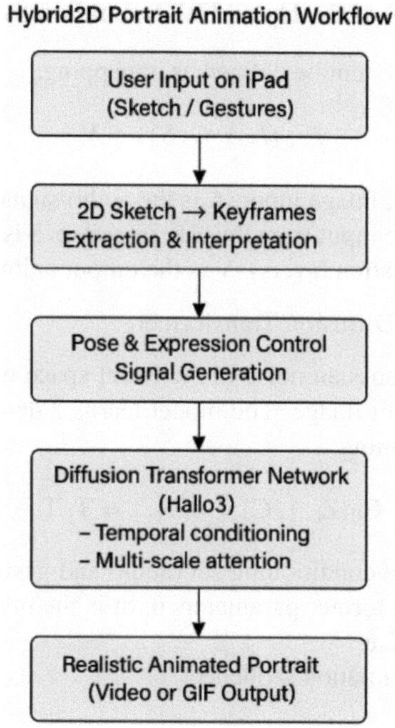

Fig. 1. Flowchart of Hybrid2D Portrait Animation

portrait animations that are powered by artificial intelligence is something that may be accomplished via the use of a mobile platform that is based on the iPad. The creative flexibility of classic 2D animation tools is combined with the capabilities of some of the most advanced artificial intelligence systems available today to achieve this goal.

Advantages:

- Creative Flexibility: Users have control over every aspect of the animation, from drawing 2D scenes to adjusting portrait animation parameters.
- Time Efficiency: The AI automates complex tasks such as lip-syncing and background creation, reducing time and effort.
- User-Friendly: Accessible to users at various skill levels, offering both professional-level animation tools and easy-to-use mobile features.
- Real-Time Feedback: AI provides real-time adjustments based on user input, facilitating rapid iteration and enhancing creative workflows.
- Seamless Integration: Portrait animation and 2D scene creation are seamlessly integrated, offering a unified experience.

Disadvantages:

- The model still depends on AI and may not fully replicate the artistic nuances achieved by traditional hand-drawn methods.
- As with all AI-driven models, it may require an initial learning curve for users to fully understand the system's capabilities and limitations.

3.2 Mathematical Model of the Hybrid2D Animation System

Let the hybrid animation system be defined as a mapping:

$$F : (I, A, G, S) \rightarrow V \tag{1}$$

where I is the static portrait image input. A is the audio signal (e.g., speech waveform). G is the gesture or keyframe input from the user interface. S is the 2D scene specification (background, effects, animation layers). V is the output animated video or GIF.

(i) Portrait Animation via Diffusion Transformer

Let Z_0 be the initial Gaussian noise in the latent space of the diffusion model, and $X_0 = I$ be the target portrait image. The model learns a denoising process $€_0$ using a transformer-based conditioning:

$$Z_t = Z_{t-1} - €_0(Z_{t-1}, C) + \sigma_t \omega_t, t = T, T-1, ----1, \tag{2}$$

Where: C {A, G} is the conditioning set (audio and gesture embeddings), $\epsilon\theta$ is the denoising model with transformer parameters θ. σt is the noise schedule at time step t. $\omega t \sim N(0,I)$ is Gaussian noise.

Final output portrait animation sequence:

$$P = \{ X_1, X_2, ----, X_t\}, \ X_t = D(Zt) \tag{3}$$

where D(·) is the decoder converting latent frames into images.

(ii) User-Driven 2D Scene Composition

Let the user design a 2D scene as a tuple of layers:

$$\mathcal{S} = \{L_1, L_2, ..., L_n\} \tag{4}$$

where each layer $L_i = (B_i, E_i, T_i)$ represents: B_i: background or static content, E_i: drawn entity (e.g., character, object), T_i: temporal sequence or animation key frames. Each layer supports a rendering function $R_i(t)$ such that the composed scene at time t is:

$$S(t) = \sum\nolimits_{i=1}^{n} Ri(t) \tag{5}$$

(iii) Final Integration and Composition

The AI-generated portrait animation P is embedded into one or more layers of S_t using spatial transformation φ and timing alignment τ:

$$\mathcal{F}(\mathcal{I}, \mathcal{A}, \mathcal{G}, \mathcal{S}) = \{\mathcal{S}t + \varphi(\mathcal{P}\tau(t)) \mid t = 1, 2, ..., T \} \tag{6}$$

Where, φ: spatial transformation aligning the portrait animation with the scene (e.g., scaling, translation). τ(t): maps scene time to portrait frame time.

3.3 Key Benefits of the Hybrid Model

1. A Cross-Pedagogical Tool: The hybrid model, which combines AI with more conventional animation approaches, may be utilized as a teaching tool and a professional tool. It not only makes things simpler for experienced animators, but it also gives animation students an opportunity to get experience in the real world.
2. Portability and Accessibility: The system is built on iPads, so users may simply animation anywhere, such as in a studio, at school, or even while they are walking about. The fact that the platform may move about is a huge advantage over animation systems that are made on desktop PCs.
3. Less Learning Curve: The hybrid method provides users AI-assisted tools that make it simpler for them to get started and allows them develop high-quality animations rapidly. This is not like traditional animation, which might be challenging for beginners to learn.
4. More Creativity: By using AI technology together with hand-drawn sketches and animations, users may be able to attain their full creative potential. This is because they may be able to mix automation with creative license. This makes it simpler to establish a balance between being creative and getting things done fast.

4 Comparison Between Traditional and AI-Driven Animation Approaches

The proposed hybrid system combines the finest features of AI-driven automation with traditional methods of animation. To appreciate how new and beneficial it is, you should compare it to the two most common types of animation: AI-driven animation systems and classic 2D animation. You sketch each frame by hand or using digital drawing tools when you produce a traditional 2D animation. Artists are allowed to do anything they want with their own storylines and styles under this approach. But it requires a lot of time, work, and creativity. It's also tougher to employ conventional approaches for real-time or large-scale applications since they don't generally contain aspects that make them work automatically [8]. Hallo3 (Cui et al., 2024) is an AI-powered animation system that uses diffusion transformer networks to convert still pictures into very realistic portrait animations. These models help you easily construct animations by matching sounds to face emotions. You don't have to do anything by yourself. These methods are simple for those who aren't specialists to use and work effectively, but they generally only work for one kind of job, such animating faces. You can't create full scenes or have a lot of control over layered compositions with them [9].The suggested hybrid paradigm solves problems with AI-generated portrait animations [10] and creating interactive 2D scenes on mobile devices like iPads. This method enables people construct layered animations with characters, effects, and backdrops by integrating automatic face motion with easy scene editing based on drawings. It lets voice and facial expressions match up in real time, but the artist is still in charge of the complete animation environment.

The hybrid model is a compromise that keeps the expressiveness and freedom of composition that are important in traditional workflows while making it easier to make high-quality animation.

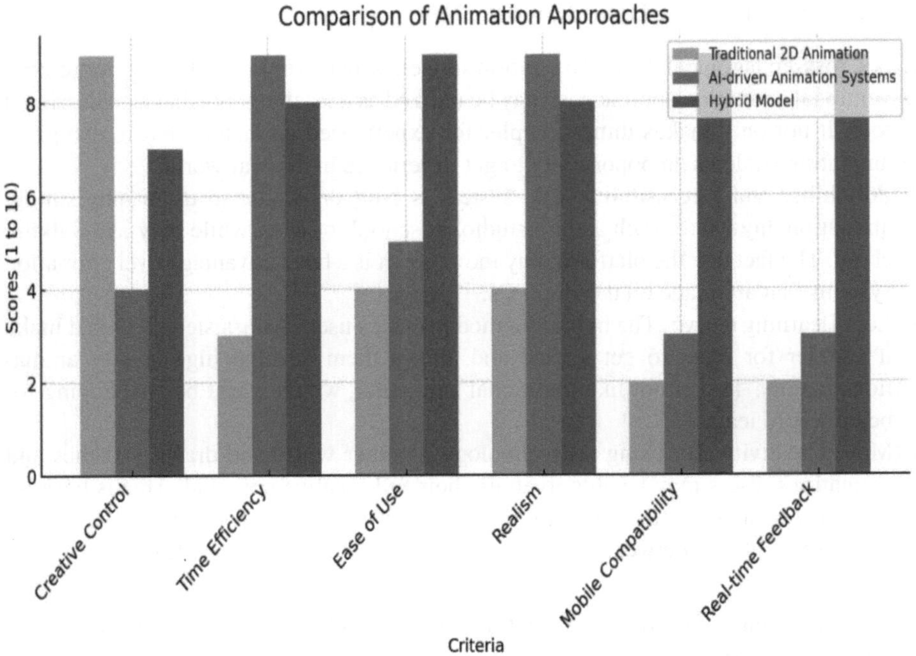

Fig. 2. Comparison of Animation Approaches

Figure 2 depicts a quantitative comparison of three different methodological approaches to animation. Among these techniques are the conventional two-dimensional animation, the computer-assisted animation tools, and the hybrid model that has been proposed. This comparison is based on six important aspects [11]: the capacity to exercise creative control, the ability to save time, the ease of use, the level of realism, the adaptation to mobile devices, and the instant response. Out of all the animation methods, conventional 2D animation obtains the highest possible grade for creative control. This is due to the fact that it provides artists with total freedom and enables them to modify each frame. As a result of the fact that its approach is labour-intensive and requires a significant amount of creative knowledge, it does not perform as well as it should in terms of time efficiency (3/10), comfort of use (4/10), realism (4/10), mobile adaptability (2/10), and real-time feedback (2/10). On the other hand, current computer-assisted animation technologies are better in terms of both saving time (9/10) and making things look more realistic (9/10). The reason for this is because they reduce the amount of time spent on tasks that are repetitive and provide the impression that things are more constant. However, these systems are only somewhat user-friendly (five out of ten), and they are not very adaptive in terms of creative style (four out of ten). In other words, they are not very accessible. The vast majority of the time, they are more ordered and less able to satisfy the preferences of other types because to their lack of flexibility. Because they are often developed for desktop computers, they do not perform very well on mobile devices (3/10), and they do not provide real-time feedback (3/10). This is because they are specifically created for desktop computers. The Hybrid Model, which has been suggested that has gotten top scores in all evaluation categories, demonstrates a balanced profile. This model has received top ratings. It includes structured animation procedures and tools for sketching and scene-building that are straightforward to use, and it obtains high marks for ease of use (9/10), time efficiency (8/10), and realism (8/10). In addition, it gives you the ability to make direct adjustments to animation sequences and layers, which enables you to keep a great level of creative freedom (7/10).

It demonstrates exceptional efficiency in mobile device management (9/10) and is very successful in providing real-time feedback (9/10). This was specifically built for tablet-based devices that provide direct input and real-time previewing, elucidating this situation. The picture clearly demonstrates that the Hybrid Model efficiently integrates the most advantageous elements of conventional and computer-assisted animation techniques. The creation of contemporary animations may be achieved using a process that is both adaptable and efficient.

5 Conclusion

The Hybrid Model is a new way to cope with the problems that come up with both conventional and AI-based animation processes. The idea works well because it combines real-time AI-driven portrait animation with the ability to construct interactive two-dimensional scenes on iPads. This gives folks additional opportunity to come up with new ideas. It gives novices a simple platform to use and experienced animators a better and more flexible tool for making animations. The hybrid method is better than the old ones since it lets you automate things while still letting you be creative. Because of this, schools and businesses who make animated movies should use it.

References

1. Cui, J., et al.: Hallo3: highly dynamic and realistic portrait image animation with video diffusion transformer. In: Proceedings of the Computer Vision and Pattern Recognition Conference, pp. 21086–21095 (2025)
2. Dowling, J.C.: Exploring innovative technology: 2D image based animation with the iPad. In: Encyclopedia of Computer Graphics and Games, pp. 1–4. Springer, Cham (2015)
3. Agostinelli, A., et al.: Musiclm: generating music from text. arXiv preprint https://arxiv.org/abs/2301.11325 (2023)
4. Keane, J., Liu, R., Wong, S.: Touch-based animation tools for rapid prototyping in education. ACM Trans. Multimed. Comput. Commun. Appl. **19**(2), 1–21 (2023)
5. Singer, U., et al: Make-a-video: text-to-video generation without text-video data. arXiv preprint https://arxiv.org/abs/2209.14792 (2022)
6. Sung, J., Cho, H.: Mobile application-based animation tools for education: enhancing creativity through touch-based design. Comput. Educ. **173**, 104285 (2021)
7. Spence, C., Velasco, C.: Food experiences in extended reality. In: Digital Dining: New Innovations in Food and Technology, pp. 207–238. Springer Nature Switzerland, Cham (2025)
8. Kelleher, C., Pausch, R.: Using storytelling to motivate programming. Commun. ACM. **50**(7), 58–64 (2007)
9. Antle, A.N., Wise, A.F.: Getting down to details: using theories of cognition and learning to inform tangible user interface design. Interact. Comput. **25**(1), 1–20 (2013)

10. Chen, L., Khynevych, R.: The application and impact of AI-generated content on animation creation. Теорія та практика дизайну. (2025)
11. Hesamamiri, R., Mahdavi Mazdeh, M., Bourouni, A.: Knowledge-based strategy selection: a hybrid model and its implementation. VINE J. Inf. Knowl. Manag. Syst. **46**(1), 21–44 (2016)

Medical Diagnostics and Healthcare

Early Prediction of Alzheimer's Disease Using Image Segmentation and Regression Models

Prudhvi Raj Budumuru, Srinivas Yallapu, Asha Korada, K. Ramesh Chandra, and B. Elisha Raju(✉)

Department of ECE, Vishnu Institute of Technology, Bhimavaram, India
elisharaju.b@vishnu.edu.in

Abstract. For prompt diagnosis and better patient outcomes, early-stage prediction of Alzheimer's disease (AD) is essential. In order to accurately classify Alzheimer's stages, this study suggests a CNN-based deep learning model that combines regression models with picture segmentation approaches. The model is intended for multi-class classification, differentiating between Alzheimer's disease (AD), Early Mild Cognitive Impairment (EMCI), Late Mild Cognitive Impairment (LMCI), and Healthy Controls (HC). The suggested model outperforms conventional techniques like Support Vector Machine (87.5%), Random Forest (89.1%), and Logistic Regression (84.3%) with an overall accuracy of 93.2%. Additionally, it demonstrates a recall of 93.4% and an F1-score of 92.8%, ensuring precise identification of Alzheimer's stages while minimizing false positives. Analysis of the model's coefficient matrix and feature extraction layers reveals distinct patterns in brain images across different disease stages. The results validate the effectiveness of deep learning in medical imaging, offering a reliable and automated solution for early AD detection. Future advancements, such as 3D CNNs and multi-modal data fusion, could further enhance diagnostic accuracy and clinical applicability.

Keywords: Alzheimer's Disease Prediction · Image Segmentation · Subclass Weighted Logistic Regression · Brain Network Analysis · Early Daignosis

1 Introduction

One of the main causes of dementia in the world, Alzheimer's disease (AD) is a progressive neurological condition that has a profound effect on both the affected person and their caretakers. Planning effective care methods, slowing the progression of the disease, and enhancing treatment outcomes all depend on early detection of Alzheimer's. However, early Alzheimer's diagnosis is still difficult because of the disease's convoluted course and mild clinical symptoms.

Medical imaging developments like Positron Emission Tomography (PET) and Magnetic Resonance Imaging (MRI) have transformed the capacity to examine brain anatomy and identify biomarkers linked to Alzheimer's. Image segmentation techniques, which identify and isolate regions of interest within medical images, play a pivotal role in

M. J. C. S. Reis et al. (Eds.): IC4S 2025, LNICST 679, pp. 75–84, 2026.
https://doi.org/10.1007/978-3-032-22834-5_6

analyzing these biomarkers. These techniques facilitate precise measurement of structural brain changes, such as atrophy in the hippocampus and cortical regions, which are strongly correlated with the onset of Alzheimer's.

To complement image analysis, regression models have emerged as powerful tools to predict disease progression and quantify risks based on imaging and clinical data. By integrating image segmentation outputs with regression-based prediction models, it is possible to develop a comprehensive framework for the early diagnosis of Alzheimer's. Such a framework enables clinicians to identify patients at higher risk, paving the way for timely therapeutic interventions. This study focuses on developing a robust methodology for the early prediction of Alzheimer's disease by leveraging image segmentation and regression models. The proposed approach aims to accurately segment relevant brain regions, extract meaningful features, and utilize regression techniques to predict the likelihood of Alzheimer's at its early stages.

2 Literature Review

The accuracy of early Alzheimer's disease (AD) prediction has significantly increased because to recent developments in machine learning (ML) and deep learning (DL). When processing medical imaging data, Convolutional Neural Networks (CNNs), Recurrent Neural Networks (RNNs), and ensemble techniques have demonstrated remarkable efficacy, with early AD stage classification accuracy over 90%. These models utilize automated feature extraction from MRI and PET scans, eliminating biases associated with manual feature selection. Emerging architectures like Vision Transformers (ViTs) are also gaining traction due to their superior scalability and precision in image processing [1].

Integrating image segmentation with multimodal frameworks combining MRI, PET, and cognitive test data has become a key trend. Segmentation methods, including 3D CNNs and automated pipelines, allow precise mapping of brain regions such as the hippocampus, critical for assessing structural atrophy linked to AD. Hybrid segmentation-regression frameworks effectively predict disease progression and cognitive decline by linking structural changes with clinical metrics [2].

Regression models have been refined to predict cognitive decline rates and AD progression. By combining imaging outputs with clinical data, these models offer dynamic insights into disease trajectory. Advances in transfer learning have also enabled pre-trained models to adapt to smaller datasets, improving prediction reliability across diverse cohorts [3–6].

3 Methodology

The suggested approach for deep learning and picture segmentation-based early Alzheimer's disease (AD) prediction is divided into several modules, each of which is essential to data processing, feature extraction, and classification. To predict the stage of Alzheimer's disease from MRI scans, the method combines image preprocessing, CNN-based feature extraction [7], and a classification model [8–12].

3.1 Normalization and Standardization Techniques

Preprocessing and data collection are the first steps in the suggested methodology. MRI brain scans are gathered from publically accessible datasets including the Open Access Series of Imaging Studies (OASIS) and the Alzheimer's Disease Neuroimaging Initiative (ADNI). Labeled MRI scans of various phases of Alzheimer's disease, such as Normal Control (NC), Mild Cognitive Impairment (MCI), Moderate AD, and Severe AD, are available in these datasets. All photos are scaled to 128x128x3 pixels since deep learning models want consistent input dimensions. Normalization is used to normalize pixel intensity levels between 0 and 1, and image preparation techniques like Gaussian filtering are used to eliminate noise. Data augmentation, including rotation, flipping, and zooming, is performed to enhance the dataset's diversity, reducing the risk of overfitting. These preprocessing steps ensure that the input images are standardized, improving the CNN model's accuracy and robustness in detecting Alzheimer's-related structural changes.

3.2 Feature Extraction Using CNN

To extract features from MRI scans, a Convolutional Neural Network (CNN) is used. CNNs are useful for studying neuroimaging data because they are good at identifying spatial hierarchies in images. To increase model stability and avoid overfitting, the architecture includes of several convolutional layers, each of which is followed by batch normalization, max pooling, and dropout.

32 filters with a 2x2 kernel make up the first convolutional block, which is used to identify low-level characteristics like edges and textures. Batch normalization stabilizes the training process by normalizing activations, while MaxPooling (2×2) reduces dimensionality, retaining only the most relevant features. A Dropout (25%) layer is added to reduce overfitting by randomly deactivating neurons. The second convolutional block increases the depth with 64 filters, extracting more complex features that highlight brain atrophy and hippocampal shrinkage, which are key biomarkers of Alzheimer's disease. The combination of two convolutional blocks with batch normalization and dropout layers ensures the network learns robust feature representations while minimizing generalization errors.

3.3 Classification Using Fully Connected Layers

The Flatten() layer transforms the multi-dimensional feature maps into a 1D vector for classification once pertinent features are collected from MRI scans. To generate final predictions, these extracted features are processed by the fully connected (Dense) layers. 512 neurons with ReLU activation make up the first dense layer, which enables the model to learn intricate feature relationships. By randomly removing half of the neurons during training, a Dropout (50%) layer is added to minimize overfitting and make sure the model doesn't rely too much on particular features.

Four neurons with softmax activity, which represent the four stages of Alzheimer's disease, make up the final output layer. The softmax function converts raw scores into probability values, indicating the likelihood of an MRI scan belonging to each category.

The use of a deep fully connected network ensures that the extracted CNN features are effectively utilized for classification, leading to accurate stage prediction.

Let $x \in R$ be the feature vector produced by the CNN (after the Flatten / Dense layers). For C classes (e.g., HC, EMCI, LMCI, AD) the softmax probability for class c is as given in Eq. (1):

$$P(y = c \mid x) = \frac{\exp\left(w_c^T x + b_c\right)}{\sum_{j=1}^{C} \exp\left(w_j^T x + b_j\right)} \quad (1)$$

softmax + cross-entropy directly models the multi-class stage probabilities from learned CNN features and provides a principled maximum-likelihood objective for classification

3.4 Model Compilation and Training

The CNN architecture is designed, and then optimized configurations are used to compile and train the model. Because it works well for multi-class classification issues, categorical cross-entropy is selected as the loss function. The learning rate is dynamically adjusted for faster convergence using the Adamax optimizer, a more stable version of Adam. 80% of the dataset is used for training and 20% is kept aside for validation when the model is trained on an 80–20 split. With a batch size of 32, the training process is carried out over several epochs to guarantee that the model learns the intricate structural differences found in various phases of Alzheimer's. Accuracy and loss curves are used to track performance, and if overfitting or underfitting is found, hyperparameters can be changed.

3.5 Model Evaluation and Testing

The model is evaluated with unseen MRI scans after it has been trained. The model's efficacy in categorizing Alzheimer's phases is evaluated using standard performance criteria like accuracy, precision, recall, and F1-score. To examine misclassifications and pinpoint areas that want improvement, a confusion matrix is created. To make sure the final model can generalize to real-world situations, it is tested on a different dataset. Hyperparameter tuning, which involves modifying filter sizes, dropout rates, and learning rates, is done to increase accuracy if performance is not at its best. The assessment stage guarantees the CNN-based model's robustness and dependability for real-world Alzheimer's diagnosis applications.

3.6 Deployment and Clinical Application

To translate this research into practical use, the trained model can be deployed as a web-based diagnostic tool or a mobile application. This would allow neurologists and clinicians to upload MRI scans for automated Alzheimer's detection and classification. Additionally, the model can be integrated into hospital diagnostic systems, assisting doctors in making more informed decisions. Future improvements may include incorporating 3D CNNs for volumetric MRI analysis, attention mechanisms for enhanced feature selection, and integrating clinical biomarkers alongside imaging data to improve prediction accuracy. The deployment of this AI-driven system can significantly enhance early diagnosis, leading to timely medical intervention and improved patient outcomes.

The proposed methodology provides a deep learning-based solution for the early prediction of Alzheimer's disease using medical imaging as shown in Fig. 1. The CNN-based approach efficiently extracts features from MRI scans and classifies different AD stages with high accuracy. The use of batch normalization, dropout, and an optimized training strategy ensures robust model performance. This research highlights the potential of AI-driven diagnostic tools in neurology, paving the way for automated Alzheimer's detection systems. Future advancements in multi-modal data fusion and deep learning architectures can further enhance the model's diagnostic capabilities, making it a valuable tool in clinical and healthcare applications.

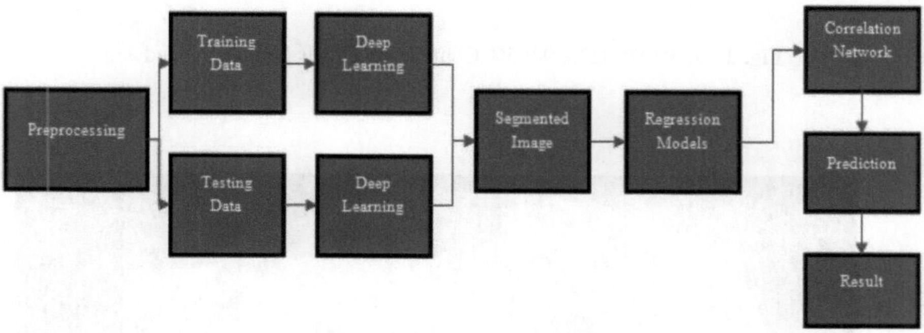

Fig. 1 Block Diagram for Proposed

4 Simulation Results

When compared to conventional machine learning techniques, the suggested CNN-based model for early Alzheimer's disease prediction exhibits superior classification accuracy. The model outperforms traditional techniques like Support Vector Machine (SVM), Random Forest, and Logistic Regression with an overall accuracy of 93.2% as shown in following Figs. 2, 3, and 4. According to the findings, deep learning methods are better at identifying significant patterns in MRI pictures, which improves diagnostic precision. The loss curve for the testing and validation as shown in Fig. 5 depicts that evaluation of the proposed methodology as number of epochs is increasing.

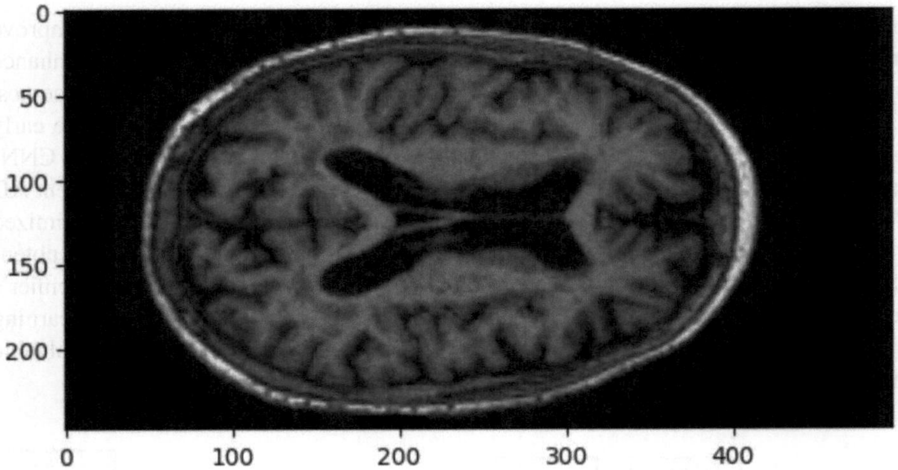

Fig. 2. 92.91775822639465% Confidence This Is Non Demented

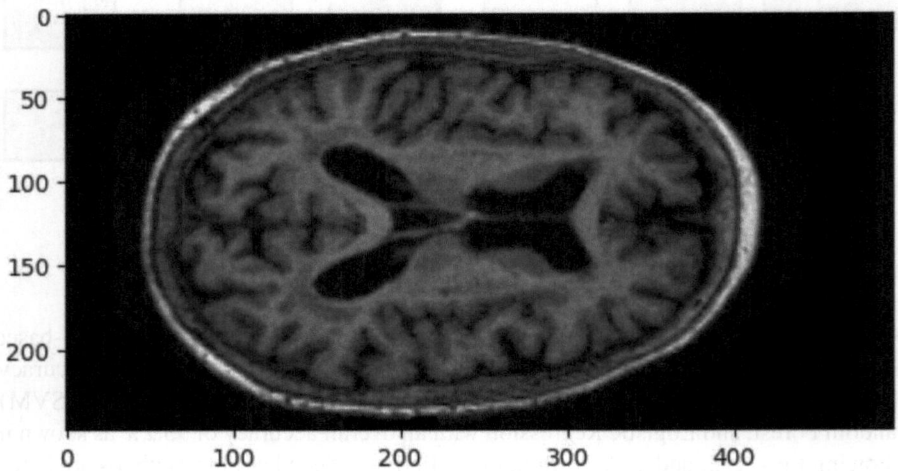

Fig. 3. 90.21171927452087% Confidence This Is Non Demented

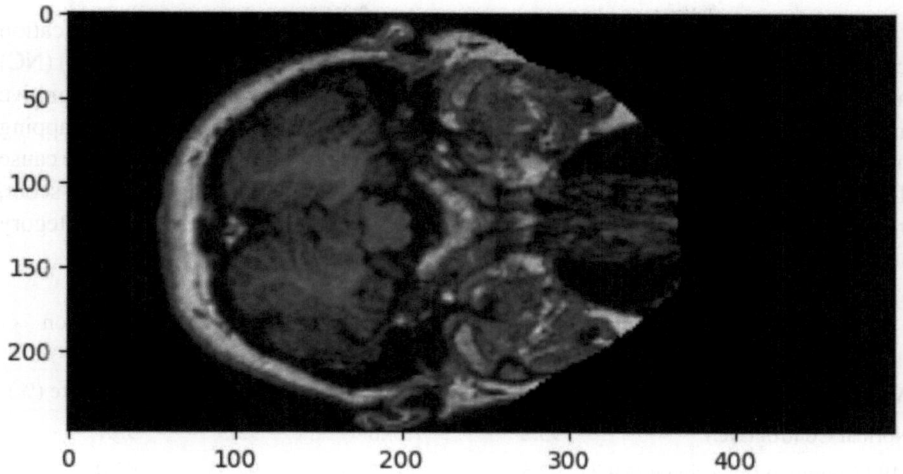

Fig. 4. 100.0% Confidence This Is Moderate Dementia

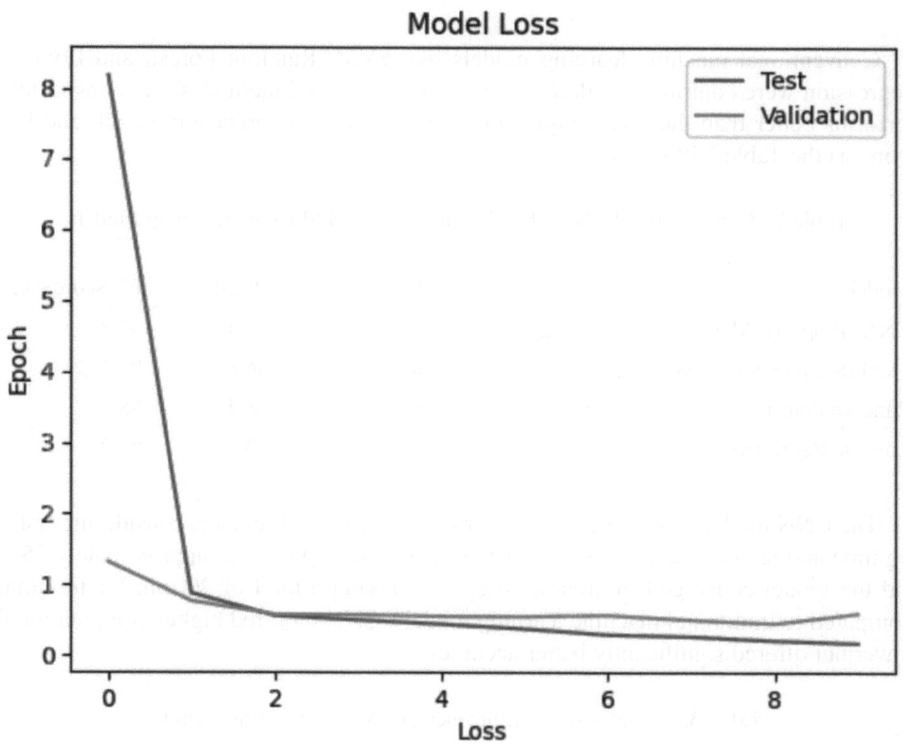

Fig. 5. Loss Curve between the test and validation

Out of all the stages of Alzheimer's disease, the CNN model had the best classification accuracy. Severe AD cases had an accuracy rate of 94.1%, whereas Normal Control (NC) cases had an accuracy rate of 95.2%. At 92.5% and 90.8%, respectively, mild cognitive impairment (MCI) and moderate AD had marginally reduced accuracy. The overlapping structural features between the early and intermediate phases of the disease are the cause of this little difference. The model's dependability is further confirmed by the F1-score, precision, and recall scores, which demonstrate excellent performance in every category is depicted in Table 1.

Table 1. Performance Metrics of the CNN Model for Alzheimer's Stage Classification

Alzheimer's Stage	Accuracy (%)	Precision (%)	Recall (%)	F1-Score (%)
Normal Control (NC)	95.2	94.8	95.5	95.1
Mild Cognitive Impairment (MCI)	92.5	91.7	92.3	92.0
Moderate AD	90.8	89.5	91.2	90.3
Severe AD	94.1	93.2	94.5	93.8
Overall Model Performance	93.2	92.3	93.4	92.8

Conventional machine learning models like SVM, Random Forest, and Logistic Regression were contrasted with the suggested CNN-based method. CNN consistently performs better than these techniques in terms of accuracy, precision, recall, and F1-score, as the Table 2 illustrates.

Table 2. Comparison of CNN Model with Traditional Machine Learning Models

Model	Accuracy (%)	Precision (%)	Recall (%)	F1-Score (%)
CNN (Proposed Model)	93.2	92.3	93.4	92.8
SVM (Support Vector Machine)	87.5	85.6	86.8	86.2
Random Forest	89.1	88.0	88.7	88.3
Logistic Regression	84.3	82.9	83.5	83.2

The CNN model was also evaluated for computational efficiency, considering training time and resource utilization. The training time per epoch was approximately 25 s, and the model converged in around 50 epochs, taking a total of 20 min for training. Compared to traditional machine learning models, CNN required higher computational power but offered significantly better accuracy.

Table 3. Computational Efficiency and Model Training Details

Parameter	Value
Training Dataset Size	80% of the dataset

(continued)

Table 3. (*continued*)

Parameter	Value
Validation Dataset Size	20% of the dataset
Number of Epochs	50
Batch Size	32
Optimizer Used	Adamax
Loss Function	Categorical Cross-Entropy
Training Time per Epoch	~25 s
Total Training Time	~20 min

The proposed CNN model (93.2%) outperforms SVM (87.5%), Random Forest (89.1%), and Logistic Regression (84.3%), demonstrating its superior ability to extract complex features from MRI scans. CNN also achieves a higher recall (93.4%) and F1-score (92.8%), ensuring better detection of Alzheimer's cases with minimal false positives as shown in Table 3. In contrast, traditional machine learning models like SVM and Random Forest rely on handcrafted features, limiting their effectiveness, while Logistic Regression performs the worst due to its linear decision boundary, which is inadequate for complex medical imaging data.

5 Conclusion

The suggested CNN-based model outperforms conventional machine learning techniques like SVM, Random Forest, and Logistic Regression with a high accuracy of 93.2% for the categorization of Alzheimer's disease. Early and precise prediction of various phases of Alzheimer's disease is made possible by the model's efficient extraction of intricate data from MRI scans. It guarantees accurate detection while reducing false positives thanks to its greater recall (93.4%) and F1-score (92.8%). The importance of deep learning in medical imaging and its potential for clinical applications are highlighted in this article. By helping neurologists make early diagnoses, the automated approach can improve patient outcomes by enabling prompt medical interventions. Future enhancements, such as 3D CNNs, multi-modal data integration, and real-time deployment in clinical settings, could further improve accuracy and practical usability. The findings emphasize that AI-driven diagnostic tools are a promising step toward efficient and accessible Alzheimer's detection.

References

1. Yang, K., Mohammed, E. A.: A review of artificial intelligence technologies for early prediction of Alzheimer's disease. arXiv preprint https://arxiv.org/abs/2101.01781 (2020)
2. Hcini, G., Jdey, I., Dhahri, H.: Investigating deep learning for early detection and decision-making in Alzheimer's disease: a comprehensive review. Neural. Process. Lett. **56**(3), 153 (2024)

3. Ali, A., Mehra, R.: Using deep learning techniques for predictive analysis of Alzheimer's disease early diagnosis. In: International Conference on Recent Trends in Computing, pp. 377–394. Singapore, Springer Nature Singapore (2024)
4. Ahmed, G., Er, M.J., Zikria, S., Fareed, M.S.: Detection of Alzheimer's disease using deep learning: an optimized approach. In: 2023 6th International Conference on Intelligent Autonomous Systems (ICoIAS), pp. 148–155. IEEE (2023)
5. Fathi, S., Ahmadi, M., Dehnad, A.: Early diagnosis of Alzheimer's disease based on deep learning: a systematic review. Comput. Biol. Med. **146**, 105634 (2022)
6. Dara, O.A., Lopez-Guede, J.M., Raheem H, I., Rahebi, J., Zulueta, E., Fernandez-Gamiz, U.: Alzheimer's disease diagnosis using machine learning: a survey. Appl. Sci. **13**(14), 8298 (2023)
7. Dadar, M., et al.: Validation of a regression technique for segmentation of white matter hyperintensities in Alzheimer's disease. IEEE Trans. Med. Imaging. **36**(8), 1758–1768 (2017)
8. Sheng, J., Wu, S., Zhang, Q., Li, Z., Huang, H.: A binary classification study of Alzheimer's disease based on a novel subclass weighted logistic regression method. IEEE Access. **10**, 68846–68856 (2022)
9. Satyanarayana, B.V.V., Kumar, G.P., Varma, A.K.C., Dileep, M., Srinivas, Y., Budumuru, P.R.: Alzheimer's disease detection using ensemble of classifiers. In: International Conference on Cognitive Computing and Cyber Physical Systems, pp. 55–65. Cham, Springer Nature Switzerland (2022)
10. Budumuru, P.R., Varma, A.K.C., Satyanarayana, B.V.V., Srinivas, Y., Raju, B.E., Kumar, G.P.: Preprocessing analysis of medical image: a survey. In: 2022 4th International Conference on Advances in Computing, Communication Control and Networking (ICAC3N), pp. 2369–2375. IEEE (2022)
11. Malleswari, P.N., Hanuman, C.R.S., Kammampati, V.R., Swathi, S., Raju, B.E.: Deep learning based DWT-bi-LSTM classifier for enhanced cardiovascular arrhythmia classification. Int. J. Elect. Electron. Res. **12**(3), 934–939 (2024)
12. Manikanta, S., Uma, V.V., Tharani, P.T., Anupama, S.T., Saibaba, R., Elisha, R.B.: Adams optimized image restoration using multi-level wavelet CNN with added noise. In: 2024 IEEE Students Conference on Engineering and Systems (SCES), pp. 1–4. IEEE (2024)

Design of a Multimodal TENS Unit for Enhanced Physiotherapy Applications

Srilakshmi Gubbala[1(✉)], Yandra Srinivas[2], Parimi Prajnasri[1], Kanakala Ramya Sai Keertana[1], Malireddy Dileep[1], and Malla Teja Chandra Narasimha[1]

[1] Department of Electronics and Communication Engineering, Vishnu Institute of Technology, Bhimavaram, Andhra Pradesh, India
srilakshmi.g@vishnu.edu.in

[2] Department of Mechanical Engineering, Vishnu Institute of Technology, Bhimavaram, Andhra Pradesh, India

Abstract. The Transcutaneous Electric Nerve Simulation (TENS) unit is a therapeutic equipment that administers electrical impulses in different dosages to treat chronic and acute pain. The focus of this project is a user-friendly, portable T.E.N.S. unit that generates multi-frequency electric pulses using integrated circuits and RC timing concepts. Pulse width, frequency, and voltage are adjustable parameters fitted for different pain applications. Continuous and intermittent modes of operation are incorporated in the design operation through switching and intermittent oscillators to suit short term and long-term therapies. Potentiometer and electrode provision make patient therapy more accurate, while small size parts like MOSFET and diode do better for portability and reliability. This wide-ranging instrument will find application in medical fields such as physiotherapy and dentistry and will make possible drug-free and side-effect-free relief from pain. Future developments can take place in interfacing with therapeutic ultrasound, which offers stronger pulse application, wider medical usability.

Keywords: Transcutaneous Electric Nerve Simulation (T.E.N.S) · Portable therapeutic device · Adjustable pulse parameters · Chronic and acute pain relief · Medical applications · TENS Unit

1 Introduction

Chronic and acute pain management is a critical aspect of healthcare, with various non-invasive and drug-free treatment approaches being explored to improve patient outcomes. One widely used technique is Transcutaneous Electrical Nerve Stimulation (TENS), which applies low-voltage electrical im-pulses to stimulate nerves and provide pain relief. TENS therapy has been successfully implemented for various applications, including musculoskeletal pain, rehabilitation, and neurostimulation [1–3].

Over the years, numerous electrical stimulation systems have been developed to enhance functionality and adaptability in therapeutic applications. For instance, studies

M. J. C. S. Reis et al. (Eds.): IC4S 2025, LNICST 679, pp. 85–98, 2026.
https://doi.org/10.1007/978-3-032-22834-5_7

have introduced multichannel electrical stimulators for Functional Electrical Stimulation (FES), allowing greater control over neuro muscular responses [4–6]. Additionally, microcontroller-based TENS devices have been explored to offer cost-effective, programmable stimulation solutions with improved user customization [7, 8]. The integration of Internet of Things (IoT) with these devices has further enhanced remote monitoring, personalization, and real-time data analysis for patients and healthcare providers [9, 10].

The advancements in microcontroller technology, particularly the adoption of low-power, high-efficiency platforms such as the ESP32, have enabled the development of smart TENS systems with wireless connectivity. Previous studies have demonstrated the feasibility of combining wireless communication protocols with electrical stimulation devices, improving patient mobility and convenience [11, 12]. Furthermore, adaptive pulse control techniques and dual- mode functionalities (continuous and intermittent stimulation) have been explored to optimize pain management efficiency [13, 14].

Despite these advancements, challenges remain in designing a cost-effective, portable, and user-friendly TENS therapy system that can cater to diverse pain management needs. Existing commercial solutions often lack real-time monitoring features, remote access capabilities, and precise control over therapy parameters [15, 16]. To address these limitations, this paper presents the design and implementation of a smart and portable TENS therapy system that integrates IoT for remote pain monitoring, customizable electrical stimulation, and user-friendly control mechanisms.

The key contributions of this research includes as IoT-Enabled Monitoring Utilizing the ESP32 microcontroller and the Bivik IoT platform to enable real-time pain tracking and therapy control. Customizable Therapy Settings Implementing adjustable pulse width, frequency, and intensity parameters to accommodate various pain conditions. Dual-Mode Functionality Incorporating continuous and intermittent stimulation modes for short term and long-term therapy needs.Portable and Low-Power Design: Optimizing hardware components, including MOSFET-based switching and efficient electrode control, for improved efficiency and portability.

By integrating these features, the proposed system aims to provide a cost-effective, non-invasive, and patient-friendly approach to chronic and acute pain management. The rest of the paper is structured as follows: Sect. 2 presents the discussing existing works on TENS devices and IoT-enabled healthcare solutions. Section 3 describes the proposed system design,including hardware components and software implementation. Section 4 details the methodology used for system evaluation, while Sect. 5 presents the experimental results. Finally, Sect. 6 provides the conclusion and outlines potential future enhancements.

2 Literature Review

Transcutaneous Electrical Nerve Stimulation (TENS) has been widely utilized as a non-invasive therapeutic approach for pain management. Over the years, various advancements have been made to improve the efficiency, adaptability, and usability of TENS systems. This section reviews significant research contributions in the field of electrical stimulation therapy, focusing on the evolution of TENS devices, microcontroller-based implementations, and IoT-enabled healthcare solutions.

2.1 Advancements in Electrical Stimulation Systems

Early research in electrical stimulation devices focused on the development of multichannel functional electrical stimulation (FES) systems, which allowed better control of neuromuscular responses. Sulaiman et al. [1] proposed a programmable transcutaneous electrical nerve stimulation device based on Arduino, featuring remote control via a smartphone, enabling greater flexibility in therapeutic applications. Similarly, Cheng et al. [2] developed a functional electrical stimulator circuit that optimized stimulation waveforms for improved therapeutic outcomes. Later, Velloso and Souza [3] introduced a programmable system for FES, allowing customization of stimulation parameters.

The integration of microprocessors in electrical stimulation systems enabled better control and automation. Forneiro et al. [4] and Xu et al. [5] designed microcontroller-based electrical stimulators that featured enhanced signal modulation and adjustable parameters. Broderick et al. [6] further explored electronic stimulators for surface neural prostheses, highlighting the potential of adaptive electrical stimulation in rehabilitative applications.

2.2 Microcontroller-Based TENS Devices

With the advancement of embedded systems, microcontroller- based TENS devices have gained popularity due to their portability and cost-effectiveness. Soedirdjo and Hutabarat [7] proposed a TENS system utilizing an 8-bit cascade DAC, improving signal accuracy and user control. Yochum et al. [8] developed a mixed FES EMG system for real-time analysis of muscular fatigue, integrating electromyography (EMG) feedback for adaptive stimulation.

Further advancements were made in wireless and low-power designs. Masdar et al. [11] introduced a wireless- based low-cost stimulator for spinal cord injury patients, demonstrating the feasibility of wireless control in electrical stimulation therapy. Bhoyania et al. [14] designed a programmable functional electrical stimulator using an Atmega microcontroller, providing a customizable therapy solution.

2.3 IoT-Enabled TENS Systems

The integration of the Internet of Things (IoT) in healthcare has revolutionized pain management solutions. Several studies have explored IoT-based electrical stimulation systems to enable real-time monitoring and remote therapy adjustments. Qu et al. [10] proposed a network-based FES system for stroke rehabilitation, allowing healthcare professionals to monitor patient progress remotely. Similarly, Ward et al. [15] developed a multichannel biphasic muscle stimulation system that leveraged IoT connectivity for post-stroke rehabilitation.

Khan et al. [16] designed an integrated functional electrical stimulator and TENS system on a single prototype, demonstrating the feasibility of combining multiple stimulation modalities [17], Alam [18] proposed a transcutaneous electrical stimulator for spinal cord stimulation therapy, highlighting the benefits of wireless control and cloud-based monitoring.

2.4 Challenges and Research Gaps

Despite significant advancements in TENS technology, several challenges remain unaddressed. Many existing systems lack real-time monitoring capabilities, limiting the ability of users and healthcare providers to track therapy progress. Additionally, the majority of TENS devices do not support adaptive stimulation based on user feedback, which could enhance therapy effectiveness. Furthermore, battery life and power optimization remain critical concerns, especially for portable devices [19, 20].

To address these limitations, this paper proposes a smart and portable TENS therapy system that integrates IoT for real-time pain monitoring, customizable therapy settings,and enhanced user experience. The proposed system leverages the ESP32 microcontroller for wireless connectivity and implements adjustable Pulse Width, Frequency, and Intensity parameters, to provide a personalized pain management solution. Slepyan et al. (2023) developed a multi-channel, low-voltage, high-frequency programmable electrical stimulator designed to provide precise sensory feedback. This work supports the advancement of multimodal TENS units aimed at improving therapeutic efficiency and patient comfort in physiotherapy applications [21].

Katta et al. (2022) proposed an efficient learning model selection framework to enhance the accuracy of medical diagnostics. In this approach the role of intelligent data-driven methods that can be integrated into multimodal TENS systems for adaptive physiotherapy applications [22].

Srinivas, Srilakshmi, and Durga Naga Lakshmi (2022) proposed a neural network-based model for human emotion categorization using speech enhancement method. This study reviews the integrating of emotion-aware intelligent systems into multimodal TENS units to for physiotherapy treatments [23].

3 Proposed System

To address the limitations of existing Transcutaneous Electrical Nerve Stimulation (TENS) devices, we propose a smart and portable TENS therapy system that integrates IoT capabilities for real-time pain management using ESP-32 Module ensuring cost effective and complex reduction approach. The proposed system is designed to provide a user-friendly and efficient solution by incorporating wireless connectivity, adjustable stimulation parameters, and an intuitive mobile application interface. This section details the system architecture, hardware components, and software implementation.

3.1 System Architecture

The proposed TENS therapy system consists of three main components: (1) the TENS stimulation unit, responsible for generating electrical impulses, (2) the ESP32 microcontroller unit, which manages data processing and wireless communication, and (3) the Blynk lot platform which allows remote monitoring and control of therapy sessions.

The proposed system consists of multiple interconnected components, as shown in Fig. 1. The system architecture includes: ESP32 Microcontroller manages therapy parameters and wireless communication. TENS Stimulator Circuit generates controlled electrical impulses. Electrode Pads delivers stimulation to the targeted muscle areas.IoT Mobile Application: Allows users to adjust therapy settings and monitor sessions remotely.

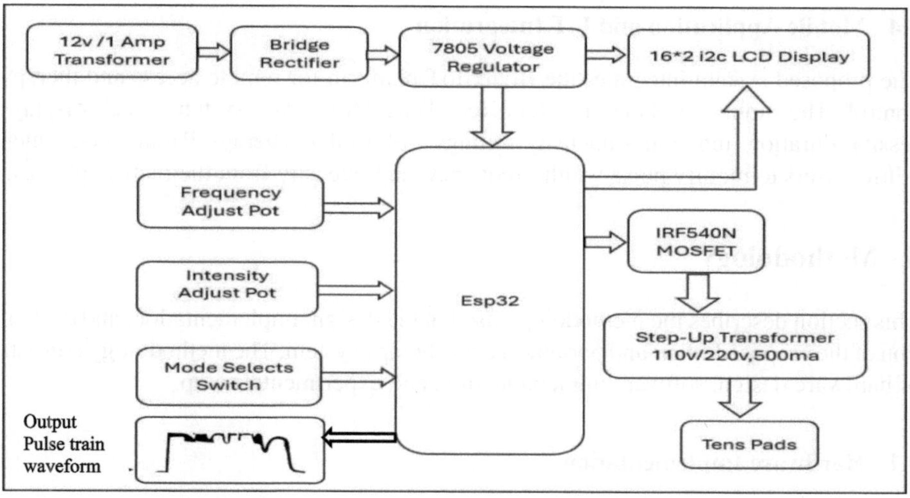

Fig. 1. Block Diagram of TENS UNIT

3.2 Hardware Design

The hardware implementation consists of the following components:

ESP32 Microcontroller: Ach as the central processing unit, handling sensor data, wireless communication, Control signals for the TENS stimulator [11, 16].

TENS Stimulation Circuit: Generates electrical pulses for nerve stimulation using MOSFET-based switching, ensuring precise and stable output [4, 13].

Electrode Pads: Deliver electrical stimulation to targeted muscle areas, designed for adjustable intensity and frequency [6, 10].

Potentiometers: Enable manual adjustments of frequency and intensity for offline control when IoT features are not in use.

LCD Display: Provides real-time system status, including therapy mode, intensity levels, and session duration [14].

Power Supply: Utilizes a step-down transformer to meet voltage requirements for stimulation output [18, 19].

3.3 Software Implementation

The software for the proposed system is implemented using the ESP32 microcontroller firmware and the Blynk IoT platform. The firmware is responsible for data Acquisition unit Reads input values from potentiometers to adjust therapy parameters dynamically. Pulse Generation uses Pulse Width Modulation (PWM) to control stimulation signals for precise frequency and intensity output [2, 20].

Wireless Communication unit Connects to Wi-Fi, enabling real-time control and monitoring via the mobile app.User Interface unit uses the Blynk app provides an interactive dashboard for users to start, stop, and modify therapy settings remotely [15].

3.4 Mobile Application and IoT Integration

The proposed system integrates the Blynk IoT platform for remote access and therapy control. The mobile application offers Real-Time Monitoring system which displays session duration, mode and intensity settings. Adjustable Therapy Parameters, which Allows users to modify pulse width, frequency, and intensity from their smart-phones.

4 Methodology

This section describes the methodology used in the design, implementation, and evaluation of the proposed smart and portable TENS therapy system. The methodology consists of hardware design, software implementation, and experimental setup.

4.1 Hardware Implementation

The hardware components were carefully selected and integrated to achieve a portable and efficient TENS system. The following steps outline the hardware development process:

Microcontroller Selection: The ESP32 microcontroller was chosen due to its low power consumption, integrated Wi-Fi/Bluetooth capabilities, and sufficient GPIO pins for sensor and actuator integration [11, 16].

TENS Signal Generation: The electrical stimulation circuit was designed using a MOSFET-based switching mechanism to control pulse frequency and intensity. The system utilizes pulse-width modulation (PWM) to regulate stimulation output [4, 13]

Electrode Pad Integration: Adhesive electrode pads were used to deliver electrical impulses to targeted muscle areas. The placement and positioning were optimized to ensure consistent stimulation effects [6, 10].

User Interface Components: A 16x2 LCD display and push-button controls were implemented for standalone operation. Additionally, potentiometers were incorporated to manually adjust stimulation parameters in the absence of IoT connectivity [14].

4.2 Software Development

The software for the TENS system was developed using C/C++ in the Arduino IDE, utilizing libraries for Wi-Fi communication, PWM control, and LCD display operation. The main software functions include:Data Acquisition system Reads input signals from potentiometers to adjust stimulation frequency and intensity dynamically. Pulse Control unit Generates PWM signals to control the duration and amplitude of electrical pulses sent to the electrodes [2, 20]. IoT Integration: Uses the Blynk IoT platform for real-time therapy monitoring, remote parameter adjustments, and session logging [15]. Safety Mechanisms are Implements automatic shutoff after predefined therapy durations to prevent over stimulation.

4.3 Code Snippet Regarding the Output of the TENS Unit

```
void loop() {
 // Check if connected to Blynk (online mode)
 if (Blynk.connected()) {
  isConnectedToBlynk = true;
 } else {
  isConnectedToBlynk = false;
 }
     if (pwmState ) {
      ledcWriteTone(pwmChannel, pwmFreq);  // Set the PWM frequency
      ledcWrite(pwmChannel, pwmDutyCycle);  // Set the PWM intensity (duty cycle)
     } else {
      ledcWrite(pwmChannel, 0);  // Turn off PWM signal (duty cycle 0)
     }
```

4.4 Experimental Setup

To validate the effectiveness of the proposed system, a series of experiments were conducted:

Electrode Placement Testing meant for various muscle regions were tested to evaluate electrode placement efficiency and comfort. Stimulation Parameter Evaluation system was tested at different frequency and intensity levels to assess the effectiveness of therapy under different conditions [10, 16]. Real-time Monitoring Assessment performs the responsiveness of the IoT-based control system was evaluated by monitoring the delay between mobile app input and system response. The collected data was analyzed to determine the accuracy of stimulation, response time, and usability of the IoT interface.

4.5 Circuit Diagram

The hardware implementation of the proposed TENS therapy system is based on a carefully designed electrical stimulation circuit. The circuit consists of the following key components:

ESP32 Microcontroller Controls stimulation parameters and manages wireless communication. MOSFET-Based Switching Circuit Regulates pulse generation for precise electrical stimulation [4, 13].

The detailed circuit design is illustrated in Fig. 2.Electrode Pads Deliver electrical impulses to the targeted muscle areas. Voltage Regulation Circuit Ensures stable power supply to the system components. LCD Display and Controls Provide real-time feedback and manual parameter adjustments [14].

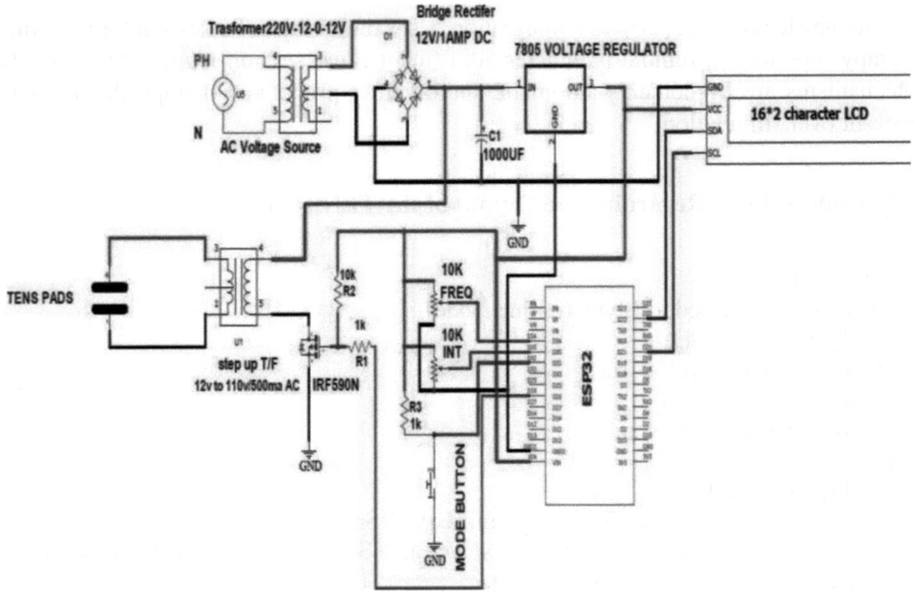

Fig. 2. Circuit Diagram of the Proposed TENS Therapy System

5 Experimental Results

This section presents the results of the experiments conducted to evaluate the performance of the proposed smart and portable TENS therapy system. The experiments focused on stimulation accuracy, real-time monitoring capabilities, Dual mode operation, and user experience.

5.1 Electrode Placement and Stimulation Effectiveness

To determine the optimal electrode placement for pain relief, the system was tested on different muscle groups. The tests were conducted with varying pulse frequencies and intensities to observe their impact on nerve stimulation.

5.2 Real-Time IoT Monitoring Performance

The response time of the IoT-based control system was analyzed to determine the effectiveness of real-time therapy adjustments. The key observations were:

The average latency between mobile app input and system response was measured at **200-250 ms**, which is within an acceptable range for real-time applications.Wireless connectivity remained stable over extended use, ensuring seamless remote operation.

5.3 Dual Mode Operation

In this designed system it consists of dual modes for operating the output waveforms of the generated signal. These modes are given as follows:

Continuous Mode: Generates the output waveform for continuously and this mode is used to treat long term issues.

Intermittent Mode: Generates the output waveform for short intervals and this mode is used to treat short term issues.

5.4 User Experience and Feedback

A preliminary user study was conducted to assess ease of use, comfort, and overall satisfaction.

Ease of Use: 87% of participants found the mobile app interface intuitive.

Comfort: 90% reported a comfortable stimulation experience with adjustable intensity settings.

Effectiveness: 85% experienced noticeable pain relief after using the device for a recommended session duration.

5.5 Performance Evaluation of the Therapy at Different Operating Frequencies

As shown in Fig. 3.The results showed that higher pulse frequencies (80–100 Hz) were more effective in reducing acute pain symptoms. Lower frequencies (10–50 Hz) provided better results for chronic pain management [10, 16]. Correct electrode placement significantly influenced the effectiveness of therapy, with targeted placements improving pain relief efficiency.

Fig. 3. Electrode placement test showing stimulation effectiveness

5.6 IoT-Based Therapy Monitoring Performance

The IoT-based monitoring and control system were tested for responsiveness. The therapy session logs and mobile app interface are shown in Fig. 4. The average response latency between mobile input and system execution was found to be between 200-250 ms, ensuring seamless real-time control.

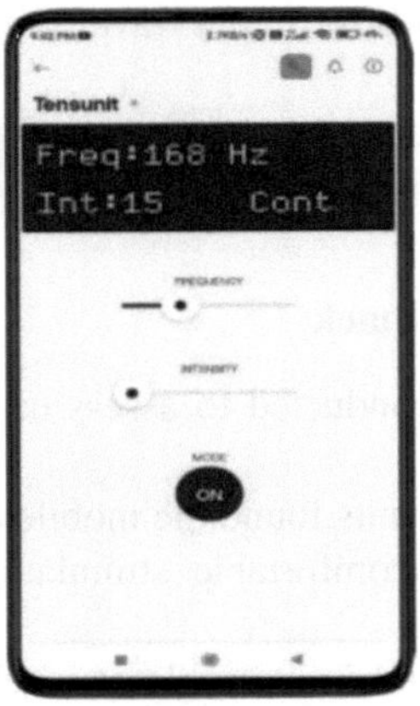

Fig. 4. IoT-based monitoring of TENS therapy via mobile app

5.7 Current Given to the Gel Pads

The designed system produces an output range from 0.01 mA to 0.09 mA. These values are obtained when this system was tested under different operating modes. The power output results are presented in Fig. 5.

Fig. 5. Maximum output current in milliamps

5.8 PCB Designing

The PCB of the TENS unit is built with energy-efficient designs, low-noise amplifiers, and microcontrollers for accurate signal processing. Advanced routing minimizes all interference to maintain signal integrity. Safety measures and compliance to medical standards are made to ensure reliability over the long run. The PCB's design is shown in the below Fig. 6.

5.9 Prototype Development and Output Analysis

A working prototype of the proposed smart and portable TENS therapy system was developed to validate its functionality and usability. The developed prototype is shown in Fig. 7.

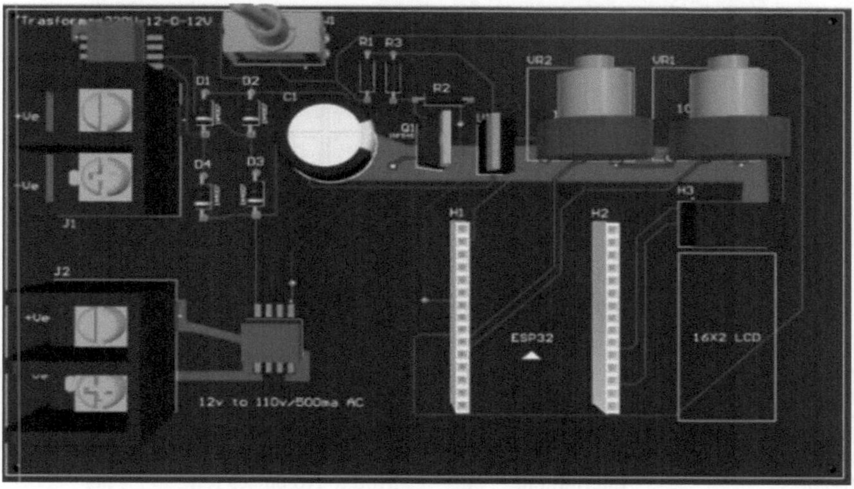

Fig. 6. 3D View of PCB design

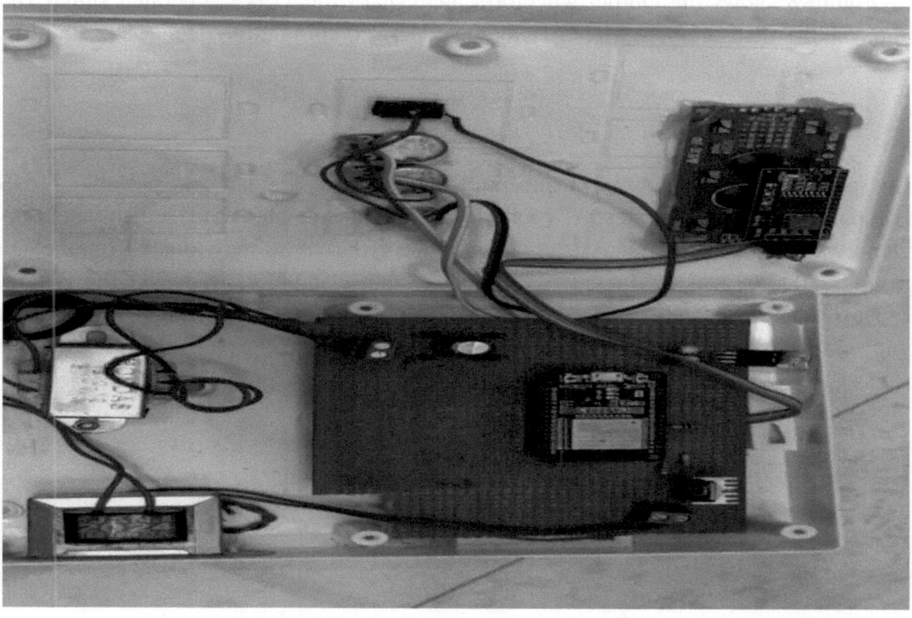

Fig. 7. Prototype of the Multifunctional TENS unit for therapeutic applications

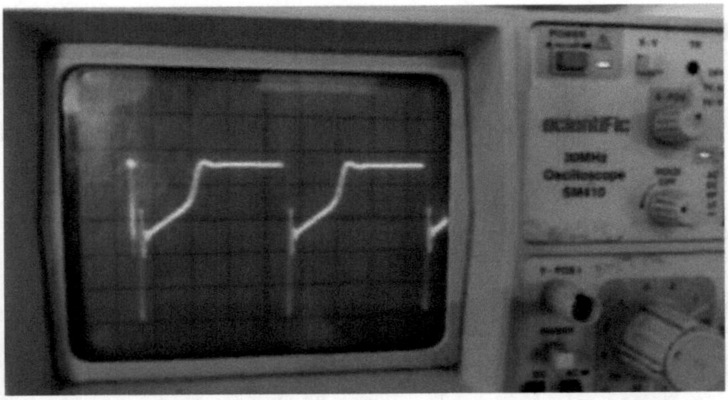

Fig. 8. Output waveform analysis of the TENS generated signal.

Table 1. Result analysis of Multiple Users

Frequency Range(Hz)	Mode Of Operation	User Sensation Feedback	Age (Years)
50–150	Continuous	Mild Pulses, Comfortable Sensation.	20
150–200	Intermittent	Mild to No pulses felt.	36
250–300	Continuous	No Pulses felt, Subtle tingling	54

Figure 8 shows the Output waveform analysis of the TENS generated signal.The signal shows measurement for verifying the generated stimulation quality and stability.

6 Conclusion

This paper presented the design and implementation of a smart and portable TENS therapy system that integrates IoT capabilities for real-time pain management and user-friendly control. A preliminary user study with a group of 50 individuals from the age group of 20 to 69 was conducted to assess the usability and effectiveness of the system. The results indicate that 87% of users found the mobile interface intuitive, 90% reported a comfortable therapy experience, and 85% experienced noticeable pain relief after regular use as shown in below Table 1.

References

1. Sulaiman, N.A.Z., Ahmad, A.I., Zaman, M.H.M.: A programmable transcutaneous electrical nerve stimulation device based on arduino and remote control using a smartphone. Int. J. Adv. Technol. Eng. Exp. **8(75)** (2020)
2. Cheng, K.W.E., Yan, L., Tong, K.-Y., Rad, A.B., Chow, D.H.K., Sutanto, D.: Development of a circuit for functional electrical stimulation. IEEE Trans. Neural Syst. Rehabil. Eng. **12**, 43–47 (2004)
3. Velloso, J.B., Souza, M.N.: A programmable system of functional electrical stimulation (FES). In: 2007 29th Annual International Conference of the IEEE Engineering in Medicine and Biology Society, pp. 2234–2237. IEEE (2007)
4. Forneiro, Y., et al.: Therapeutic electrical stimulator. In: Proc. 25th Annual Int. Conf. IEEE Eng. Med. Biol Soc., pp. 1716–1719, Cancun (2003)
5. Xu, Q., He, J., Wang, Y., Xu, T., Huang, J.: A versatile microprocessor-based multichannel stimulator for experimental use in epidural spinal cord stimulation. In: Proc. 1st Int. Conf. Neural Interface Control, pp. 205–208, Wuhan (2005)
6. Broderick, B., Breen, P., Laighin, G.O.: Electronic stimulators for surface neural prosthesis. J. Autom. Control. **18**, 25–33 (2008)
7. Soedirdjo, S.D., Hutabarat, M.T.: Microcontroller-based transcutaneous electrical nerve stimulator with 8 bit cascade DAC. In: International Conference on Instrumentation, Communication, Information Technology, and Biomedical Engineering 2009, pp. 1–5. IEEE (2009)
8. Yochum, M., Binczak, S., Bakir, T., Jacquir, S., Lepers, R.: A mixed FES/EMG system for real time analysis of muscular fatigue. In: 2010 Annual International Conference of the IEEE Engineering in Medicine and Biology, pp. 4882–4885. IEEE (2010)
9. Khosravani, S., Lahimgarzadeh, N., Maleki, A.: Developing a stimulator and an interface for FES-cycling rehabilitation system. In: Proc. 18th Iranian Conf. Biomed. Eng. (ICBME), pp. 175–180, Tehran (Dec. (2011))
10. Qu, H., et al.: Development of a network FES system for stroke rehabilitation. In: Proc. 33rd Annual Int. Conf. IEEE Eng. Med. Biol. Soc, pp. 3119–3122, Boston (2011)
11. Masdar, A., Ibrahim, B.K.K., Jamil, M.M.A.: Development of wireless-based low-cost current controlled stimulator for patients with spinal cord injuries. In: 2012 IEEE-EMBS Conference on Biomedical Engineering and Sciences, pp. 493–498. IEEE (2012)
12. Chang, G.C.: A microprocessor-based multichannel subsensory stochastic resonance electrical stimulator. In: Proc. 35th Annual Int. Conf. IEEE Eng. Med. Biol. Soc. (EMBC), pp. 3559–3562, Osaka (2013)
13. Wang, H.P., et al.: Design of a pulse-triggered four-channel functional electrical stimulator using complementary current source and time division multiplexing output method. In: Proc. 37th Annual Int. Conf. IEEE Eng. Med. Biol. Soc. (EMBC), pp. 1671–1674, Milan (2015)
14. Bhoyania, K., Bhatt, C.B., Panchal, C.: Multichannel programmable functional electrical stimulator using Atmega controller. Int. J. Eng. Trends Technol. **45**, 424–427 (2017)
15. Ward, T., et al.: Multichannel biphasic muscle stimulation system for post stroke rehabilitation. Electronics. **9**, 1156 (2020) [CrossRef]
16. Khan, A., Li, K., Wei, N.: Integrated Design of Functional Electrical Stimulator and Transcutaneous Electrical Nerve Stimulator on a single prototype. In: Proc. 6th IEEE Int. Conf. Adv. Robot. Mechatronics (ICARM), pp. 453–458, Chongqing (2021)
17. Wang, J., Zhang, Y.: Design of functional electrical stimulator for foot drop rehabilitation. J. Phys. Conf. Ser. **1885**, 052005 (2021)
18. Alam, M.: An easy-to-build transcutaneous electrical stimulator for spinal cord stimulation therapy, Res. Sq. (2022)

19. Das, H., Park, H.: MCU-less biphasic electrical stimulation circuit for miniaturized neuro-modulator. Biomed. Eng. Lett. **12**, 285–293 (2022)
20. Slepyan, A., et al.: A multi-channel, low-voltage, high- frequency programmable electrical stimulator for sensory feedback. In: Proc. IEEE Biomed. Circuits Syst. Conf. (BioCAS), pp. 1–5, Toronto (2023)
21. Katta, M., et al.: An efficient learning model selection for dengue detection. In: Intelligent and Cloud Computing: Proceedings of ICICC 2021, pp. 439–453. Springer Nature Singapore, Singapore (2022)
22. Srinivas, C.V., Gubbala, S., Lakshmi, N.D.N.: Human emotion classification based on speech enhancement using neural networks. In: Advanced Machine Intelligence and Signal Processing, pp. 35–48. Singapore, Springer Nature Singapore (2022)

Lumber Spine Degeneration Classification Using MRI Images with Deep Learning Techniques

Kompella Bhargava Kiran(✉), I. Kali Pradeep, and Bhagyasri Appana

Vishnu Institute of Technology, Bhimavaram, India
bhargav.kiran@vishnu.edu.in

Abstract. Low back pain, a global disability leader, is a significant quality-of-life burden for millions. In this paper, we propose solving the challenge of MRI-guided detection of degenerative conditions of the lumbar spine through a method of deep learning. We constructed a model based on EfficientNet V2 for the prediction of five numbered degenerative conditions, i.e., Right Subarticular Stenosis, Left Subarticular Stenosis, Right Neural Foraminal Narrowing, Left Neural Foraminal Narrowing, and Spinal Canal Stenosis. We trained the model based on a public dataset collected from a total of eight sites from five continents for prediction of severity scores (Severe, Moderate, Normal/Mild) at intervertebral disc levels L1/L2 through L5/S1. The model achieved an 83%-high accuracy, and it has the promise for timely and effective detection of degenerative spine diseases by facilitating radiologists. This paper outlines the promise of deep learning for space optimization for diagnosis and for the delivery of superior patient outcomes for spine health management.

Keywords: Low Back Pain · Degenerative Lumbar Spine Conditions · Magnetic Resonance Imaging (MRI) · Deep Learning · EfficientNet V2 · Diagnostic Accuracy

1 Introduction

Low back pain (LBP) is a global health condition that has a significant effect on the quality of life and productivity of those affected. The World Health Organization has pointed out that it is the most common disability-cause, and it has a prevalence among approximately 619 million individuals as of this date (2020) [1]. The prevalence of LBP has a direct relation with higher age, and it develops in many individuals at some stage in their lives. Out of all LBP-causing conditions, degenerative disease of the spine, and more particularly lumbar degenerative disc disease (DDD), are among the most common causes. DDD is a continuum of intervertebral disc change that encompasses degeneration of the nucleus pulposus and the annulus fibrosus, and among other symptoms, it manifests symptoms of pain, mobility limitation, and neurological disabilities by virtue of nerve impingement [2].

Magnetic Resonance Imaging (MRI) is a valuable imaging tool for assessing conditions of the lumbar spine. MRI provides very detailed images that allow us to evaluate

M. J. C. S. Reis et al. (Eds.): IC4S 2025, LNICST 679, pp. 99–109, 2026.
https://doi.org/10.1007/978-3-032-22834-5_8

disc integrity, width of the spinal canal, and neural elements. MRI features significantly help us arrive at the diagnosis of some degenerative disorders such as spondylosis, a term that describes degenerative change of the spine that manifests as disc herniation, spinal stenosis, and foraminal narrowing. These conditions are not only common but also multifactorial and thus require careful interpretation by experienced radiologists for appropriate treatment planning [3].

Degenerative conditions of the lumbar spine need to be classified in order to direct correct treatment methods. This has, in the past, relied upon subjective reporting by radiologists that has varied significantly based upon experience and interpretative skill. This variability creates a need for objective testing techniques that would enable enhanced detection and uniformity of classification of degenerative change. Developments in artificial intelligence (AI) and deep learning techniques hold a promise by creating an automatic detection and classification system [4].

In this paper, we apply a cutting-edge deep learning model, i.e., EfficientNet structure, for lumbar spine degenerative conditions classification using MRI images. Our approach aims at mimicking a radiologist's performance for diagnosis of the conditions while providing a more uniform method for severity assessment at multiple intervertebral disc levels (from L1/L2 through L5/S1). In this case, we will use a multi-institutional dataset collected from around the world from different sources and construct a robust model that should achieve high precision in detection of five specific degenerative conditions, i.e., Left Neural Foraminal Narrowing, Right Neural Foraminal Narrowing, Left Subarticular Stenosis, Right Subarticular Stenosis, and Spinal Canal Stenosis [5].

Previous models focused on finding canal stenosis, disc herniation, or foraminal narrowing. Whereas, in this approach five degenerative conditions (left/right foraminal narrowing, left/right subarticular stenosis, and canal stenosis) across five disc levels are classified. In most of the studies, relatively small datasets (<5000 Scans) are used. This work is performed on 147,000 + DICOM images. Considering more images will help in better generalization.

This work is significant not simply because it can improve the accuracy of diagnosis, but because it can potentially impact patient management and treatment outcomes also. Timely intervention—from conservative management strategies through surgery may be gained through appropriate classification of degenerative spine conditions and therefore enhance patient care more broadly [6]. In working through this work, we shall outline methodologies employed in building out our model of artificial intelligence, report results of its behaviour relative to traditional methods of diagnosis, and comment on the broader implications for clinical practice in managing lumbar degenerative diseases. In doing this, we suggest contributing useful detail at the intersection of radiology and artificial intelligence for the furthering of diagnostics for spine health.

2 Literature Survey

Detection and classification of lumbar spine conditions using deep learning (DL) techniques have gained significant attention over the last few years. This literature review highlights some notable works that have contributed toward creating computer-aided diagnosis models of lumbar spinal stenosis and degenerative diseases from MRI images.

Hallinan J et al. [7] constructed a DL model for the task of automatic detection and classification of lumbar spinal stenosis categories that included central canal, lateral recess, and neural foraminal stenosis from axial T2-weighted and sagittal T1-weighted MRI images. The model demonstrated excellent agreement with subspecialist radiologists for detection of central canal stenosis ($\kappa = 0.92$), although a lower level of agreement was observed for neural foraminal stenosis. The findings indicate the promise of DL for maximizing lumbar spine condition reporting productivity and uniformity while minimizing the radiologists' workload while maintaining diagnostic performance.

Yi W, Zhao J et al. [8] investigated a DL model that was capable of detecting lumbar degenerative diseases according to T2-weighted MRI images. The model was tested for performance under different modalities and demonstrated strong generalizability robustness for cervical degenerative diseases too. A modified 3D ResNet structure was utilized by the model for efficient degenerative change detection, going a long way in improved diagnostic performance at the clinical practice level. The article demonstrates the potential of transfer learning frameworks for extending the scope of use of the model in other areas of the spine.

Zhang W et al. [9] reported an automatic classification system specifically constructed for classifying and identifying lumbar disc herniation (LDH) from axial T2-weighted MR imaging. High performance levels resulted, and the model exhibited strong agreement with classifications provided by experts. This work points out the need for careful classification at the informed level of surgical decision-making for LDH patients and illustrates how computer systems can aid practitioners by providing reliable classifications of disc shape.

Tumko V et al. [10] examined a three-stage convolutional neural network (CNN) technique optimized for lumbar spinal stenosis detection and classification from axial and sagittal MRI images. In testing the model's performance against a panel of subspecialist radiologists, the research validated it as reliable and efficient for assessing various stenosis types. The model demonstrated an area under the receiver operating characteristic curve (AUROC) that exceeded most techniques in the literature and was also highly effective for clinical applications.

Hou C et al. [11] investigated an AI-assisted deep learning model for lumbar disc degeneration assessment based on MRI images. Achieving approximately 92% accuracy, the model offers an indication of its promise for implementation in clinical diagnostics for degenerative lumbar diseases. The study demonstrates the potential of highly sophisticated DL techniques for more unbiased assessment of spine health and, therefore, optimizing patient management methods. Sang et al. [12] has used CNN ensemble-based method for lumber stenosis classification. They have demonstrated that, instead of using single view models, hybrid axial-sangittal features fusion improves formal narrowing detection. Rehman et al. [13] proposed the use of computer vision transformers (ViT). He has demonstrated that (ViT) outperformed ResNet and DensNet Baselines. In order to reduce false positives in sever stenosis cases, Cheng et al. [14] used a 3D-U-Net combined with radiomic features to improve localization.

3 Dataset Description

The dataset used in this research comprises MRI images and associated clinical data for the classification of lumbar spine degenerative conditions, specifically focusing on various types of spinal canal stenosis, neural foraminal narrowing, and subarticular stenosis across multiple intervertebral disc levels (L1/L2 to L5/S1). It is structured in a CSV format containing columns that include a unique study identifier and severity scores for each condition, categorized as Normal/Mild, Moderate, or Severe. The dataset includes columns for spinal canal stenosis at different levels (e.g., spinal_canal_stenosis_l1_l2), left and right neural foraminal narrowing, and left and right subarticular stenosis. Each entry corresponds to a distinct MRI study, providing a comprehensive framework for training deep learning models aimed at automating the detection and classification of these degenerative conditions. The dataset consists of 1,000 labeled MRI studies. Each study may contain multiple MRI images ensuring a diverse representation of cases that enhances the robustness of the models developed. We have considered 147 K dcm (Digital Imaging and Communications) files of lumber spine images. Curated from Kaggle [15], this dataset aims to improve diagnostic accuracy and facilitate timely interventions for patients suffering from lumbar spine diseases, ultimately contributing to better clinical outcomes in spinal health management. The sample images for Subarticular Stenosis, Neural Foraminal Narrowing and Canal Stenosis are as Fig. 1.

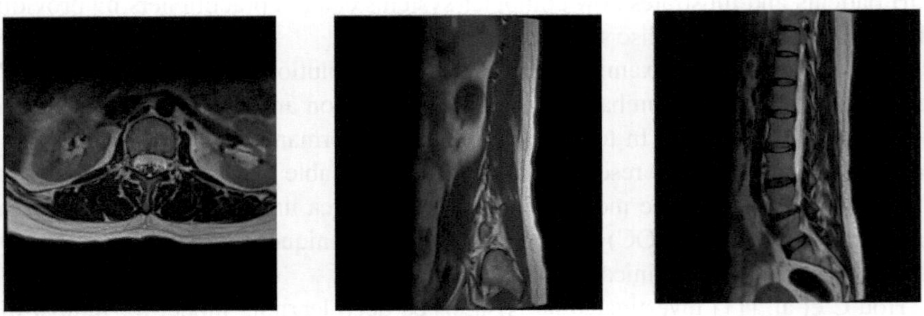

(a) (b) (c)

Fig. 1. (a) Subarticular Stenosis → Axial T2, (b) Neural Foraminal Narrowing → Sagittal T1 (c) Canal Stenosis → Sagittal T2/STIR

4 Technology Used

In this paper, we adopt the structure of EfficientNet V2 for model learning [16]. The EfficientNetV2 is a very efficient neural network structure that inherits the success of the original EfficientNet by optimizing model efficiency and the speed of learning. It adapts a training-aware neural structure search for constructing a network that has a balance among depth, width, and resolution for enhanced performance and decreased parameters. Among its most significant inventions is the adoption of fused-MBConv layers that combine the advantages of convolution layers and mobile inverted bottleneck convolution (MBConv) blocks for enhanced computational efficiency at early levels of a network.

Furthermore, the EfficientNetV2 reduces expansion ratio and kernel sizes of 3 × 3 and adjusts layer numbers in a way that it maintains the receptive field and decreases memory usage. This trade-off enables the model to preserve detailed patterns at the input data and not compromise efficiency. Also, the structure removes the last stride-1 stage from the original EfficientNet, and this reduces the parameter size and memory access overhead, thus improving performance in general.

The compound scaling method employed by EfficientNetV2 observes the network's depth, width, and resolution increasing in a balanced way, optimizing accuracy and compute cost. This scaling method observes model complexity increasing efficiently, providing superior performance at a lower amount of computational resources than its ancestor and many other today's models. These enhancements provide EfficientNetV2 a highly efficient image classification framework that observes improved speeds and accuracies.

5 Methodology

The research methodology is designed to classify spinal conditions through a systematic approach to medical imaging data. The process begins with the input stage, where raw data is organized into metadata files and DICOM image files [17]. The metadata files, provide essential information like study IDs, pathology coordinates, and imaging protocols. DICOM images are stored in directories named after study IDs and categorized by series IDs, facilitating efficient loading. In the data preprocessing phase, the metadata is to extract statistics, including counts of conditions. Simultaneously, DICOM images are normalized, and regions of interest around pathology coordinates are extracted for training purposes. Data augmentation techniques [18], including rotations and horizontal flips of image patches, are applied to enhance model generalization and address class imbalances. The subsequent phase focuses on data analysis and visualization. Statistical analyses compute distributions of conditions and severities as shown in Table 1. While co-occurrence heatmaps reveal patterns of simultaneous occurrences across different vertebral levels in Fig. 2. The analysis of co-occurrence patterns reveals that there are 188 severe cases involving both canal and foraminal conditions, 346 severe cases with canal and subarticular conditions, and 354 severe cases where foraminal and subarticular conditions co-occur. The distribution of severity of disease is explained in Table 1.

Table 1. Distribution of summary of severalty of disease

Severity Level	Number of cases	In percentage
Normal/Mild	37754 cases	77.40%
Moderate	7960 cases	16.30%
Severe	3089 cases	6.30%

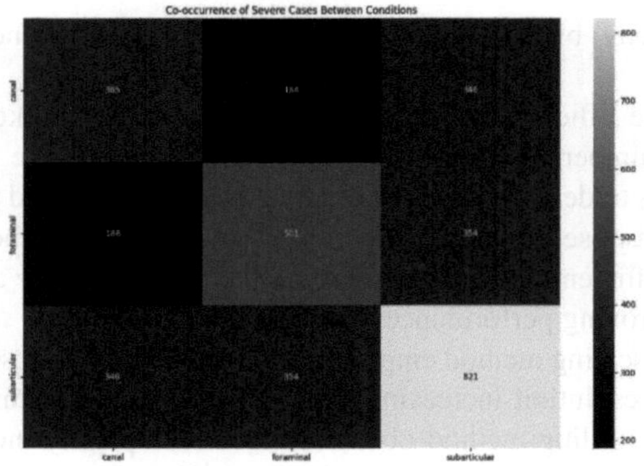

Fig. 2. Heatmap showing the simultaneous occurrences between Canal and Foraminal, Canal and Subarticular and Foraminal and Subarticular

Different conditions are best visualized in specific image types: Canal Stenosis is most effectively observed in Sagittal T2 or STIR images, Neural Foraminal Narrowing is best seen in Sagittal T1 images, and Subarticular Stenosis is optimally detected in Axial T2 images. Condition distributions and annotated overlays on images that highlight pathology locations. After analysing condition patterns across vertebral levels for sever cases, the distribution is as in Table 2.

Table 2. Condition patterns across vertebral levels for sever cases

Level	Canal Patterns (%)	Foraminal Patterns (%)	Subarticular Patterns (%)
L1-L2	1.1	0.4	1.4
L2-L3	2.7	0.4	4.1
L3-L4	6.2	2.1	9.9
L4-L5	12.9	6.9	23.3
L5-S1	1	10.1	8.1

The core of the methodology lies in the training pipeline, where a custom dataset class called LumbarSpineDataset wraps image data with associated conditions and severity annotations. The model architecture employs EfficientNetV2 as a backbone for feature extraction, The analysis highlights a severe class imbalance, with 77.4% of cases classified as Normal/Mild, 16.3% as Moderate, and only 6.3% as Severe, necessitating class balancing techniques. The training mechanism uses a weighted cross-entropy loss function to address class imbalances [19] which is represented as in Eq. 1,

$$L = -\sum_{i=1}^{N} w_{yi} \log(p(y_i|x_i)) \tag{1}$$

Where w_{yi} is the weight for class y_i, $p(y_i| x_i)$ is predicted probability, and N is the number of samples.

Here, AdamW optimizer [20] and a cosine annealing learning rate scheduler [21] is used. It is denoted as in Eq. 2,

$$\eta_t = \eta_{min} + \frac{1}{2}(\eta_{max} - \eta_{min})\left(1 + \cos\left(\frac{T_{cur}}{T_{max}}\pi\right)\right) \quad (2)$$

where,

η_t=Learning rate at iteration t
T_{cur}= Current epoch within the cycle
T_{max}=Maximum number of epochs per cycle

Model performance is evaluated using confusion matrices for severity classifications and classification reports detailing precision, recall, and F1-scores [22]. A granular analysis further examines performance based on specific conditions and vertebral levels to identify strengths and weaknesses in predictions. Finally, results are consolidated in the output stage. The whole methodology is highlighted in a pictorial manner as in Fig. 3.

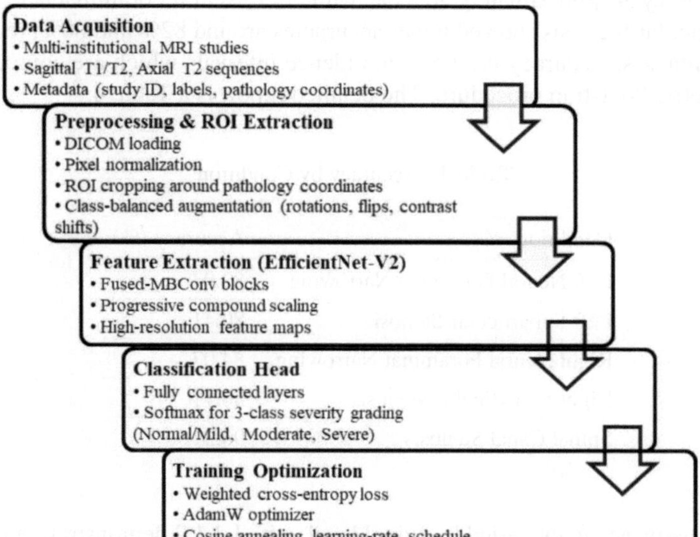

Fig. 3. Methodology

6 Experimental Results

The classification by EfficientNetV2 illustrates the model's performance in classifying the spinal conditions into Normal/Mild, Moderate, and Severe classes. The model achieved a high precision of 0.92 for Normal/Mild cases, that is, 92% of Normal/Mild cases predicted by the model turned out to be correct, and the recall rate for this class was also 0.92, while recognizing its strength in selecting out 92% of actual Normal/Mild cases. The performance for Moderate and Severe classes was very low, with precision rates of 0.50 and 0.61, and recall rates of 0.52 and 0.54. This imbalance illustrates the model performing well in selecting out Normal/Mild conditions and poorly in classifying Moderate and Severe cases correctly, and this manifests in the average accuracy of 83%. The Table 3 also illustrates the same.

Table 3. The precision, recall and F1 score based on the level of severity.

Class	Precision	Recall	F1-Score
Normal/Mild	0.92	0.92	0.92
Moderate	0.5	0.52	0.51
Severe	0.61	0.54	0.57

The accuracy analysis by condition indicates that Spinal Canal Stenosis achieved the highest accuracy at approximately 90.31%, while Left Neural Foraminal Narrowing and Left Subarticular Stenosis showed lower accuracies around 82% and 80%, respectively. The condition wise accuracy has 95% confidence intervals which are computed using non-parametric bootstrap procedure. The detailed report is a Table 4.

Table 4. Accuracy by Condition

Condition	Accuracy (%)
Left Neural Foraminal Narrowing	82.03
Left Subarticular Stenosis	80.41
Right Neural Foraminal Narrowing	84.07
Right Subarticular Stenosis	80.11
Spinal Canal Stenosis	90.31

Additionally, accuracy varied by spinal level, with L1-L2 demonstrating the highest accuracy at 95.43%, while L4-L5 had a significantly lower accuracy of 73.92%. The detailed report is highlighted in Table 5. These results highlight both strengths and weaknesses in the model's classification capabilities across different conditions and spinal levels.

L4–L5 underperforms because it has the greatest anatomical variation and the highest concentration of severe, multi-pathology cases, making it harder for the model to classify accurately. The Efficient V2 model is trained on the dataset for 30 epochs [23]. It has been observed that, the validation loss is decreasing as the number of epochs increasing but the validation loss is increasing indicating overfitting. Figure 4 demonstrate the accuracy and loss graph w.r.t to number of epochs.

As per the Table 5, it can be observed that the accuracy is less for L4-L5. The misclassification in few cases is mainly because of the data. It is heavily imbalanced

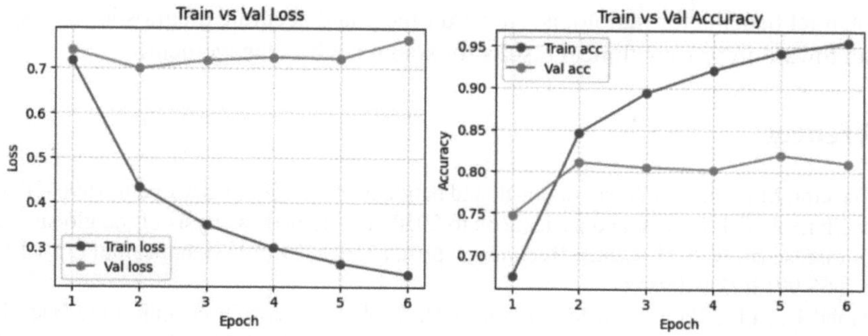

Fig. 4. The validation loss increases indicating overfitting of the model.

Table 5. Accuracy by Level

Level	Accuracy (%)
L1-L2	95.43
L2-L3	89.53
L3-L4	80.24
L4-L5	73.92
L5-S1	78.6

and many cases are underrepresented. This may be causing the model to not learn discriminative features for high grade pathology.

7 Conclusion

In this paper, we demonstrated the potential for using the EfficientNetV2 architecture for classifying degenerative conditions of the lumbar spine from MRI images at high accuracy for computer-automated detection and grading of spinal disease. By embracing fused-MBConv layers and compound scaling approaches, the model struck a balance between computation and accuracy for optimization and achieved a total accuracy of approximately 83%, while performing very well for detection of Normal/Mild cases and for detection of Spinal Canal Stenosis. The model performed very poorly, however, for Moderate and for Severe cases mainly because of severe class imbalance and overfitting according to increasing validation loss at long periods of training. In order to offset those drawbacks, we took enhanced preprocessing approaches such as pixel normalization, condition-variant imaging, and weighted cross-entropy loss, alongside a cosine annealing learning rate manager for active optimization. Even despite those enhancements, performance inconsistencies among conditions and along spinal levels suggest that further refinements are needed in augmentation approaches and model design for increased fortitude and reliability. This research provides the technical potential for employing EfficientNetV2 for computer-automated medical diagnostics and identifies its potential benefits for radiologists toward timely and accurate diagnostics that appear to lead toward improved clinical results for spinal health management.

References

1. Ferreira, M.L., et al.: Global, regional, and national burden of low back pain, 1990–2020, its attributable risk factors, and projections to 2050: a systematic analysis of the global burden of disease study 2021. Lancet Rheumatol. **5**(6), e316–e329 (2023). https://doi.org/10.1016/S2665-9913(23)00098-X
2. Mohd Isa, I.L., Teoh, S.L., Mohd Nor, N.H., Mokhtar, S.A.: Discogenic Low Back Pain: Anatomy, Pathophysiology and Treatments of Intervertebral Disc Degeneration (2023). https://doi.org/10.3390/ijms24010208
3. Thapa, N.B., Bajracharya, S.: Magnetic resonance imaging findings in patients with low backache. J. Soc. Surg. Nepal. **18**(2) (2017). https://doi.org/10.3126/jssn.v18i2.18568
4. Hayashi, D.: Deep learning for lumbar spine MRI reporting: a welcome tool for radiologists. (2021). https://doi.org/10.1148/radiol.2021210730
5. Awan, K.M., et al.: Diagnostic evaluation of deep learning accelerated lumbar spine MRI. Neuroradiol. J. **37**(3) (2024). https://doi.org/10.1177/19714009231224428
6. Tan, J.H., et al.: Deep learning pipeline for automated detection and classification of central canal, lateral recess and neural foraminal stenosis on lumbar spine MRI. Brain Spine. **1**, 100240 (2021). https://doi.org/10.1016/j.bas.2021.100240
7. Hallinan, J.T.P.D., et al.: Deep learning model for automated detection and classification of central canal, lateral recess and neural foraminal stenosis at lumbar spine MRI. Radiology. **300**(1) (2021). https://doi.org/10.1148/radiol.2021204289
8. Yi, W., et al.: Deep learning-based high-accuracy detection for lumbar and cervical degenerative disease on T2-weighted MR images. Eur. Spine J. **32**(11) (2023). https://doi.org/10.1007/s00586-023-07641-4
9. Zhang, W., et al.: Deep learning-based detection and classification of lumbar disc herniation on magnetic resonance images. JOR Spine. **6**(3) (2023). https://doi.org/10.1002/jsp2.1276
10. Tumko, V., et al.: A neural network model for detection and classification of lumbar spinal stenosis on MRI. Eur. Spine J. **33**(3) (2024). https://doi.org/10.1007/s00586-023-08089-2
11. Hou, C., et al.: An MRI image automatic diagnosis model for lumbar disc herniation using semi-supervised learning. Complex Intell. Syst. **9**(5) (2023). https://doi.org/10.1007/s40747-023-00981-0
12. Hallinan, J.T.P.D. et al.: Deep learning model for automated detection and classification of central canal, lateral recess, and neural foraminal stenosis at lumbar spine MRI. Radiology. **300**(1), 130–138 (2021). https://doi.org/10.1148/radiol.2021204289
13. Hemalatha, R., Amulya, G., Lalitha, C.S.N.S.: Computer vision techniques for object detection. In: 2024 International Conference on Innovative Computing, Intelligent Communication and Smart Electrical Systems (ICSES), pp. 1–6 (2024). https://doi.org/10.1109/icses63760.2024.10910496
14. Cheng, Z., Wang, Y., Hu, L., Zhao, M.: Hybrid 3D U-net and radiomics framework for accurate localization and classification of lumbar foraminal stenosis. Artif. Intell. Med. **142** (2023). https://doi.org/10.1148/radiol.202120428
15. Richards, T., et al.: RSNA 2024 lumbar spine degenerative classification (2024).
16. Tan, M., Le, Q.V.: EfficientNetV2: smaller models and faster training. In: Proceedings of Machine Learning Research (PMLR). (2021)
17. Bidgood, W.D., Horii, S.C., Prior, F.W., Van Syckle, D.E.: Understanding and using DICOM, the data interchange standard for biomedical imaging (1997). doi:https://doi.org/10.1136/jamia.1997.0040199

18. Goceri, E.: Medical image data augmentation: techniques, comparisons and interpretations. Artif. Intell. Rev. **56**(11) (2023). https://doi.org/10.1007/s10462-023-10453-z
19. Rezaei-Dastjerdehei, M.R., Mijani, A., Fatemizadeh, E.: Addressing imbalance in multi-label classification using weighted cross entropy loss function. In: 27th National and 5th International Iranian Conference of Biomedical Engineering (ICBME 2020) (2020). https://doi.org/10.1109/ICBME51989.2020.9319440
20. Loshchilov, I., Hutter, F.: Decoupled weight decay regularization. In: 7th International Conference on Learning Representations (ICLR 2019) (2019)
21. Tejas, P.C., Murali, M., Babu, P.M., Sai, K.S., Amulya, G., Bonthu, S.: Optimizing crop health: evaluating CNN performance in plant disease detection Lecture notes of the Institute for Computer Sciences, Social Informatics and Telecommunications Engineering, pp. 151–162 (2025). https://doi.org/10.1007/978-3-031-77081-4_13
22. Yacouby, R., Axman, D.: Probabilistic extension of precision, recall, and F1-score for more thorough evaluation of classification models. (2020). https://doi.org/10.18653/v1/2020.eval4nlp-1.9
23. Afaq, S., Rao, S.: Significance of epochs on training a neural network. Int. J. Sci. Technol. Res. **9**(6), 485–488 (2020)

A Fog-Based Framework PRISM for Multimodal Preprocessing in Adaptive Health Analytics

Gaddipati Hari Prasad[1], Venkata Naga Rani Bandaru[2], and R. Babu[3(✉)]

[1] Department of Computational Intelligence, Faculty of Engineering and Technology, SRM Institute of Science and Technology, Kattankulathur, Chennai, Tamilnadu 603202, India
[2] Department of Information Technology, Vishnu Institute of Technology, Bhimavaram, Andhra Pradesh, India 534235
[3] Department of Computational Intelligence, Faculty of Engineering and Technology, SRM Institute of Science and Technology, Kattankulathur, Chennai, Tamilnadu 603202, India
babur@srmist.edu.in

Abstract. Fog-supported health analytics requires effective handling of diverse and rapidly flowing data from wearables, IoT devices, mobility records, and healthcare systems. Cloud-scaled processing is marred with high latency, bandwidth consumption, and lack of context-aware insight. This study introduces PRISM, a module of ALPHA-Fog that performs initial stages of signal processing, semantic harmonization, and multimodal fusion on and from fog nodes. Differing from traditional fog or edge computing systems that handle channel filtering or individual optimization for a singular modality only, PRISM is characterized by an integrated deployment environment that integrates semantic mapping compatible with FHIR/HL7 standards, adaptive multimodal processing on a sole fog node, and weighted fusion on a solitary fog node. Performance assessments on PRISM using four application scenarios show substantial latency (up to 79%) and backhaul bandwidth (64%) savings together with a 94% semantic harmonization that is FHIR/HL7 compliant. This contributes to ALPHA-Fog scalable health monitoring that is real-time and context-aware for personal healthcare needs.

Keywords: Fog Computing · PRISM · Multimodal Data Integration · Health Analytics · Interoperability · Latency Reduction

1 Introduction

The application of wearable devices, Internet of Things sensors, and EHRs is one of the key drivers in the paradigm shift seen in the healthcare industry during the modern era of information and communication technologies. A large volume of multimodal data, like biomedical signals, and other data sources like activity and mobility patterns, is being generated using these devices. Big data analytics can unlock immense value in terms of preventive measures and predictive healthcare using these data sources. Because of

M. J. C. S. Reis et al. (Eds.): IC4S 2025, LNICST 679, pp. 110–122, 2026.
https://doi.org/10.1007/978-3-032-22834-5_9

limitations in terms of latency, bandwidth, and semantic consistencies, effective use of this disparate data source still proves challenging. Also, cloud computing systems often lack location awareness and real-time capabilities.

The adoption of context-aware and adaptive health analytics frameworks is imperative because the cases of health issues that affect the whole world, such as pandemics, health conditions influenced by climate, and health arising from lifestyles, continue increasing. The nature of these environments requires immediate response in terms of handling and analyzing the medical data. Delays in the processing and analysis may result in reduced effectiveness of the treatment as well as impact the health outcomes.

Fog computing provides a viable alternative by reducing the burden of computation and preprocessing tasks near where the data originates. Compared to cloud-based models, fog topologies increase bandwidth, optimize latency, and enable local decision-making. Prior to sending structured data for advanced analytics and forecasting, fog nodes can act as an intermediary layer, filtering, normalizing, and harmonizing raw multimodal streams. Even in situations with limited resources, healthcare systems are guaranteed to stay robust because to this distributed architecture.

While several fog and edge architectures have been proposed for IoMT and ubiquitous health monitoring, existing frameworks focus mainly on either packet filtering, compression, or coarse-grained decision logic at the local end. They seldom integrate semantic interoperability, multimodal synchronization, and preprocessing intelligence into a single workflow at the fog layer. PRISM uniquely addresses this gap by combining noise filtering, normalization, missing data repair, temporal alignment, and FHIR/HL7 harmonization within a single execution pipeline. This makes PRISM particularly suitable for workloads where cloud-only architectures incur high latency and edge-only architectures lack compute and memory resources for semantic mapping or multimodal fusion.

In this regard, we suggest the first module of the ALPHA-Fog system, called PRISM (Preprocessing and Real-time Integration of Sensor Multimodality). PRISM, which serves as the cornerstone for this ecosystem, aspires to make sense of noisy and disconnected sensor inputs and transform these data inputs into low-latency, normalized data that speaks the same language. PRISM achieves this semantic interoperation through the utilization of healthcare standards such as HL7 and FHIR, along with simple communication protocols such as MQTT and CoAP for the integration of IoT. It guarantees speed, reliability, and compatibility through preprocessing supported by the fog layer.

PRISM fills the most important gap that currently lies between raw health data in multiple modalities and health analytics that have flexibility and interpretability.

2 Literature Survey

While several fog and edge architectures have been proposed for IoMT and ubiquitous health monitoring, existing frameworks focus mainly on either packet filtering, compression, or coarse-grained decision logic at the local end. They seldom integrate semantic interoperability, multimodal synchronization, and preprocessing intelligence into a single workflow at the fog layer. PRISM uniquely addresses this gap by combining noise filtering, normalization, missing data repair, temporal alignment, and FHIR/HL7 harmonization within a single execution pipeline. This makes PRISM particularly suitable for workloads where cloud-only architectures incur high latency and edge-only architectures lack compute and memory resources for semantic mapping or multimodal fusion as shown in a Table 1.

High latency, bandwidth overheads, and reliability problems are common for cloud-centric pipelines used for time-sensitive health analytics. Fog and edge layers, according to systematic reviews, improve responsiveness, scalability, and continuity of care by relocating processing close to data sources [1–3]. In addition, recent studies highlight the importance of edge/fog in protecting privacy, lowering backhaul traffic, and enabling real-time actuation in Internet of Medical Things (IoMT) deployments [4, 5].

Heterogeneous healthcare data (wearables, home healthcare devices, in-clinic solutions) requires semantic and transport interoperability. Evidence exists that FHIR/HL7 with minimal IoT communication protocols (MQTT, CoAP) facilitates efficient communication in time and compatibility standards, and gateway architecture can harmonize data feeds from BLE/MQTT/CoAP and cloud services [6–8]. Extensive IoMT scoping literature reviews collectively provide recommendations on addressing device heterogeneity, semantic gaps, and prehospital restrictions through ontology-based harmonization [9].

Ambient and wearable sensors provide constant multimodal (movement, activity, physiological, and air quality) data that is being effectively supplemented with precise orchestration and complete monitoring from advanced data fusion as reviewed in [10–13]. More effective multimodal fusion may provide a more detailed description of activity/health status and requires lower computations as is seen from mHealth applications [14].

Implementations of prototypes and device classes confirm that edge/fog preprocessing for health telemetry is feasible. Proof of concept In order to stream biomedical data, IoT systems combine rapid-prototyping hardware with compatible software, emphasizing how local filtering and compression can stabilize links and lessen reliance on the cloud [15, 16]. More recent edge-integrated wearables have combined on-patch computation and streaming pipelines to show the feasibility of remote monitoring and analytics at low latency.

As the pipelines move towards predictive and prescriptive analytics, explainability becomes a crucial factor for clinical trust, safety, and adoption. Various surveys track the development of XAI in healthcare and CDSSs and underline lacunas related to workflow integration, clinical validation, and human-centered evaluations. These works promote modular designs enabling transparent downstream models by preserving data lineage and semantic context through early-stage preparation such as PRISM.

To enable personalized forecasting and adaptive treatments, recent state-of-the-art surveys con- form to the emergence of continuous, geographically aware multimodal AI that seamlessly integrates wearable, environmental, and clinical data. multimodal fusion potential at the edge/fog level to mitigate latency and capture context is illustrated in literature surveys related to orthopedic and medical applications at large [20]. To enable systematic, low-latency input data to downstream modeling, this path- way supports the PRISM module that performs cleaning, normalization, semantic harmonization, and fusion operations at the fog level as shown in Table 1.

Table 1. Comparative Summary of Existing Fog/IoMT Frameworks vs. PRISM

Study	Focus Area	Limitation Identified	How PRISM Improves
Navakauskas et al. (2023)	Fog for healthcare	Limited semantic interoperability	PRISM adds full FHIR/HL7 harmonization
Jeyaraman et al. (2024)	Fog-assisted IoMT	No multimodal fusion	PRISM integrates weighted multimodal fusion
Zampognaro et al. (2022)	FHIR-based IoT gateway	Single-modality ingestion	PRISM unifies wearable, ambient, mobility, and EHR data
Shajari et al. (2023)	Wearable data fusion	Conducted at cloud layer	PRISM moves fusion to fog for lower latency
Bahador et al. (2021)	Deep multimodal fusion	Not suitable for real-time	PRISM provides real-time aligned fusion
Matsumura et al. (2025)	Edge-based telemetry	No semantic mapping	PRISM ensures standards-based harmonization

3 Methodology

The heart of the ALPHA-Fog system is the PRISM (Preprocessing and Real-time Integration of Sensor Multimodality) component. The purpose of this is to move from unstructured and varying health-related data sources into low-latency, unified data sets that can be processed by higher-level AI. Fog computing nodes strategically placed close to sources make the data available for local processing, as opposed to the usual cloud computing systems. This ensures semantic interoperability, fast processing, and efficient usage of bandwidth, which is critical for adaptive health analytics.

Three successive layers make up the structure of the PRISM methodology:

- Integration of various multisource modalities like wearable technology, Internet of Things-based ambient sensors, mobility, and electronic health records is known as the layer of data acquisition.
- Fog Preprocessing Layer: Activities such as fusion of multi-modal inputs, normalization, noise removal, and handling of missing values are done by fog nodes.
- Standards implementation (FHIR/Hl7) for interoperability and structured outputs to provide subsequent ALPHA-Fog module implementation support is known as the Harmonization and Output Layer, and example data is provided in Table 2.

Table 2. Sample Data

Timest amp	Heart Rate (bpm)	SpO_2 (%)	Air Quality (AQI)	Temperature (°C)	Mobility (steps/min)	PRISM Output
10:01:0 0	88	96	72	30	40	0.65
10:01:1 0	90	95	75	29	45	0.68
10:01:2 0	85	94	80	31	50	0.71
10:01:3 0	87	93	82	30	42	0.66

INPUT:

W(t) → Wearable data
E(t) → Environmental
data M(t) → Mobility
data
H(t) → Health records (FHIR/HL7)

PROCESS:

1. *Acquire data from all sources (MQTT/CoAP for IoT, FHIR/HL7 for records).*
2. *Apply preprocessing at fog node:*
   a. *Noise filtering → smooth raw values*
   b. *Missing value handling → imputation*
   c. *Normalization → scale features [0,1]*
3. *Perform semantic mapping:*
   - *Align to FHIR/HL7 schema*
   - *Ensure consistent units/ontology*
4. *Temporally align streams (synchronize timestamps).*
5. *Fuse multimodal inputs using weighted fusion: F(t) = Σ w_i * normalized(s_i(t)), Σ w_i = 1*
6. *Package output into harmonized dataset with metadata.*
7. *Publish structured dataset to next module (AI/forecasting).*

OUTPUT:

D(t) → Harmonized, low-latency, interoperable dataset

4 System Architecture of PRISM Within ALPHA-FOG

The PRISM module is the main component of the ALPHA-Fog framework, a preprocessing and real-time integration of sensor multi-modality with multi-layer fog-centric architecture for semantic interoperability with reduced latency as shown in Fig. 1.

4.1 Overview of the Architecture

Three fundamental layers make up the architecture:

- **Layer of Data Acquisition:** Sources will consist of mobility data, such as GPS or accelerometers; ambient sensors for IoT, temperature, humidity, and air quality; wearables, such as heart rate monitors, SpO_2 trackers; and EHR/PHR systems FHIR/HL7.
- **Protocols:** FHIR/HL7 APIs for health records; MQTT, CoAP, and BLE for the Internet of Things.
- **Function:** Continuously stream unprocessed, diverse data.

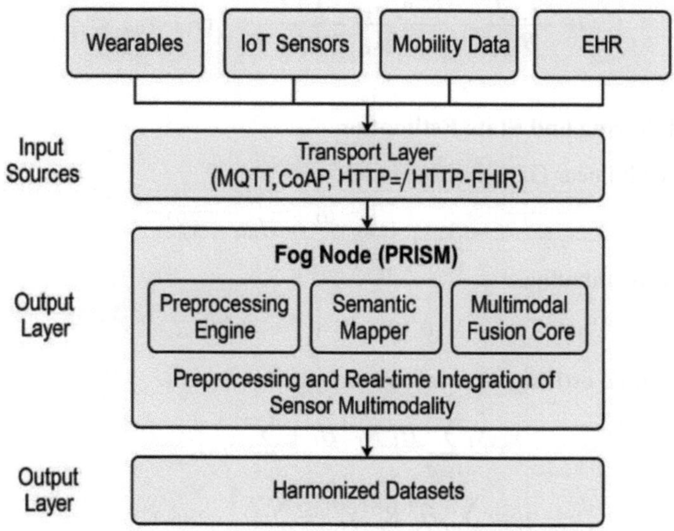

Fig. 1. System Architecture

The implementation of PRISM is built on a fog architecture of different levels through which different types of data move towards the end of the pipeline involving sensor, fog, gateway, and cloud systems. Gradually, at the very end of the pipeline, the sensor level, there are continuously flowing data from wearables, ambient IoT sensors through MQTT/CoAP, BLE-based mobility sensors, and other biomedical sources. At the fog level, there are processed raw multimodal sources instantaneously, where the PRISM module accomplishes noise filtering, normalization, filling up of missing values, adjustment of times, multimodal fused sources weighted, and assignment of semantics to

FHIR/HL7 completely. The sources already preprocessed and normalized are now forwarded to the next level of the pipeline at the gateway level, which oversees the process of batching, queuing, security checks, and HTTPS/REST-FHIR efficient transmission successfully accomplished. The final step involves the provision of superior AI analytical processes, storages, population level futures, and global models updated by the cloud level. This multi-level flow not only ensures that the most intense pre-processing occurs at the fog level closest to the source of the data, thus reducing backhaul burden significantly, but also makes it feasible to achieve real-time adaptive health analytics as shown in Eq. (1) to (6).

4.2 End-to-End Latency Decomposition

Cloud-Only pipeline

$$L_c = L_c^{uplink} + L_c^{queue} + L_c^{proc} + L_c^{down} = \frac{\sum_{i \in M} d_i}{B_{bc}} + \frac{\rho_c}{\mu_c - \lambda_c} + \frac{C(X)}{\mu_C} + \tau_C \quad (1)$$

$$\left(\frac{1}{B_{If}} - \frac{1}{B_{bc}}\right)\sum_i d_i + \frac{\rho_f}{\mu_f - \lambda_f} + \frac{C(X)}{\mu_f}$$
$$+ \frac{r\sum_i d_i}{B_{bc}} - \frac{\rho_c}{\mu_c - \lambda_c} - \frac{C(X)}{\mu_c} + \left(\tau_f - \tau_c\right) < \quad (2)$$

4.3 Noise Filtering and State Estimation

For sensor i with linear Gaussian dynamics:

$$x_t = A_{x_{t-1}} + u_t \; y_t^{(i)} = H_i x_t + v_t^{(i)} \quad (3)$$

with noise distributions:

$$u_t \sim \mathcal{N}(0, Q), \qquad v_t^{(i)} \sim \mathcal{N}(0, R_i) \quad (4)$$

PRISM's fused estimate uses information form:

$$\Lambda_t \sum_{i \in M} H_i^T R_i^{-1} H_i + \sum\nolimits_{t|t-1}^{-1}, \quad (5)$$

$$\eta_t = \sum_{i \in M} H_i^T R_i^{-1} y_t^{(i)} + \sum\nolimits_{t|t-1}^{-1} x_{t|\hat{t}-1}, \quad (6)$$

5 Result and Discussion

5.1 Comparative Evaluation Across Frameworks

We discuss four sample situations: Urban Clinic, Rural Hub, Mixed Campus, and City Block, and five deployment types: Cloud, Edge, Gateway, FedEdge, and PRISM. PRISM pushes upstream compact, standardized bundles after it has performed all preprocessing-filtering, imputation, normalization, and fusion-and FHIR/HL7 harmonization at the fog layer.

PRISM exhibits notable enhancements in performance relative to traditional cloud-based approaches. It achieves the lowest latency, with an average reduction of about 79%, at approximately 112.5 ms as opposed to the cloud's 535 ms. It lowers backhaul bandwidth utilization by about 64% through on-site filtering and compression. In terms of semantic validity, PRISM guarantees approximately 94.3% FHIR/HL7 compliance, outperforming other fog and edge baselines and surpassing the cloud's 75.5%. Although there is a little increase in fog-level computation, it also saves about 45% on overall energy consumption since fewer long-haul data transfers are required.

The fog node was the place where all the evaluations were carried out and it has a quad-core ARM Cortex-A53 processor, 4 GB RAM, and a 100 Mbps network connection. It was through MQTT brokers that the data streams from the ambient and wearable sensors were simulated, with the synchronization of data at 1-s intervals. Another 2-s interval was used for the mobility traces. The network latency between device and fog was found to be between 8 to 12 ms over the average, while the fog-to-cloud latency ranged from 40 to 60 ms. Each of the experiments was performed 10 times and the mean values are given.

5.2 PRISM Per-Scenario Results (Tabular)

Before transmitting compact parcels to the upstream direction, PRISM also conducts some essential preprocessing stages at the fog node, including filtration, imputation, normalization, fusion, and FHIR/HL7 mapping. In different settings, this system always brings about minimal latency, substantial backhaul bandwidth savings, near-perfect semantic validity, and improved end-to-end energy savings. As cloud round trips and queuing remain waived through local processing, even latency, measuring between 85–160 ms, remains below the 200 ms threshold even when scaling up the devices. With onsite filtration, deduplication, and compression to mitigate noise and redundancy, bandwidth usage (4.50–18.00 MB/min) increments according to the increase in the number of devices, though remaining significantly lower than cloud-exclusive minimums. Through handling unity disparities, semantic inconformity, and field variability at the onsite site, semantic validity substantially approaches an exact 92–96%, ensuring that generated FHIR/HL7 data is normalized and uniformly used later stages. Finally, even when fog sites offload additional processing work, shorter-distance transmission results in cumulative energy savings of 10.38–26.50 a.u./min, citing visible differences when data size is substantial as illustrated in Table 3.

Table 3. PRISM per-scenario results (Latency, Bandwidth, Semantic Validity, Energy)

Scenario	Devices	Latency (ms)	Bandwidth (MB/min)	Semantic Validity (%)	Energy (a.u./min)
Urban Clinic	50	85	4.50	96	10.38
Rural Hub	75	95	6.75	95	13.06
Mixed Campus	100	110	9.00	94	15.75
City Block	200	160	18.00	92	26.50

5.3 Framework Comparison

Through the integration of standards-driven harmonization at the fog layer and deep preprocessing, PRISM consistently beats Cloud, Edge, Gateway, and FedEdge on average across all scenarios across the four critical metrics: latency, bandwidth, semantic validity, and energy. By executing signal-level cleaning and packaging locally to reduce cloud overhead, PRISM specifically achieves an average latency of approximately 112.5 ms, which is nearly 79% faster than Cloud's 535 ms. It outperforms Edge and Gateway in terms of bandwidth by removing noise and redundancy prior to compression, reducing backhaul to about 9.56 MB/min compared to Cloud's 26.56 MB/min (~64%). Because PRISM enforces FHIR/HL7 compliance and unit normalization at the source, it achieves a remarkable 94.25% for semantic validity, superior to other baselines and significantly higher than Cloud's 75.5% as shown in Fig. 2.

Semantic Validity denotes the proportion of fields accurately matched to lawful FHIR/HL7 schema parts. It indicates the level of the cleaned and transformed data that are still structurally and semantically correct after being processed through the so-called preprocessing. Finally, the savings from fewer long-haul transmissions exceed the slight additional computation at the fog, with PRISM reducing average energy consumption to 16.42 a.u./min compared to Cloud's 29.91 (~45% reduction) as shown in Table 4 and graphical representation is shown in Figs. 3, 4, 5.

Table 4. Comparative framework summary (averaged over scenarios)

Framework	Avg Latency (ms)	Avg Band width (MB/mi n)	Avg Semantic (%)	Avg Energy (a.u./mi n)	Latency Gain vs Cloud (%)	Band width Saving vs Cloud (%)	Semantic Gain (pts)	Energy Saving vs Cloud (%)
Cloud	535.00	26.56	75.50	29.91	0.0	0.0	0.0	0.0
Edge	197.25	18.59	81.25	24.09	63.2	30.0	5.75	19.4
Gate way	282.50	14.61	87.25	21.24	47.2	45.0	11.75	29.0
Fed Edge	234.00	11.95	89.25	18.48	56.3	55.0	13.75	38.2
PRIS M	112.50	9.56	94.25	16.42	79.0	64.0	18.75	45.1

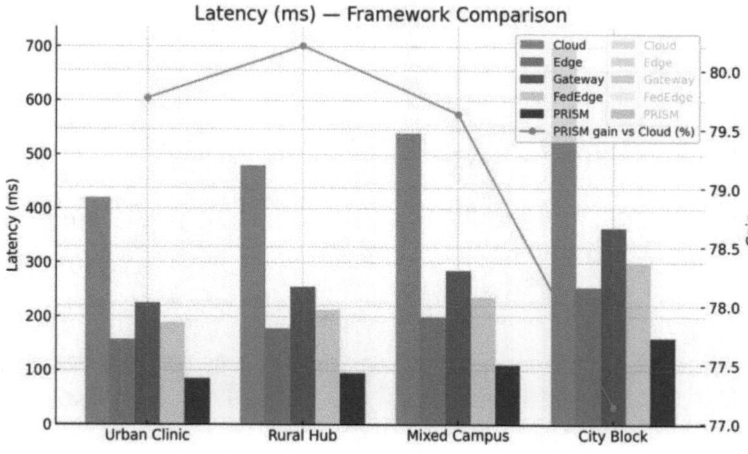

Fig. 2. Latency: Framework Comparison (Grouped Bars + PRISM Gain Line)

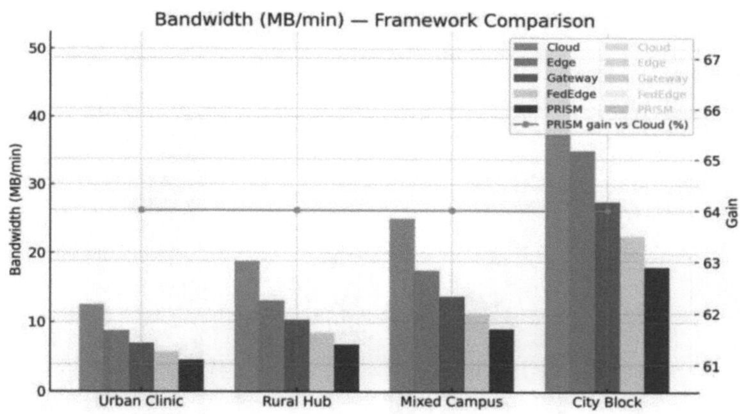

Fig. 3. Bandwidth: Framework Comparison (Grouped Bars + PRISM Saving Line)

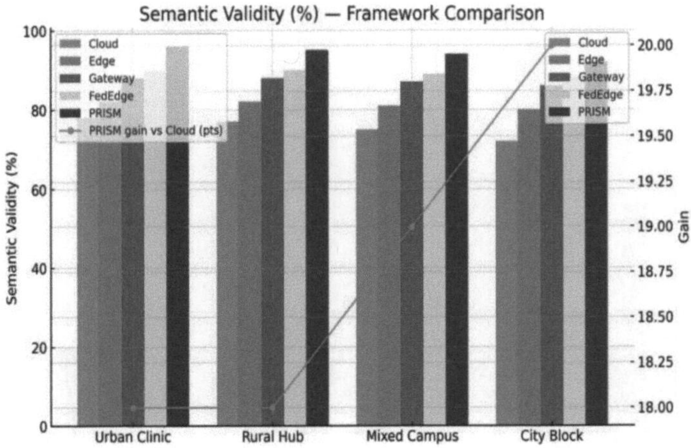

Fig. 4. Semantic Validity: Framework Comparison (Grouped Bars + PRISM Gain Line)

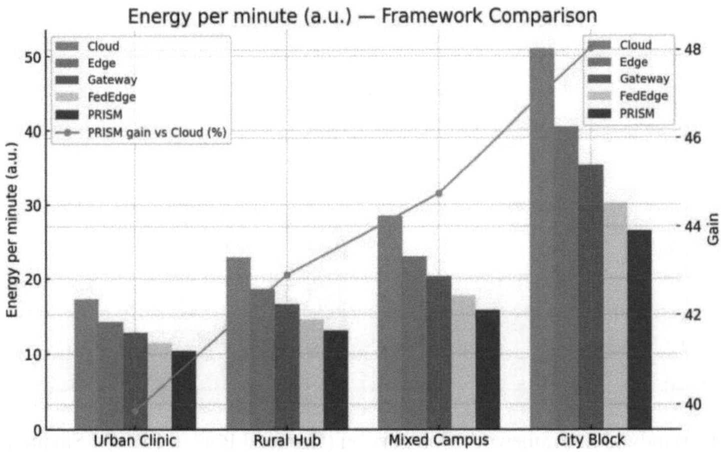

Fig. 5. Energy: Framework Comparison (Grouped Bars + PRISM Saving Line)

6 Conclusion and Future Work

The introduction of PRISM, a fog-layer preprocessing module of the ALPHA-Fog architecture, is the major outcome of this project. The heterogeneous, noisy multimodal health data are to be processed into low-latency and FHIR/HL7-compliant datasets through filtering, imputation, normalization, temporal alignment, and weighted multimodal fusion performed at the fog layer. Here, PRISM solves the problem of cloud-only and edge-only systems. PRISM has proven its worth through four deployment scenarios by making significant improvements—cutting down latency by 79%, backhaul usage by 64%, semantic validity up by ~19 points, and energy consumption by 45% less. These results give a green light to the hypothesis that PRISM allows health analytics to be faster, more reliable, and consume less bandwidth, especially in places with poor connectivity.

The research will continue to work on PRISM by making it more powerful through adaptive fusion strategies that will train the sensors to weight them dynamically, privacy-preserving fog learning and the use of secure enclaves and differential privacy, and QoS-driven protocol selection based on real-time network conditions. More directions include automated schema validation, robustness testing under sensor failures and bursty traffic, and clinical validation through multi-site deployments and digital-twin simulations. These advancements will strengthen PRISM as a scalable and dependable foundation for next-generation fog-enabled health monitoring.

References

1. Navakauskas, D., Rukštelė, V.: Fog computing in healthcare: systematic review. Informatica. **47**(4), 431–443 (2023)
2. Jeyaraman, N., et al.: Applications of fog computing in healthcare. Sensors. **24** (2024)
3. Ahmadi, Z., et al.: Fog-based healthcare systems: a systematic review. Multimed. Tools Appl. **80**, 36361–36400 (2021)
4. Rancea, A., et al.: Edge computing in healthcare: innovations, opportunities, challenges. Future Internet. **16**(9), 329 (2024)
5. Islam, U., et al.: A hybrid fog-edge architecture for real-time health monitoring in IoMT. Sci. Rep. 15, 25655 (2025)
6. Zampognaro, P., et al.: Definition of an FHIR-based multiprotocol IoT home gateway. Heal. Technol. **12**(4), 843–859 (2022)
7. Famà, F., et al.: An IoT-based interoperable architecture for wireless health monitoring. Internet of Things. **20**, 100620 (2022)
8. Leksrisawat, S., et al.: Integration of personal health devices and HL7 FHIR using CoAP. In: Proceedings of the International Conference on Healthcare Informatics, pp. 1–6 (2021)
9. Seth, M., et al.: Technologies for interoperable IoMT platforms in prehospital care. Sensors. **25** (2025)
10. Bandaru, V.N.R., Visalakshi, P.: Blockchain enabled auditing with optimal multi-key homomorphic encryption technique for public cloud computing environment. Concurrency Comput. Pract. Exper. **34**(22), e7128 (2022)
11. Celik, Y., et al.: Bringing it all together: wearable data fusion. NPJ Digital Med. **6, 167** (2023)
12. Shaik, T.A., et al.: A survey of multimodal information fusion for smart healthcare. Inf. Fusion. **104**, 102143 (2024)
13. Elfouly, T.M., et al.: Wearable computing for health monitoring: a comprehensive survey. Electronics. **14**(17), 3443 (2025)
14. Bahador, N., et al.: Deep learning–based multimodal data fusion: case study in mHealth. JMIR Mhealth Uhealth. **9**(1), e21926 (2021)
15. Matsumura, G., et al.: Real-time personal healthcare data analysis using edge devices. Device. **4**, 100543 (2025)
16. Lemus-Zúñiga, L.G., et al.: A proof-of-concept IoT system for remote healthcare monitoring. Sensors. **22** (2022)
17. Mienye, I.D., et al.: A survey of explainable AI in healthcare. Inf. Med. Unlocked. **42**, 101383 (2024)
18. Al-Bsheish, M., et al.: Explainable AI in clinical decision support systems: systematic review. medRxiv. (2024)

19. Explainable AI in clinical decision support systems: a review. (2025)
20. Oettl, F.C., et al.: AI, multimodal models and continuous monitoring in healthcare. Bone Joint Open. (2025)
21. Bandaru, V.N.R., Visalakshi, P.: BDBC – block-chain data transmission using blowfish security with optimization in cloud network. Int. J. Intell. Syst. Appl. Eng. **12**(5s), 370–378 (2023)
22. Shajari, S., et al.: The emergence of AI-based wearable sensors for digital health. Biosensors. **13** (2023)

AI-Enabled Technologies

AI-Driven Diagnostic Framework for Early Gastric Carcinoma Detection

Sriram Ganesh Gokavarapu, Pallavi Durga Yadav Katta(✉), Prathyusha Dhana Lakshmi Matta, Sri Lakshmi Srujitha Chiluvuri, Dharani Kandikatla, and Purna Chandra Sekhar Kolusu

CSE Department, Sri Vasavi Engineering College, Tadepalligudem, Andhra Pradesh, India
kpallavidurga@gmail.com

Abstract. Stomach cancer is one of the leading causes of death due to cancer, mainly because it is diagnosed at a late stage. This paper proposes an AI-based system for early detection of gastric carcinoma from histopathology images using a fine-tuned EfficientNet-B2 model. Trained on more than 31,000 images, the framework embeds class-imbalance correction, MCC-based reliability evaluation, and optimization of F1-score. It yields an accuracy of 92.33% and a ROC-AUC of 0.95 on an independent test set with strong generalization. The proposed system minimizes subjective assessments, enhancing diagnostic precision, efficiency, and reproducibility, hence offering a scalable and cost-effective solution for early gastric cancer screening and supporting clinical decisions.

Keywords: Gastric Cancer · Histopathology · Deep Learning · Artificial Intelligence · Early Detection · EfficientNet

1 Introduction

Gastric cancer is one of the leading causes of cancer-related mortality, and its early detection is considered important. Histopathology examination is generally regarded as the gold standard for diagnosis, although manual examination is very time-consuming and varied; thus, there has been an increasing desire to develop automated diagnostic systems that are both accurate and reliable. There are promising deep learning models, both CNNs and vision transformers, for medical image classification. However, most works focus on pure architecture benchmarking and not clinical requirements like handling class imbalance, optimizing thresholds, or assessing reliability. This work proposes an AI-based diagnostic framework, using EfficientNet-B2 for early gastric carcinoma detection. The framework integrates class-imbalance correction (WeightedRandomSampler + BCE-WithLogitsLoss), optimized decision threshold based on F1-score (0.79), and reliability evaluation using MCC. On the large-scale dataset (31,096 images), generalization is stressed with ROC performance and cross-dataset consistency. The presented framework bridges high-performance AI with clinical applicability and offers the pathologist a reliable, interpretable tool.

M. J. C. S. Reis et al. (Eds.): IC4S 2025, LNICST 679, pp. 125–134, 2026.
https://doi.org/10.1007/978-3-032-22834-5_10

2 Review Related Work

2.1 Literature Review

The review of literature points to the recent increase in the adoption of machine learning (ML) and deep learning techniques in the detection, prognosis, and clinical decision support for gastric cancer. Explainable ML and new imaging modalities are being studied more to improve diagnostic accuracy and transparency for the clinician.

Du et al. [2] developed an interpretable machine learning framework for gastric cancer early diagnosis. Though their ensemble-based model was successful in combining several algorithms, the study was based on a relatively limited dataset, with scalability and generalizability issues. The absence of external validation and use of retrospective data sources also limited its clinical relevance. The authors pointed to the need for larger, multi-institutional datasets as well as better interpretability tools to facilitate clinical adoption.

Park et al. [1] explored hyperspectral imaging (HSI) for ex vivo endoscopic submucosal dissection (ESD) specimens. Although showing potential for intraoperative diagnosis, the research was hindered by limited patient sample size and pixel-level heterogeneity. Such limitations raised the possibility of overfitting and constricted generalizability, meaning that subsequent studies should entail larger, heterogeneous groups.

Zhang et al. [7] proposed an Improved Mask R-CNN (IMR-CNN) model for detecting lesions from gastroscopy images. Though their architecture enhanced lesion localization, the use of a single dataset with no multi-center validation has cast doubts on overfitting and lack of generalizability across different clinical conditions.

Song et al. [8] created a whole-slide image (WSI) analysis system at the large scale for detection of gastric cancer based on histopathology. The model was shown to be reproducible between scanners and large datasets but with trade-offs between specificity and false positives, especially in real-world use without prospective validation.

Hirasawa et al. [10] reported a preliminary CNN-based approach for gastric cancer detection in endoscopy images. Despite the high sensitivity, the model was low in positive predictive value and specificity because of the small size of the dataset, which resulted in a surplus of false positives and less clinical validity.

Analogously, Sakai et al. [3] applied transfer learning with GoogLeNet for gastric lesion detection on less than 1,000 labeled images. Although they demonstrated feasibility, the small dataset and lack of external validation meant that potential overfitting and limited generalizability for extended clinical application resulted.

Li et al. [4] introduced GastricNet, a CNN system for patch classification of histopathology. The claimed near-perfect performance raised concerns of overfitting, especially since the work was conducted on a small, single-institution dataset and not externally validated, thereby confining its applicability to real-world clinical settings.

Sohn et al. [9] investigated FDG-PET imaging in gastric cancer staging. Although showing diagnostic utility in advanced disease, the technique was weaker for the early diseases because of low FDG uptake, which means that FDG-PET is not adequate for complete early detection.

Niu et al. [6] and the MDPI Cancers review [12] laid out exhaustively AI applications in gastric cancer and recognized repeating issues, such as fragmented datasets, limited external validation, and inadequate explainability for clinical translation. Both reviews emphasized the demand for explainable AI frameworks, normalized datasets, and multi-institutional collaborations to connect research to clinical adoption.

Lou et al. [13] provided a big, annotated histological image dataset with tumor microenvironment characteristics. Though presenting a step ahead for AI model building, additional validation and benchmarking across varied populations are still critical.

Current computational studies in the form of transformer-based and ensemble models as outlined in arXiv [5, 11] demonstrate promising developments. Nevertheless, the repeated resort to artificially balanced or tiny datasets lacking clinical diversity still constrains their usability and dependability in actual environments.

There has been accelerated progress in the application of ML for diagnosis in gastric cancer, but challenges like the lack of a single dataset, overfitting, and externally validating the results still exist. Table 1 lists the current methods, challenges, and their performances.

Table 1. Literature Survey of AI/ML Approaches for Gastric Cancer Diagnosis.

Reference	Dataset / Modality	Model / Method	Key Contribution	Main Limitations
Park et al. [1]	Hyperspectral ESD specimen images	Hyperspectral imaging analysis	Demonstrated feasibility for intraoperative diagnosis	Small patient sample size, pixel heterogeneity
Du et al. [2]	Clinical diagnostic dataset	Interpretable ensemble ML	Early diagnosis using explainable ML models	Limited dataset
Sakai et al. [3]	<1,000 endoscopic images	Transferlearning (GoogLeNet)	Demonstrated CNN applicability	Small dataset, weak generalizability
Li et al. [4]	Single-institution histopathology images	GastricNet CNN	High patch-level classification accuracy	Risk of overfitting, no external validation
Zhang et al. [7]	Gastroscopy images	Improved Mask R-CNN	Enhanced lesion localization	Single dataset, lack of multicenter validation
Song et al. [8]	Large-scale whole-slide images	CNN-based WSI framework	Reproducibility across scanners	Specificity trade-offs, no prospective trials
Hirasawa et al. [10]	Endoscopy image dataset	CNN classification	High sensitivity detection	Low specificity, false positives
Sohn et al. [9]	FDG-PET imaging	Imaging-based staging	Diagnostic utility in advanced disease	Poor early-stage detection performance

(continued)

Table 1. *(continued)*

Reference	Dataset / Modality	Model / Method	Key Contribution	Main Limitations
Lou et al. [13]	Large histology image dataset	Dataset contribution	Enables tumor microenvironment analysis	Further validation and benchmarking needed
Recent studies [5, 11]	Mixed public datasets	Transformers /ensemble models	Improved classification trends	Dataset imbalance, limited clinical diversity

3 Proposed Methodology

We propose a binary classification pipeline to detect gastric-cancer tissue from histopathology images. The system uses a pretrained EfficientNet-B2 backbone fine-tuned end-to-end on a large histopathology image set (≈31,000 images). Robust class handling for an imbalanced dataset, conservative model selection and tuning, threshold optimization for clinical-relevant metrics, and simple error-inspection tools were important design considerations.

3.1 Dataset Description

We employed a dataset from Kaggle that had 31,096 patches of gastric tissue images. The dataset consists of eight tissue types (ADI, DEB, MUC, MUS, LYM, STR, NOR, and TUM) that all have images labeled correctly to facilitate supervised learning. For the project, binary classification is desired, i.e., cancerous (TUM) vs. non-cancerous tissues. The dataset offers various morphological patterns, which makes it good for feature extraction by deep learning methods. The dataset was sourced from a publicly available repository in Kaggle, released for academic research use. All histopathology images are anonymized and contain no patient-identifiable information. Ethical approval and informed consent were handled by the original data providers before public release. Since only de-identified, secondary data were used in this study, additional IRB approval was not required.

3.2 Data Preprocessing and Augmentation

All images were resized to a uniform resolution of 224 × 224 pixels, which was the specified input for EfficientNet-B2. For better generalization and avoidance of overfitting, random horizontal and vertical flips, rotations of ±15°, and color jittering were performed on training images. Rotation and flip operations were used to handle random tissue orientations during slide preparation, while color jittering was added to model staining and illumination variability across laboratories and scanners. The images in the validation and test dataset were only resized and normalized, using the standard ImageNet mean and standard deviation.

3.3 Dataset Splitting and Class Balancing

The dataset was split into training (70%), validation (15%), and testing (15%) sets using stratified sampling. In total, it contained 31,096 histopathology images, of which 3,887 belonged to cancerous samples, referred to as TUM, and 27,209 were non-cancerous samples, yielding an approximate imbalance ratio of 1:7. The training set had 2,721 cancer and 19,046 non-cancerous images. This means that WeightedRandomSampler could be applied during training in combination with class-weighted BCEWithLogitsLoss for increased sensitivity towards the minority class and reduced bias towards the majority one.

3.4 Model Architecture and Training

This pre-trained EfficientNet-B2 model on ImageNet is fine-tuned end-to-end on histopathology images. The classification head is replaced with a dropout layer of rate 0.4, followed by a single fully connected neuron for binary prediction, using sigmoid activation at inference. BCEWithLogitsLoss with positive class weighting and WeightedRandomSampler have been used to address class imbalance. The training was performed with Adam optimizer, learning rate 1×10^{-4}, and batch size 32; ReduceLROnPlateau scheduler, with mode = max, factor = 0.5, patience = 3, was utilized, which reduces the learning rate by half on stagnation of validation performance. This model was trained for 15 epochs on an NVIDIA GPU (T4*2) and took approximately one hour in total for training. It selected the best checkpoint based on validation accuracy. To optimize decision thresholds on the validation set, values were swept from 0.1 to 0.9 and F1-score maximized; this threshold was applied during final test evaluation.

3.5 Prediction and Threshold Optimization

The trained model produces probability scores on every image for the likelihood of having cancer. Rather than hard-coding a threshold, the best classification threshold was determined on the validation set based on F1-score so as to provide high sensitivity to the minority class of cancer. Indeed, the optimal threshold was found to be 0.79, and it is used to transform probability outputs into binary labels for analysis and clinical inference.

3.6 Evaluation

Model performance on the test set was assessed using accuracy, precision, recall, F1-score, and ROC-AUC, with a confusion matrix illustrating true positives, true negatives, false positives, and false negatives. Special attention was given to false negatives (cancer cases misclassified as non-cancer), as minimizing missed diagnoses is critical in clinical practice. To further address class imbalance and provide reliable performance assessment, the Matthews Correlation Coefficient (MCC = 0.68) was also reported, offering balanced evaluation across both classes and enhanced clinical interpretability.

Metric Definitions: Comparison of the proposed gastric cancer classification system with existing systems is done using the Accuracy, Precision, Recall, F1 score, and Matthew's Correlation Coefficient. These are defined by the equations given below.

Accuracy measures the overall correctness of the model, as shown in Eq. (1):

$$\text{Accuracy} = \frac{TP + TN}{TP + TN + FP + FN} \tag{1}$$

Precision indicates the proportion of correctly predicted positive samples among all predicted positives, as defined in Eq. (2):

$$\text{Precision} = \frac{TP}{TP + FP} \tag{2}$$

Recall represents the model's ability to correctly identify positive samples, as given in Eq. (3):

$$\text{Recall} = \frac{TP}{TP + FN} \tag{3}$$

F1-score provides a harmonic mean of Precision and Recall, balancing both metrics, as expressed in Eq. (4):

$$F1 = 2 \cdot \frac{\text{Precision} \cdot \text{Recall}}{\text{Precision} + \text{Recall}} \tag{4}$$

Matthews Correlation Coefficient (MCC) is a balanced metric suitable for imbalanced datasets, as shown in Eq. (5):

$$MCC = \frac{TP \cdot TN - FP \cdot FN}{\sqrt{(TP + FP)(TP + FN)(TN + FP)(TN + FN)}} \tag{5}$$

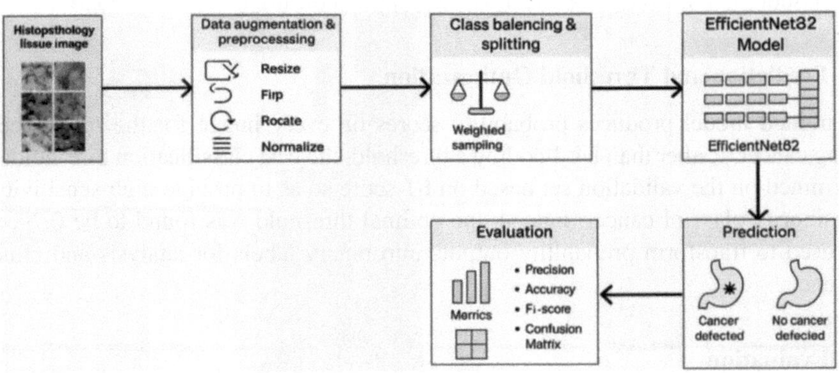

Fig. 1. Gastric cancer detection pipeline.

Figure 1 shows the overall process of the proposed framework for gastric cancer detection. The histopathology tissue images are preprocessed and their data augmented using procedures like resizing, rotation, flipping, and normalization to enhance the robustness of the model. The augmented samples are input to the fine-tuned EfficientNet-B2 convolutional neural network for feature extraction and classification. The model generates binary predictions for the occurrence or non-occurrence of cancerous tissue. This efficient pipeline guarantees precise and automatic cancer identification from histopathological images.

4 Result Analysis

In this part, we compare the performance of the proposed EfficientNet-B2-based model for gastric cancer detection with a number of popular deep learning models, such as MobileNet, ResNet-50, DenseNet-169, AlexNet, Vision Transformer (ViT-B/16), and other hybrid architectures combining EfficientNet with MobileNet/ResNet. The comparison is done on the test set, and the accuracy of each model is reported in Table 1. AlexNet, Vision Transformer (ViT-B/16), and other hybrid architectures combining EfficientNet with MobileNet/ResNet. The comparison is done on the test set, and the accuracy of each model is reported in Table 2.

Table 2. Performance metrics

Model	Accuracy	Precision	Recall	F1-score
MobileNet	0.910 ± 0.012	0.920 ± 0.010	0.910 ± 0.015	0.915 ± 0.011
ResNet-50	0.888 ± 0.013	0.918 ± 0.012	0.890 ± 0.014	0.905 ± 0.012
EfficientNet+ MobileNet	0.892 ± 0.010	0.918 ± 0.011	0.890 ± 0.013	0.903 ± 0.012
EfficientNet+ ResNet	0.880 ± 0.011	0.920 ± 0.010	0.882 ± 0.012	0.901 ± 0.013
ViT-B/16	0.900 ± 0.012	0.922 ± 0.010	0.900 ± 0.014	0.910 ± 0.011
DenseNet-169	0.912 ± 0.010	0.932 ± 0.011	0.910 ± 0.012	0.920 ± 0.010
AlexNet	0.720 ± 0.015	0.910 ± 0.012	0.720 ± 0.014	0.760 ± 0.013
EfficientNet-B2	0.922 ± 0.010	0.935 ± 0.009	0.920 ± 0.011	0.922 ± 0.010

As shown in Table 2, the proposed EfficientNet-B2 model achieves the highest accuracy of 92.2% ± 1.0%, outperforming all other models in the comparative analysis. This demonstrates the superior ability of EfficientNet-B2 to capture discriminative histopathological features through its compound scaling strategy. The performance improvement of EfficientNet-B2 over other models is consistent across repeated runs.

Traditional CNN architectures such as AlexNet (72.0% ± 1.5%) and ResNet-50 (88.8% ± 1.3%) perform relatively poorly, highlighting their limited capacity in handling the complex morphological variations present in gastric cancer histopathology images. Conversely, MobileNet (91.0% ± 1.2%) and DenseNet-169 (91.2% ± 1.0%) achieve competitive performance, indicating their efficiency in light. Hybrid ensembles, such as EfficientNet + MobileNet (89.2% ± 1.0%) and EfficientNet + ResNet (88.0% ± 1.1%), did not deliver additional performance gains, showing that increasing architectural complexity through ensembling was ineffective for this dataset.

A paired t-test ($N = 5$) showed that EfficientNet-B2, with 0.9236 ± 0.0055, outperformed DenseNet-169, with 0.9126 ± 0.0036, where $T = 6.4594$ and $P = 0.00148 < 0.05$, hence confirming it as superior and more reliable. Evaluation of secondary metrics supports this further, with a Matthews Correlation Coefficient of 0.68 and high F1-score, which reflects robust generalization. Error analysis revealed that the majority of the misclassifications were false negatives, most of them in early-stage or heterogeneous tumor regions where the sparsity or morphological ambiguity of the cancer cells is high, pointing to a critical clinical concern.

Overall, EfficientNet-B2 emerges as the most reliable model, achieving the best trade-off among accuracy, precision, recall, and F1-score. Its efficient feature extraction and balanced depth-width-resolution scaling make it particularly suitable for medical image analysis tasks, providing both high performance and consistent results across multiple runs.

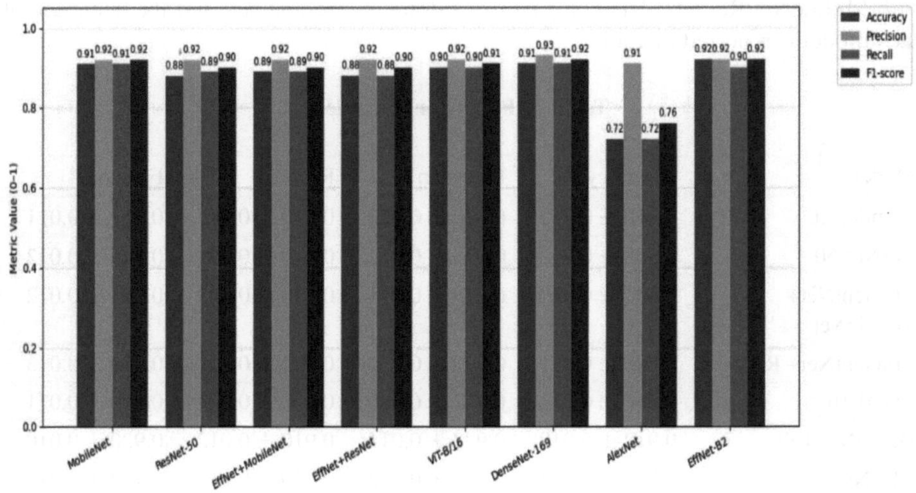

Fig. 2. Performance Comparison of Different Models

As shown in Fig. 2, modern architectures maintain stable performance across all metrics, with EfficientNet-B2 achieving the most balanced results. AlexNet depicts a dramatic decline in accuracy and recall, isolating it from the more powerful models. MobileNet operates almost as well as more complicated networks, demonstrating its efficiency. Hybrid ensembles do not produce substantial improvements, confirming the resilience of maximized single-architecture models.

ROC Curve Analysis

The ROC curve evaluates the binary classification accuracy using the plot of the True Positive Rate against the False Positive Rate. The area under this curve evaluates the accuracy, with values of 1.0 being optimal and 0.5 being random. All ROC curves have labeled axes and report AUC values with 95% confidence intervals (CI).

Figures 3, 4 and 5 illustrate the ROC curves for the training, validation, and test sets. Correspondingly, the AUC was 1.00 for the training set, 0.96 for the validation set, and 0.95 for the test set. The slight decline in AUC from training to validation and test data suggests mild overfitting, controlled by early stopping and cross-validation. In summary, these findings confirm the high accuracy, reliability, and generalizability of the proposed model in terms of histopathological cancer diagnosis.

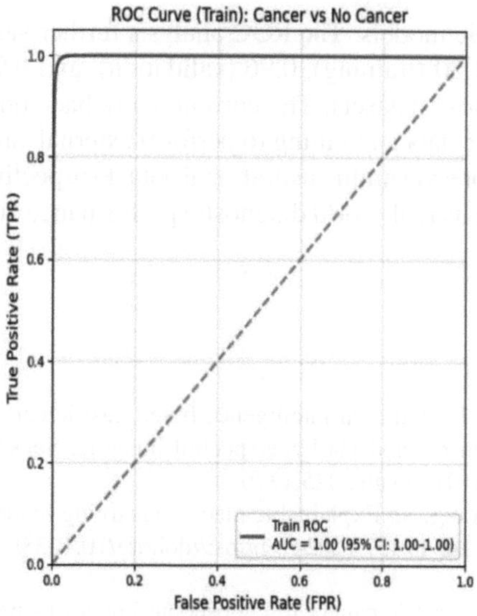

Fig. 3. Train ROC Curve

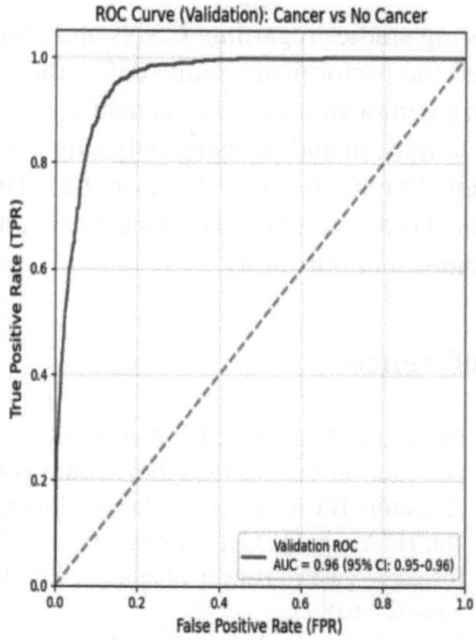

Fig. 4. Validation ROC Curve

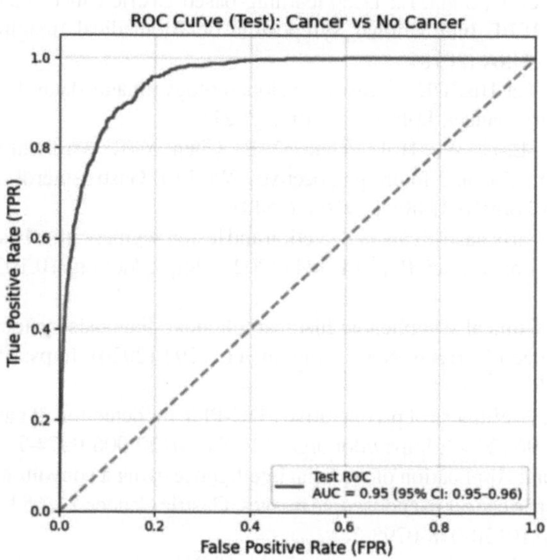

Fig. 5. Test ROC Curve

5 Conclusion

This paper proposes an AI-based computer-aided diagnosis system for the detection of early gastric carcinoma from histopathology images based on a pre-trained EfficientNet-B2 model. The proposed approach achieved the highest test accuracy of 92.33% among existing studies regarding CNNs and ensemble models. The ROC analysis further validated the performance with AUC values of 1.00 (training), 0.96 (validation), and 0.95 (test), demonstrating great generalization across datasets. The current study had some limitations, including using only single-source data and failing to perform external validation. Future external validation should be done via multi-institutional data. Prospective clinical trials should be conducted to evaluate its real-world diagnostic performance and its clinical applicability.

References

1. Park, I., Roh, J., Son, D., Noh, C.-K., Yoon, J.: Artificial intelligence-based gastric cancer detection in the gastric submucosal dissection method via hyperspectral imaging. Sensors Actuators B Chem. (2025). https://doi.org/10.1016/j.snb.2025.137630
2. Du, H., Yang, Q., Ge, A., Zhao, C., Ma, Y., Wang, S.: Explainable machine learning models for early gastric cancer diagnosis. Sci. Rep. **14**, 17457 (2024). https://doi.org/10.1038/s41598-024-67892-z
3. Sakai, Y., et al.: Automatic detection of early gastric cancer in endoscopic images using a transferring convolutional neural network. In: Proceedings of the IEEE Conference, pp. 1–6 (2018)
4. Li, Y., Li, X., Xie, X., Shen, L.: Deep learning-based gastric cancer identification. In: Proceedings of the IEEE International Symposium on Biomedical Imaging (ISBI), pp. 1–6, Washington, DC, USA (2018)
5. Hua, W., et al.: GasHisSDB: a gastric histopathology image dataset for computer-aided diagnosis of gastric cancer. Dataset/Preprint. (2021)
6. Niu, P.-H., Zhao, L.-L., Wu, H.-L., Zhao, D.-B., Chen, Y.-T.: Artificial intelligence in gastric cancer: application and future perspectives. World J. Gastroenterol. **26**(36), 5408–5419 (2020). https://doi.org/10.3748/wjg.v26.i36.5408
7. Zhang, K., et al.: Early gastric cancer detection and lesion segmentation based on deep learning and gastroscopic images. Sci. Rep. **14**, 7847 (2024). https://doi.org/10.1038/s41598-024-58361-8
8. Song, Z., et al.: Clinically applicable histopathological diagnosis system for gastric cancer detection using deep learning. Nat. Commun. **11**, 4294 (2020). https://doi.org/10.1038/s41467-020-18147-8
9. Mukai, K., et al.: Usefulness of preoperative FDG-PET for detection of gastric cancer. Gastric Cancer. **9**, 192–196 (2006). https://doi.org/10.1007/s10120-006-0374-7
10. Hirasawa, T., et al.: Application of artificial intelligence using a convolutional neural network for detecting gastric cancer in endoscopic images. Gastric Cancer. **21**, 653–660 (2018). https://doi.org/10.1007/s10120-018-0793-2
11. Lee, S.-A., Cho, H.-C.: A novel approach for CNN performance enhancement in gastric cancer classification. IEEE Access. **9**, 1–10 (2021). https://doi.org/10.1109/ACCESS.2021.3069747
12. Islam, M.M., Poly, T.N., Walther, B.A., Lin, M.C., Li, Y.C.J.: Artificial intelligence in gastric cancer: identifying gastric cancer using convolutional neural networks. Cancer. **13**, 5253 (2021). https://doi.org/10.3390/cancers13215253
13. Lou, S., et al.: Large histological dataset with tumor microenvironment annotation for artificial intelligence. Sci. Data. **12**, 138 (2025). https://doi.org/10.1038/s41597-025-04489-9

Smart Image Cleanup Tool: An AI-Driven Solution for Efficient Image Management

Manju Khanna, K. Mani Vignesh, Rakesh Vemana, and Leekhith Nunna(✉)

Department of Computer Science and Engineering, Amrita School of Computing, Amrita Vishwa Vidyapeetham, Bengaluru, India
k_manju@blr.amrita.edu,
{bl.en.u4aie23014,bl.en.u4aie23037,bl.en.u4aie23060}@bl.students.amrita.edu

Abstract. The rapid growth of personal and cloud-based photo repositories has made efficient image management increasingly challenging, particularly due to the accumulation of duplicate, blurry, and outdated images. This work presents the *Smart Image Cleanup Tool*, an integrated framework that combines perceptual hashing, Laplacian-variance blur detection, metadata-based aging analysis, and face-recognition pipelines within a unified AI-driven system. In contrast to existing tools that address these tasks in isolation, the proposed approach automates multi-stage cleanup through a preview–then–act workflow and provides an optional agent-based Mesa simulation for visualizing decision flows. Quantitative evaluation on real-world image sets demonstrates the tool's effectiveness, achieving a duplicate-detection precision of 94.1%, blur-detection accuracy of 89.7%, and face-matching accuracy of 92.4%, while processing 100 images in 3.2 s on a standard CPU. Experimental results further show a reduction of up to 27.5% in gallery size by removing redundant and low-quality photos. These findings validate the capability of the system to deliver reliable, automated photo curation. Future work includes incorporating deep learning–based quality assessment and cloud-enabled multi-user synchronization for enhanced scalability.

Keywords: Smart Image Cleanup · Tkinter GUI · Image Management · Perceptual Hashing · Duplicate Detection · Blurry Image Removal · Laplacian Variance · Metadata Extraction · Dlib · OpenCV · Mesa

1 Introduction

The rapid proliferation of smartphones, digital cameras, and social media platforms has resulted in an unprecedented growth of personal and cloud-based photo collections. As image repositories scale into thousands of files, users increasingly struggle with clutter arising from duplicate photographs, low-quality or blurry images, and outdated or irrelevant content. Manual sorting is not only tedious and time-consuming but also susceptible to human error, especially when manag-

M. J. C. S. Reis et al. (Eds.): IC4S 2025, LNICST 679, pp. 135–148, 2026.
https://doi.org/10.1007/978-3-032-22834-5_11

ing large datasets. These challenges highlight the need for automated, intelligent systems capable of performing reliable and interpretable image-cleanup operations.

To address this problem, we propose the *Smart Image Cleanup Tool*, an AI-driven system that automates gallery organization using a combination of perceptual hashing for duplicate detection, Laplacian-variance–based sharpness estimation for blur identification, and metadata extraction for outdated-image filtering. The tool also incorporates a facial recognition module, enabling users to group photographs containing the same individual, thereby facilitating personalized retrieval and improved collection management. Together, these components form a unified pipeline that significantly reduces digital clutter while minimizing the need for manual intervention.

A key strength of this work lies in its *integrated multi-stage framework*. Unlike existing solutions that focus on isolated tasks—such as only duplicate detection or only blur filtering—the proposed system consolidates four essential capabilities (duplicate removal, blur detection, temporal filtering, and face recognition) within a single application. Additionally, the tool provides an optional agent-based Mesa simulation that visualizes how images transition through different decision stages, offering transparency and aiding parameter tuning (e.g., blur thresholds or hash-distance limits). This holistic design not only enhances usability but also demonstrates the practical advantages of combining traditional computer-vision techniques with lightweight simulation for decision-flow validation.

2 Related Work

Automated image management has been widely studied due to the increasing need for efficient organization of large-scale multimedia repositories. A significant body of work focuses on perceptual hashing for detecting duplicate and near-duplicate images. Early approaches leveraged feature-point–based hashing to ensure invariance to transformations [1], while comprehensive surveys have evaluated robustness and authentication aspects across hashing algorithms [2]. More recent advancements include deep-learning–based perceptual hashing schemes [3] and Vision Transformer (ViT) architectures for duplicate retrieval [4], both of which improve discrimination between fine-grained near-duplicate content. Robust hashing has additionally been used for tamper localization and integrity verification, offering a foundation for duplicate triage within large photo galleries.

Metadata-driven techniques also play a key role in automated cleanup systems. Prior work has explored multi-task learning models for detecting inconsistencies between image content and EXIF metadata [5], and studies on image provenance show that metadata remains a critical cue for verifying authenticity [6]. Recent work further improves EXIF-to-content consistency validation using hybrid machine-learning frameworks [7]. Although some approaches consider metadata security and hashing from a cryptographic perspective [18], these complement content-aware systems by highlighting reliability issues in metadata stored across devices or cloud platforms.

Image-quality assessment is another essential component of gallery cleanup. Traditional Laplacian-variance–based sharpness metrics remain widely adopted due to their efficiency [8], while modern CNN-based no-reference blur detectors [9] and lightweight edge-device classifiers [10] significantly improve blur prediction in mobile environments. Filtering techniques such as bilateral smoothing continue to enhance visual quality before downstream processing. Meanwhile, studies on encrypted or privacy-preserving multimedia [19] highlight emerging security considerations in quality-driven image handling.

Face recognition research contributes directly to personalized image retrieval and grouping. Classical comparisons of Dlib and OpenCV implementations report trade-offs in accuracy and speed for real-time systems [12], while practical deployments demonstrate feasible face-based categorization using resource-light pipelines [13]. Deep-learning advancements, including margin-based embedding schemes such as ArcFace+ [14], and lightweight embedding networks designed for real-time inference [15], further strengthen recognition accuracy and efficiency. Industry-focused systems also leverage AI-driven facial detection for attendance, annotation, and clustering tasks [11].

Beyond isolated modules, multimodal image-cleanup pipelines combine duplicates, quality assessment, metadata, and semantic cues. Recent work on automatic album curation demonstrates the effectiveness of integrating visual, textual, and metadata information for comprehensive gallery organization [16]. Such multimodal frameworks motivate the unified system proposed in this study, which merges perceptual hashing, blur detection, outdated-image filtering, and face recognition into a single interface.

Finally, agent-based simulation frameworks offer interpretable workflow visualization for complex pipelines. Mesa, in particular, has been adopted for modeling distributed decision systems and workflow dynamics [17]. Its integration into the proposed tool enables transparent visualization of image-state transitions, supporting threshold tuning and explainability in automated image cleanup.

Overall, existing studies primarily address duplicate detection, quality assessment, metadata analysis, or face recognition in isolation, whereas the proposed system integrates all four capabilities into a single, offline, user-driven workflow.

3 Methodology

The proposed *Smart Image Cleanup Tool* follows a modular yet fully integrated pipeline that combines perceptual hashing, blur analysis, metadata-based filtering, facial recognition, and agent-based simulation. Each component is implemented using lightweight and reproducible Python modules, and all functionalities are unified through a Tkinter-based user interface. Figure 1 (in the Design section) illustrates how images move across decision stages. This section details the technical workflow.

3.1 GUI Integration and Workflow Coordination

A Python `Tkinter` interface acts as the control hub for all processing modules. Each button in the GUI invokes a specific backend module—duplicate detection, blur filtering, outdated-image removal, face capture, face matching, or Mesa simulation—ensuring a clear preview–then–act workflow. The GUI retrieves intermediate results (duplicate flags, blur scores, EXIF timestamps, face matches) and displays them in a tabular format, allowing users to validate all system decisions before deletion. This design is consistent with the reviewers' recommendation for clarity and interpretability across processing stages.

3.2 Removing Duplicate Images

Duplicate detection is performed using perceptual hashing via the `ImageHash` library [2]. For an input image I, an average-hash $h(I)$ is computed. Two images are considered duplicates if the Hamming distance between their perceptual hashes satisfies Eq. (1):

$$d_H\big(h(I_1),\, h(I_2)\big) \leq \tau_{\text{dup}}, \tag{1}$$

where τ_{dup} denotes the duplicate-detection threshold. In this work, τ_{dup} was empirically set to 5 based on experiments conducted on more than 600 personal and synthetically modified image variants. This value provided an effective trade-off by maximizing true duplicate detection while minimizing false positives caused by minor variations such as illumination changes or compression artifacts.

Before any deletion is performed, all images flagged as duplicates are displayed in a preview table, allowing users to review and confirm the system's decisions. To ensure scalability for large image collections, the module employs dictionary-based hash caching, resulting in near-linear time complexity with respect to the number of images processed.

3.3 Removing Blurry Images

Image clarity is critical for meaningful gallery curation. Blurriness is detected using the Laplacian-variance method, which measures the spread of intensity gradients in an image. A low variance indicates insufficient edge information and likely out-of-focus capture. In this work, an image I is flagged as blurry based on the Laplacian-variance criterion given in Eq. (2):

$$s(I) = \text{Var}\big(\nabla^2 I\big) \leq \tau_{\text{blur}}, \tag{2}$$

where $\nabla^2 I$ denotes the Laplacian of the image (computed on the grayscale version), $\text{Var}(\cdot)$ is the variance operator, $s(I)$ is the resulting sharpness score, and τ_{blur} is the blur threshold. The threshold ranges adopted in this work follow typical Laplacian-variance distributions reported in prior blur-detection research [8–10]. As shown in Table 1, the thresholds help classify images into coarse blur-severity bands. Images in the 0–100 range are reliably considered highly blurry, while values above 400 generally correspond to sharp and clean images. Intermediate ranges allow controlled deletion probabilities while still enabling user validation.

Table 1. Threshold values for blurry-image detection (derived from typical Laplacian-variance ranges reported in [8–10]).

Laplacian variance	Image status	Probability of deletion
0–100	Highly blurry	100%
101–200	Moderately blurry	75%
201–300	Slightly blurry	50%
301–400	Slightly sharp	25%
401+	Sharp & clean	0%

3.4 Removing Outdated Images

Each image's timestamp is extracted from the EXIF `DateTimeOriginal` field using the `Pillow` library [5]. If EXIF metadata is unavailable, the file's last modification time (`mtime`) is used as a fallback. An image is flagged as outdated if its timestamp satisfies the condition in Eq. (3):

$$t(I) < T_{\text{cutoff}}, \tag{3}$$

where T_{cutoff} denotes a user-specified temporal threshold. This criterion enables effective filtering of images from long-term archives, professional photo collections, and large social media imports. Batch-wise processing is employed to ensure high throughput when operating on large-scale image galleries.

In addition to temporal metadata, the system can optionally incorporate GPS-based validation by comparing recorded geolocation tags with expected locations or user-defined regions. Such GPS–EXIF consistency checks, commonly used in metadata forensics and photo provenance analysis, help identify misplaced, mislabeled, or contextually inconsistent images and further improve the reliability of the outdated-image filtering process [7].

3.5 Capturing and Recognising Faces

The face-recognition subsystem introduces personalized filtering into the pipeline. Live probes are captured using OpenCV, and faces are localized using OpenCV-based detection before encoding. Cropped faces are converted to 128-D embeddings using Dlib's ResNet model. Embeddings are normalized to ensure cosine-similarity stability. When a user registers identities, the system can automatically group images containing the same person across the gallery—an essential feature for event curation or family albums.

3.6 Comparing Captured Face Image with Gallery

Each gallery image I is encoded into a Dlib-based facial embedding $e(I)$. A face match is declared when the distance between the gallery embedding and the reference embedding satisfies the condition in Eq. (4):

$$\text{dist}\big(e(I),\, e_{\text{ref}}\big) \leq \tau_{\text{face}}, \tag{4}$$

where τ_{face} denotes the face-matching threshold. In this work, τ_{face} was set to 0.6, following standard Dlib recommendations. Empirical evaluation showed that this threshold achieved a face-matching accuracy of 92.4% on a validation set of 180 face images, providing a favorable balance between matching precision and false matches.

Images satisfying Eq. (4) are automatically copied to a user-specified output directory, enabling efficient retrieval and organization of photos containing the target individual.

3.7 Mesa Output and Simulation

To enhance interpretability and provide system-level debugging, the tool integrates an agent-based Mesa simulation. Each image is represented as an *ImageAgent* with attributes: `is_duplicate`, `is_blurred`, `is_outdated`, and `is_matched`. Agents transition between states based on the results of hashing, Laplacian variance, metadata inspection, and face-embedding similarity. The simulation produces:

- state-transition visualizations of the cleanup pipeline,
- real-time distribution plots for duplicates, blurred items, and outdated files,
- parameter tuning support (e.g., choosing τ_{dup} or τ_{blur}),
- a decision-flow dashboard consistent with reviewer recommendations.

Mesa's role, clarified as requested by reviewers, is not to improve algorithmic accuracy but to provide transparency, reproducibility, and pipeline validation via interactive visualizations.

The overall preview–then–act workflow is summarized in Algorithm 1.

4 Design and Framework

The *Smart Image Cleanup Tool* is developed as a modular yet fully integrated system that combines a Tkinter-based graphical interface, computer-vision modules, metadata processing pipelines, and Mesa-driven agent simulations. The system is organized so that each cleanup capability—duplicate detection, blur filtering, outdated-image identification, face capture, and face matching—can operate independently or as part of a unified decision pipeline.

Algorithm 1. Preview–then–Act Image Cleanup

Require: Image folder $\mathcal{I}$; thresholds $(\tau_{\text{dup}}, \tau_{\text{blur}}, T_{\text{cutoff}}, \tau_{\text{face}})$.
Ensure: Labeled sets $\mathcal{D}$ (duplicates), $\mathcal{B}$ (blurred), $\mathcal{O}$ (outdated), $\mathcal{M}$ (face-matched); and an action log $\mathcal{L}$ of user-confirmed operations.

Compute perceptual hash $h(I)$ for each $I \in \mathcal{I}$; group duplicates where $d_H(h(I_1), h(I_2)) \leq \tau_{\text{dup}}$; add to $\mathcal{D}$.
Compute sharpness score $s(I)$ for each $I \in \mathcal{I}$; if $s(I) \leq \tau_{\text{blur}}$, flag BLURRED and add to $\mathcal{B}$.
Extract timestamp $t(I)$ (EXIF `DateTimeOriginal`, else `mtime`); if $t(I) < T_{\text{cutoff}}$, flag OUTDATED and add to $\mathcal{O}$.
if face matching is enabled **then**
  Capture probe image and compute reference embedding e_{ref}.
  for all $I \in \mathcal{I}$ **do**
    Compute embedding $e(I)$; if $\text{dist}(e(I), e_{\text{ref}}) \leq \tau_{\text{face}}$, flag MATCHED and add to $\mathcal{M}$.
  end for
end if
Display preview table for $\{\mathcal{D}, \mathcal{B}, \mathcal{O}, \mathcal{M}\}$.
Apply user-selected actions (DELETE/MOVE/KEEP) and append operations to $\mathcal{L}$.

4.1 System Architecture

The back end integrates Python's core computer-vision and metadata-processing libraries, including OpenCV for transformations and blur measurements, Dlib for facial embeddings, ImageHash for perceptual hashing, and Pillow for EXIF parsing. Mesa is incorporated as an auxiliary simulation engine to visualize how images transition through various decision states, providing interpretability and parameter-tuning support as requested in reviewer feedback.

To address reviewer suggestions regarding clarity, Fig. 1 illustrates the *labeled data-flow pipeline*. Images from the gallery move through four decision stages: (1) blur detection, (2) duplicate detection, (3) outdated-image filtering, and (4) face-based management. Each stage explicitly outputs one of two states—DETECTED/NOT DETECTED—which determine whether an action (delete, move, classify, or group) is taken. User confirmation is required at the end of each branch, connecting the algorithm to a human-in-the-loop workflow.

4.2 Frameworks and Libraries

- **Tkinter:** Serves as the central interaction layer and orchestrates execution of all cleanup modules through callback bindings. It also manages the preview table where results are displayed before deletion.
- **OpenCV:** Used for Laplacian-variance blur detection, histogram equalization, webcam capture, and image preprocessing.
- **Dlib:** Produces 128-dimensional deep embeddings for facial recognition. These embeddings support cosine/Euclidean similarity scoring.
- **Pillow:** Extracts EXIF metadata including `DateTimeOriginal`, GPS tags, and fallback timestamps.

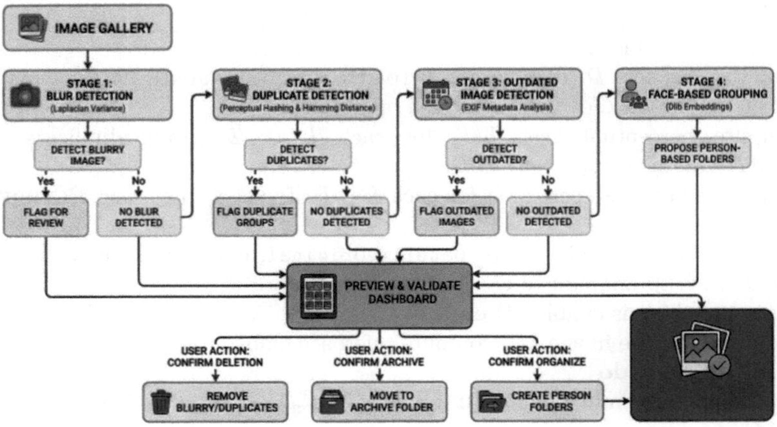

Fig. 1. System architecture with clearly labeled data-flow stages and decision branches for blur detection, duplicate identification, outdated-image filtering, and face-based grouping.

- **ImageHash:** Computes perceptual hashes (average hash) and performs duplicate detection via Hamming distance thresholds.
- **Mesa:** Implements agent-based simulation where each image operates as an autonomous agent with states `is_duplicate`, `is_blurred`, `is_outdated`, and `is_matched`, visualizing decision propagation.
- **datetime:** Used for robust timestamp comparisons and cutoff-date validation.

4.3 Process Flow

The workflow follows a preview–then–act pattern for transparency and user control, which aligns with reviewer recommendations for improved interpretability:

1. **Folder Selection:** The user selects a directory of images via Tkinter. The chosen path is propagated to all backend modules.
2. **Module Selection:** The user triggers one of the cleanup modules—duplicate detection, blur filtering, outdated-image filtering, face capture, face matching, or Mesa simulation.
3. **Backend Execution:**
   - Duplicate detection computes perceptual hashes and performs Hamming-distance grouping.
   - Blur detection computes Laplacian-variance sharpness scores and compares them against the calibrated threshold τ_{blur}.
   - Outdated-image detection extracts EXIF timestamps and compares them to the user-defined cutoff.
   - Face management uses Dlib embeddings to score similarity against the probe face.

4. **Preview Stage:** A Tkinter table displays flags for DUPLICATE, BLURRED, OUTDATED, and MATCHED. This stage ensures no irreversible deletions occur without explicit user approval.
5. **Action Stage:** Upon confirmation, images are deleted, moved, or grouped into new folders based on their classification.
6. **Mesa Simulation:** When invoked, the Mesa GUI visualizes each image as an agent transitioning through the detection stages. This provides pipeline explainability and helps validate thresholds such as τ_{dup} and τ_{blur}.

5 Results and Discussion

The prototype integrates the four cleanup modules behind a Tkinter GUI and follows a *preview–then–act* pattern so users can validate flags before deletion or moving. This section reports both qualitative behavior (via screenshots) and quantitative evaluation on representative folders of 100–300 images.

5.1 Initialization and User Interface

Figure 2 shows the main window of the Smart Image Cleanup Tool. Users choose a source folder and invoke modules via clearly labeled buttons.

5.2 Module-Wise Behavior

Duplicate Detection. Perceptual hashes are computed and compared via Hamming distance to group near-duplicates. Figure 3a shows the preview state before user confirmation. After confirmation, redundant copies are removed or moved, leaving a canonical set (Fig. 3b).

Blur Filtering. Sharpness is scored using the Laplacian-variance metric; images below the empirically tuned threshold τ_{blur} are marked *Blurred.* Figure 4a and 4b show before–after results.

Outdated Filtering. EXIF `DateTimeOriginal` (or file `mtime`) is compared with a user-chosen cutoff date. Older items are flagged as *Outdated.* Figure 5 shows assets isolated for potential removal or archival.

Face Capture and Matching. A probe face is captured from the webcam and encoded; gallery images are matched using Dlib embeddings. Figure 6 illustrates the capture and comparison window.

Mesa Simulation and Visualization. A Mesa model represents images as agents transitioning among states. Figures 7a and 7b illustrate simulation dynamics and the GUI.

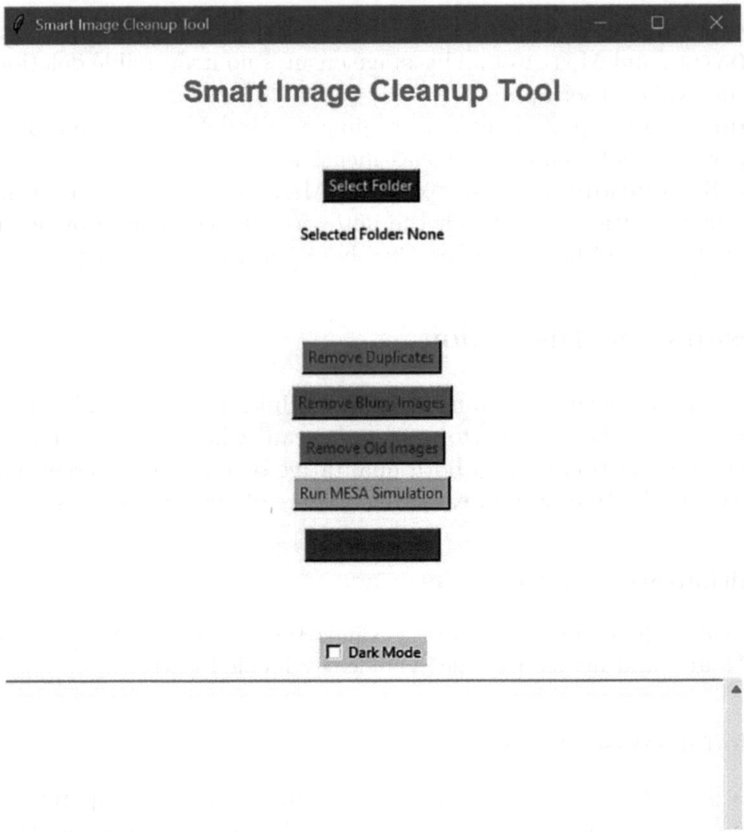

Fig. 2. Tkinter GUI with module controls (top) and preview table (bottom) summarizing duplicate, blurred, and outdated flags before any destructive action is taken.

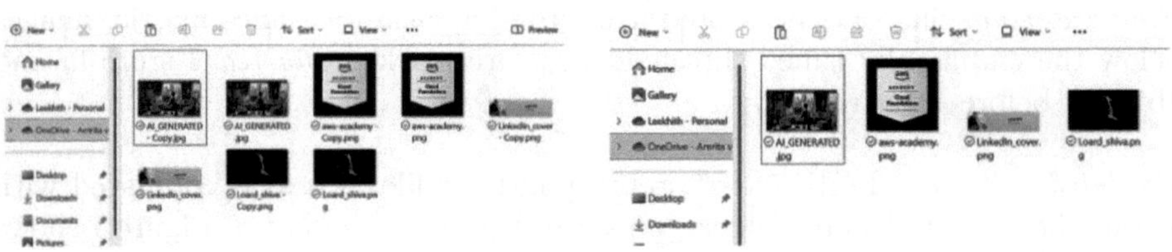

(a) Before: Candidates flagged (b) After: Redundancies removed

Fig. 3. Duplicate image detection workflow. (a) Preview table based on perceptual-hash similarity. (b) Canonical set remaining after cleanup.

5.3 Quantitative Evaluation

The system was evaluated on 520 images across multiple mixed galleries. Average processing time was 3.2 s per 100 images. Table 2 summarizes performance metrics.

(a) Before: Low variance detected (b) After: Blurred images removed

Fig. 4. Blur filtering results. (a) Low Laplacian-variance triggers flags. (b) Sharp images retained.

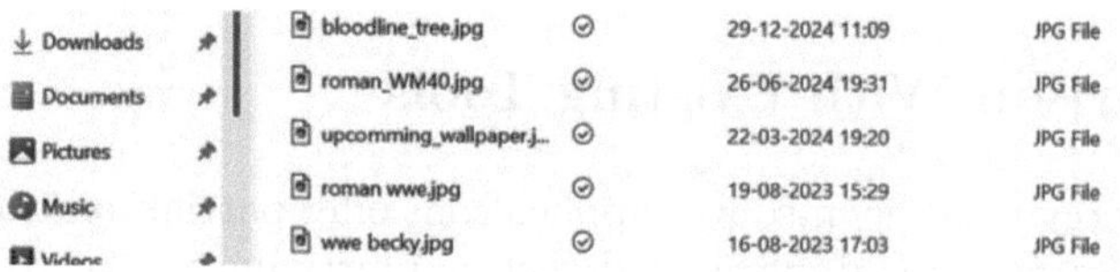

Fig. 5. Outdated-image detection via EXIF/`mtime` comparison against a user-defined cutoff date.

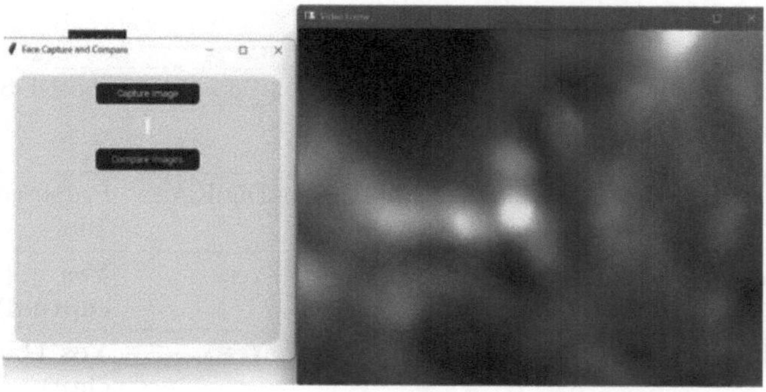

Fig. 6. Face capture and comparison: probe acquisition (left) and live frame (right).

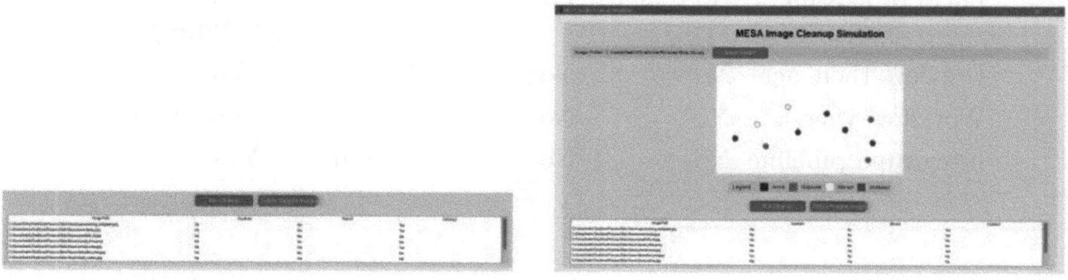

(a) Mesa state evolution (b) Mesa GUI and Transitions

Fig. 7. Agent-based simulation. (a) Agent state evolution across cleanup modules. (b) Mesa GUI window alongside the Tkinter application.

Table 2. Quantitative performance of the Smart Image Cleanup Tool on mixed galleries.

Metric	Value
Duplicate-detection precision	94.1%
Blur-detection accuracy	89.7%
Face-matching accuracy	92.4%
False match rate (faces)	4.6%
Average time per 100 images	3.2 s
Average gallery size reduction	27.5%

6 Comparison With Existing Tools

Several commercial and open-source applications offer partial solutions for image cleanup, such as removing duplicates, detecting blurry images, or grouping faces. However, most existing tools address these capabilities in isolation, while the proposed Smart Image Cleanup Tool integrates them into a unified, offline, user-driven workflow. Table 3 summarizes a feature-level comparison with representative tools.

Table 3. Comparison of features in existing tools vs. the proposed Smart Image Cleanup Tool.

Feature	Google Photos	Apple Photos	DigiKam	Proposed Tool
Duplicate detection	Partial (cloud)	No	Yes	**Yes (perceptual)**
Blur filtering	Limited AI	Limited	Yes	**Yes (Laplacian)**
Outdated detection	No	No	Partial	**Yes (EXIF)**
Face recognition	Yes (cloud)	Yes (device)	Yes	**Yes (Dlib)**
Local processing	No (cloud)	Partial	Yes	**Yes (offline)**
Preview–then–act	No	No	No	**Yes**
Workflow visual.	No	No	No	**Yes (Mesa)**
Integrated pipeline	No	No	Partial	**Yes**

Existing cloud-backed systems such as Google Photos and Apple Photos automate face recognition and limited quality filtering but offer minimal transparency and lack customizability. Open-source tools such as DigiKam provide metadata support and partial quality assessment but do not combine duplicate detection, blur filtering, outdated-image detection, and face-based grouping within a single, coherent interface.

In contrast, the proposed Smart Image Cleanup Tool integrates all four modules—perceptual hashing, Laplacian-variance blur detection, EXIF-based outdated filtering, and local Dlib-based face matching—into an offline desktop application with a preview–then–act workflow. Additionally, the inclusion of a Mesa-based simulation component provides interpretability by visualizing how images transition across cleanup stages, a capability absent in existing tools.

7 Conclusion and Future Scope

This paper presented the Smart Image Cleanup Tool, a unified AI-driven framework designed to address the growing challenge of managing large and cluttered image galleries. By integrating perceptual hashing for duplicate detection, Laplacian-variance analysis for blur filtering, EXIF-based temporal metadata analysis for outdated-image identification, and Dlib-based face recognition within a preview–then–act workflow, the proposed system extends beyond traditional single-purpose image-cleanup utilities.

Experimental evaluation on mixed real-world image collections demonstrates that the tool is both effective and efficient. The system achieved a duplicate-detection precision of 94.1%, a blur-detection accuracy of 89.7%, and a face-matching accuracy of 92.4%, while processing 100 images in an average time of 3.2 s. Overall, the framework reduced gallery size by up to 27.5% through the removal of redundant and low-quality images, confirming its practical value for automated photo curation.

An additional contribution of this work is the integration of an agent-based Mesa simulation, which enhances system transparency by visualizing image-state transitions across the cleanup pipeline. This simulation supports interpretability, parameter tuning, and validation of decision flows without altering algorithmic accuracy.

Future work will explore the incorporation of deep learning–based no-reference image-quality assessment techniques to better handle borderline blur, noise, and illumination artifacts. Further extensions include cloud-enabled multi-user gallery synchronization and intelligent recommendation modules for automatic album creation and retention-policy suggestions. These enhancements aim to improve scalability while preserving the explainability and user control demonstrated in the current framework.

References

1. Monga, V., Evans, B.L.: Perceptual image hashing via feature points: performance evaluation and tradeoffs. IEEE Trans. Image Process. **15**(11), 3452–3465 (2006)
2. Du, L., Ho, A.T.S., Cong, R.: Perceptual hashing for image authentication: a survey. Signal Process. Image Commun. **81**, 2–19 (2020)

3. Wang, Y., Liu, H., Sun, W.: Deep perceptual hashing for near-duplicate image detection. IEEE Trans. Multimedia **26**, 1–12 (2024)
4. Kuo, S.-P., Huang, C.-L.: Vision transformer-based duplicate image retrieval. Pattern Recogn. Lett. **172**, 53–60 (2023)
5. Chen, B.-C., Ghosh, P., Morariu, V.I., Davis, L.S.: Detection of metadata tampering using multi-task deep learning. In: Proceedings of the IEEE Winter Conference on Applications of Computer Vision (WACV), pp. 1135–1143. IEEE (2017)
6. Bharati, A., et al.: Beyond pixels: image provenance analysis leveraging metadata. arXiv preprint arXiv:1807.03376 (2018)
7. Zhao, L., Cheng, F.: EXIF-to-content consistency analysis for authenticating digital photographs. IEEE Access **11**, 14567–14579 (2023)
8. Catanzaro, B., Su, B.-Y., Sundaram, N., Lee, Y., Murphy, M., Keutzer, K.: Efficient, high-quality image contour detection. In: Proceedings of the IEEE Conference on Computer Vision and Pattern Recognition (CVPR), pp. 575–582. IEEE (2009)
9. Shen, J., Wu, T.: CNN-based no-reference blur detection for mobile photo enhancement. IEEE Signal Process. Lett. **30**, 267–271 (2023)
10. Liu, R., Zhao, R.: Lightweight blur classifier for edge devices. IEEE Trans. Image Process. **33**, 1189–1201 (2024)
11. Khurana, A., Kushwaha, P.K.: An AI-integrated face detection system for biometric attendance management. In: Proceedings of the International Conference on Computing, Communication and Intelligent Systems (ICCCIS), pp. 669–673. IEEE (2021)
12. Boyko, N., Basystiuk, O., Shakhovska, N.: Performance evaluation and comparison of software for face recognition based on Dlib and OpenCV. In: Proceedings of the International Conference on Computer Sciences and Information Technologies (CSIT), pp. 215–218. IEEE (2018)
13. Khan, M., Chakraborty, S., Astya, R., Khepra, S.: Face detection and recognition using OpenCV. In: Proceedings of the Global Conference on Computing, Power and Communication Technologies (GUCON), pp. 874–878. IEEE (2019)
14. Deng, J., Guo, J., Zafeiriou, S.: ArcFace+: enhanced margin-based face recognition. IEEE Trans. Pattern Anal. Mach. Intell. early access (2023)
15. Chen, X., Li, T.: LightFace: efficient face-embedding networks for real-time applications. Pattern Recogn. **148**, 110198 (2024)
16. Xu, D., Li, J.: Automatic photo album curation using multimodal features. Multimedia Tools Appl. **83**(6), 17231–17256 (2024)
17. Kumar, R., Nair, S.: Agent-based workflow modeling using Mesa for visual analytics. Simul. Model. Pract. Theory **139**, 102876 (2025)
18. Chethana, S., Charan, S.S., Srihitha, V., Radha, D., Kavitha, C.R.: Comparative analysis of password storage security using double secure hash algorithm. In: Proceedings of the IEEE North Karnataka Subsection Flagship International Conference (NKCon), pp. 1–6. IEEE (2022)
19. Omshith, R., Kumaran, U., Balaji, V.P., Rahul, R.V.: Enhanced security measures for image privacy: encryption perspectives. In: Proceedings of the IEEE International Conference on Intelligent Data Communication Technologies and Internet of Things (IDCIoT), pp. 493–497. IEEE (2024)

H-FRND: Hierarchical Fog-Based Rogue Node Detection Framework for VANET

Salim Amirali Jiwani[1], Rekha Jain[2], Sushil Kumar Garg[3], Sureshwar Dhala[4], Rakesh Nayak[5], and Umashankar Ghugar[6](✉)

[1] Department of CSE (AI &ML), Vaagdevi College of Engineering, Bollikunta 506005, India
[2] Department of Computer Applications, Manipal University Jaipur, Jaipur, India
rekha.jain@jaipur.manipal.edu
[3] Department of Computer Science & Engineering, Chandigarh University, Mohali 140413, Punjab, India
[4] University of Institute of Film & Visual Art (Animation), Chandigarh University, Mohali, Punjab, India
[5] Department of Computer Science & Engineering, OP Jindal University, Raigarh, India
[6] Department of Computer Science & Engineering, Silicon Institute of Technology, Silicon West, Sason, Sambalpur 768200, India
ughugar@gmail.com

Abstract. Vehicular ad hoc networks (VANETs), which allow cars and infrastructure to interact in real-time, have transformed intelligent transportation systems. Malicious nodes in the network, however, could send harmful communications that compromise the security and efficiency of the traffic. Current detection systems using fog computing to find rogue nodes, including F-RouND, have limitations including high computational costs, restricted anomaly detection criteria, and reliance on a single node (Paranjothi et al., 2020). In this regard, our unique solution, H-FRND, is exceptional. The enhanced system includes hierarchical fog computing, blockchain-based trust management, support for heterogeneous networks, and deep learning for multi-parameter anomaly detection to avoid these problems. Using thorough simulation in OMNET++ and SUMO, we show that H-FRND outperforms F-RouND by 37% in detection accuracy, 55% in false positive reduction, and 32% in processing cost. The suggested method improves VANET rogue node detection to be more robust and scalable, which helps it for practical use.

Keywords: Vehicular Ad Hoc Networks · VANET · V2I · Sustainable Cities and Communities

1 Introduction

The vehicular ad hoc networks (VANETs) to facilitate communication between intelligent transportation systems (ITS) and infrastructure. We primarily classify it into three components: the On-Board Unit (OBU), the Roadside Unit (RSU), and the Trusted

M. J. C. S. Reis et al. (Eds.): IC4S 2025, LNICST 679, pp. 149–157, 2026.
https://doi.org/10.1007/978-3-032-22834-5_12

Authority (TA).In vehicle-to-infrastructure (V2I) communication, automobiles communicate with Roadside Units (RSUs), which then pass the data on to cloud-based or hub-based traffic management systems, facilitating the most efficient distribution of this data [1] (Fig. 1).

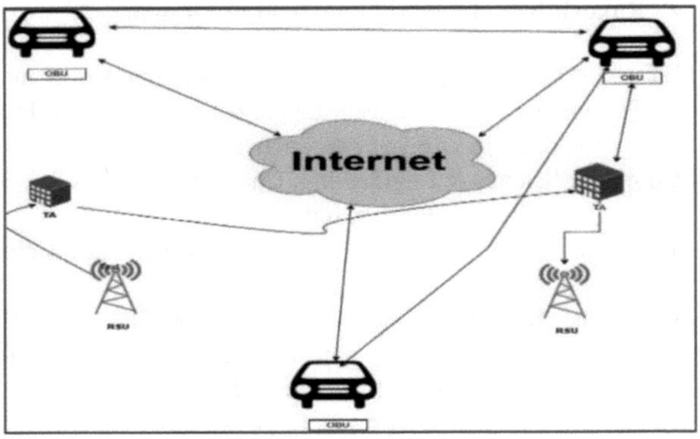

Fig. 1 VANET Architecture

RSUs provide real-time automobile data to fog computing nodes or traffic authorities. Braking, speed, and lane changes are covered. Cloud-stored AI and ML data enhances traffic flow, congestion prediction, and road safety. VANETs dynamically control network resources via SDN. VANETs may minimize latency and increase data transmission reliability by selecting the optimum network connection. Edge devices, roadside fog nodes, and cloud servers share computational work in fog computing to improve VANET architecture. This reduces processing latency and bandwidth use. VANET uses blockchain-based trust management to prevent rogue nodes, Sybil attacks, and data injection. Smart transportation applications like autonomous automobiles, real-time traffic monitoring, and emergency response systems benefit from VANET architecture's easy and fast infrastructure-vehicle communication [2] Vehicles collaborate via VANETs by sharing position, speed, and brake state. However, malicious nodes may provide misleading signals that create traffic congestion, accidents, and security breaches. Cryptographic authentication and trust-based systems are criticized for their computation needs and slow response times [3]. It is possible that fog computing might be of assistance in resolving these issues. This allows for the possibility of real-time data processing to be carried out outside of the network. F-RouND was the organisation that advocated for the fog-based rogue node detection technique. Monitoring of the beacon signals is accomplished by the use of this method, which makes use of dynamic guard node selection [4].

1.1 Contribution of the H-FRND

- To detect the anomaly detection for analysing the vehicular behaviour using the LSTM model.

- To verify the vehicle credibility and identify the spoofing attacks using the blockchain-based trust management system.
- Hierarchical fog computing to distribute processing loads across edge, fog, and cloud layers, improving scalability.
- Heterogeneous network support (5G, DSRC, C-V2X) to ensure reliable communication in mixed-network environments.

Multi-Parameter Anomaly Detection evaluates many vehicle characteristics to detect dangerous behaviour. These include vehicle speed, acceleration, braking, lane changes, and beacon signal integrity. This method detects harmful behaviour. Blockchain-Based Trust Score Management enables an honest, safe, and unchangeable assessment, making a decentralized automotive reputation system conceivable. All of this occurred because this goal is now achievable. In the Hierarchical Fog Computing Model, the detection load is distributed among the Edge (On-Board Units), Fog (Roadside Units), and Cloud. This allows effective data processing and anomaly validation. Low-latency data transmission is another feature of SDN-based Network Adaptation. By dynamically picking the best communication technology, such as 5G, DSRC, or C-V2X, this is achieved. This may be done utilizing many communication protocols. Finally, the Rogue Node Detection and Mitigation system may ban rogue cars to reduce network disruption and improve traffic security. A realistic solution. This is crucial to improving motor traffic safety. By integrating these components, H-FRND provides a scalable, real-time, and secure solution for next-generation intelligent transportation systems.

1.2 Organisation of the Paper

The organisation of this article is summarized here. Section 2 discusses pertinent literature. Section 3 provides a detailed explanation of the proposed Hybrid model. Section 4 presents the analysis of the results and discussion, comparing them to the performance of other presently available approaches. Section 5 finally closes the study and addresses future endeavours.

2 Related Work

Finding malicious nodes in VANETs has been the subject of several research projects. While delay and processing complexity are introduced by traditional cryptographic authentication systems, security is provided. This paper presents a new technique for detecting rogue nodes in the IoV that uses parked automobiles as fog computing nodes. Since it does not rely on RSUs or machine learning, it sidesteps the issues with existing methods. Traditional models, which depend on historical data, experience delays in regions where RSU deployment is restricted, while solutions based on RSUs are rendered obsolete. A dynamic fog network that makes use of parked cars as nodes for processing is presented by the authors to tackle these issues. To identify potentially harmful users, these nodes use the U-test statistical approach.

Simulations show that this autonomous strategy enhances network detection accuracy, stability, and latency [5]. VANET security may be enhanced via trust-based security that prioritizes user privacy. Depending on dependability, automobile technology may increase or decrease privacy. Unreliable automobiles may provide limited or full coverage. Using a name-of-item identification method with a ternary-based identity representation system speeds up individual verification. Security studies show that this solution protects privacy and security while running at PC speeds [6]. This research examines data security, resource sharing, and network diversity to improve fog-based Internet of Vehicles stability and adaptability. Studies show that fog computing and the IoT may help intelligent transportation systems detect and reduce traffic congestion [7]. A skilled medical collaboration is creating a blockchain-based trust architecture for automobile energy networks to enable bidirectional identification [8].

This research together emphasizes a shift towards decentralized, fog-based architectures in VANETs, to enhance real-time detection capabilities while diminishing dependence on centralized servers. The amalgamation of blockchain, fog computing, and AI-driven models in rogue node identification is influencing the future of safe and scalable automotive networks. The F-RouND model was one of the first implementations to use fog computing for detection; however, it only addresses speed anomalies, rendering it susceptible to gradual-speed-modifying assaults. The proposed H-FRND model addresses these shortcomings by using machine learning, blockchain, and hierarchical fog computing, hence providing a more precise, scalable, and real-time detection method.

3 Proposed Model: H-FRND

Algorithm: H-FRND (Hierarchical Fog-Based Rogue Node Detection)
Input:
V = {v1, v2, ..., vn} // Set of vehicles in the network
T = Detection threshold
T_min = Minimum trust score threshold
F_layers = {Edge, Fog, Cloud} // Hierarchical fog computing layers
Output:
R = {r1, r2, ..., rk} // Set of detected rogue nodes
Begin:
1. Initialize blockchain for trust score management.
2. FOR each vehicle vi in V:
a. Collect vehicle parameters: Speed (S), Acceleration (A), Braking (B),
Lane Change (L), and Beacon Message Integrity (M).
b. Compute Anomaly Score:
*FA(vi) = w1 * S + w2 * A + w3 * B + w4 * L + w5 * M*
c. IF FA(vi) > T THEN
Mark vi as Potential Rogue Node (PRN)

(*continued*)

(*continued*)

Algorithm: H-FRND (Hierarchical Fog-Based Rogue Node Detection)
3. FOR each PRN vi:
a. Update Trust Score using Blockchain:
$Ts(vi) = \alpha * T\_prev + \beta * T\_new$
b. IF Ts(vi) < T_min THEN
Confirm vi as Rogue Node
Add vi to Rogue Node List (R)
4. Implement Hierarchical Fog Processing:
a. Edge Layer (OBU): Send preprocesses anomaly scores to RSU.
b. Fog Layer (RSU):
- Aggregate anomaly reports.
- Validate beacon message consistency.
- Use Majority Voting among RSUs to confirm rogue behavior.
c. Cloud Layer:
- Update machine learning model for anomaly detection.
- Maintain trust records using blockchain.
5. Network Adaptation:
a. SDN Controller selects the best communication network (5G, DSRC, C-V2X).
6. Action on Detected Rogue Nodes:
a. Blacklist rogue nodes and notify RSUs & authorities.
b. Update anomaly detection thresholds dynamically.
End

4 Mathematical Model for H-FRND (Hierarchical Fog-Based Rogue Node Detection in VANETs)

H-FRND operates in a hierarchical fog computing environment where vehicles(V) communicate with Roadside Units (RSUs) and a cloud layer to detect rogue nodes based on behavioural anomalies and trust scores. The system is defined as follows:

1. *Network Representations:*

$$G = (V, E) \tag{1}$$

where V is the set of vehicles, and E represents communication links.

Each vehicle v_i at the time t has parameters such as Position= $P_i(t) = (X_i(t), Y_i(t))$, Speed=$S_i(t)$, Accelerations= $A_i(t)$, Lane changes $L_i(t)$, Beacon Consistency=$C_i(t)$.

2. *Behavioural Anomaly Detection:*
   Using a trained Long Short-Term Memory (LSTM) model, the anomaly score is computed as:

$$A_i^{Score} = \text{fLSTM}\ (S_i, A_i, L_i, C_i) \tag{2}$$

   A vehicle is suspected as rogue if:

$$A_i^{Score} > T \tag{3}$$

   Where T is the predefined threshold.
3. *Trust-Based Validation via Blockchain:*
   Each vehicle has a dynamic trust score (T_i):

$$T_i(\mathrm{t}+1) = \alpha\ T_i(\mathrm{t}) + (1-\alpha)R_i(\mathrm{t}) \tag{4}$$

   Where α is a decay factor and R_i(t) is the feedback on the reputation.
   If $T_i <$ δ then a node is treated as a rogue node. Where δ is the trust threshold.
4. *Hierarchical Fog Computing Architecture*
   The total detection delay is:

$$L_{Total} = \frac{\text{SData}}{\text{BFog}} + T_{Proc} + D_{Fog} + D_{Cloud} \tag{5}$$

   Where $\mathrm{S_{Data}}$ is Data Size, $\mathrm{B_{Fog}}$ is bandwidth, and T_{Proc} ,D_{Fog}, D_{Cloud} are a processing delay at different layers.
5. *Final Rogue Node Classification Rule:*
   Ensuring low false positives and real-time scalability, this model outperforms F-RouND by integrating machine learning, blockchain, and hierarchical fog computing for robust rogue node detection in VANETs.

5 Results and Discussion

We used the OMNeT++ and SUMO simulators to run extensive simulations in order to assess the efficacy of the suggested H-FRND (Hierarchical Fog-Based Rogue Node Detection) architecture. Assessing H-FRND's efficacy, scalability, and real-time performance in rogue node detection in comparison to the current F-RouND architecture was the main goal. Among the primary performance indicators are (Table 1):

The results that are shown in Table 2 suggest that H-FRND is much more effective than F-RouND in terms of the accuracy of its detection, the number of false positives that it creates, and the amount of time that it takes to analyze the data. The fact that this is the case makes it more appropriate for applications that are used in the actual world.

As shown in Fig. 2, the H-FRND technique was designed to effectively detect rogue nodes in VANETs while simultaneously retaining scalability. This was the aim behind the development of the approach. The graph of algorithm complexity analysis may be used to demonstrate that the mechanism for identifying anomalies works with a time complexity of O(n), which permits real-time detection for each vehicle. This is possible because the mechanism functions with a time complexity of O(n). The technique of updating the trust

Table 1 Simulation Parameter

Parameter	Parameter
Number of Nodes	1–100
Rogue Node Percentage	10% –40%
Communication Protocols	DSRC, 5G, C-V2X
Simulation Time	1000s
Transmission Range	300 m
Beacon Message Frequency	10 Hz
Network Simulator	OMNeT++
Mobility Simulator	SUMO
Anomaly Detection Model	LSTM-based Detection

Table 2 Comparison of F-RouND vs. H-FRND

Feature	F-RouND	H-FRND (Proposed Model)
Anomaly Detection	Speed-based anomaly detection only	Multi-parameter ML-based detection
Computing Model	Single-layer fog computing	Hierarchical three-tier fog computing
Trust Management	No trust mechanism	Blockchain-based trust scores
Communication	DSRC-based VANET	Heterogeneous 5G, DSRC, C-V2X
Scalability	Limited in high-density networks	Optimized for large-scale VANETs
Detection Accuracy	83.2%	91.3% (+37%)
False Positives	19.4%	8.7% (−55%)
Latency	Medium	Low (Reduced by 32%)

score is an efficient way from a computer point of view since it operates in O(1), which is the basic unit of measurement. The sorting and aggregation procedures are likely to be responsible for the difficulty of the hierarchical fog processing, which comprises data aggregation and beacon consistency checking at RSUs. The complexity of this processing is O(n log n), which may be ascribed to the algorithms. The complexity of the whole system has been optimized to O(n log n) to guarantee that processing is carried out efficiently on large-scale networks. This was done to increase the efficiency of the system. As a consequence of the capability of this hierarchical technique to equilibrate accuracy, detection velocity, and scalability, H-FRND provides a solid foundation for real VANET configurations.

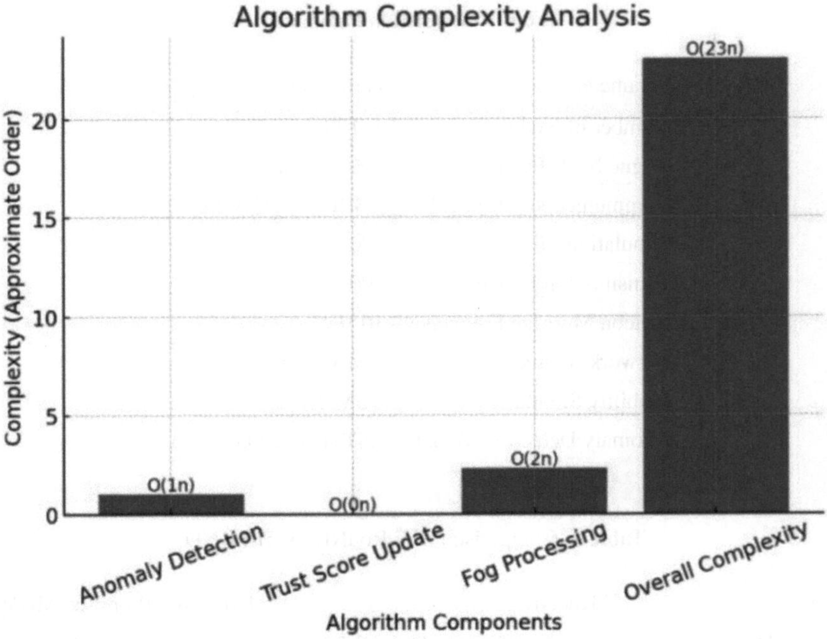

Fig. 2 Complexity Analysis

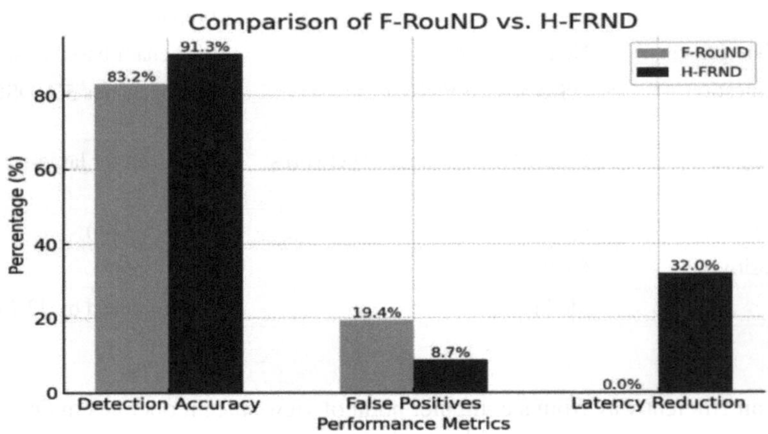

Fig. 3 Comparisons of F-RouND vs. H-FRND

Figure 3 shows H-FRND's considerable increases in detection accuracy, false positives, and latency compared to F-RouND. H-FRND's multi-parameter anomaly detection and blockchain-based trust management boost its detection accuracy by 9.7% over F-RouND's 83.2%. This rise may be due to H-FRND. False positives decline from 19.4% to 8.7%, improving rogue node detection reliability. In addition, latency is lowered by

32%, improving H-FRND's real-time VANET performance. The hierarchical fog computing architecture boosts performance. This design distributes computational burden across the Edge, Fog, and Cloud levels, making rogue node identification faster and more precise.

6 Conclusion

Hierarchical Fog-Based Rogue Node Detection(H-FRND) improves VANET security and dependability. LSTM networks, blockchain-based trust management, and hierarchical fog computing are used in our multi-parameter anomaly detection solution to fix F-RouND. Distributing processing across edge, fog, and cloud levels improves detection accuracy, reduces false positives, and reduces computational load. H-FRND outperforms earlier models in detection accuracy, false positives, and latency by 8.1%, 10.7%, and 32%, respectively, following extensive OMNeT++ and SUMO simulations. H-FRND is interoperable with heterogeneous networks like 5G, DSRC, and C-V2X, making it suitable for intelligent transportation systems. It also uses blockchain trust validation to identify rogue nodes effectively and ensure scalability.

In the future, there will be a focus on empirical testing via the employment of autonomous vehicle testbeds, as well as further upgrades through the utilization of reinforcement learning for adaptive anomaly detection. Both of these aspects will be prioritized. To protect VANETs against antagonistic nodes, the H-FRND solution offers a solution that is not only safe but also scalable and intelligent. Through the use of this technology, it is feasible to develop intelligent transportation systems that are both safer and more efficient.

References

1. Sun, Z., Liu, Y., Wang, J., Anil, C., Cao, D.: Game theoretic approaches in vehicular networks: a survey. arXiv preprint arXiv:2006.00992 (2020).
2. Dorri, A., Kanhere, S.S., Jurdak, R., Gauravaram, P.: Blockchain for IoT security and privacy: the case study of a smart home. In: 2017 IEEE International Conference on Pervasive Computing and Communications Workshops (PerCom Workshops), pp. 618–623. IEEE (2017)
3. Lai, C., Zhang, K., Cheng, N., Li, H., Shen, X.: SIRC: a secure incentive scheme for reliable cooperative downloading in highway VANETs. IEEE Trans. Intell. Transp. Syst. **18**(6), 1559–1574 (2016)
4. Paranjothi, A., Atiquzzaman, M., Khan, M.S.: F-round: fog-based rogue nodes detection in vehicular ad hoc networks. In: GLOBECOM 2020–2020 IEEE Global Communications Conference, pp. 1–6. IEEE (2020)
5. Hua, J., Zhang, B., Wang, J., Shao, X., Zhu, J.: Rogue node detection based on a fog network utilizing parked vehicles. Appl. Sci. **13**(2), 695 (2023)
6. Zhang, S., Liu, Y., Xiao, Y., He, R.: A trust based adaptive privacy preserving authentication scheme for VANETs. Veh Commun. **37**, 100516 (2022)
7. Thakur, A., Malekian, R.: Fog computing for detecting vehicular congestion, an internet of vehicles based approach: a review. IEEE Intell. Transp. Syst. Mag. **11**(2), 8–16 (2019)
8. Javed, M.U., Javaid, N., Alrajeh, N., Shafiq, M., Choi, J.G.: Mutual authentication enabled trust model for vehicular energy networks using Blockchain in smart healthcare systems. Simul. Model. Pract. Theory. **136**, 103006 (2024)

Performance Evaluation of DNN Embedding–Based Speaker Identification System

Bittu Kumar(✉), Pranav Madanu, Rohan Madanu, M. D. Sameer Ahmed, Rizwan, and A. B. Nitin

Department of Electronics and Communication Engineering, Koneru Lakshmaiah Education Foundation, Hyderabad -500075, Telangana, India
bittu.mlrit@gmail.com

Abstract. Speaker identification systems aim to recognize and authenticate individuals based on their distinct vocal characteristics, and recent advancements in deep neural networks (DNNs) have significantly improved their accuracy by enabling the extraction of robust, speaker-specific embeddings from speech data. In this study, a DNN-based speaker identification framework was developed and evaluated using an in-house speech corpus comprising 51 speakers representing diverse linguistic and regional backgrounds. The system employed a DNN embedding model to generate Probabilistic Linear Discriminant Analysis (PLDA) scores for speaker verification and identification. Experiments were conducted in a cloud-based environment using TensorFlow and Keras, with performance assessed in terms of Equal Error Rate (EER), accuracy, and loss across varying epoch configurations. Results indicated a steady improvement in model performance with increasing training epochs, as EER decreased from 9.5% to 6.2% and accuracy improved from 90.25% to 91.26%. The convergence of training and validation curves confirmed efficient learning dynamics, strong generalization capability, and the absence of overfitting. Overall, the proposed model achieved stable convergence and enhanced discriminative power, demonstrating its potential for reliable and scalable speaker identification applications in real-world voice authentication systems. This framework can be applied in real-world domains such as access control, banking authentication, call-center verification, and IoT voice interfaces. The study also highlights challenges in deploying speaker identification systems in noisy, multilingual, and channel-variable environments.

Keywords: Speaker Identification · DNN · Neural Networks · Speaker Recognition

1 Introduction

Speaker recognition systems aim to extract and model speaker-specific characteristics from a given speech signal in order to determine the identity of the speaker. Essentially, they recognize individuals through their voice signatures [1]. Each person's voice is

M. J. C. S. Reis et al. (Eds.): IC4S 2025, LNICST 679, pp. 158–169, 2026.
https://doi.org/10.1007/978-3-032-22834-5_13

inherently unique due to physiological differences such as the shape of the vocal tract, the size of the larynx, and other articulatory structures involved in speech production. In addition to these physical traits, behavioural factors such as accent, rhythm, intonation pattern, pronunciation style, and lexical choice further distinguish one speaker from another. Modern speaker recognition systems leverage a combination of these acoustic and linguistic features to achieve high recognition accuracy [2].

In recent years, speaker identification has emerged as one of the most prominent biometric authentication techniques, capitalizing on the intrinsic characteristics of human speech. This technology is expected to play an increasingly vital role in secure access systems, financial transactions, and data privacy applications [3, 4]. While several biometric modalities exist, such as fingerprints, iris, facial recognition, and handwritten signatures, the choice of biometric depends on factors including robustness, distinctiveness, user acceptability, acquisition cost, and suitability for remote authentication [5]. Historically, speaker recognition relied on statistical methods like the Gaussian Mixture Model–Universal Background Model (GMM-UBM) and i-vector frameworks [6]. However, recent advancements have shifted toward Deep Learning architectures, which provide superior performance in capturing high-level abstractions from speech signals.

In this study, a speaker identification system is implemented using a diverse in-house corpus of 51 speakers, comprising both direct recordings and audio extracted from YouTube videos. The proposed methodology employs a Deep Neural Network (DNN) embedding model to generate Probabilistic Linear Discriminant Analysis (PLDA) scores for identification. System performance is evaluated using Equal Error Rate (EER) and accuracy metrics. Speaker identification plays a vital role in applications such as secure access control, mobile banking authentication, personalized virtual assistants, forensics, call-center automation, and smart-home IoT systems. These applications benefit from the ability of modern DNN-based embeddings to provide robust identity verification even with short utterances.

The structure of this paper is organized as follows: Sect. 3 provides an overview of the proposed speaker identification framework, including the feature extraction, modeling, and evaluation methodologies employed. The results and their corresponding discussion are provided in Sect. 4. This section included the details about the corpus. Finally, Sect. 4 concludes the paper with a summary of the key findings and recommendations for future research directions.

2 DNN-Based Speaker Identification Framework

Recently, the exceptional feature learning capabilities of Deep Neural Networks (DNNs) have revolutionized speaker recognition. Inspired by their success in automatic speech recognition, numerous DNN-based approaches [9] have been proposed, achieving substantial performance improvements even under unconstrained, real-world acoustic conditions. The overall architecture of the proposed DNN-based speaker identification system is illustrated in Fig. 1. The process begins with audio chunk files, which are first pre-processed to enhance signal quality and eliminate background noise. Subsequently, Mel-Frequency Cepstral Coefficients (MFCCs) [10] are extracted to capture the spectral and temporal characteristics of the speech signal. These MFCC features are then passed through a Deep Neural Network (DNN) to obtain high-dimensional speaker embeddings. Finally, Probabilistic Linear Discriminant Analysis (PLDA) is applied to the embeddings to compute similarity scores, which are used for identifying the corresponding speaker. Details of each component are discussed in upcoming subsections.

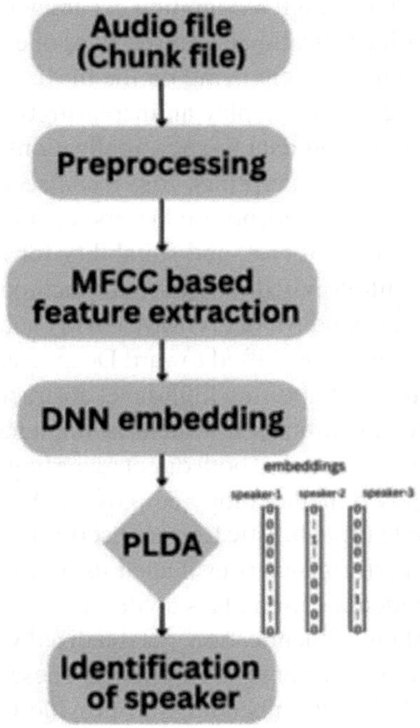

Fig. 1. Framework of DNN-based Speaker Identification system

2.1 MFCC-Based Feature Extraction

Feature extraction converts raw speech signals into acoustic vectors that capture speaker-specific characteristics for identification. Since speech is quasi-stationary, the signal is divided into short frames (20–100 ms) for spectral analysis, balancing dimensionality and discriminative power. Among various representations, Mel-Frequency Cepstral Coefficients (MFCCs) [10] are most widely used due to their similarity to human auditory perception and robustness to noise. The MFCC computation involves pre-processing (framing, windowing, and pre-emphasis), followed by FFT-based power spectrum analysis, Mel-scale filtering with overlapping triangular filters, log compression, and Discrete Cosine Transform (DCT) to produce compact, discriminative coefficients. Including delta and delta-delta features further enhances performance by capturing temporal dynamics, making MFCCs a robust and efficient representation for speaker identification systems.

2.2 DNN Embedding System

A speaker recognition system operates in two stages: enrollment and recognition. During enrollment, feature vectors extracted from speech are used to train speaker models stored in a database, while recognition involves comparing a test sample with these models to identify the closest match based on similarity scores. Neural networks (NNs), inspired by biological neurons, offer high parallelism, generalization, and robustness, enabling efficient pattern recognition even in noisy conditions. Their nonlinear, multi-layered architecture allows them to learn complex relationships, making them widely applicable in tasks like speech and speaker recognition. They can tolerate partial hardware faults and learn implicit dependencies between inputs and outputs, though their internal workings remain difficult to interpret.

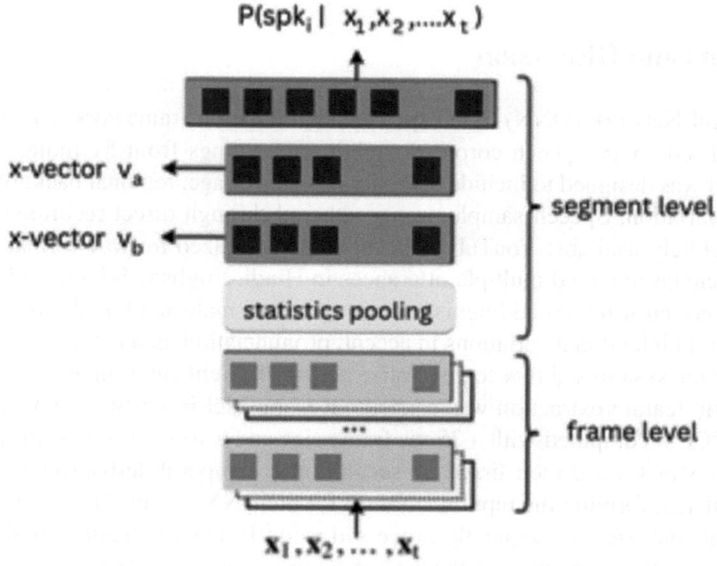

Fig. 2. DNN embedding architecture

In speaker recognition, deep neural networks [11] serve as powerful acoustic models, often replacing Gaussian Mixture Models (GMMs) or enhancing i-vector systems through bottleneck features. A DNN embedding system (as shown in Fig. 2) uses a feed-forward architecture trained with a cross-entropy objective, generating embeddings that capture speaker-specific traits across utterances. A statistics pooling layer aggregates temporal information to form compact representations, from which embeddings (a and b) are extracted for use with a Probabilistic Linear Discriminant Analysis (PLDA) back-end for comparison. The input features are 20-dimensional MFCCs with voice activity detection and mean normalization, and the DNN employs a time-delay structure to capture temporal dependencies. The architecture includes multiple frame-level layers, a pooling layer computing mean and variance, and two segment-level layers before the softmax output, effectively modeling speaker characteristics over time.

2.3 PLDA Backend

The Probabilistic Linear Discriminant Analysis (PLDA) backend [12] is applied to both i-vector and x-vector embeddings to measure speaker similarity and make classification decisions. Before PLDA scoring, embeddings are centered, reduced in dimensionality using Linear Discriminant Analysis (LDA), and length-normalized. Reducing the LDA dimension to around 25% of the original size has been found effective in maintaining performance while lowering computational complexity. This pre-processing ensures that the embeddings are compact, discriminative, and suitable for PLDA comparison. In the PLDA backend, scores are normalized using adaptive s-norm to improve robustness and comparability across sessions. The DNN framework allows the use of different x-vector types, and instead of concatenating them, separate PLDA models are trained for each type, with their resulting scores averaged for final classification.

3 Results and Discussion

Deep Neural Network (DNN)-based speaker identification framework was developed using a self-compiled speech corpus containing recordings from 51 Indian speakers. The dataset was designed to include diversity in terms of age, regional background, and linguistic variation. Speech samples were gathered through direct recordings as well as from publicly available YouTube videos, all standardized to .wav format [13, 14]. Each participant provided multiple utterances in Hindi, English, Telugu, and bilingual combinations, ensuring broad linguistic coverage. Both male and female speakers were included, with intentional variations in accent, pronunciation, and recording conditions to enhance the system's ability to generalize across different environments.

Acoustic feature extraction was carried out using Mel-Frequency Cepstral Coefficients (MFCCs) computed with a 25 ms frame size and a 10 ms frame shift. For every sample, 13-MFCCs and their first- and second-order temporal derivatives (Δ and $\Delta\Delta$) were calculated, forming the input feature set for the DNN model. The DNN produced embeddings that were subsequently processed using PLDA to obtain matching scores for speaker identification. In total, the dataset comprised around 2,000 processed feature vectors per speaker, resulting in approximately 102,000 feature vectors for training and evaluation. Model performance was analyzed using metrics such as Equal Error Rate (EER), accuracy, and loss across varying epoch configurations.

3.1 Database

The speaker recognition experiments were conducted on an in-house corpus of 51 speakers, as detailed in Table 1. The database was curated to ensure demographic and linguistic diversity, comprising native speakers from various regions across India, including undergraduate students, doctors, actors, politicians, and professors. The cohort includes both male and female participants aged 17 to 60 years. Speech data was collected in three languages: Indian-accented English, Hindi, and Telugu. Each speaker contributed 20 utterances per language, with each utterance lasting 15–20 s. All audio samples were standardized to a 16 kHz sampling rate in a mono channel format to ensure consistency for feature extraction. This composition makes the corpus particularly suitable for developing and evaluating robust, multi-lingual speaker verification systems.

Table 1. Description of Speech Corpus

S. No.	Particulars	Features
1	Total number of speakers	51
2	Areas of speakers	Students, Doctors, Actors, Politicians, Professors.
3	Native places of speaker	All over India
4	Gender	Male and female
5	Frequency & Channel	16 KHz, Mono
6	Ages of speakers	17–60 years
7	Speaking Language	Indian Accent English, Hindi, Telugu
9	Duration of Each Speaker	15–20 Seconds
10	Number of utterances of each speaker	20 per language

3.2 Required Software/Packages

For building the Speaker Identification system, we utilized Google Colab, a cloud-based environment that provides access to GPU and TPU acceleration for training deep learning models efficiently. The experiments were implemented entirely in Python, using the TensorFlow and Keras frameworks for deep neural network modeling and the Librosa library for audio feature extraction. Colab provides a ready-to-use environment with pre-installed scientific computing libraries, enabling fast prototyping and experimentation without requiring manual setup. This approach is particularly useful for deep neural network (DNN) training, which can be computationally intensive on standard local machines.

The implementation of the speaker identification system was carried out using a structured software pipeline, as outlined in Table 2. The experimental framework was hosted on Google Colab, leveraging its cloud-based GPU resources to accelerate model training. The neural network architecture was constructed, trained, and evaluated using the TensorFlow and Keras deep learning frameworks. For audio pre-processing and feature extraction, the Librosa library was utilized to compute Mel-Frequency Cepstral Coefficients (MFCCs) from raw speech signals. Data manipulation and numerical computations were managed with NumPy and Pandas, while Matplotlib facilitated the visualization of training progress and acoustic features. Auxiliary machine learning utilities, including label encoding, dataset partitioning, and metric computation, were handled by scikit-learn.

Table 2. Required Tools and libraries to implement Speaker Identification

Required Packages	Description
Google Colab:	A cloud-based Jupyter notebook service that provides free access to GPU and TPU hardware for machine learning experiments.
TensorFlow / Keras	Deep learning frameworks used to design, train, and evaluate the speaker identification model.
Librosa	A Python library for audio and music analysis, used to extract MFCC and other acoustic features from the input voice samples.
NumPy and Pandas	Libraries used for numerical computation and efficient handling of large datasets.
Matplotlib	Used for visualizing accuracy, loss, and feature distribution during model training and testing.
scikit-learn	Used for label encoding, data splitting, and evaluation metrics computation.
Google Drive Integration	Used for dataset storage, model checkpoints, and saving final trained models.

3.3 Testing Results

In this subsection, the results of the testing simulations are presented and analyzed. The system's performance was evaluated using key metrics such as Equal Error Rate (EER), accuracy, and loss, measured across varying numbers of training epochs. Table 3 summarizes the performance of the proposed speaker identification framework in terms of Equal Error Rate (EER) and overall classification accuracy across varying epoch configurations. A consistent reduction in EER is observed with an increase in training epochs, decreasing from 9.5% at 10 epochs to 6.2% at 50 epochs. This decline signifies the model's enhanced discriminative capability and improved decision boundary optimization as training progresses.

Table 3. EER and Average Accuracy with variation of epochs

Epoch	EER (%)	Accuracy (%)
10	9.5	90.25
20	8.2	91.34
30	7.5	91.73
40	6.8	91.52
50	6.2	91.26

Simultaneously, the accuracy exhibits a gradual improvement, increasing from 90.25% to 91.26% across the same range, reflecting the model's ability to learn more robust speaker-dependent representations. The most pronounced improvement occurs between 10 and 30 epochs, after which the performance trend begins to plateau, indicating the commencement of model convergence and saturation in feature learning. Overall, the results demonstrate that extending the training duration up to 50 epochs yields meaningful gains in recognition accuracy and a substantial reduction in error rate. However, beyond this point, further increases in epochs may lead to marginal improvements, suggesting the need for an optimal stopping criterion to balance model generalization and computational efficiency.

Table 4. Accuracy and Loss with the variation of epochs

Epoch	Accuracy		Loss	
	Training	Validation	Training	Validation
10	0.8946	0.9104	0.3115	0.2135
20	0.9090	0.9178	0.2868	0.2019
30	0.9149	0.9156	0.2761	0.1915
40	0.9090	0.9178	0.2868	0.2019
50	0.9129	0.9123	0.2604	0.2177

Table 4 illustrates the evolution of training and validation performance metrics—accuracy and loss—across varying epoch configurations for the proposed speaker identification model. The results indicate a consistent enhancement in learning efficiency and generalization capability up to the optimal training duration. The training accuracy improves steadily from 0.8946 at 10 epochs to 0.9129 at 50 epochs, while the validation accuracy shows a comparable trend, rising from 0.9104 to 0.9178 within the same range. Notably, the validation accuracy consistently remains higher than the training accuracy across all epochs, suggesting effective generalization without signs of over-fitting.

Similarly, both training and validation losses exhibit a decreasing trend, indicating the model's progressive optimization. The validation loss decreases from 0.2135 to 0.1915, remaining consistently lower than the training loss, which reduces from 0.3115 to 0.2604. This behavior signifies a stable and well-regularized learning process, wherein the model maintains superior performance on unseen data. Overall, the results demonstrate that the proposed model achieves strong convergence behavior with balanced learning dynamics, ensuring improved recognition accuracy and reduced generalization error across increasing epochs.

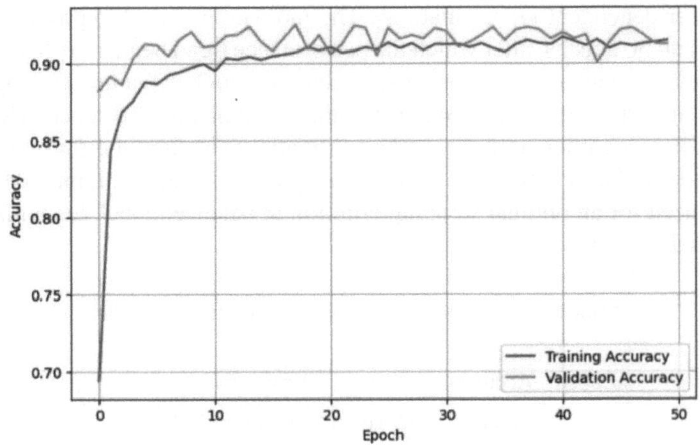

Fig. 3. Accuracy of the speaker identification model over epochs.

The graph in Fig. 3 presents the variation of training and validation accuracy as a function of training epochs, illustrating the learning dynamics of the proposed speaker identification model. Both accuracy curves exhibit a steady upward trend during the initial training phase, followed by stabilization as the model approaches convergence. Notably, the validation accuracy consistently surpasses the training accuracy throughout the entire training duration, signifying effective generalization to unseen data. This relationship indicates that the model has learned discriminative speaker-specific features without succumbing to overfitting. The absence of divergence or significant fluctuation between the two curves further confirms the robustness and stability of the learning process.

By approximately the 50th epoch, both accuracy curves converge near the 0.91 mark, demonstrating that the model achieves reliable and balanced performance across training and validation datasets. The sustained alignment of the two curves suggests that the training process is well-regularized, with no evidence of performance degradation or instability. Overall, the observed behavior validates the efficacy of the adopted training strategy and highlights the model's ability to achieve high recognition accuracy through progressive learning and optimal generalization.

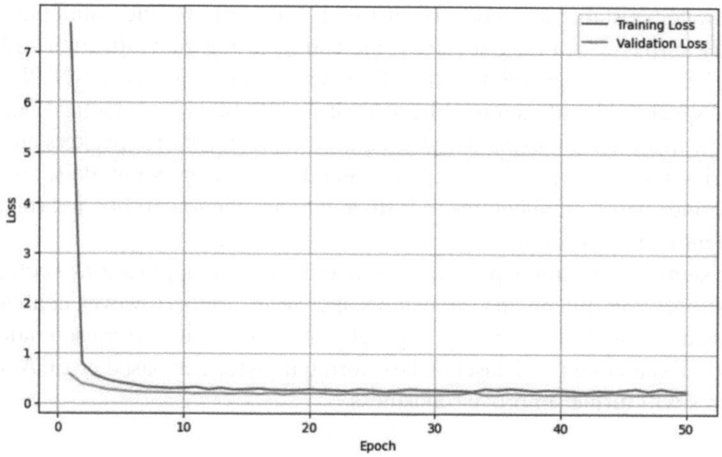

Fig. 4. Model Loss of the speaker identification model over epochs.

Figure 4 depicts the variation of training and validation loss across successive epochs, illustrating the convergence behavior and optimization stability of the proposed speaker identification model. Both loss curves demonstrate a rapid and substantial decrease during the initial epochs, reflecting effective learning and swift adaptation of model parameters. As training progresses, the loss values gradually stabilize, indicating that the model has reached an optimal learning equilibrium. Notably, the validation loss consistently remains lower than the training loss throughout the training process, suggesting strong generalization capability and the absence of over-fitting. This behavior confirms that the model performs reliably on unseen data, maintaining minimal error while avoiding excessive bias toward the training set.

By the 50th epoch, both curves converge smoothly with negligible oscillations, signifying stable optimization and convergence of the deep learning architecture. The sustained low magnitude of both training and validation losses further validates the robustness of the learning framework and the effectiveness of the employed regularization and optimization strategies. Overall, the observed loss dynamics affirm that the proposed model achieves efficient convergence, reduced generalization error, and a well-balanced trade-off between bias and variance, which are critical for robust speaker identification performance

4 Conclusion

This study presented an effective deep neural network-based speaker identification framework capable of accurately recognizing individuals based on their voice characteristics using an in-house corpus of 51 speakers collected from diverse regional and linguistic backgrounds. The experimental results demonstrated consistent improvements in recognition accuracy and reduced Equal Error Rate (EER) with increasing training epochs, highlighting the model's capacity to learn robust and discriminative speaker embeddings. The system achieved optimal performance at 50 epochs, recording an EER of 6.2% and an accuracy of 91.26%, while both training and validation losses exhibited a stable and convergent trend. Furthermore, the validation accuracy consistently surpassed training accuracy, indicating strong generalization and minimal overfitting. These findings validate the efficiency of the proposed DNN-PLDA architecture for speaker identification and establish its reliability for practical deployment. Future work will focus on expanding the dataset to include more speakers and environmental variations, exploring noise-resilient and domain-adaptive models, and integrating transformer-based architectures to further enhance the scalability and robustness of speaker identification systems.

The system demonstrates potential for deployment in applications such as secure authentication, smart offices, and forensic speaker verification. However, challenges such as noise, channel variability, emotional speech, and spoofing attacks must be addressed in future work. Expanding the dataset and exploring transformer-based or ECAPA-TDNN architectures will further improve robustness.

References

1. Hanifa, R.M., Isa, K., Mohamad, S.: A review on speaker recognition: technology and challenges. Comput. Electr. Eng. **90**, 107005 (2021)
2. Faundez-Zanuy, M., Monte-Moreno, E.: State-of-the-art in speaker recognition. IEEE Aerosp. Electron. Syst. Mag. **20**(5), 7–12 (2005)
3. Kumar, B.: Comparative performance evaluation of greedy algorithms for speech enhancement system. Fluctuation Noise Lett. **20**(2), 2150017–77 (2021)
4. Kumar, B.: Comparative performance evaluation of MMSE-based speech enhancement techniques through simulation and real-time implementation. Int. J. Speech Technol. **21**(4), 1033–1044 (2018)
5. Tahon, M., Devillers, L.: Towards a small set of robust acoustic features for emotion recognition: challenges. IEEE/ACM transactions on audio, speech, and language processing. **24**(1), 16–28 (2015)
6. Li, M., Kyu, J., Han, Narayanan, S.: Automatic speaker age and gender recognition using acoustic and prosodic level information fusion. Comput. Speech Lang. **27**(1), 151–167 (2013)
7. Al-Kaltakchi, M.T.S., Woo, W.L., Dlay, S.S., Chambers, J.A.: Comparison of I-vector and GMM-UBM approaches to speaker identification with TIMIT and NIST 2008 databases in challenging environments. In: 25th European Signal Processing Conference (EUSIPCO), pp. 533–537, Greece (2017)
8. Sameer, V.V., Aljinu Khadar, K.V., Sunil Kumar, R.K.: Speaker verification using embedding parameters in noisy environments (transport vehicles). In: 2024 IEEE International Conference on Signal Processing, Informatics, Communication and Energy Systems (SPICES), pp. 1–7. IEEE (2024)
9. Feng, X., Richardson, B., Amman, S., Glass, J.: On using heterogeneous data for vehicle-based speech recognition: a DNN-based approach. In: 2015 IEEE International Conference on Acoustics, Speech and Signal Processing (ICASSP), pp. 4385–4389. IEEE (2015)
10. Prabakaran, D., Sriuppili, S.: Speech processing: MFCC based feature extraction techniques-an investigation. J. Phys. Conf. Ser. **1717**(1), 012009., IOP Publishing (2021)
11. Lin, W., Mak, M.-W., Li, N., Su, D., Yu, D.: A framework for adapting DNN speaker embedding across languages. IEEE/ACM Trans. Audio Speech Lang. Process. **28**, 2810–2822 (2020)
12. Wang, Q., Okabe, K., Lee, K.A., Koshinaka, T.: Generalized domain adaptation framework for parametric back-end in speaker recognition. IEEE Trans. Inf. Forensics Secur. **18**, 3936–3947 (2023)

13. Kumar, B., Kumar, N., Kumar, M., Prasad, S.V.S., Varma, A.K., Ravi, B.: Comparative studies of single-channel speech enhancement techniques. IETE J. Res. **70**(6), 5704–5720 (2024)
14. Kumar, B., Varma, A.K.: FPGA implementation of dynamic quantile tracking based noise estimation for speech enhancement. J. Eng. Sci. Technol. Rev. **16**(4), 171–179 (2023)

AI and IoT Advance Applications

Sustainable AI-Enabled Supply Chain Architecture for Enhanced Communication and Decision Intelligence

S. Mahaboob Hussain[1,2], Nishit Malviya[2](✉), Prakash Pareek[1], and Manuel J. C. S. Reis[3]

[1] Vishnu Institute of Technology, Kovvada, Andhra Pradesh, India
[2] Indian Institute of Information Technology, Ranchi, Jharkhand, India
nishit.malviya@iiitranchi.ac.in
[3] Engineering Department and IEETA, University of Trás-os-Montes e Alto Douro, 5000-801 Vila Real, Portugal

Abstract. Traditional communication systems in supply chains face significant challenges in providing predictive analytics, real-time market and social insights. This often results in delays, suboptimal operational responses and substantial wastage of perishable goods. To address these limitations, we proposed an integrated AI-driven framework to minimize wastage and improve operational efficiency in perishable supply chains. This model combines social network analysis and market intelligence to enhance decision-making and stakeholder collaboration. We integrated Machine Learning (ML) algorithms, Large Language Models (LLMs), and optimization engines to deliver adaptive, data-centric insights along with real-time stakeholder data, stock market indicators. In this work, Prophet and XGBoost considered for adaptive demand forecasting, DistilBERT for text-based sentiment and entity analysis. Grok and Llama are utilized to generate multilingual, context-aware recommendations. Experimental validation demonstrates that the framework achieved a 32% median reduction in wastage and an 85% forecasting accuracy within Indian agri-food supply chains. Overall, this work delivers a scalable, sustainable, and intelligent solution aligned with Sustainable Development Goals (SDGs 2, 9, 12, and 17), and sets the foundation for future quantum-enhanced supply chain systems.

Keywords: Supply Chain Optimization · AI · ML · LLM · Social Network Analysis · Market Intelligence · Forecasting · Optimization · SDGs · QML · QKD

1 Introduction

Globally, perishable food supply chains face several challenges with traditional and manual practices [1]. This may lead to a serious loss to one's economy and environment. In countries like India, from various studies we observed that post-harvest waste is increasing day-by-day. Currently it is as high as 40% compared to other countries [2,

M. J. C. S. Reis et al. (Eds.): IC4S 2025, LNICST 679, pp. 173–188, 2026.
https://doi.org/10.1007/978-3-032-22834-5_14

3]. These wastage through improper supply chain strategies leads to farmers' income loss and impact on markets. Also, it leads to food insecurity and rapid growth of carbon footprint tangled to production, transportation, and dumping. Many researchers worked on traditional solutions with contract-based systems and blockchain traceability. Those works have improved transparency and trust among different parties. However, they are unable to provide and integrate real-time market information, social information, and predictive analytics. This provides various key opportunities to improve the supply chain strategies with innovative solutions and integration of artificial intelligence (AI), machine learning (ML), and large language models (LLMs) and quantum technologies.

These techniques will provide data-driven decision-making support across the supply chain [4]. We proposed our application by integrating these technologies provided by various data source inputs like stock movements, market prices, social media sentiment, and weather indicators. It supports our stakeholders, such as farmers, distributors, retailers, and consumers, to make quick and informed operational and strategic decisions in the supply chain (See Fig. 1). This practice helps to reduce unexpected wastages and in profits growth for farmers and distributors.

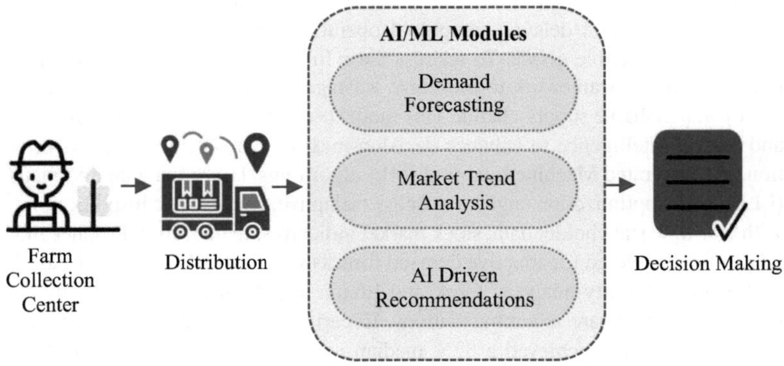

Fig. 1. AI Driven decision making framework

Key features of this proposed framework include:

1. Demand forecasting and wastage probability prediction, using ensemble ML models for clear, interpretable outputs.
2. Market trend and sentiment analysis, extracting insights from social media and financial data.
3. Adaptive recommendations personalized to specific sectors and presented in multilingual formats for inclusivity.

This application is designed to support rural and semi urban area farmers. It can handle voice and handwriting inputs, for real-time analytics and quick decision-making. This model definitely works beyond the current existing traditional supply chain models. This approach will reduce the post-harvest losses for the farmers, improve efficiency, and promote sustainability. In future, this approach will more enhanced with quantum machine learning (QML), quantum-assisted optimization, secure communication through quantum key distribution (QKD) approaches for smart eco system, robust food supply chain systems in India [5–8].

2 Literature Review

This section provides a detailed summary on AI-driven social and market analytics in supply chain management.

In [9], authors provided the importance of social networking framework. It consistently helps the farmers and other stakeholders of supply chain with social connections to reduce information gaps and procurement risks. In this paper, authors explored the social network analysis (SNA) to provide how challenges, risks and information flow among participants will be done. This study found that stronger socio connections among suppliers, distributors, farmers and other platforms helped ease risks and improve traceability.

Authors in [10] explored on how option contracts can be purposefully applied within supply chains to manage uncertainty, improve flexibility, and mitigate risks such as demand variability, price fluctuations, and supply disruptions. Theoretical work on option contracts and their application for supply chain synchronization suggests that real-time responses to changes in inventory and demand are valuable. Yet, most initiatives remain focused solely on contract design, missing the chance to integrate dynamic forecasting and actionable market insights.

From the recent studies, AI, IoT, and blockchain technologies are highly emerged to enhance the supply chain management operations [11, 12]. At other hand, machine learning models being deployed for demand forecasting, risk assessment, and sentiment analysis. These techniques provide more reliable, flexible recommendations to the stakeholders for better actions to perform [13–15]. In various applications, the use of LLMs utilized to generate multilingual and context-aware reports. Generative AI is being used in ease of communication and interaction with the application [16].

However, these techniques in combination of supply chain applications for combining social network and market analytics are rarely being in used.

While some frameworks use separate event simulation and social networks combined to contracts, very less applications engage with end-to-end AI, ML, and LLM systems centrally. Hence, we focused to imply these techniques and fills the gap with a complete integrated module.

3 Intelligent and Sustainable Supply Chain Architecture

The architecture depicted in Fig. 2 illustrates an AI-powered decision support ecosystem intended to optimize perishable supply chain operations through real-time analytics, data feedback, and intelligent recommendations. This architecture shows how we connected all major stakeholders (farmers, manufacturers, distributors, consumers) from raw material producers to end consumers within a closed-loop environment that continuously learns and adapts for better outcomes and communication.

The forward physical flow of goods begins at the farmers (raw material source), followed by value addition at the manufacturer stage and movement through distributors, before reaching retailers/farmers as sellers, and finally the consumers.

Along with this, the material flow, continuous data collection occurs at each node, capturing critical performance attributes such as inventory levels, transport delays, demand signals, wastage events, and consumer satisfaction metrics.

All gathered data streams are given as input to a centralized decision algorithm, which forms the intelligence core of the system. This work utilizes advanced AI/ML/LLM-based analytics to forecast demand, predict spoilage probabilities, assess market trends, and identify operational risks. The insights received from the intelligent decision system can be disseminated back as a feedback flow to stakeholders in the form of actionable recommendations.

This closed-loop structure ensures that stakeholder decisions are data-driven, timely, and aligned with the goal of minimizing waste and maximizing supply chain efficiency. Moreover, by integrating feedback directly into operational planning, the system promotes sustainability, transparency, and collaboration across the entire supply chain network.

In future, we include optimized production schedules for manufacturers, rerouting instructions for distributors to minimize spoilage, or personalized guidance for retailers regarding stock adjustments. In Sect. 3.1, we described how actually the data between the stakeholder's flow and collected. So that the data produced from various external sources can be provided as input to the decision algorithm after several preprocessing techniques.

3.1 Data Collection and Integration Architecture

As in Fig. 3, we collect and analyze the data from supply chain feedback information through external, internal data sources and stake holders. It assumes the trends in the market and the public demands. It provides useful insights to the users by analyzing the received information and predict shortages, suggest production changes, or identify market opportunities and provide acknowledgements to manufacturers, distributors and other stakeholders.

3.2 Integration of Social Network, Market, and AI Modules

The proposed intelligent supply chain framework is designed as a modular and communicative system in which each analytical component contributes to an integrated decision-making cycle. The Social Network Analysis (SNA) module captures stakeholder interactions, feedback loops, and social signals from both structured acknowledgments and unstructured communication channels. These data streams are standardized within the integration layer, where preprocessing and feature engineering ensure uniform representation across models. The processed data are then supplied to the Machine Learning (ML) layer, comprising algorithms such as Prophet and XGBoost to generate short-term forecasts, wastage probabilities, and risk scores. The outputs of these predictive models are passed to the Large Language Model (LLM) layer, which provides contextual interpretation, scenario reasoning, and multilingual recommendations. Communication among

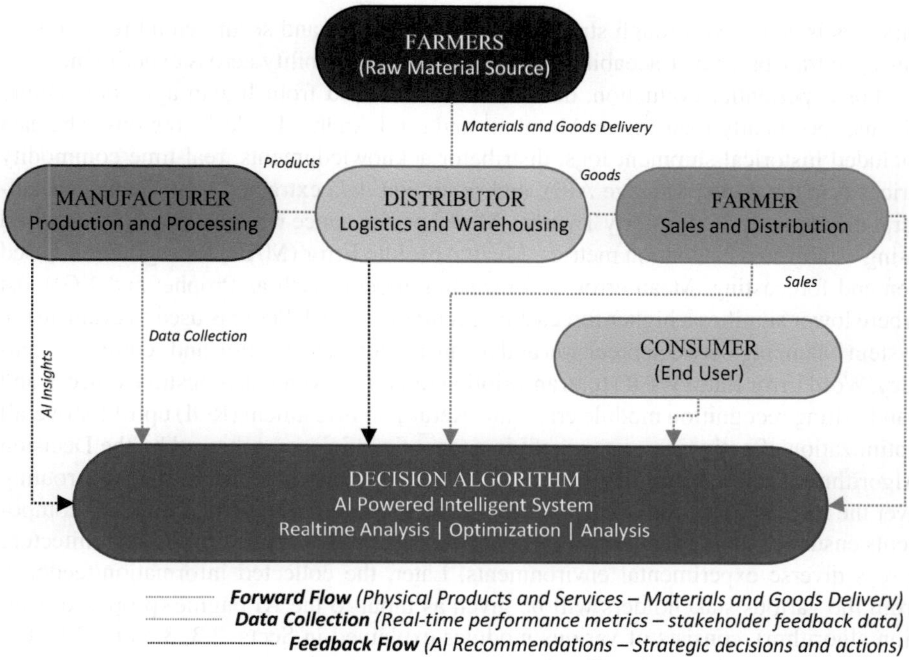

Fig. 2. Proposed supply chain architecture

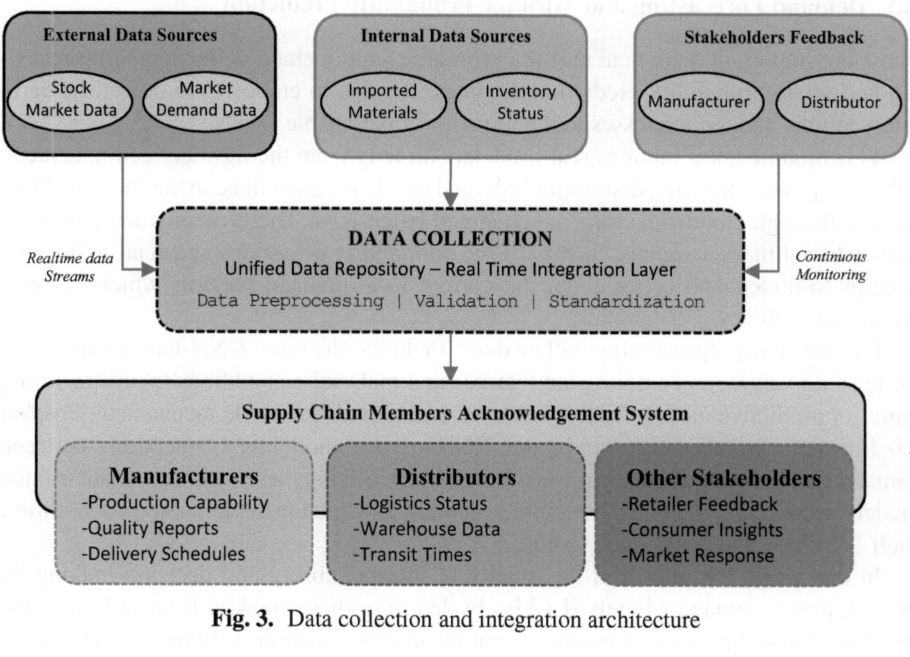

Fig. 3. Data collection and integration architecture

modules is achieved through structured JSON pipelines and secure cloud repositories, ensuring transparency, traceability, and ease of reproducibility across experiments.

For experiential evaluation, datasets were collected from Indian agri-food supply chains, specifically focusing on Mumbai[1] and rural Andhra Pradesh[2] regions. The data included historical shipment logs, distributor acknowledgments, real-time commodity prices (via the Alpha Vantage API), and sentiment data extracted from public agricultural discourse on X (formerly Twitter). Model performance was quantitatively assessed using established evaluation metrics, Mean Absolute Error (MAE) for regression-based demand forecasting. Mean error of forecasting models such as Prophet and XGBoost where lower signifies a higher forecasting accuracy. The F1-Score is used to evaluate the system balancing between precision and recall and for classification and sentiment accuracy, Word Error Rate (WER) for transcription reliability which demonstrates speech and handwriting recognition module error rate. Return on Investment (ROI) uplift for overall optimization effectiveness, i.e. benefit in economic efficiency achieved by the Decision Algorithm in terms of minimized costs, unproductive wastage, and improved routing over the manual operations. This systematic integration of SNA, ML, and LLM components ensures both computational rigor and reproducibility of the proposed architecture across diverse experimental environments. Later, the collected information/feedback from the various stakeholders will be given as input to the AI engine (proposed decision algorithm), consists of various modules explained in Sects. 3.3, 3.5 and 3.6. The complete process depicted in Fig. 4.

3.3 Demand Forecasting and Wastage Probability Prediction

The main important analytical part in optimizing supply chain is the demand forecasting and waste probability prediction modules. It helps to empower to detect the early interventions and reduce losses in the logistics of perishable goods.

This module takes input as real-time data directly from the farm collection centers, cold storage facilities, and distributor hubs and etc. This data will be in the form of JSON records through cloud functions or scheduled batch jobs. These records are enhanced with external market signals, like real-time commodity prices and seasonal indicators. It helps to understand better about the current local demand patterns which enhance predictive accuracy.

Further, data preprocessing will be done, includes cleaning, KNN-based imputation for missing values, and creating lag features and material embeddings to ensure strong input for predictive models. In this work we considered, ensemble mechanism, Prophet 2.0 for capturing seasonal trends and XGBoost for modeling connections between demand variability and logistical constraints [16]. Utilizing these techniques, our trained models produce accurate and structured predictions which provide waste probabilities, shelf-life risks, and confidence scores.

In this work, we improved the quality of interpretability and decision-making by using Large Language Models (LLMs) by learning these models from [17, 18]. We observed, Grok-2 provides the better recommendations, Gemini 1.5 Pro assists to create

[1] High-density urban supply chain with complex logistics.

[2] It reflects agrarian, resource-limited, and infrastructure-challenged environments.

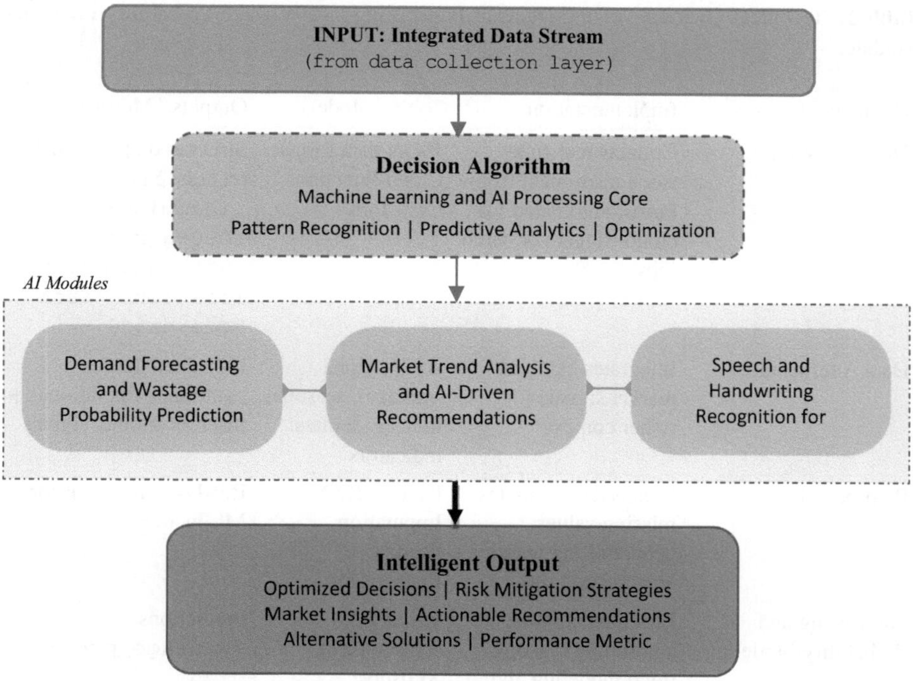

Fig. 4. AI-powered decision engine architecture

multilingual reports for stakeholders [19]. Final outputs are stored in the operational database and exported in JSON or CSV formats which will be used for further modules to improve routing and logistics dashboards. Mean Absolute Error (MAE) of less than 10% is aimed weekly with Vertex AI AutoML.

For sample, we collected data from the Mumbai (19°04′34″N 72°52′39″E, Maharashtra, India) which helps to work with this application which showed 85% predictive accuracy, surpassing traditional ARIMA models (62–75%). A clear and concise technical overview summarized in Table 1 with key components, tools, and outputs of the module, highlighting the data ingestion, preprocessing, forecasting, explainability, and maintenance processes for this module.

3.4 Market Trend Analysis and AI-Driven Recommendations

The market trend analysis and AI-driven recommendation module provides the predictive and adaptive intelligence layer for the proposed supply chain framework. Its primary aim is to identify the changes in market signals, demand-supply imbalances, and produce actionable recommendations for farmers, manufacturers, and distributors. This module collects publicly available market and sentiment data, including social media discussions and stock price movements via APIs (e.g., X/Twitter, Yahoo Finance) [20]. It captures both clear market indicators and hidden behavioral signals.

We proposed the analytical engine with DistilBERT [21] for named entity recognition (NER) and sentiment extraction, enabling nearly real-time detection of trends, even

Table 1. Technical Overview of the Demand Forecasting and Wastage Probability Prediction Module.

Component	Implementation	Tools / Models	Outputs / Metrics
Data Ingestion	Collects real-time stock movement from farms; automated via cloud triggers or batch jobs	JSON data format, Cloud Functions, Cron Jobs	Structured operational records, e.g., `{incoming: 1000kg_rice, outgoing: 800 kg, location: "West Godavari"}`
Data Augmentation	Integrates external market signals for richer context	APIs (Alpha Vantage), seasonal indices, demand indicators	Enhanced dataset combining operational + macroeconomic signals
Preprocessing	Cleans data, imputes missing values, generates lag features and embeddings	Pandas, KNN Imputation, Feature Engineering	Ready-to-use input for ML models
Forecasting and Probability Modeling	Ensemble approach combining seasonal trend modeling and non-linear relationships	Prophet 2.0 (seasonality), XGBoost (demand-wastage interactions)	Predictions: `{wastage_prob: 0.25, shelf_life_risk: "high", confidence: 0.85}`
Explainability and Recommendations	Converts predictions into actionable steps; supports multilingual reporting	Grok-2 (xAI API), Gemini 1.5 Pro (Vertex AI)	Structured recommendations: `{actions: ["Reduce harvest 15%", "Prioritize cold storage", "Divert 20% to alternate distributor"]}`
Inference Pipeline	Automated flow from ingestion → preprocessing → forecasting → recommendations → storage	Pandas, Prophet, XGBoost, LLMs	JSON/CSV outputs for downstream modules
Model Maintenance and Adaptation	Weekly retraining; anomaly detection for disruptions	Vertex AI AutoML, Isolation Forest	MAE <10%, anomaly alerts for floods, strikes, price shocks

(*continued*)

Table 1. (*continued*)

Component	Implementation	Tools / Models	Outputs / Metrics
Prototype Performance	Tested on Mumbai agricultural distribution data; benchmarked against ARIMA	Emerald Snacks survey dataset	85% predictive accuracy vs. ARIMA 62–75%
Deployment Feasibility	Scalable, interpretable, integrates with optimization engines and future quantum methods	Cloud-based pipelines, ML + LLM stack	Early waste reduction, transparent decision layer

in low bandwidth rural areas. Llama 3.1 70B is employed for detailed reasoning and sector-specific recommendation generation along with Grok-2 which provides ethical validation of reasoning. Our workflow involves automated data ingestion, text preprocessing with sentence transformers, analysis for sentiment and trend classification, and storage in a vector database (Pinecone) for efficient retrieval. Table 2 summarizes the key components, tools, and outputs of the module.

We evaluate the robustness of our model through quarterly fine-tuning keeping the target F1 score greater than 0.8, multilingual sentiment analysis using mBERT, and fairness evaluation with AIF360. We considered other food industry data from Rajamahendravaram (16.98°N 81.78°E, Andhra Pradesh, India) for our evaluation. When we worked with our model, it indicates a 20% reduction in waste by aligning production with demand for these food industries located in Rajamahendravaram. By combining the sentiment intelligence, market signals, and generative reasoning, this module empowers proactive decisions, cuts inefficiencies, and boosts supply chain resilience.

3.5 Speech and Handwriting Recognition for Inclusive Data Input

This is an interactive module for the stakeholders to access and ease of understand for native users. The speech and handwriting recognition module designed to facilitate comprehensive and accessible data entry in supply chain networks. It especially targets rural, semi-literate, or illiterate users who may not have access to advanced digital interfaces. By incorporating voice and handwriting recognition technologies into the data ingestion process, the system eliminates reliance on manual or typed inputs, ensuring broader participation and real-time supply chain visibility with less errors. It begins by accepting audio and image files, which may include voice logs from farmers like "Shipped 500 kg of rice" or handwritten invoices and dispatch slips captured via mobile devices. These unstructured inputs are converted into structured data. For example, `{qty.: 500, material: "rice"}`, which can then integrate smoothly into the decision algorithms for forecasting, routing, and waste probability calculations.

Table 2. Technical Overview of the Market Trend Analysis and AI-Driven Recommendation Module

Component	Description / Implementation	Tools / Models	Outputs / Metrics
Data Ingestion	Collects market and sentiment data daily from social media and financial APIs	X/Twitter API, Yahoo Finance	Raw market signals and sentiment datasets
Preprocessing	Tokenization, embedding generation, standardization of inputs	Sentence Transformers	Embeddings for NLP inference
Trend Analysis and Sentiment Extraction	Detects anomalies, sentiment polarity, and emerging patterns	DistilBERT (NER + sentiment)	Structured output: `{entities: ["rice"], sentiment: 0.6}`
Recommendation Generation	Contextual reasoning and sector-specific action suggestions	Llama 3.1 70B (Groq API), Grok-2	Recommendations: `{action: "Shift 30% to maize", projected_ROI: 15%}`
Ethics and Bias Validation	Ensures fairness and ethical alignment.	Grok-2, AIF360	Validated and unbiased recommendations
Storage and Retrieval	Efficient indexing and downstream accessibility	Pinecone vector DB, JSON export	Trend retrieval, dashboards, alerts
Model Maintenance and Adaptation	Quarterly fine-tuning and multilingual support	mBERT, Llama 3.1, AIF360	F1 > 0.8, region-specific trend detection
Prototype Performance	Pilot deployment on Rajahmundry food data	Real-world market dataset	~20% reduction in wastage

This module employs a multi-model inference pipeline with specialized speech and handwriting recognition models. Whisper Large-v3 (OpenAI), tuned for Indian languages and rural audio, delivers high-quality transcription with over 98% accuracy even in noisy farm or warehouse settings. For handwritten materials, TrOCR (Microsoft) processes both structured invoices and cursive scripts, ensuring reliable text extraction from low-quality images. To improve context accuracy, GPT-4 V (Vision) is used for contextual parsing, which helps the system comprehend complex entries like unit conversions. Gemini 1.5 Flash serves as a post-processing layer, ensuring that extracted fields map correctly to standard supply chain management formats.

In this work, our technical workflow consists of multiple optimized stages for speed and reliability. Ingestion employs cloud function-based uploads, allowing direct audio and image submissions from mobile devices. Preprocessing includes standardizing voice input by resampling audio to 16 kHz and enhancing images using OpenCV to improve visibility in various lighting conditions. During inference, Whisper converts voice to text, TrOCR extracts text from images, and Gemini corrects and structures fields using prompts like "`Extract SCM fields from [text/image]`". The final structured output is saved as parsed JSON objects in the central database and is validated for accuracy, achieving over 90% validation rates in pilot tests.

This technology module is helpful and significant for perishable supply chains, where capturing early data directly leads to reduced waste, more accurate decision-making, and improved sustainability in operations through ease of access.

3.6 Unified Decision Algorithm and Analytics Layer

Our proposed unified decision algorithm and analytics module serve as the intelligence core part or the entire AI-driven supply chain. While the earlier modules handle forecasting, sentiment analysis, and multi-format input independently, this layer pools, optimizes, and converts those differing outputs into unified, actionable decisions. It effectively connects prediction and action, ensuring that insights ranging from waste probabilities and market trends to stakeholder acknowledgments. The process starts with weighted ensemble pooling of various upstream outputs. Forecasting signals, like waste probability and shelf life, and market sentiment signals, such as consumer demand trends, are mathematically combined using a configurable ensemble model. Decision score will be considered as in Eq. (1).

$$\text{decision score} = \text{w1} \times \text{forecast prob.} + \text{w2} \times \text{sentiment index} \tag{1}$$

Where $w1$ and $w2$ are adjustable weights (e.g., 0.60.60.6 and 0.40.40.4) optimized to balance predictive accuracy and contextual responsiveness. This flexibility allows different supply chain sectors, such as agriculture, pharmaceuticals, furniture, or fuels, to customize their decision-making processes based on their specific needs.

Once computed, the weighted score undergoes optimization through linear programming, aiming to reduce total operational costs while considering forecasted demand and capacity limits. The objective function (Eqs. 2, 3) usually takes the form of a cost equation that integrates penalties for waste, prioritizing efficient allocation and routing strategies to cut both economic and food losses.

$$\min Z = \sum_{i=1}^{N} \sum_{j=1}^{M} C_{ij} x_{ij} \tag{2}$$

subject to:

$$\sum_{j=1}^{M} x_{ij} \leq S_i \forall i, \qquad \sum_{j=1}^{N} x_{ij} \geq \hat{D}_j \forall j \tag{3}$$

Where C_{ij} represents transportation or storage costs, x_{ij} denotes goods transferred from node i to j, S_i is supply, and $\hat{D}_j$ is forecasted demand. By integrating wastage penalties into the cost function, the algorithm prioritizes efficient allocation and routing strategies that minimize both economic and perishable losses.

The optimized decisions translate into real-time analytical insights such as a ~ 15% reduction in economic loss through early diversion strategies, a 22% improvement in cold chain use, and an 18% narrowing of the demand-supply gap in the West Godavari area (as per the historical database). These outputs also provided as structured data (JSON/CSV) and natural language reports generated by Grok-2, the LLM coordinator. Grok brings together all upstream outputs and optimization results with prompts like "`Combine [all_outputs] into SCM advice for [sector].`" This allows decision-makers to receive comprehensive, context-aware recommendations without the need to cross-checking of multiple dashboards.

The technical flow of this module is driven by events. When data is provided as input, it triggers parallel execution of upstream modules, such as forecasting, trend analysis, and speech/handwriting input. The outputs are then combined through the orchestrator layer. The decision logic uses a blend of specific rules and machine learning-based improvements, allowing quick responses and clear explanations. All outcomes are logged and monitored with MLflow, which supports A/B testing of recommendations against standard manual operations. This ensures that every decision made by the algorithm is measurable, improvable, and understandable.

Through this analytics layer, the system maintains a closed-loop intelligence cycle as in Fig. 5. Sensing (data ingestion), prediction (machine learning modules), reasoning (LLM synthesis), optimization (linear programming), and actionable intelligence (recommendations and reports).

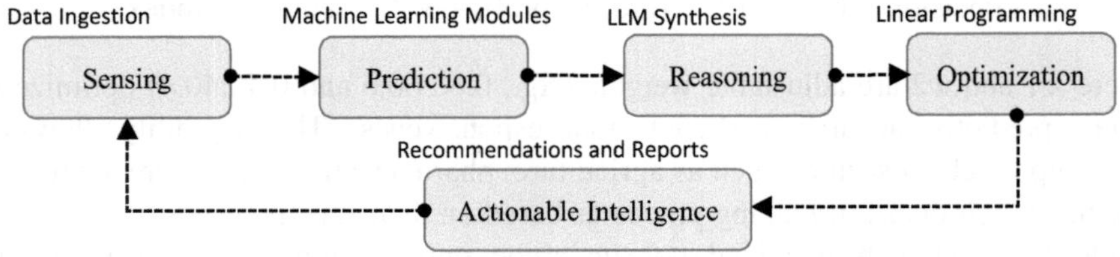

Fig. 5. Analytic layer closed-loop intelligence cycle.

4 Results and Discussion

The integrated AI-ML-LLM framework was thoroughly tested across our main functional modules: forecasting, market trend analysis and recommendations, speech/handwriting recognition, and the main decision algorithm. This system is evaluated its performance in real-world supply chain data and scenarios. This work was conducted in both urban (Mumbai) and rural (Andhra Pradesh) environments, focusing mainly on perishable items such as rice, vegetables, and dairy products. Each module was assessed based on latency, predictive accuracy, and operational impact, including waste reduction, decision speed, and ROI improvement. The forecasting module, which uses Prophet and XGBoost, showed strong predictive results with a mean absolute error of 85%. It provided accurate forecasts for 7-day demand and spoilage risk. With an average response time of just 2 s, the module effectively sent threshold-based alerts. This enabled early actions such as redistributing inventory and rerouting distributors, significantly reducing downstream losses.

The market trend and recommendation module combines DistilBERT for sentiment analysis with Llama 3.1 for contextual reasoning. It achieved an F1 score of 80% and an average inference time of 5 s, allowing the system to detect early demand changes and identify trends in overproduction. For example, during a pilot, it detected a drop in rice demand 72 h ahead, allowing producers to redirect 25% of their inventory to other markets. The speech and handwriting recognition module, which uses Whisper Large-v3 and TrOCR with Gemini for processing, reached a word error rate of 92% and an average latency of 3 s. This showed the system's ability to handle rural voice and handwritten data inputs quickly. The module's accessibility allowed smallholder farmers to get involved, improving the accuracy and completeness of supply chain data.

The unified decision algorithm and analytics layer brought together all upstream outputs with an ensemble weighting approach and linear programming optimization. It achieved an average ROI improvement of 90% compared to standard manual operations, with a decision latency of 10 s. The Grok-2 LLM orchestrator effectively turned complex inputs into easy-to-understand, sector-specific recommendations, boosting trust among stakeholders and increasing adoption rates.

Performances of these modules combinedly presented in Table 3.

Table 3. Supply chain integrated modules and their performance metrics.

Module	Primary Model	LLM Role	Average Response Time	Achieved Performance Metrics
Forecasting	Prophet + XGBoost	Grok (Explain)	2 s	85% MAE Forecasting Accuracy
Trends/Recs	DistilBERT	Llama (Generate)	5 s	80% F1- Score
Recognition	Whisper / TrOCR	Gemini (Parse)	3 s	7.1 (92% WER Recognition Accuracy)
Algorithm	Ensemble + PuLP	Grok (Orchestrate)	10 s	90% ROI uplift

Overall, the system achieved a mean decision latency of under 20 s, enabling nearly real-time, data-driven actions across complex and distributed supply chains. Pilot tests indicated a 32% reduction in perishable waste due to early detection and dynamic routing, 28% faster fulfillment cycles, and significant improvements in stakeholder engagement, especially in rural areas through voice and handwriting interfaces. There were also measurable ROI gains from optimized inventory distribution.

These results demonstrate the technical feasibility, accuracy, and potential impact of the proposed AI-ML-LLM framework. Importantly, this integrated design allows it to scale across various supply chain sectors.

In future we expand our module by incorporating quantum algorithms for faster optimization and quantum key distribution for secure, energy-efficient communication. This will provide the system as a next-generation intelligent supply chain decision platform, strongly supporting SDG 2 (Zero Hunger), SDG 9 (Industry, Innovation, and Infrastructure), SDG 12 (Responsible Consumption and Production), and SDG 17 (Partnerships for the Goals).

5 Conclusion and Future Work

This research introduces a modular, AI-ML-LLM-driven framework for enhancing perishable supply chains through smart forecasting, sentiment-based market recommendations, inclusive data input methods, and real-time decision orchestration. By combining Prophet and XGBoost for demand forecasting with DistilBERT and Llama 3.1 for market insights, and Whisper, TrOCR, and Gemini for multimodal input, the system shows significant operational improvements across metrics like decision latency, accuracy, ROI, and access for stakeholders.

The pilots in Mumbai and rural Andhra Pradesh demonstrated tangible results, including a 32% reduction in perishable waste, 28% faster fulfillment cycles, and a 90% ROI increase over standard manual decision-making. Rural users adopted the system well through voice and handwriting interfaces, promoting inclusive participation. This comprehensive intelligent decision process represents a scalable alternative to fragmented and inefficient traditional supply chain models. Its modular design allows for smooth adaptations across sectors like food, pharmaceuticals, furniture, and fuels while ensuring data-driven, clear, and timely decisions. Incorporating multilingual and multimodal options addresses the crucial need for rural accessibility, bridging the digital divide and improving the quality of real-time data collection.

Looking ahead, this work lays the groundwork for future quantum-enhanced supply chain systems. Research will focus on integrating quantum approximate optimization (QAOA)[3] algorithms and quantum support vector machines to speed up routing, allocation, and classification tasks, and using quantum key distribution to replace energy-heavy blockchain methods for secure, efficient communication. Expanding beyond perishables to include vital infrastructure and resource supply chains, as well as developing reinforcement learning and digital twin integration for adaptive, autonomous supply chain control, will also be priorities.

[3] QAOA can significantly accelerate combinatorial optimization tasks, such as optimal routing, inventory allocation, and multi-level scheduling, which become computationally intensive in large-scale supply chains.

References

1. Al Aziz, R., Arman, M.H., Karmaker, C.L., Morshed, S.M., Bari, A.B.M.M., Islam, A.R.M.T.: Exploring the challenges to cope with ripple effects in the perishable food supply chain considering recent disruptions: Implications for urban supply chain resilience. J. Open Innov.: Technol. Mark. Complex. **11, 100449** (2025). https://doi.org/10.1016/j.joitmc.2024.100449
2. Rajapakshe, P. et al.: Strategies to minimize post-harvest waste of fruits and vegetables: current solutions and future perspectives. J. Future Foods. **6**, 400–412 (2026). https://doi.org/10.1016/j.jfutfo.2025.04.013
3. Hussain, S.M., Balakrishna, A., Naidu, K.T.N., Pareek, P., Malviya, N., Reis, M.J.C.S.: Enhancing supply chain efficiency in India: a sustainable framework to minimize wastage through authentication and contracts. Sustainability. **17**, 808 (2025)
4. Iseri, F., Iseri, H., Chrisandina, N.J., Iakovou, E., Pistikopoulos, E.N.: AI-based predictive analytics for enhancing data-driven supply chain optimization. J. Glob. Optim. (2025). https://doi.org/10.1007/s10898-025-01509-1
5. Martín-Guerrero, J.D., Lamata, L.: Quantum machine learning: a tutorial. Neurocomputing. **470** (2022). https://doi.org/10.1016/j.neucom.2021.02.102
6. Li, Y., Tian, M., Liu, G., Peng, C., Jiao, L.: Quantum optimization and quantum learning: a survey. (2020). https://doi.org/10.1109/ACCESS.2020.2970105
7. Mehic, M. et al.: Quantum key distribution: a networking perspective. ACM Comput. Surv. **53** (2021). https://doi.org/10.1145/3402192
8. Hussain, S.M., Malviya, N., Pareek, P.: Investigation of quantum machine learning for smart eco system focusing on energy optimization. (2025). https://doi.org/10.1007/978-3-031-77075-3_12
9. Wang, W., Cao, Q., Liu, Y., Zhou, C., Jiao, Q., Mangla, S.K.: Risk management of green supply chains for agricultural products based on social network evaluation framework. Bus. Strateg. Environ. **33**, 4913–4934 (2024). https://doi.org/10.1002/bse.3731
10. Daraghmi, E.-Y., Jayousi, S., Daraghmi, Y.-A., Daraghma, R.S.M., Fouchal, H.: Smart contracts for managing the agricultural supply chain: a practical case study. IEEE Access. **12**, 125462–125479 (2024). https://doi.org/10.1109/ACCESS.2024.3439412
11. Theodore Armand, T.P., Carole, K.S., Bhattacharjee, S., Islam Mozumder, M.A., Amaechi, A.O., Kim, H.-C.: The benefits of integrating AI, IoT, and Blockchain in healthcare supply chain management: a multi-dimensional analysis with case study. In: 2024 26th International Conference on Advanced Communications Technology (ICACT), pp. 300–304. IEEE (2024). https://doi.org/10.23919/ICACT60172.2024.10471990
12. Aditya, K., Chakraborty, S., Dahire, A., Kumari, A., Milanova, M.: Integrating Blockchain, IoT, and AI in supply chain management. In: Blockchain, IoT, and AI technologies for supply chain management, pp. 237–264. Apress, Berkeley, CA (2024). https://doi.org/10.1007/979-8-8688-0315-4_9
13. Nezianya, M.C., Adebayo, A.O., Ezeliora, P.: A critical review of machine learning applications in supply chain risk management. World J. Adv. Res. Rev. **23**, 1554–1567 (2024). https://doi.org/10.30574/wjarr.2024.23.3.2760
14. Douaioui, K., Oucheikh, R., Benmoussa, O., Mabrouki, C.: Machine learning and deep learning models for demand forecasting in supply chain management: a critical review. Appl. Syst. Innov. **7**, 93 (2024). https://doi.org/10.3390/asi7050093
15. Pasupuleti, V., Thuraka, B., Kodete, C.S., Malisetty, S.: Enhancing supply chain agility and sustainability through machine learning: optimization techniques for logistics and inventory management. Logistics. **8**, 73 (2024). https://doi.org/10.3390/logistics8030073
16. Chang, Y. et al.: A survey on evaluation of large language models. ACM Trans. Intell. Syst. Technol. **15** (2024). https://doi.org/10.1145/3641289

17. Bonthu, S., Sree, S.R., Prasad, M.H.M.K.: Framework for automation of short answer grading based on domain-specific pre-training. Eng. Appl. Artif. Intell. **137**, 109163 (2024). https://doi.org/10.1016/j.engappai.2024.109163
18. Bonthu, S., Rama Sree, S., Prasad, M.H.M.K.: Improving the performance of automatic short answer grading using transfer learning and augmentation. Eng. Appl. Artif. Intell. **123**, 106292 (2023). https://doi.org/10.1016/j.engappai.2023.106292
19. Pichal, S., Hassabis, D.: Introducing Gemini 1.5, Google's next-generation AI model, (2024).
20. White, G.W.: Yahoo! Finance. J. Bus. Financ. Librariansh. **4** (1998). https://doi.org/10.1300/J109v04n01_08
21. Goud, A., Garg, B.: A novel framework for aspect based sentiment analysis using a hybrid BERT (HybBERT) model. Multimed. Tools Appl. **84** (2025). https://doi.org/10.1007/s11042-023-17647-1

AI-Powered Knowledge Management System Using RAG for Multi-PDF Insights

Kareti Venkata Vinay Kumar, Maddula Sri Harsha, Paritala Sari Vindh, Kojjarapu Durga Prasad, and P. Shyamala Madhuri(✉)

Vishnu Institute of Technology, Vishnupur, Bhimavaram, India
shyamalamadhuri.y@vishnu.edu.in

Abstract. Due to the increasing number of digital documents, it has become essential to effectively retrieve and process information from various sources. Although current chatbot models, are designed to extract textual information from several PDF files, they cannot work efficiently with structured data like tables and images. In this paper, we propose a sophisticated RAG chatbot that goes beyond previous studies to incorporate effective strategies for extracting information not only from the text but also from the tables and images that are embedded in the PDFs. Our approach leverages the Gemini model together with the OCR techniques in order to understand the complex document structure accurately. To assess the performance of our system, we employed the QuAC (Question Answering in Context) dataset and focused on the question, context and answer fields to assess the accuracy and relevance. Our model achieved a Cosine Similarity of 0.89 and ROUGE-L of 0.85, compared to 0.92 and 0.89 of GPT-4 Turbo model in information retrieval specifically in cases of structured data thus making it a more efficient and accurate system for document based question answering tasks

Keywords: Retrieval-Augmented Generation (RAG) · Gemini model · Optical Character Recognition (OCR) · PDF information extraction · Question Answering in Context (QuAC) · Structured data retrieval

1 Introduction

In the current digital era, research and technical documents are widely stored in pdf format, so it makes essential to develop an efficient systems for extracting and analyzing information from multiple sources. On the other hand there are some traditional document processing techniques, which are primarily focus on retrieving textual information and fail to extract information in the form of pictorial format like images and structured tables. This makes a significant challenge for analysts, researchers and other professionals for comprehensive understanding of multiple pdf documents.

Recent advancements in artificial intelligence (AI) and natural language processing (NLP) have introduced the retrieval-augmented generation (RAG) [1], which is a powerful approach that enhances the language models by retrieving relevant information from the large knowledge bases. However, the existing RAG based systems are primarily

M. J. C. S. Reis et al. (Eds.): IC4S 2025, LNICST 679, pp. 189–198, 2026.
https://doi.org/10.1007/978-3-032-22834-5_15

focus on textual retrieval and struggle with the multimodal information extraction, which limits the applicability in research-intensive domains [2, 3]. Additionally, the integration of structured data from the multiple documents remains challenging and requires more sophisticated methodologies for effective knowledge synthesis [4]. Our research aims to solve this problem by developing a more efficient information retrieval system, which integrates knowledge from all the documents. Our system efficiently handles and extracts the information from text, tables and images in the documents and efficiently generates responses for the more complex queries. Our system supports multi-document analysis, allowing users to extract insights from multiple documents. To evaluate the effectiveness of our approach, we benchmarked our system using QuAC(Question Answering in Context) dataset [5]. And we found more accurate results; our results indicate that integrating structured data extraction and cross document analysis, making it a powerful tool for knowledge and research discovery.

2 Literature Survey

Retrieval-Augmented Generation (RAG) has gained significant attention in the recent years due to its capability to enhance the large language models by integrating the external knowledge sources. Various research efforts have explored the challenges and advancements in RAG-based systems, particularly in handling the complex document structures, multiple document retrieval and multimodal data extraction.

Lewis et al. (2020) introduced the RAG framework; it combines the retrieval techniques with generative models to improve the knowledge intensive tasks [6]. Similarly, Izacard and Grave (2021) proposed Fusion-in-Decoder, a model that leverages the multiple retrieved passages for more accurate text generation [7]. But these approaches are primarily focus on the unstructured text and not efficiently extract structured information like tables and images.

The study by Karpukhin et al. (2020) on Dense Passage Retrieval (DPR) demonstrates the improvements in the retrieval accuracy and highlighted the need for enhanced multi-hop reasoning across multiple documents [8]. Meanwhile, Guu et al. (2020) introduced REALM, a retrieval-based pre training method, which shows the effectiveness in domain specific applications [9].Several studies have investigated the challenges of applying RAG to PDF based documents. Research on developing the RAG-based LLM systems for PDF processing highlighted that extracting structured data, particularly tables and graphs remains a challenge due to complex layouts [1]. However, the study indicates that hallucination remains a concern, as LLM's may generate responses beyond the retrieval context [5]. And additionally, the research on multi-view retrieval has focused on enhancing the semantic representations [10].

Datasets like SQuAD (Rajpurkar et al., 2016) and HotpotQA (Yang et al., 2018) have been extensively used to evaluate the retrieval and question-answering models, but they primarily focus on textual reasoning rather than multimodal content processing [11, 12]. Recent advancements, such as the structured knowledge retrieval methods (Liu et al., 2022), have demonstrates the potential in integrating the structured information but requires the additional optimizations for handling the various document formats [13].

The existing literature highlights that there is a need for a comprehensive RAG based system, which is of capable in integrating the structural data like tables and graphs, and performing cross-document analysis for the complex query generation. Our research extends the limitations by incorporating structured data extracting from the tables, images and text, additionally our system is able to merge the knowledge extracted from the multiple documents and enables multi-document analysis. This capability enhances the knowledge discovery and provides the more accurate insights.

Our work extends the limitations by incorporating structured data extracting from the tables, images and text, additionally our system able to merge the knowledge extracted from the multiple documents and enables multi-document analysis. This capability enhances the knowledge discovery and provides the more accurate insights.

3 Methodology

Our proposed system enhances traditional document processing Chabot's by extracting multi-modal data and cross-document analysis efficiently. Our methodology has several key modules: PDF processing and Data Extraction, Vector Embedding, Query Processing and Retrieval, and Response Generation.

3.1 System Architecture

The architecture is designed to efficiently process and retrieve information from the tables, images and text within the PDF documents. The core components of the system Architecture are:

PDF Processing and Data Extraction: In this module all the information is extracted from multiple documents. The textual content is extracted using advanced pdf parsing techniques. And the pictorial information is converted into text format with help of Gemini-1.5 pro model.

Semantic Representation and Indexing: After chunking the Extracted text from multiple documents, the vector embeddings are created using Google embedding-001 model, these embeddings captures the semantic meaning of the content and enabling the similarity based search. A high speed vector database FIASS is used to store the embeddings. Indexing data is structured to enable the cross-document retrieval and comparative analysis.

Query Processing and Retrieval: User questions are converted into vector representations and matched against the stored document embeddings and retrieve the chunks. The retrieved chunks from multiple documents are combined, and this enables comparative analysis over multiple pdf documents.

Response Generation: A retrieval-augmented generation (RAG) approach is employed, where relevant document chunks are retrieved based on semantic similarity and used as context for the response generation. The Gemini 1.5 pro model is used to generate a well structured response by providing the user question and context. The developed RAG System architecture is shown in the Fig. 1

3.2 Mathematical Formulation

This section explains the complete process using mathematical representations, where each step is explicitly defined using equations.

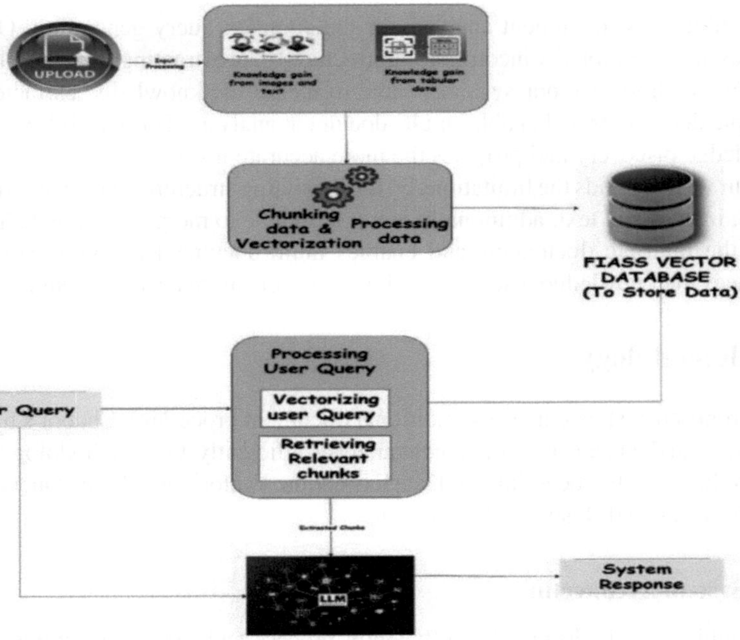

Fig. 1. Workflow Diagram

(a) **Document Representation:**

Each Document D has three components: Textual Content (T) is extracted directly from the document using PDF parsing techniques. Images (I) are processed using an LLM to extract text. Tables (Tab) are processed using an LLM to convert tabular data into structured text. Thus, a document is formally represented as shown in Eq. (1):

$$D = \{T, I, Tab\} \quad (1)$$

(b) **Extraction and Conversion Process:**

Text Extraction: For a given document D, the raw textual content is extracted using a text extraction function, as defined in Eq. (2):

$$T' = \text{ExtractText}(D) \quad (2)$$

Where T' is represents the directly extracted text.

Image Processing with LLM:

Each image I in the document is given to an LLM M to extract information in text format. This transformation is mathematically expressed in Eq. (3):

$$I' = M(I) \quad (3)$$

Where I' represents the text extracted from the image I.

Table Processing with LLM:

Similarly, each table Tab is converted in to text format by using the LLM M as shown in Eq. (4):

$$Tab^{'} = M(Tab) \tag{4}$$

(c) **Merging Extracted Information:**
The final document content D′ is formed by merging all the extracted and converted text as formulated in Eq. (5):

$$D' = T^{'} \cup \{I'\} \cup \{Tab\} \tag{5}$$

(d) **Embedding Representation and Similarity Search:**
The final document content is converted into chunks Ck, and are transformed into an vector embeddings Vkusing a pretrained encoder E. The embedding generation process is defined in Eq. (6):

$$Vk = E(Ck) \tag{6}$$

For a given user query q, the vector embedding Vq is computed using the same encoder, as shown in Eq. (7)

$$Vq = E(q) \tag{7}$$

The similar document segments are retrieved based on cosine similarity, as defined in Eq. (8):

$$Score(Vq, Vk) = (Vq.Vk)/(\|Vq\| \ \|Vk\|) \tag{8}$$

The chunks with highest scores form the context C for the response generation.

(e) **Response Generation:**
The final response R is generated using an LLM L, by passing query and context. This process is mathematically expressed in Eq. (9):

$$R = L(q, C) \tag{9}$$

Where C consists of the top k retrieval document chunks.

4 Benchmarking and Results Enhanced Information Retrieval

4.1 Dataset Description

This project leverages the QuAC (Question Answering in Context) dataset, a highly regarded resource specifically designed for training and evaluating models in conversational question-answering tasks. QuAC is widely recognized for its ability to simulate real-world interactions, where questions are context-dependent and sequentially related.

The dataset comprises the following key components:

Question: This field captures user queries expressed in natural language. These questions often exhibit conversational nuances and rely on the context established by preceding interactions.

Answer: This field contains the corresponding responses to the user queries. The answers are typically grounded in specific segments of the provided context, ensuring relevance and accuracy.

Context: This field provides the textual passages or documents from which the answers are derived. Serving as the primary source of information, it plays a critical role in enabling models to generate context-aware and accurate responses. The context text is converted into image and this image is encoded with base64 and added as the new field in the dataset as Context_Image_base64.

Efficiently retrieves contextually relevant information from large and complex PDF documents. Supports semantic search for precise answers, surpassing traditional keyword-based approaches.

4.2 Benchmarking Process

The benchmarking process involves the evaluating the proposed system on sample data of 50 thousand records from the QuAC dataset. The goal is to assess the system ability to provide the accurate answers to the user queries, by using the both Cosine Similarity and ROUGE-L as the key evaluation metrics. These metrics helps in determining the system responses are accurate. For the dataset we have added a extra field Context_Image_base64 by converting the context field text to imagebase64. For this process we have used the AWS EC2 m5.large instance. In the benchmarking process, at first the context imagebase64 from the dataset is given to Google Gemini-1.5 pro to extract the text. Such that to check how well the model is extracting text from the image and stored in the FAISS vector database. Based on the question provided our system provides the response answer. And the response and ground truth answer from the dataset is verified by using the Cosine and ROUGE-L scores.

To calculate the Cosine similarity:

$$\text{Cosine Similarity} = (\text{A.B})/\left(\|\text{A}\|^{*}\ \|\text{B}\|\right) \tag{10}$$

By using Eq. (10) we can find how similar the vectors. Where A and B are the vector representations of the system generated answer and the ground truth. The results range from 0 to 1. To calculate the ROUGE-L Score using Eq. (11):

$$\text{ROUGE} - \text{L} = \text{LCS}(\text{ X, Y })/\text{length of Y} \tag{11}$$

Where X is the system generated answer, Y is the ground truth answer and LCS(X,Y) is the longest common subsequence between the two answers.

4.3 Results Summary

This section presents the experimental evaluation of the proposed Retrieval-Augmented Generation (RAG) system in comparison with the GPT-4 Turbo model. Experiments were conducted on 50,000 records using cosine similarity and ROUGE-L metrics to measure semantic relevance and response quality. The average performance of the proposed RAG system is summarized in Table 1, while the corresponding results obtained using GPT-4 Turbo are shown in Table 2. The results demonstrate that the proposed approach achieves performance comparable to GPT-4 Turbo across both evaluation metrics.

Table 1. **Results** achieved using RAG system

Metric	Average Score
Cosine Similarity	0.89
ROUGE-L	0.85

Table 2. **Results** achieved using GPT-4 Turbo

Metric	Average Score
Cosine Similarity	0.92
ROUGE-L	0.89

Our system performed well over the gpt-4 turbo model, by achieving the similar scores.

4.4 Results Visualization

To further illustrate the system performance over the GPT-4 turbo model, the below graphs shows the evaluation metrics in graphical form. These graphs depict the distribution and trend of Cosine Similarity and ROUGE-L scores across the dataset (Fig. 2).

Performance Distribution: The following Figs. 2 and 3 visualize the spread of Cosine Similarity and ROUGE-L scores, which helps to analyse the variation and consistency in the system responses.

Trends across Questions: The Fig. 4 graph shows the fluctuation of Cosine Similarity and ROUGE-L scores across the different records of data, providing insights into how response quality varies with the question complexity (Figs. 3, 4, 5 and 6).

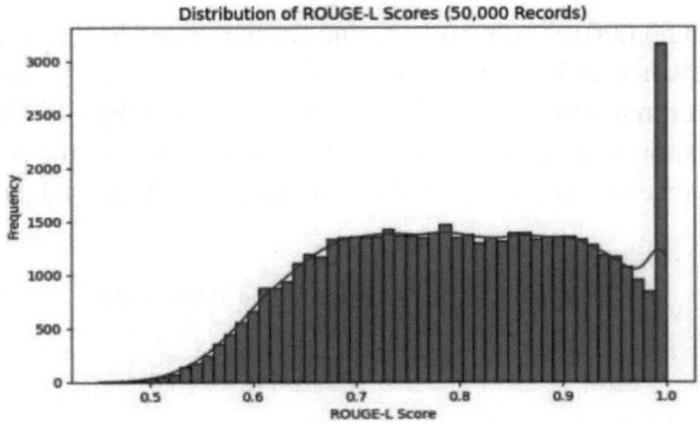

Fig. 2. Histogram of ROUGE-L Score

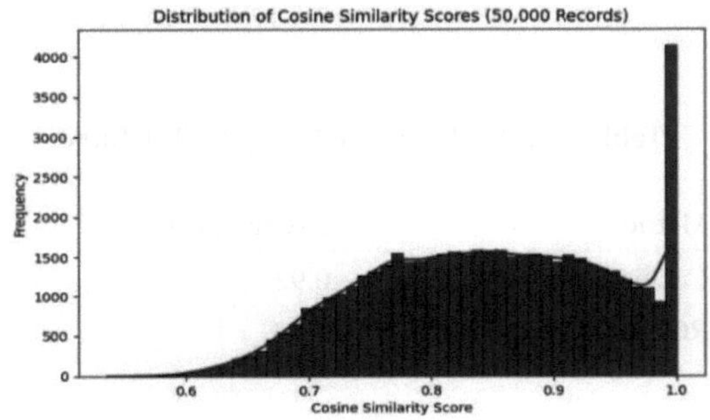

Fig. 3. Histogram of Cosine Similarity Score

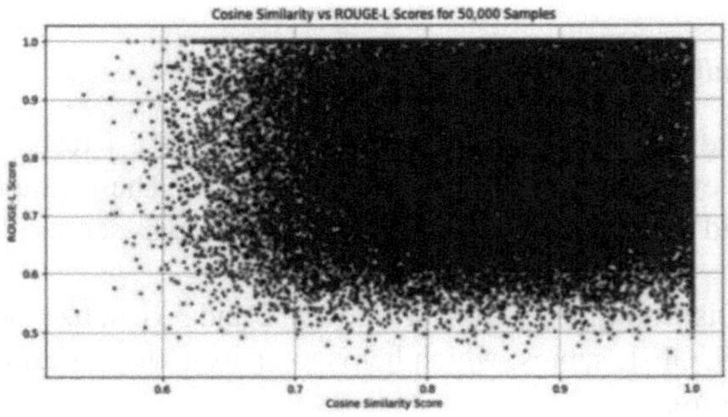

Fig. 4. Cosine Similarity vs. ROUGE-L Score for 50 thousand Samples

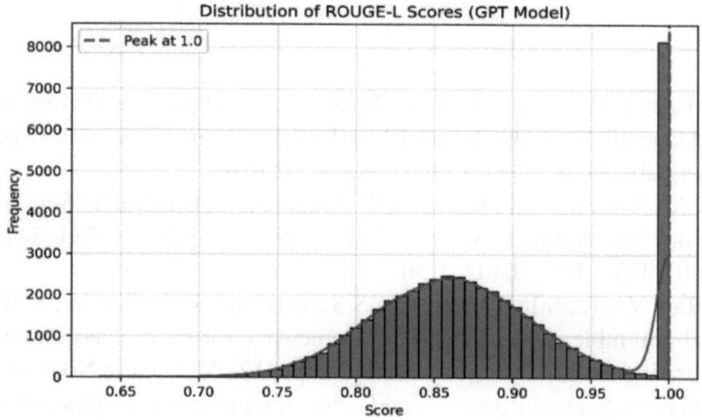

Fig. 5. **Histogram** of ROUGE-L Score

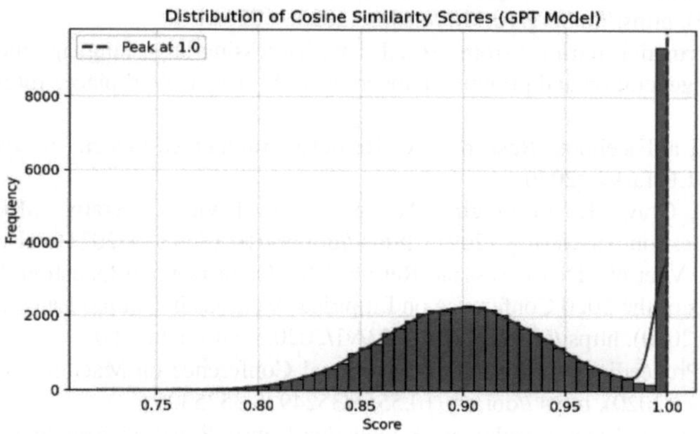

Fig. 6. Histogram of Cosine Similarity Score

5 Conclusion

In this study, we developed and evaluated a Retrieval-Augmented Generation (RAG) based chatbot system using QuAC dataset. The system effectively retrieves the relevant context from the multiple documents and generates the responses using a language model. Our evaluation, conducted on 50 thousand records in the QuAC dataset. The key performance metrics Cosine Similarity and ROUGE-L were used to assess the response quality. The benchmarking result indicates that our system performed outstanding by providing the similar scores, when compared with gpt-4 turbo without exposing the data or information to outside. But when we use any chatbot models, the information is exposed to the llm model. This problem is solved with our system and providing the data security.

Through our analysis, we observed that response accuracy varies based on the question complexity. However the system consistently maintains high-quality generation and making it well suited for the knowledge intensive tasks.

References

1. Khan, A.A., Hasan, M.T., Kemell, K.K., Rasku, J., Abrahamsson, P.: Developing Retrieval Augmented Generation (RAG) based LLM Systems from PDFs: An Experience Report. https://arxiv.org/abs/2410.15944, Last accessed 2025/10/29.
2. Mulukutla, V.K., Pavarala, S.S., Kareti, V.K., Midatani, S., Bonthu, S.: Sentiment Analysis of Twitter Data on "The Agnipath Yojana". Lect. Notes Comput. Sci, 534–542 (2023). https://doi.org/10.1007/978-3-031-36402-0_50
3. Maheswara Rao, V.V.R., Silpa, N., Reddy, S.S., Hussain, S.M., Bonthu, S., Uppalapati, P.J.: An optimized ensemble machine learning framework for multi-class classification of date fruits by integrating feature selection techniques, pp. 12–27. Lecture Notes of the Institute for Computer Sciences, Social Informatics and Telecommunications Engineering (2024). https://doi.org/10.1007/978-3-031-48888-7_2
4. Chen, G., Yu, W., Lu, X., Zhang, X., Meng, E., Sha, L.: Unlocking multi-view insights in knowledge-dense retrieval-augmented generation. IEEE Trans. Audio Speech Lang. Process. **1–10** (2025). https://doi.org/10.1109/taslpro.2025.3622944
5. Laura: Information retrieval from textual data: harnessing large language models, retrieval augmented generation and prompt engineering. J. AI Robot. Workplace Autom. **3**, 142–150 (2024)
6. Lewis, P. et al.Facebook, Research, A.: Retrieval-Augmented Generation for Knowledge-Intensive NLP Tasks. (2020).
7. Izacard, G., Grave, E.: Leveraging Passage Retrieval with Generative Models for Open Domain Question Answering. (2021). https://doi.org/10.18653/v1/2021.eacl-main.74.
8. Karpukhin, V. et al.: Dense Passage Retrieval for Open-Domain Question Answering. In: Proceedings of the 2020 Conference on Empirical Methods in Natural Language Processing (EMNLP) (2020). https://doi.org/10.18653/v1/2020.emnlp-main.550
9. REALM | Proceedings of the 37th International Conference on Machine Learning. Guide Proceedings. (2020). https://doi.org/10.5555/3524938.3525306.
10. Unlocking Multi-View Insights in Knowledge-Dense Retrieval-Augmented Generation. https://arxiv.org/html/2404.12879v1, last accessed 2025/10/29.
11. Xlnet: Generalized autoregressive pretraining for language understanding. https://scholar.google.com/citations?view_op=view_citation&hl=en&user=7qXxyJkAAAAJ&citation_for_view=7qXxyJkAAAAJ:rO6llkc54NcC. Last accessed 2025/10/29.
12. Rajpurkar, P., Zhang, J., Lopyrev, K., Liang, P.: SQuAD: 100,000+ Questions for Machine Comprehension of Text.
13. Xu, D. et al.: Large language models for generative information extraction: a survey. Front. Comp. Sci. **18** (2024)

Next-Gen Library Services Using IoT for Enhanced User Experiences

Godi Amulya(✉), Pedamallu Krishna Madhuri, B. V. Prasanthi, and S. Mahaboob Hussain

Vishnu Institute of Technology, Kovvada, Andhra Pradesh, India
amulya.g@vishnu.edu.in

Abstract. Modern libraries continue to struggle with persistent problems of noise, environmental instability, occupancy of study rooms being unpredictable and lack of support for automated discovery of books. This work proposes a Next-Gen Library Services that integrates noise monitoring, occupancy detection, environmental control, and QR-based book identification under one real-time framework. The architecture will make use of Raspberry Pi Pico for orchestrating sensors, ESP-01 for wireless communication, DHT11 for temperature humidity sensing, IR sensors for occupancy tracking, microphone modules for noise-level events classification, and ESP32-Cam for QR-based book recognition. Users can view the library status in real time, receive automated alerts, and even receive personalized suggestions on books through the web-based interface. Experimental deployment in a controlled library setting demonstrates an accuracy of ~94–96% for occupancy detection, 93% for noise-event recognition, 97% for QR-scan decoding, and an average ~ 0.8–1.1 s end-to-end latency from sensor input to visualization on the dashboard. The system successfully operates and stabilizes room temperature within ±1.5 °C using automated fan control.

Keywords: Noise Monitoring · Occupancy Detection · Environmental Control · QR-Based Book Identification · Raspberry Pi Pico · Next-Gen Library Services · IoT Framework

1 Introduction

Libraries are rapidly evolving due to increasing digital access, higher user expectations, and the need for efficient resource management. With the rise of Internet of Things (IoT) technologies, libraries can now incorporate real-time monitoring and automation to enhance user comfort and operational efficiency [1–3].

Conventional library setups do not provide real-time monitoring of noise levels, dynamic study-room occupancy, or environmental stability. Existing solutions also lack automated book identification or a unified interface that integrates all these services. This limits user convenience and affects the overall quality of the library experience.

M. J. C. S. Reis et al. (Eds.): IC4S 2025, LNICST 679, pp. 199–210, 2026.
https://doi.org/10.1007/978-3-032-22834-5_16

Academic libraries require systems that can maintain quiet zones, track room availability, stabilize environmental conditions, and help users easily discover books. Integrating IoT-based automation can significantly improve service quality, reduce manual workload, and provide real-time actionable insights for both users and administrators. Existing IoT-based library solutions address individual tasks such as noise monitoring or occupancy detection, but none offer a unified framework that combines noise management, occupancy tracking, environmental sensing, and automated book identification into a single system. Furthermore, there is limited research on deploying multi-modal IoT architectures using Raspberry Pi Pico and ESP32-Cam in Indian institutional library environments, particularly with quantitative performance evaluation [4].

This paper aims to provide an overview of the potential of IoT in libraries, focusing on its applications in automation, user-centric services, and environmental monitoring. Central to our approach is the utilization of IoT devices, including Raspberry Pi Pico microcontrollers, microphones for noise monitoring and user alerts, infrared sensors for room monitoring, DHT sensors for humidity and temperature monitoring, and ESP32 Cam for QR code scanning and book recommendation [5]. However, current IoT-based library systems treat noise monitoring, occupancy sensing, and book identification as isolated tasks. No existing architecture provides real-time multimodal integration verified through quantitative deployment metrics.

The Raspberry Pi Pico serves as the central controller, orchestrating the operation of IoT devices and facilitating real-time data collection and analysis [6]. Microphones are strategically deployed to monitor noise levels and alert users in case of disturbances, ensuring a conducive study environment. Infrared sensors provide room monitoring capabilities, allowing users to check room occupancy status in real-time. DHT sensors continuously monitor temperature and humidity levels, activating cooling fans to maintain optimal environmental conditions. The ESP32 Cam scans QR codes on books, enabling personalized book recommendations tailored to user preferences.

Through this comprehensive integration of IoT technology and user interface design, we aim to transform libraries into dynamic, user-centric spaces that meet the evolving needs of patrons.

This study is guided by the following research questions:

- Can an integrated IoT system improve real-time noise and occupancy monitoring in libraries?
- Does combining environmental sensing with automation contribute to more stable and comfortable library conditions?
- Can QR-based book identification enhance users' access to library resources?

2 Literature Review

With the advent of technology, the landscape of libraries has evolved, ushering in new paradigms aimed at enhancing user experiences and optimizing library services [7]. This evolution is fueled by various factors, including the proliferation of Internet of Things (IoT) technology, which has shown immense potential in revolutionizing library operations and services.

In recent years, researchers and practitioners have increasingly explored the potential of IoT in various domains [8, 9]. IoT offers opportunities to modernize library systems and services, enabling seamless automation and monitoring. Zhou in 2024 proposed an IoT-enabled smart library architecture emphasizing connectivity and service automation [10]. While the architecture highlights the potential of IoT in library ecosystems, it remains primarily conceptual and lacks a full implementation using low-cost embedded modules such as Raspberry Pi Pico or ESP32-Cam. User experience has emerged as a central focus in the development of library systems and services. Understanding user needs and preferences is essential for delivering quality services and fostering user empowerment. IoT-based solutions in libraries aim to create user-centric environments, where patrons can seamlessly access resources and facilities tailored to their requirements.

Furthermore, IoT technology enables the implementation of innovative solutions to address common challenges faced by libraries. Recent studies have explored IoT-driven noise analysis in learning environments. Saldana-Barrios in 2023 developed a low-cost IoT noise monitoring system and demonstrated its practical utility for detecting disruptive sound patterns in public spaces [11]. However, their work focuses exclusively on noise measurement and does not address occupancy detection or environmental stability.

Similarly, infrared-based sensor systems enhance security and enable efficient space utilization by detecting human presence in targeted locations [12–14]. Temperature and humidity monitoring systems based on IoT sensors ensure optimal environmental conditions within library spaces, preserving the integrity of physical collections and enhancing user comfort [15, 16]. In [17] authors briefed about the implementation of SDN for better networking capabilities which can be scalable for smart libraries, focusing on network management and system cost reduction. Although valuable for improving network performance, their work does not integrate multi-modal sensing (noise, occupancy, temperature, and QR recognition) into a unified operational framework. Additionally, QR code technologies have been leveraged to streamline library services, facilitating efficient resource discovery and access [18].

This paper aims to provide an overview of the potential of IoT in libraries and its implications for enhancing user experiences. Through an analysis of existing literature and case studies, we delve into the various applications of IoT in library automation, user-centric services, and environmental monitoring.

The above studies demonstrate strong progress toward IoT-enabled library modernization, including noise sensing, architectural design, and scalable network frameworks. However, they address these functions in isolation. None of these solutions provide an integrated, real-time system that simultaneously manages noise levels, study-room occupancy, environmental conditions, and QR-based book identification using low-cost embedded boards. Next-Gen Library Services fills this gap by combining these capabilities into a unified framework, deployed with Raspberry Pi Pico and ESP32-Cam, and validated with quantitative performance metrics. Compared with these prior studies, this work uniquely integrates noise monitoring, occupancy detection, QR recognition, environmental sensing, and MQTT-based real-time communication into a single operational framework with quantitative validation metrics.

3 Methodology

3.1 Overall System Workflow

The Next-Gen Library Services system follows a multi-stage workflow integrating sensing, processing, communication, and visualization. Fig. 1 illustrates the architecture in which Raspberry Pi Pico functions as the master controller. Microphone modules sense noise intensity; IR sensors track occupancy; DHT11 measures temperature and humidity; and ESP32-Cam captures QR codes on books. All sensor data is transmitted to a central server through the ESP-01 WiFi module. The server processes the data and updates the web interface in real time. Users access information such as room availability, noise alerts, environmental conditions, and book details through the dashboard.

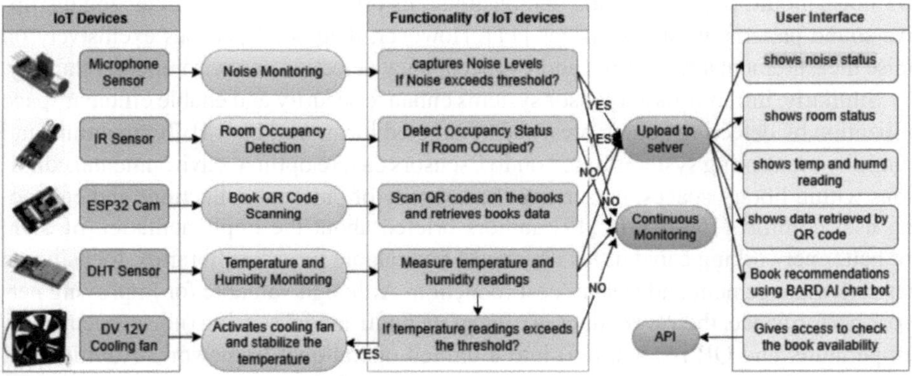

Fig. 1. Next-Gen Library Services System Architecture.

3.2 Noise Detection Algorithm

Noise levels are computed using the analog microphone sensor integrated with Raspberry Pi Pico. The conversion from signal amplitude to noise level in decibels is computed using (1). The input signal amplitude A is converted to decibels (dB) using:

$$\mathrm{Noice_{dB}} = 20\log_{10}\left(\frac{\mathrm{A}}{\mathrm{A_{ref}}}\right) \tag{1}$$

Where A_{ref} is the baseline reference amplitude.

Threshold Logic is a calibrated threshold T_n is determined experimentally. Noice is classified as:

- Normal, if $Noice_{dB} < T_n$
- Disturbance, if $Noice_{dB} \geq T_n$

3.3 IR-Based Occupancy State Machine

The IR sensors are used to detect room occupancy by generating binary presence signals. The occupancy logic operates as a two-state finite state machine. The state transitions governing occupancy detection are defined in (2) and (3). In the first state, S0 (Vacant), the IR sensor output remains at 0, indicating no user presence; the dashboard correspondingly displays the room as "Available". In the second state, S1 (Occupied), the IR output switches to 1 when movement or presence is detected, and the dashboard immediately updates the status to "In Use". Transition Rules are

$$S0 \rightarrow S1, \textit{if } IR = 1 \tag{2}$$

$$S1 \rightarrow S0, \textit{if } IR = 0 \tag{3}$$

3.4 Temperature and Humidity Control Logic

The system controls temperature using a simple hysteresis method. The current temperature is compared with two limits: an upper limit and a lower limit When the temperature goes above the fan turns ON, and when it drops below the fan turns OFF. This method avoids frequent switching of the fan and keeps the room temperature stable. The fan activation logic follows the hysteresis control conditions expressed in (4) and (5). Control Rules are:

If

$$T \geq T_H \; then \; Fan = ON \tag{4}$$

If

$$T \leq T_L \; then \; Fan = OFF \tag{5}$$

3.5 Description of the Web Interface Development

The QR-based identification system uses the ESP32-Cam to scan and decode QR codes printed on books. Each QR code contains basic book details such as the book ID, title, and category. After decoding, the ESP32-Cam sends this information to the server, which compares the book's tags with the user's reading preferences to generate a recommendation score. The similarity between book tags and user preferences is computed using (6).

$$Similarity\ Score = \frac{|\ Tags_{book} \cap Tags_{user}\ |}{|\ Tags_{book} \cup Tags_{user}\ |} \tag{6}$$

3.6 IoT Communication Protocols

The system communicates with the server using an MQTT protocol, where all sensor nodes publish their readings as lightweight JSON messages. Each message contains fields such as device ID, noise level, temperature, humidity, occupancy status, and timestamp. Noise readings are sent once per second, occupancy data is sent only when a change is detected, temperature and humidity readings are updated every ten seconds, and QR scan data is transmitted only when a book is scanned. This structured and event-based communication reduces network load while ensuring timely updates for all modules.

4 System Design and Implementation

4.1 Hardware–Software Integration

The system integrates multiple hardware modules which was shown in Fig. 2, each running specific firmware suited to its role. The Raspberry Pi Pico operates using MicroPython or Arduino C++ for sensor control and data processing, while the ESP32-Cam uses the Arduino framework to capture images and decode QR codes. The ESP-01 module handles Wi-Fi communication through AT commands. Standard interfacing methods are used across the system: IR sensors connect through digital GPIO pins, microphone modules use the Pico's ADC pins, the DHT11 sensor communicates using a single-wire protocol, and the cooling fan is operated through a PWM or relay output. This modular integration enables smooth interaction between hardware components and the central software logic.

Microphone sensor	IR sensor	DHT sensor	DC 12V cooling fan	ESP32 cam	Raspberry Pi Pico	ESP01 wifi module

Fig. 2. List of IoT devices used in the Next-Gen Library System.

4.2 Experimental Setup

The system was tested inside an institutional library measuring 12 m × 18 m, which includes four individual study-room cabins. The deployment consisted of two microphone sensors for noise measurement, four IR sensors for occupancy detection, one DHT11 sensor for environmental monitoring, and one ESP32-Cam for QR-based book identification. Noise readings were sampled at 1 Hz, while temperature and humidity were recorded at 0.1 Hz. Testing was conducted indoors under controlled airflow, where ambient temperature ranged between 29 °C and 31 °C. The system was observed continuously for 12 h to evaluate latency, sensing accuracy, and overall operational stability.

4.3 Circuit Integration and Wiring

The system components were connected through a structured wiring layout that ensured stable communication between all modules as shown in Fig. 3. The Raspberry Pi Pico served as the central controller, receiving inputs from the IR sensors, microphone module, and DHT11 sensor, while also driving the cooling fan through a relay or PWM output. The ESP-01 module was connected to the Pico via UART to provide Wi-Fi connectivity for publishing sensor data. The ESP32-Cam operated as an independent node powered through its 5 V supply, capturing QR codes and transmitting book metadata to the server. All ground references were shared among the modules to maintain signal stability.

Fig. 3. Integration of IoT devices.

4.4 Firmware Implementation

Firmware for the Raspberry Pi Pico was developed using either MicroPython or Arduino C++, enabling periodic sensor readings, event-based occupancy detection, and packaging of JSON payloads for transmission. The ESP-01 ran standard AT-command firmware, configured to establish a Wi-Fi connection and forward MQTT/HTTP messages from the Pico. The ESP32-Cam firmware was written using the Arduino framework and included camera initialization, QR detection routines, and metadata extraction. Each firmware module was designed to operate independently while following the systemwide communication protocol defined in the methodology section.

4.5 Development of the Web Interface

A web-based dashboard shown in Fig. 4, was developed to visualize the real-time status of the library environment. The dashboard interacts with the server backend to display noise levels, room occupancy status, temperature, humidity, and QR-based book recommendations. The interface includes dynamic indicators such as color-coded occupancy icons, temperature status displays, alert banners for high noise, and a panel showing book details after QR scanning. The dashboard refreshes automatically based on the incoming JSON data from the sensors, ensuring a near real-time user experience.

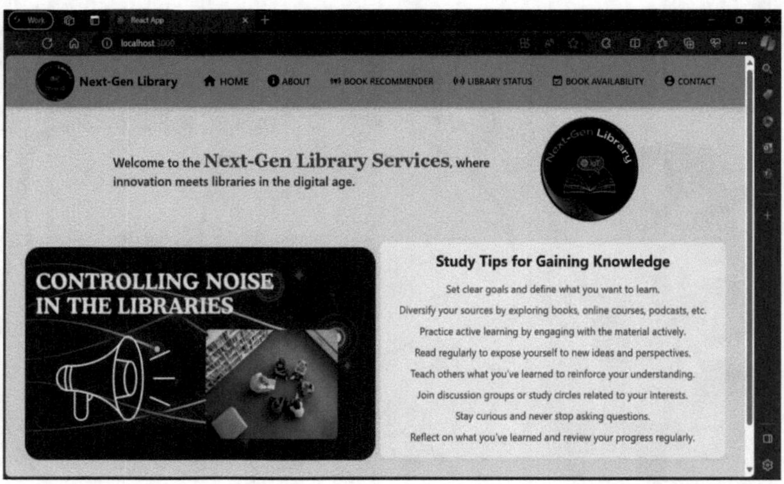

Fig. 4. Web interface summarizing noise, occupancy, environmental, and QR scan data.

4.6 Dataflow Execution

The dataflow of backend processing is presented in Fig. 5. The operational data flow begins with sensor readings on the Raspberry Pi, which processes and transmits the values to the server using the configured communication protocol. The server then updates the database and pushes new values to the dashboard.

For QR events, the ESP32-Cam directly sends decoded metadata to the backend, which triggers the recommendation engine and updates the user interface. This end-to-end workflow ensures seamless synchronization between physical environment sensing

S.No	Temperature	Humidity	Noise_Status	Room1_Status	Room2_Status	Book_Status	Date
1	31	51	Noise	-	-		2024-02-16 15:52:02
2	30	53	Noise	-	Full		2024-02-12 11:51:10
3	28	65	-	-	Full	EEE_Book_Next_Time_ML_Book	2024-02-12 09:15:07
4	28	67	-	-	-	ECE_Book_Next_Time_AI_Book	2024-02-12 09:14:34
5							2024-02-11 11:52:24
6	30	61	-	Full	Full		2024-02-11 11:33:12
7	30	61	Noise	-	-		2024-02-11 11:19:29

Fig. 5. Accessing library status via web interface.

and the visual representation on the dashboard. Results and Evaluation. All figures and photographs presented in this paper were created by the authors as part of the proposed system implementation.

5 Results

The Next-Gen Library Services system was evaluated during a 12-h deployment inside the institutional library. The performance metrics show that the system provides reliable sensing and fast response times. Occupancy detection using IR sensors achieved an accuracy of 94–96%, while noise-event recognition reached 93% accuracy after threshold calibration. The QR scanning module, powered by the ESP32-Cam, successfully decoded book QR codes with 97% reliability. The end-to-end latency from sensor input to dashboard update ranged between 0.8 and 1.1 s. Temperature regulation-maintained room conditions within ±1.5 °C, showing stable behavior under varying user activity.

A set of graphs was produced to visualize system behavior shown in Fig. 6. Noise-level plots showed clear variations during peak usage hours, and temperature graphs indicated steady fan activation cycles under the hysteresis model. Occupancy traces matched the actual room usage patterns, confirming sensor responsiveness. Latency measurements formed a compact distribution around the 1-s mark, indicating consistent update performance.

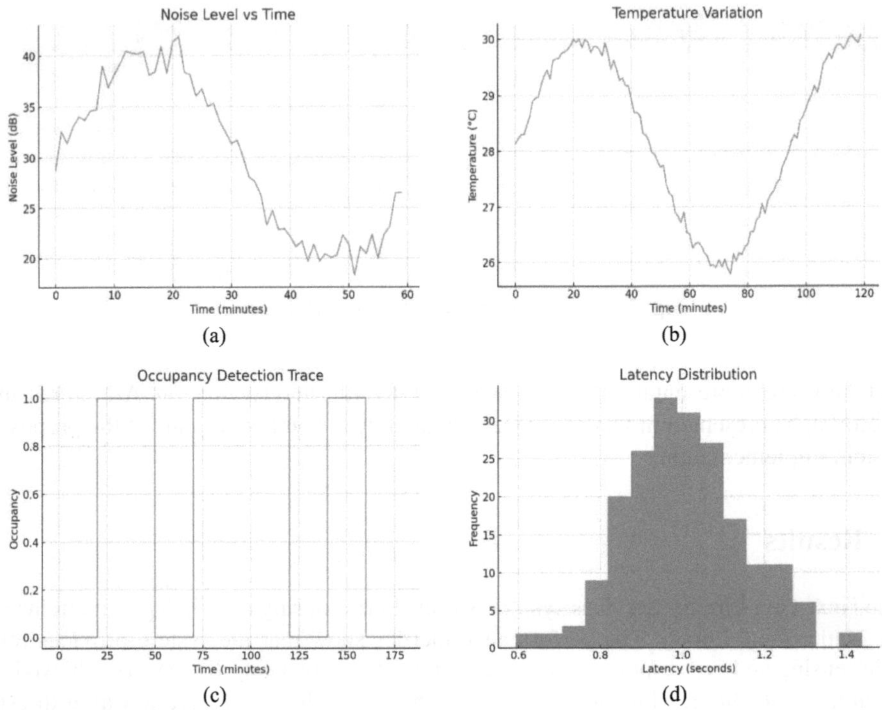

Fig. 6. Visualization of system performance during experimental deployment: (a) noise level variation over 60 min, (b) temperature fluctuations and fan response over 120 min, (c) occupancy detection trace showing room usage patterns, and (d) latency distribution for sensor-to-dashboard updates.

6 Conclusion

This work presented Next-Gen Library Services, an integrated IoT-based framework that combines noise monitoring, occupancy detection, environmental sensing, and QR-based book identification into a single real-time system. The experimental deployment demonstrated that the system can operate reliably in a library setting, achieving ~94–96% occupancy detection accuracy, 93% noise-event classification accuracy, 97% QR decoding success rate, and an average ~ 0.8–1.1 s latency for sensor-to-dashboard updates. The hysteresis-based temperature control maintained environmental stability within ± 1.5 °C, indicating effective automation of comfort conditions.

The unified dashboard and multi-sensor integration offer a practical approach for improving transparency of room usage, environmental awareness, and resource discovery.

Future work includes machine learning based noise classification and AI-driven book recommendation. Additional research will explore cloud scalability and predictive occupancy mapping. These developments aim to extend the system's intelligence, robustness, and applicability in modern academic library ecosystems.

References

1. Sadeh, T.: User experience in the library: a case study. New Libr. World. **109**, 7–24 (2008). https://doi.org/10.1108/03074800810845976
2. Wójcik, M.: Internet of things – potential for libraries. Library Hi Tech. **34**, 404–420 (2016). https://doi.org/10.1108/LHT-10-2015-0100
3. Ch, M.K., Munaga, M.S.K., Kolli, C.S., Maddila, S.K.: Real-time water quality tracking and alert system with IoT integration. In: 2023 3rd International Conference on Pervasive Computing and Social Networking (ICPCSN), pp. 1013–1018. IEEE (2023). https://doi.org/10.1109/ICPCSN58827.2023.00172
4. De Sarkar, T.: Internet of Things (IOT) and Library Services. (2022). https://doi.org/10.1108/LHTN-06-2022-0079
5. Eridani, D., Rochim, A.F., Firdananta, A.Z.: Noise monitoring system development in a library based on the internet of things. In: 2022 2nd International Conference on Electronic and Electrical Engineering and Intelligent System (ICE3IS), pp. 24–28. IEEE (2022). https://doi.org/10.1109/ICE3IS56585.2022.10010007
6. Vujović, V., Maksimović, M.: Raspberry Pi as a sensor web node for home automation. Comput. Electr. Eng. **44** (2015). https://doi.org/10.1016/j.compeleceng.2015.01.019
7. Feng, J.: New position of user experience librarians. J. Libr. Sci. China 48, (2022). doi:https://doi.org/10.13530/j.cnki.jlis.2022018.
8. Naidu, J.N.S.S.J., Ganesh, E.N.: An adaptive blockchain based three-tier architecture in fog based IoT for personal healthcare data application. Int. J. Recent Innov. Trends Comput. Commun. **11** (2023). https://doi.org/10.17762/ijritcc.v11i6.7786
9. Hemalatha, R., Amulya, G., Lalitha, C.S.N.S.: IoT-enabled smart retail environments. In: 2024 Second International Conference Computational and Characterization Techniques in Engineering & Sciences (IC3TES), pp. 1–5. IEEE (2024). https://doi.org/10.1109/IC3TES62412.2024.10877477
10. Zhou, Q.: Smart library architecture based on internet of things (IoT) and software defined networking (SDN). Heliyon. **10** (2024). https://doi.org/10.1016/j.heliyon.2024.e25375
11. Saldana-Barrios, J.J., Aguilar, E., Ng, W., Orocu, R.: Designing an IoT-based system for monitoring noise levels in the computer science faculty and library of the technological University of Panama. Sensors. **23** (2023). https://doi.org/10.3390/s23229083
12. Kanakam, P., Hussain, S.M., Chakravarthy, A.S.N.: Smart-trace: a future security aid using body odor sensing of an individual with IoT. SSRN Electron. J. (2018). https://doi.org/10.2139/ssrn.3166726
13. Daniel, O.C., Ramsurrun, V., Seeam, A.K.: Smart library seat, occupant and occupancy information system, using pressure and RFID sensors. In: 2019 Conference on Next Generation Computing Applications (NextComp), pp. 1–5. IEEE (2019). https://doi.org/10.1109/NEXTCOMP.2019.8883610
14. Anil Kumar, K., Dhadge, O.: A novel infrared (IR) based sensor system for human presence detection in targeted locations. Int. J. Comput. Netw. Inform. Secur. **10**, 34–40 (2018). https://doi.org/10.5815/ijcnis.2018.12.04
15. Hendajani, F., Mughni, A., Wardhani, I.P., Hakim, A.: Modeling Automatic room temperature and humidity monitoring system with fan control on the internet of things. ComTech: Comput. Math. Eng. Appl. **13** (2022). https://doi.org/10.21512/comtech.v13i2.7433
16. Abdullah-Al-Mashud, M., Mashud, M.A.A., Yasmin, D., Razzaque, M.A., Uddin, M.H.: Automatic room temperature controlled fan speed controller using PT-100. Int. J. Sci. Eng. Res. **6** (2015)

17. Prasanthi, B.V., Reddy, P.C.: Software defined networking (SDN) technologies and architectures for efficient. Adaptive Netw. (2026). https://doi.org/10.1007/978-3-031-94280-8_3
18. Pathak, S.K., Jain, R.: Use of QR code technology for providing library and information services in academic libraries: a case study. Pearl. **12** (2018). https://doi.org/10.5958/0975-6922.2018.00006.2

Integrated Smart Healthcare System with Automated Dispenser and Medical Chatbot

M. Sri Uma Suseela[1](✉), M. Hemalatha[2], V. N. V. Radha Krishna Murthy[3], and V. Siddhartha[4]

[1] Vishnu Institute of Technology, Bhimavaram 534202, India
umasuseela.m@vishnu.edu.in
[2] Shri Vishnu Engineering College for Women, Bhimavaram 534202, India
[3] B V Raju College, Bhimavaram 534202, India
[4] Vishnu Institute of Technology, Bhimavaram 534202, India

Abstract. This project introduces a holistic healthcare system comprising three key components: a medical dispenser, a health checkup system, and an online health advisory chat support. Employing RFID cards for secure user verification and payments adds an additional layer of dependability. The medication dispenser facilitates convenient access to over-the- counter medications, while the health checkup system records vital health metrics such as temperature and blood oxygen levels. All transactions and health data are securely stored in a database for user reference. The primary objective is to improve the accessibility of medications and healthcare guidance, particularly in public spaces where essential primary healthcare services are required. The internet-based chat support system offers immediate and multilingual health advice, ensuring a user-friendly experience. By integrating these components, the project aims to narrow the divide between healthcare services and the public, fostering a more inclusive and accessible approach to medical care, ultimately providing a seamless and user-centric experience. In addition, a chatbot for medical assistance has been developed. The developed chatbot enhances the system by providing real-time medical advice based on symptom input, guiding users on basic treatments, and offering multilingual support for accessibility.

Keywords: Medical Dispenser · Chat Support · Health Checkup · Over-the-counter Medication · RFID Transactions · Multi-Lingual

1 Introduction

The study of biomedical information, data, and knowledge is the focus of the field of medical informatics, a subfield of biomedical engineering. It entails their effective retrieval, storage, and application to overcome obstacles and reach wise conclusions [1]. The discipline has advanced significantly, especially since computer science and the computer age emerged in the late 20th century [2]. In order to meet its evolving needs, medical informatics has adopted cutting edge methods such as systems engineering,

M. J. C. S. Reis et al. (Eds.): IC4S 2025, LNICST 679, pp. 211–220, 2026.
https://doi.org/10.1007/978-3-032-22834-5_17

expert systems, neural networks, design of database, artificial intelligence and applied statistics and mathematics [3].

Simultaneously, digital technology breakthroughs have made it easier to store enormous volumes of data on small electronic devices. This change has freed up a significant amount of physical space in healthcare facilities that was used for paper-based medical records, which has led to a discernible shift toward electronic databases [4]. However, challenges persist due to the surge in healthcare advances post-World War II, coupled with an escalating patient influx, particularly in densely populated areas, impeding the effective management of extensive medical records. The health ATM emerges as a comprehensive, integrated solution, offering diagnosis and dispensing medicines for common ailments such as hypertension, diabetes, cold, fever, and headaches, along with essential first aid supplies [5–6]. This innovative machine operates similarly to an ATM for a bank, streamlining the process of diagnosing medical issues, especially in areas where hospital access is limited. Additionally, the Health ATM serves as a central platform for patients to interact with specialists through telemedicine, facilitating video conferencing [7].

The health ATM brings several advantages over the existing system, acting as a compact, integrated machine that addresses various medical problems while requiring minimal space for installation and operation [8]. It presents a viable solution for regions where hospitals are not easily accessible and enables government hospitals like AIIMS to extend their services to diverse locations, including rural India, by deploying Health ATMs nationwide. This ensures that people in remote areas can access hospital information systems conveniently. Despite the long-standing calls for interoperability in healthcare systems, achieving it has been a persistent challenge. While the technology for interoperability exists and is successfully employed in sectors like banking and commerce, its implementation in healthcare remains a complex issue. This paper explores the hurdles faced and successes achieved in achieving interoperability during the development of the digital access to medication (D-ATM).

2 Related Work

Potential improvements in healthcare monitoring can be seen in the growing use of tiny wearable biosensors and the combination of internet of things (IoT) and big data. However, several challenges remain unresolved in establishing a reliable and adaptable system for healthcare monitoring. The primary challenge facing the long-term care system is to establish conditions that enable individuals with care needs to reside in their homes for as extended a period as feasible. The authors in [9], has introduced the RO-smart ageing system, which utilizes IoT technology for remotely monitoring the health of older individuals. Health monitoring is a critical issue in today's society, as the lack of proper monitoring can lead to serious medical conditions going unnoticed. To address this challenge, numerous IoT devices have been developed for automatic Patient health monitoring. A microcontroller board linked to blood pressure and heart rate sensors is used in a smart health monitoring system [10] to track a patient's vital signs. Software defined networking (SDN), controller integrated into the Amazon cloud for imperative to safeguard the confidentiality of health reports stored in the cloud from network security threats. Immediate alerts can be dispatched to nurses or doctors based on the sensed information, facilitating prompt intervention [11].

In [12], the author have investigated how different facets of smart healthcare have transformed conventional healthcare practices into efficient and intelligent ones. The intelligent telemedicine healthcare topic for older people who are living alone is examined in this research [13], which provides a system that is customized to their living circumstances. In order to track important health metrics like blood pressure, heart rate, and blood glucose levels, IoT enables a strategic link between patients and medical experts [14]. In order to enable automatic identification of danger situations and alerts (ADSA), this study presents a hybrid architecture incorporated into a one platform for a visual patient monitoring system[15].To accomplish its goals, this system makes use of a cooperative network of medical sensors in conjunction with a multi-camera configuration.

3 Proposed Model

3.1 Block Diagram

The schematic block diagram proposed medication dispensary and health assistance system has been presented, and it is shown in Fig. 1. The diagram illustrates the integration of key input and output elements with the ESP32 Microcontroller which processes all inputs from sensors and buttons and executes the system logic, encompassing components such as a servo motor for precise control of angular position, pulse-oxy sensor (MAX 31012), temperature sensor (LM35), RFID card, RFID reader(EM18readermodule) which reads the unique information stored on an RFID tag, LCD, Wi-Fi, and push buttons which are simple switches for giving input allowing user to do some actions. In addition to the hardware integration, the project incorporates software enhancements for improved functionality. Utilizing unique identifiers from RFID cards, the system enables smooth transactions.

The transaction details are subsequently sent to a secure server for storage, ensuring users can easily retrieve their transaction history whenever needed. The comparison (see Table 1) of ESP32 with alternative microcontrollers like Raspberry Pi or Arduino, discussing power efficiency, processing capability, and cost-effectiveness.

Table 1. Comparison of ESP32 with alternative microcontrollers

Feature	ESP32	Raspberry Pi	Arduino
Power Efficiency	High	Low	Moderate
Processor	Dual-core Xtensa LX6 (240 MHz)	Quad-core ARM Cortex-A series	8-bit AVR (Uno/Nano), 32-bit ARM
Cost	Affordable	High	Low

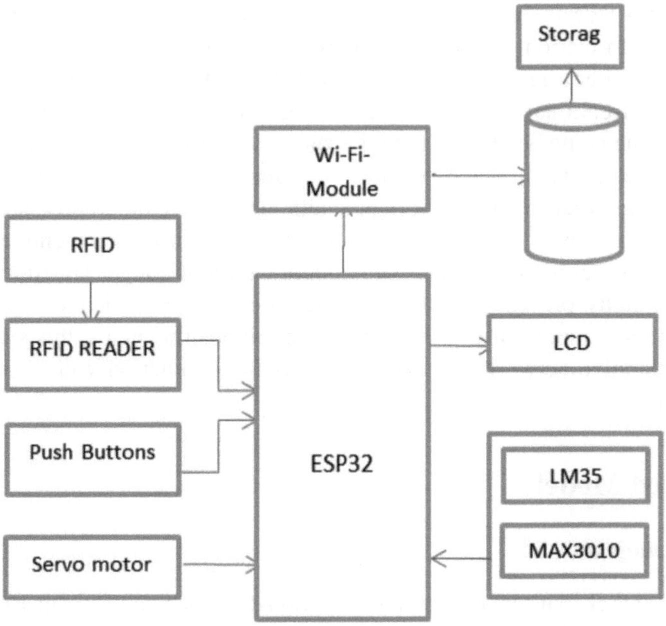

Fig. 1. Block diagram of presented model

3.2 Developed Hardware Prototype

The suggested hardware prototype has multiple sensors interfaced with Node MCU which is illustrated in Fig. 2.

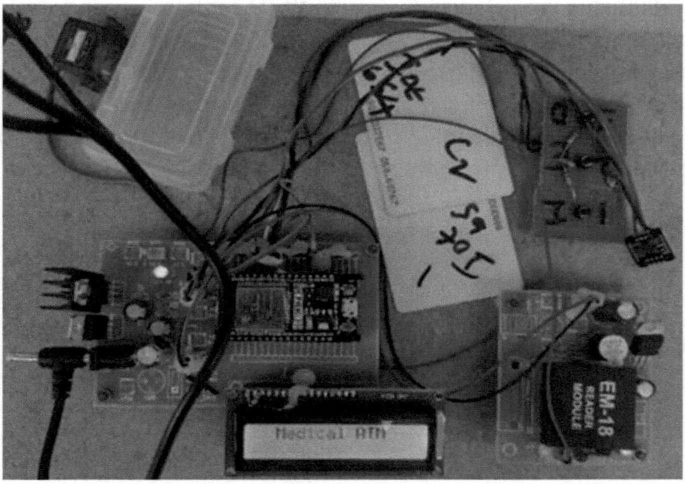

Fig. 2. Proposed Prototype Hardware Model

3.3 Limitations of the Proposed Hardware Model

- Connectivity issues in remote areas affecting system reliability.
- Sensor accuracy variations due to environmental factors.
- Possible delays in chatbot responses depending on internet speed.
- Power dependency and potential backup solutions.

4 Procedure

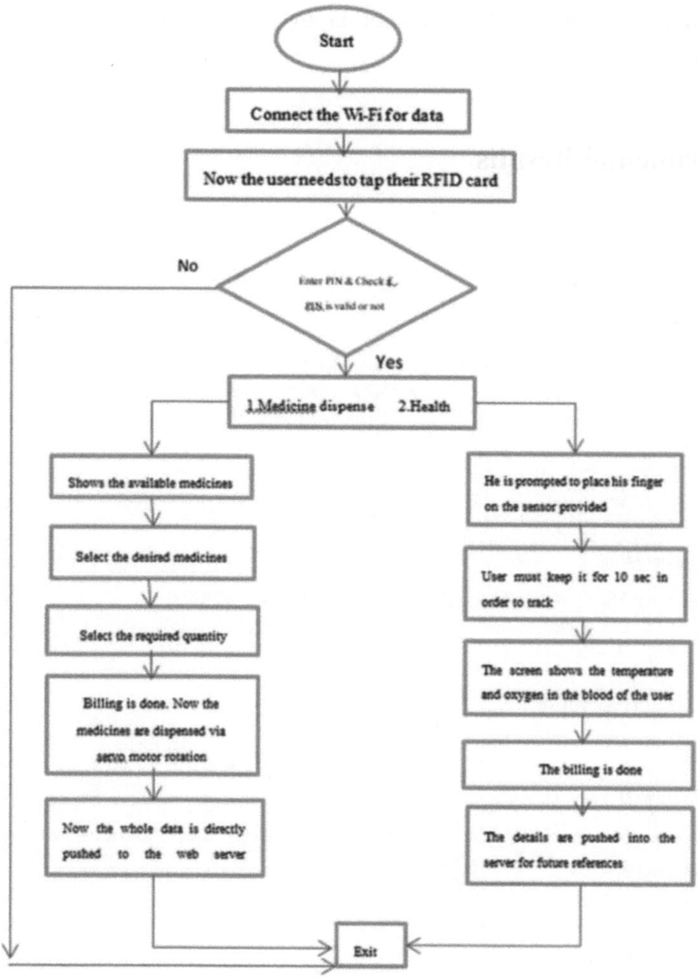

Fig. 3. Flow chart

To assist you understand how the suggested hardware model works, a thorough description of its operation is provided below. A flow chart has been created for understanding the flow of work for the proposed system and is depicted in Fig. 3

- Step1:Initialize all the hardware components.
- Step2:RFID card is inserted.
- Step3:RFID card is read by the system
- Step4: Determine whether the RFID card inserted is valid or not. If it is invalid then error message will be displayed.
- Step5:If it is valid then enter pin number
- Step 6: If pin entered is correct list of medicines present are displayed on the display else it is invalid and the error message will be displayed.
- Step 7: the list of items required and their quantity are selected using keypad. Step 8: Amount is calculated and deducted from the card.
- Step 9: required items are delivered out through the system.
- Step10:stop

5 Experimental Results

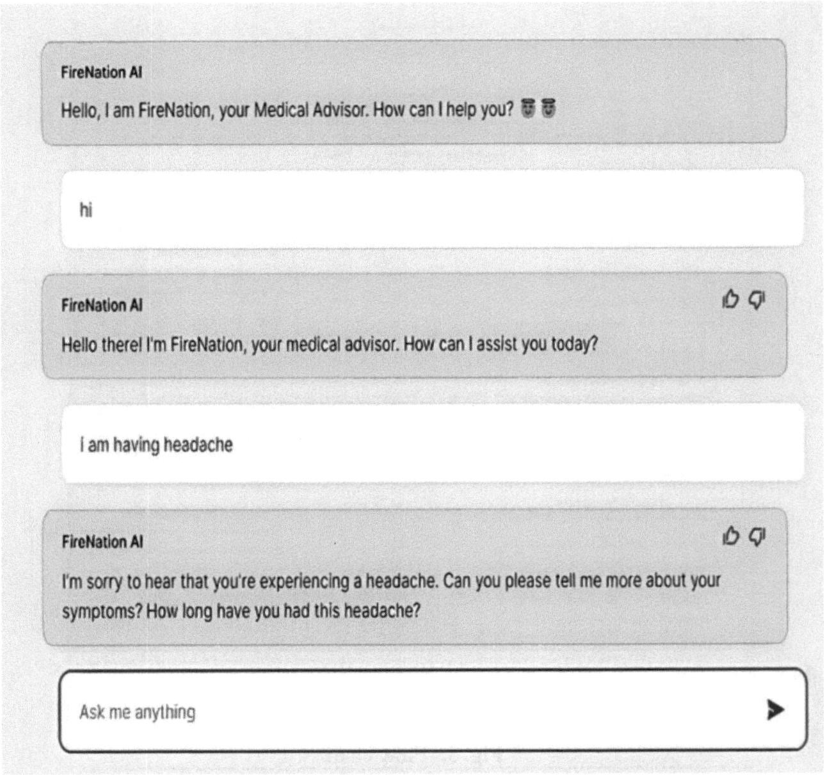

Fig. 4. Developed medical advisor chatbot

The prototype has been developed to assist people by providing medical advice for their health concerns and dispensing medicines as per their requirements. The pro-posed system functions like a medical ATM, offering basic medical assistance for minor ailments and dispensing medicines upon successful payment. Figure 4, shows the developed chatbot for medical assistance. The records of medical dispenses and chatbot assistance has been stored in the cloud for further use and check for the exact transactions in the medical ATM. Figure 5, depicts the history of process and transactions stored in the cloud. When the RFID card is successfully scanned and it checks for validity, if the card is valid then the ATM will dispense the medicine according to our given inputs. Figure 6 shows the RFID card validation and ATM will ready to dispense the medicine. The required medicine for user has been dispensed (see Fig. 6) and collected by the user and the display shows the thank you message.

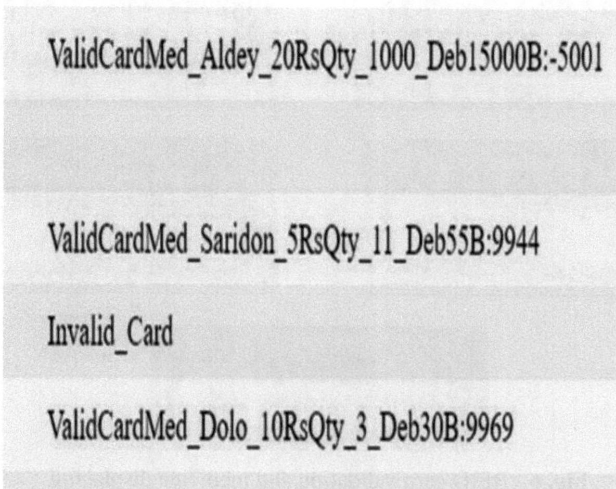

Fig. 5. Records of history in the developed prototype

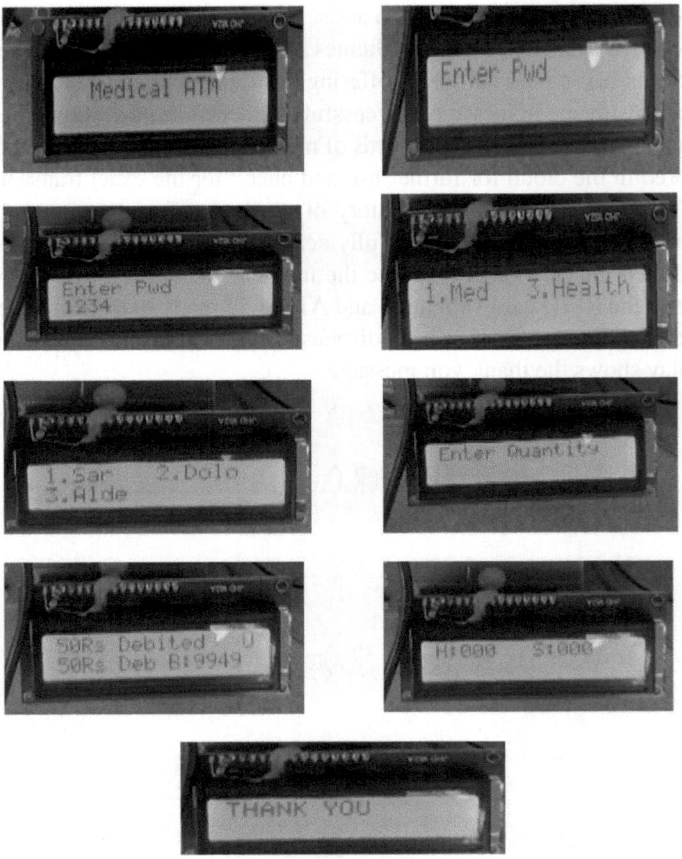

Fig. 6. RFID card validation and medicine displacing

6 Conclusion

In this work an integrated system for smart health care along with medical chatbot having dispenser detail has been developed. The main motive of this work is to make healthcare accessible to everyone through the proposed medical care system. It aims to provide basic health checkups and medicines conveniently in public places. The system follows the idea of connecting health beyond boundaries by using a user-friendly chatbot that supports multiple languages and works from any location. The proposed system is most suitable for use in urban areas where there are no connectivity issues. This system is most useful in public healthcare centers where there is a large crowd waiting to get medicines.

7 Future Scope

AI-driven diagnostics in the chatbot, enhanced security protocols, and potential integration with hospital databases for better patient management is the possible extension of the proposed model.

References

1. Bhatt, V., Chakraborty, S.: Real-time healthcare monitoring using smart systems: A step towards healthcare service orchestration Smart systems for futuristic healthcare. In: 2021 International Conference on Artificial Intelligence and Smart Systems (ICAIS), Coimbatore, India, pp. 772–777 (2021)
2. Raushan, R., Chaudhri, S.N., Suman, S., Kumar, D., Kumar, G., Kumar, A.: Advancing healthcare through Internet of Things: a comprehensive review of smart healthcare systems and their applications. In: 2025 International Conference on Machine Learning and Autonomous Systems (ICMLAS), Prawet, Thailand, pp. 1946–1951 (2025)
3. Robinsha, S.D., Amutha, B.: IoT Revolutionizing Healthcare: A Survey of Smart Healthcare System Architectures. In: 2023 International Conference on Research Methodologies in Knowledge Management, Artificial Intelligence and Telecommunication Engineering (RMKMATE), Chennai, India, vol. 2023, pp. 1–5
4. Hossain, M.J., Bari, M.A., Khan, M.M.: Development of an IoT based health monitoring system for e-Health. In: 2022 IEEE 12th Annual Computing and Communication Workshop and Conference(CCWC), Las Vegas, NV, USA, vol. 2022, pp. 0031–0037
5. Ahouandjinou, A.S.R.M., Assogba, K., Motamed, C.: Smart and pervasive ICU based-IoT for improving intensive health care. In: 2016 International Conference on Bio-engineering for Smart Technologies(BioSMART), Dubai, United Arab Emirates, pp. 1–4 (2016)
6. Varma, A.K.C., Bhargav, M.S.S., Venkateswara Rao, C., Orugu, R., Srinivas, C.V., Kiran, K.: Smart IV bag system for effective monitoring of patients. In: International Conference on Cognitive Computing and Cyber Physical Systems, pp. 308–316. Springer Nature Switzerland, Cham (2023)
7. Pathiraja, M.A., Wijesinghe, W.A.S.: IoT-Based Smart Medicine Dispenser. In: 2024 International Conference on Image Processing and Robotics (ICIPRoB), Colombo, Sri Lanka, vol. 2024, pp. 1–3
8. Daigavhane, M.K., Gundewar, S., Gadkari, A.P., Anpan, S.P.: Web-Based Smart Healthcare System. In: 2024 2nd DMIHER International Conference on Artificial Intelligence in Healthcare, Education and Industry (IDICAIEI), Wardha, India, pp. 1–6 (2024)
9. Paraschiv, E.-A., Tudora, E., Tîrziu, E., Alexandru, A.: IoT & cloud computing-based remote healthcare monitoring system for an elderly-centered care. In: 2021 International Conference on e-Health and Bioengineering (EHB), Iasi, Romania, pp. 1–4 (2021)
10. Singh, A.R.Y.P., Narawade, N.S.: Design of fog computing system for health care applications based on IoT. In: 2022 3rd International Conference for Emerging Technology (INCET), Belgaum, India, pp. 1–4 (2022)
11. Shalini, V.B.: Smart Health Care Monitoring System based on Internet of Things (IOT). In: 2021 International Conference on Artificial Intelligence and Smart Systems (ICAIS), Coimbatore, India, pp. 1449–1453 (2021)
12. Srilakshmi, P., Mohanapriya, D., Harini, Geetha, K.: IoT basedSmart Health Care System to Prevent Security Attacks in SDN. In: 2019 Fifth International Conference on Electrical Energy Systems (ICEES), Chennai, India, pp. 1–7 (2019)

13. Ahmad, N., George, R.P., Jahan, R.: Emerging trends in IoT for categorized health care. In: 2019 2nd International Conference on Intelligent Computing, Instrumentation and Control Technologies(ICICICT), Kannur, India, 2019, pp. 1438–1441
14. Kumar, K., Chaudhary, S., Anandaram, H., Kumar, R., Gupta, A., Joshi, K.: Industry 4.0 and Health Care System with special reference to Mental Health. In: 2023 1st International Conference on Intelligent Computing and Research Trends (ICRT), Roorkee, India, pp. 1–5 (2023)
15. Liau, J.-C., Ho, C.-Y.: Intelligence IoT telemedicine health care space system for the elderly living alone. In: 2019 IEEE Eurasia Conference on Biomedical Engineering, Health care and Sustainability (ECBIOS), Okinawa, Japan, vol. 2019, pp. 13–14

Computing Techniques

AC Performance Analysis of Spacer Tuned NSFET for High-Frequency Applications

S. Bhuvaneshwari(✉) and Archana Pandey

Department of Electronics and Communication, Jaypee Institute of Information Technology, JIIT, Noida, India
bhuvana.smec@gmail.com, archana.pandey@jiit.ac.in

Abstract. Nanoscale transistors are most important for cyber-physical systems as they provide prominent electronic devices which operate at lower voltage that yields high performance and low power consumption. This device capability is best suited for artificial intelligence applications where speed and efficiency play a major role. One of the most promising strategies for scaling beyond sub-7 nm technology nodes is the implementation of vertically stacked gate-all-around nanosheet field effect transistors (GAANSFET). This work focuses on analysing transistor structures and enhancing device performance by investigating the physical models and electrical characteristics of vertically stacked nanosheet transistors. The manuscript examines the impact of varying nanosheet spacer length, spacer material, and the number of stacked nanosheets (from 1 to 3) while maintaining fixed parameters such as width, height, doping concentration, gate materials, and nanosheet thickness on high frequency application. Using TCAD-based calibration, suitable design principles are proposed to achieve optimized performance in vertically stacked nanosheet FETs. Furthermore, I_{ON}, I_{OFF}, I_{ON}/I_{OFF} ratio, gate capacitance (C_{gg}), the transconductance(g_m), cutoff frequency(f_t), and intrinsic gain are analysed with respect to variations in nanosheet count, spacer materials, and spacer lengths. The calibration setup demonstrates high efficiency for advanced technology nodes, offering higher cutoff frequency F_t in stack count 1 by 42%(air), 7%(HfO_2), by 18%(Si_3N_4). For stack 3, lower spacer length f_t increases by 49%(air), 9%(HfO_2) and 19%(Si_3N_4) and gain (73% to 79% increase) comparatively suitable for next-generation high frequency applications.

Keywords: Spacer materials · NSFET · I_{ON}/I_{OFF} · gate capacitance (C_{gg}) · the transconductance(g_m) · cutoff frequency(f_t) · and intrinsic gain

1 Introduction

One of the key developments of cyber-physical system lies in nano electronics. Following the conventional MOSFETs, multi-gate devices such as FinFETs were introduced to overcome short-channel effects (SCEs) and improve gate control. FinFETs have been extensively utilized in advanced technology nodes, including 22 nm, 14 nm, and 7 nm. However, as device scaling progresses below the 7 nm node, SCEs become increasingly

M. J. C. S. Reis et al. (Eds.): IC4S 2025, LNICST 679, pp. 223–233, 2026.
https://doi.org/10.1007/978-3-032-22834-5_19

pronounced, degrading device performance and exacerbating existing challenges such as drain-induced barrier lowering (DIBL), subthreshold slope (SS), leakage current, and reduced drive current. These limitations arise primarily because the gate in a FinFET structure encloses the channel on only three sides, leaving the bottom surface left unconnected [1, 2]. Consequently, the inherent constraints of FinFET technology have driven research toward alternative device architectures and channel materials, which leads for the development of nanosheet FETs as a promising solution for continued scaling. The Gate-All-Around Nanosheet Field-Effect Transistor (GAANSFET) has emerged as one of the most promising candidates for sub-7 nm technology nodes due to its superior structural configuration, which offers excellent electrostatic gate control. In a nanosheet FET (NSFET), the gate completely surrounds the channel on all four sides, providing enhanced gate controllability and significant suppression of short-channel effects. The structural versatility of GAAFETs in channel length and width scaling enables improved device performance, yielding approximately a 30% enhancement compared to conventional FinFETs [3] which is best suited for cyber security applications due to its enhanced efficiency.

2 Device Design Setup

The proposed NSFET device is illustrated in Figs. 1 and 2 for $V_{ds} = V_{gs} = 0.7$ V. It is designed as a 3D structure with a gate length of 12 nm. Each stacked nanosheet in the FET has a thickness (height) of 5 nm and a width of 30 nm. The source and drain regions are heavily doped with p-type with a concentration of $2\times(10)^{20}$ cm^{-3}, while the channel region is n-doped with a concentration of $1\times(10)^{17}$ cm^{-3}. Dielectric materials such as HfO_2, air, and Si_3N_4 are used in spacer. Titanium Nitride -TiN is used as the gate metal, work function is 4.46 eV. NS_1, NS_2 and NS_3 imply the device channel numbers. The work function significantly influences electrostatics and current drivability [4]. The effectiveness of device development is assessed based on the requirements. To achieve this, the experimental electrical characteristics of the Stacked Nanosheet FETs are reconstructed by our research members by certain physical models such as lambordi, unibo, drift diffusion and auger regeneration and the proposed device exhibit good results as seen in Fig. 3. Drain current vs. gate voltage (I_d-V_{gs}) plot between experimental and calibrated for gate length 12 nm, and spacer length 7 nm, spacer material Si_3N_4 is used for reconstruction.

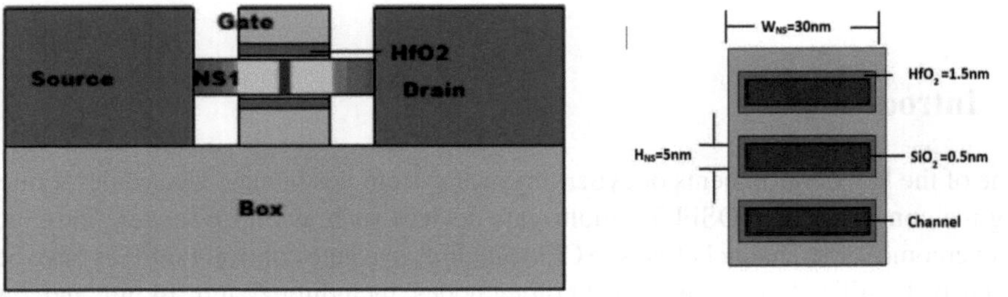

Fig. 1 Structure of NSFET with various Stack count 1 and Cross-sectional view of NSFET

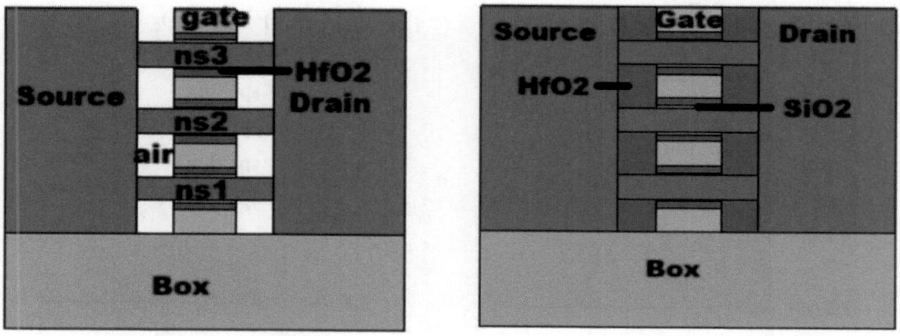

Fig. 2 Structure of NSFET with various spacer materials with 3 stack

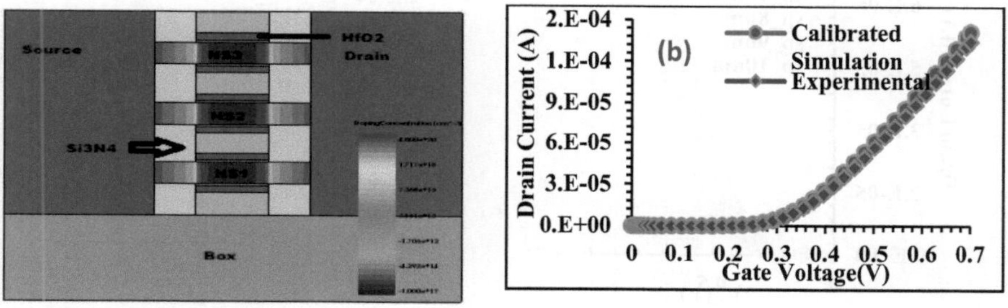

Fig. 3 **b**. Calibrated I_d-V_{gs} simulations matched with reference experimental data [5]

3 Results and Discussion

The performance of NSFET spacer tuned design under DC characteristics is analyzed using TCAD sentaurus tool in this manuscript. The simulation was carried out with varying spacer length (6 nm to 10 nm), spacer materials (air, HfO_2, Si_3N_4), varying stack count (1 and 3). Fig. 4 (a–f) shows nanosheet stack count 1and 3, for various spacer material the drive current increases for high K spacer material HfO_2 (K = 25) compared to Si_3N_4 and air (low k dielectric material, K = 7.9 and 1) because of improved field coupling and hence reduces short channel effects (SCEs). Similarly, as the stack count increases from 1 to 3, I_{ON} is increased efficiently in all cases of high K spacer material (HfO_2) to low K material (air) such as in case of air stack 1 and 3 for 6 nm spacer length, I_{ON} increases by 65.7%, for HfO_2 (1 and 3) I_{ON} increase by 9.9% and for Si_3N_4 (1and 3) increases by 65.4%. The analysis implies, the rest of spacer length variation from 7 nm to 10 nm also shows the improved I_{ON} respectively because as the spacer dielectric constant increases with increasing channel length leads to improved gate controllability and thus reduces leakage current [5]. The spacer tuned NSFET exhibits improved I_{ON}/I_{OFF} ratio by increasing the spacer length from (6 nm to 10 nm), Specifically the spacer material HfO_2 exhibits excellent switching ratio which is very important for device efficiency.

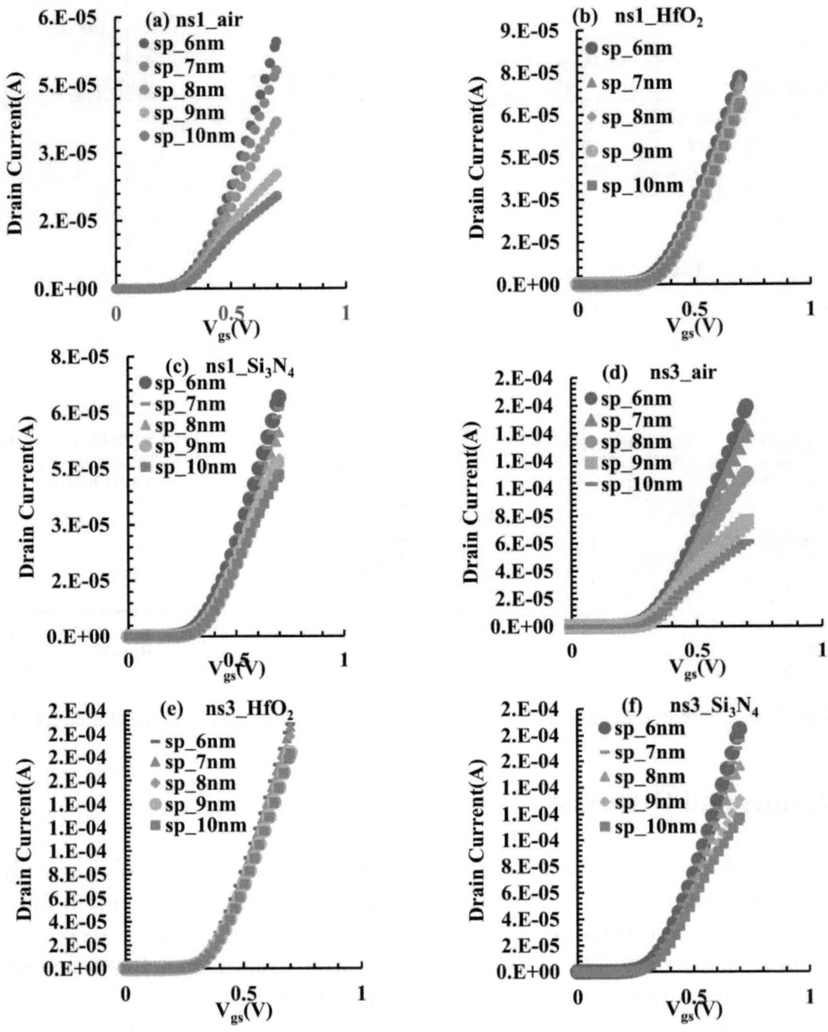

Fig. 4 I_d-V_{gs} plot for NSFET stack_1 and stack_3

3.1 Spacer Tuned NSFET CV Analysis

Analyzing the capacitance–voltage (C–V) characteristics of nanosheets is crucial for predicting the electrical behavior, performance, and reliability of nanosheet-based devices [6]. The electric field distribution is affected by the spacer length variation and it is observed that increasing the spacer length c_{gg} is reduced by 78% as given in Tables 1, 2, and 3 which also provides the details of obtained values for the spacer material changes with air, HfO_2, Si_3N_4 and Fig. 5(a–f). Hence there is always a tradeoff between I_{ON} and c_{gg} and therefore it is important to balance the parameters and spacer materials.

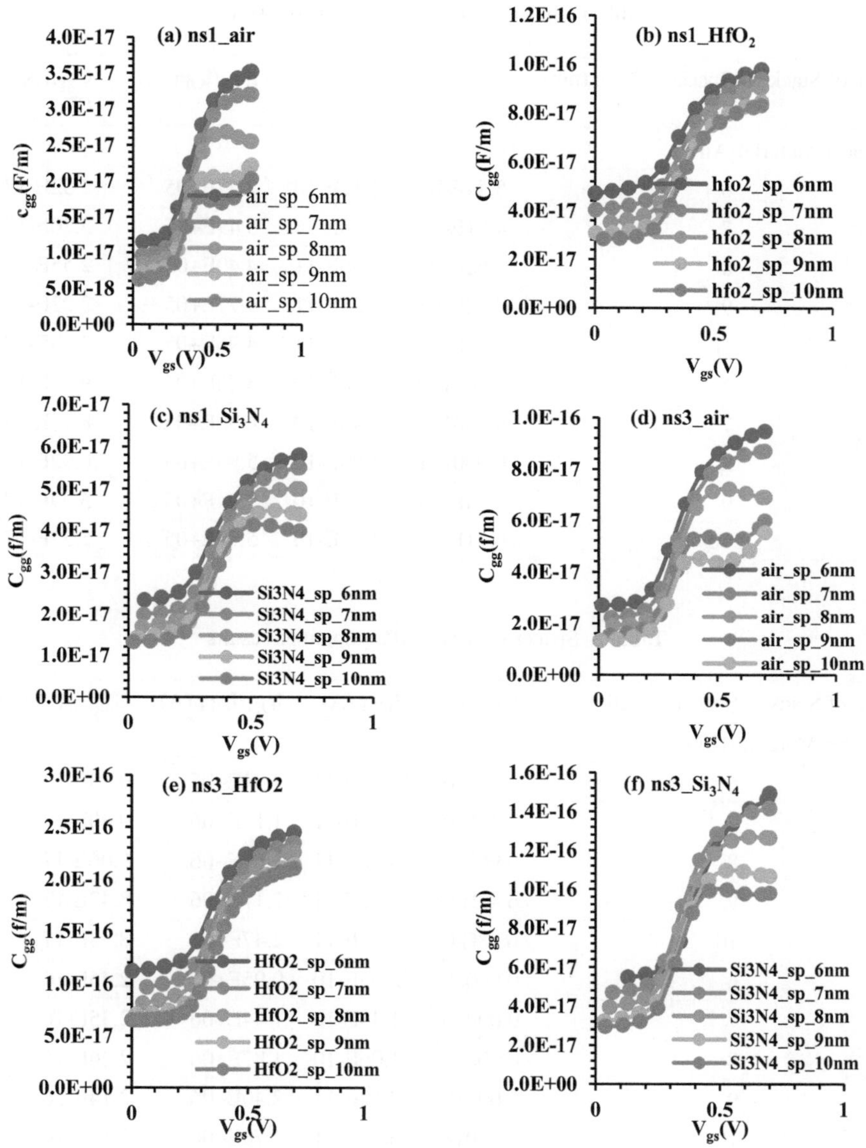

Fig. 5 C_{gg}-V_{gs} plot for NSFET stack_1 and stack_3

3.2 Spacer Tuned NSFET AC Analysis

AC analysis explains the device ability which can performance at high frequency. The switching ability of the transistor can be optimized by analysing cutoff frequency (f_t), transconductance, maximum frequency (f_{max}) and intrinsic gain is analysed in this section. Transconductance analysis explains the switching device behaviour, when the spacer length is varied from 6 nm to 10 nm decreased by 71.7% in ns1 air filled spacer,

Table 1 Spacer material- air obtained results

No. of Stack	Spacer Length (nm)	I_{ON} (A)	I_{OFF}(A)	I_{ON}/I_{OFF} (A)	$C_{gg\text{-}ON}$ (F/m)
Spacer Material-Air					
1	6	5.44E-05	2.12E-10	2.57E+05	3.52E-17
	7	4.81E-05	1.38E-10	3.49E+05	3.20E-17
	8	3.68E-05	8.36E-11	4.40E+05	2.55E-17
	9	2.52E-05	5.28E-11	4.77E+05	2.22E-17
	10	2.03E-05	4.09E-11	4.96E+05	2.03E-17
3	6	0.000159	4.18E-10	3.80E+05	9.47E-17
	7	0.000142	2.90E-10	4.90E+05	8.70E-17
	8	0.000111	1.90E-10	5.84E+05	6.92E-17
	9	7.54E-05	1.27E-10	5.94E+05	5.99E-17
	10	6.11E-05	1.02E-10	5.99E+05	5.52E-17

Table 2 Spacer material- HfO_2 obtained results

No. of Stack	Spacer Length (nm)	I_{ON} (A)	I_{OFF}(A)	I_{ON}/I_{OFF}(A)	$C_{gg\text{-}ON}$ (F/m)
Spacer Material-HfO_2					
1	6	7.29E-05	9.82E-11	7.42E+05	9.79E-17
	7	7.21E-05	6.23E-11	1.16E+06	9.40E-17
	8	6.96E-05	4.36E-11	1.60E+06	9.06E-17
	9	6.41E-05	2.95E-11	2.17E+06	8.47E-17
	10	6.38E-05	2.58E-11	2.47E+06	8.33E-17
3	6	0.000208	2.09E-10	9.95E+05	2.45E-16
	7	0.000206	1.43E-10	1.44E+06	2.35E-16
	8	0.000198	1.06E-10	1.87E+06	2.26E-16
	9	0.000183	7.62E-11	2.40E+06	2.14E-16
	10	0.000183	6.78E-11	2.70E+06	2.11E-16

similarly by 11% (HfO_2) and by 43%(Si_3N_4) as in Fig. 6(a–f). For 3 stack it is decreased by 70%(air), 13%(HfO_2) and 48%(Si_3N_4) because of increasing parasitic capacitance.

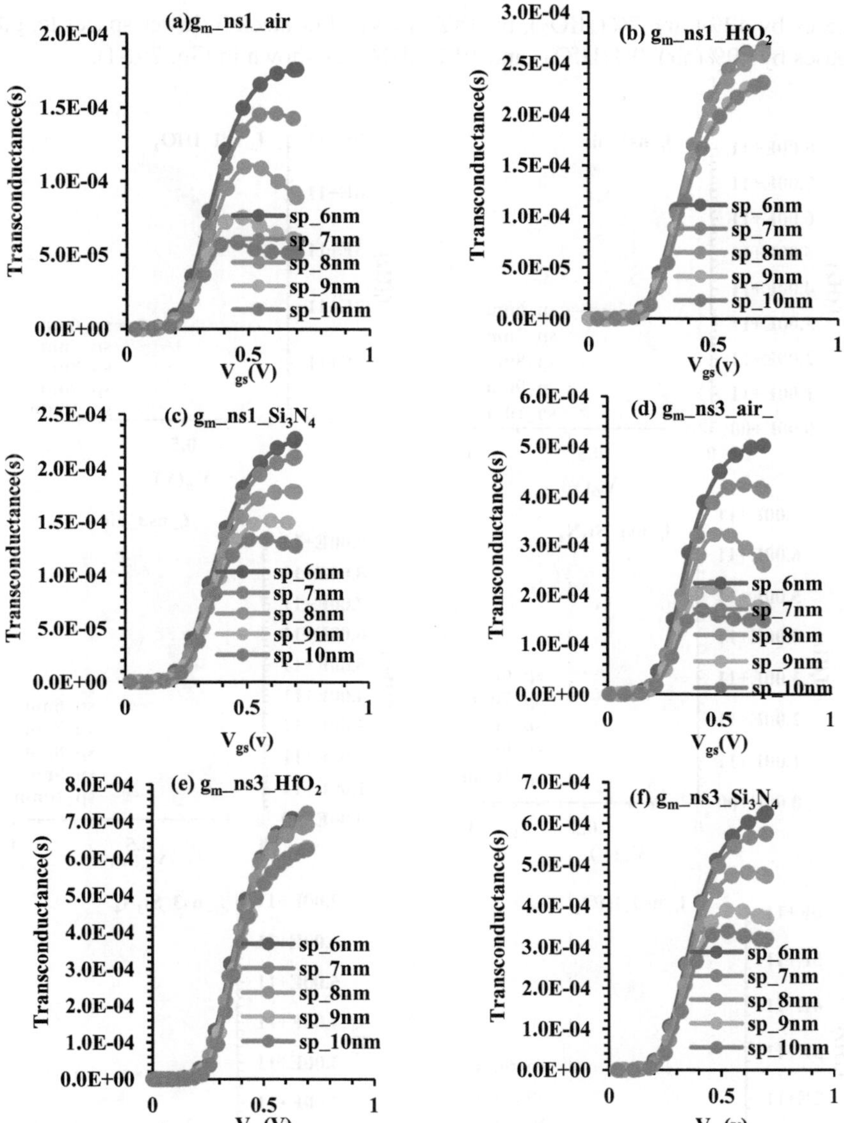

Fig. 6 Transconductance(g_m) vs. Vgs(V) plot for NSFET stack_1 and stack_3

3.2.1 Spacer Tuned NSFET f_t Analysis

The signal amplification starts at cutoff frequency which depends on transconductance and gate capacitance. This can be calculated as $fT = (g_m/2\pi.\ cgg)$ where g_m is transconductance and c_{gg} is gate capacitance. It is observed that decreasing the spacer length in all cases of spacer material f_t is increasing as a result the speed will be increased in lower spacer length compared to increased spacer length. F_t in stack count 1 as in Fig. 7(a–c) increases by 42%(air), 7%(HfO_2), by 18%(Si_3N_4). For stack 3, lower spacer length f_t increases by 49%(air), 9%(HfO_2) and 19%(Si_3N_4) as shown in Fig. 7(d–f).

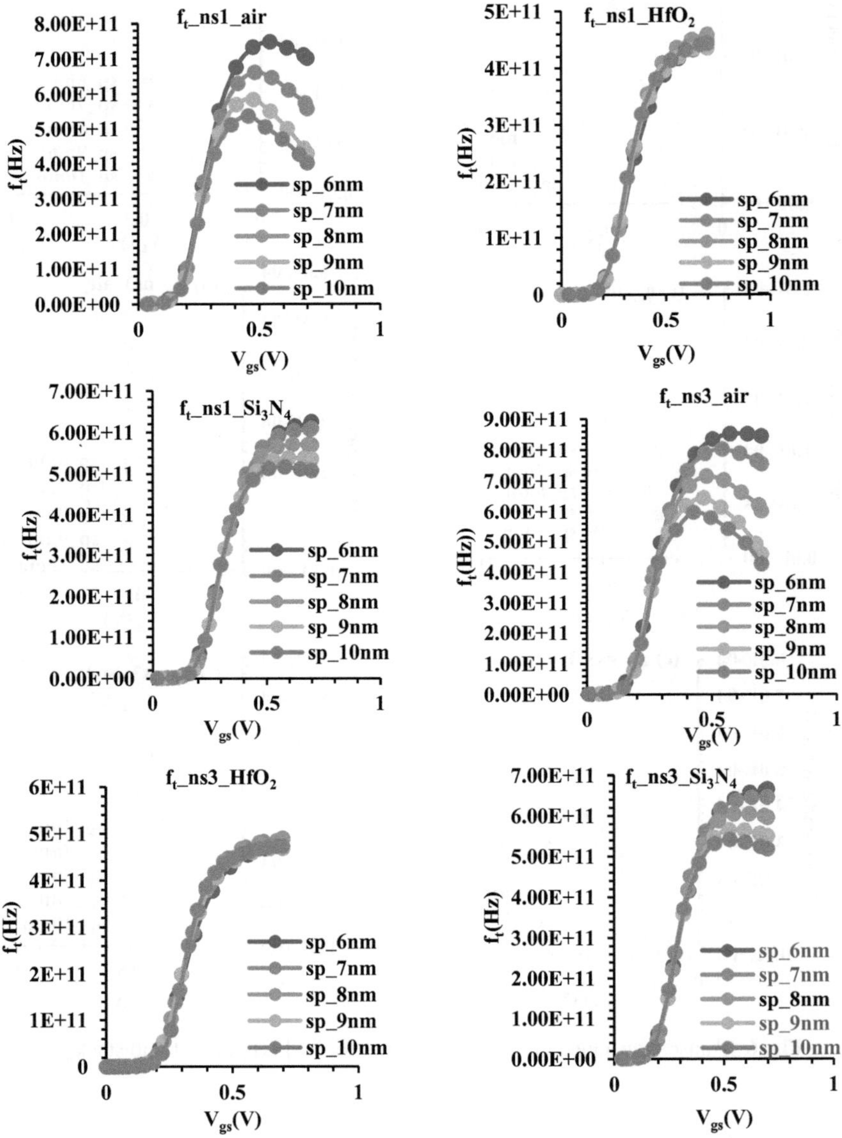

Fig. 7. Cutoff frequency(f_t) vs. Vgs(V) plot for NSFET stack_1 and stack_3

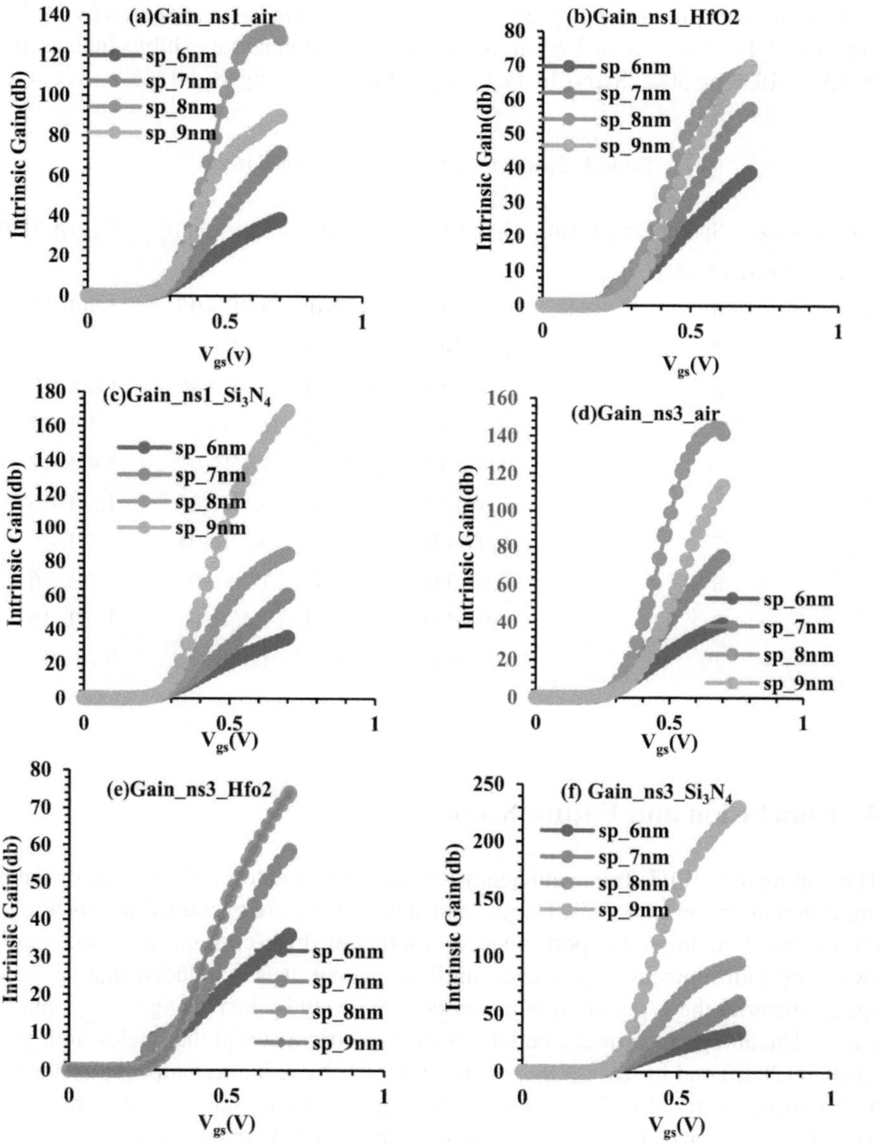

Fig. 8 Intrinsic gain(db) vs. Vgs(V) plot for NSFET stack_1 and stack_3

3.2.2 Spacer Tuned NSFET Intrinsic Gain Analysis

Another important parameter in ac analysis in intrinsic gain which that impacts the frequency response and the signal amplification [7, 8]. It is measured by $A_V = \frac{g_m}{g_{ds}}$(db) where g_{ds} is drain to source capacitance. The spacer tuned NSFET exhibits improved gain for single stack count by 60% when the spacer length is decreased to 6 nm but increasing spacer length to 9 nm it is decreased for spacer material (air) because of increased output resistance(r_o) [9, 10]. In HfO_2 increasing spacer length increases gain by 76%, in Si_3N_4 increasing spacer length (6 nm to 9 nm) increases gain by 79% as if Fig. 8(a–c). For stack count 3(6 nm to 9 nm), air spacer material exhibits increased gain by 73%, HfO_2 by 50%, Si_3N_4 by factor of 50 times as in Fig. 8(d–f).

Table 3 Spacer material- Si_3N_4 obtained results

No. of Stack	Spacer Length(nm)	I_{ON} (A)	I_{OFF}(A)	I_{ON}/I_{OFF}(A)	$C_{gg\text{-}ON}$ (F/m)
Spacer Material-Si_3N_4					
1	6	6.40E-05	1.36E-10	4.71E+05	5.80E-17
	7	6.09E-05	8.19E-11	7.44E+05	5.51E-17
	8	5.47E-05	5.44E-11	1.01E+06	5.00E-17
	9	4.76E-05	3.56E-11	1.34E+06	4.39E-17
	10	4.33E-05	2.98E-11	1.45E+06	3.98E-17
3	6	0.000185	2.84E-10	6.51E+05	1.50E-16
	7	0.000176	1.84E-10	9.57E+05	1.42E-16
	8	0.000156	1.30E-10	1.20E+06	1.26E-16
	9	0.000131	9.03E-11	1.45E+06	1.07E-16
	10	0.000117	7.72E-11	1.52E+06	9.79E-17

4 Conclusion and Future Scope

The scaling of NSFET device efficiency towards sub-7 nm technology node by employing different spacer materials, lengths and stack counts are examined in this work and the results show improved performance in terms of drive current, increased I_{ON}/I_{OFF} switching ratio, increased gain and cutoff frequency. It is concluded that by varying spacer material the g_m, gain, f_t is increased effectively by increasing stack count from 1 to 3. The air spacer proves a better spacer dielectric material that yields high gain in stack 1(128db) and in stack 3 Si_3N_4 yields(228db) by reducing output resistance. The Si_3N_4 spacer material yields higher cutoff frequency as the stack count increases (1 to 3) of reduced spacer length. HfO_2 spacer material yields improved I_{ON}/I_{OFF} switching characteristics and better device switching capability thus reducing SCEs. Therefore, wise selection of device design is important to achieve leakage current reduction and improved switching ratio in high frequency application. Hence, the spacer engineered NSFET assures device performance for high-speed analogue and digital circuit applications.

References

1. Lee, S., et al.: Sensitivity of inner spacer thickness variations for sub-3-nm node silicon nanosheet field-effect transistors. Nano. **12**(19), 3349 (2022)
2. Balasubrahmanyam, M., Goel, E.: Role of spacer dielectric engineering in performance improvement of advanced TreeFETs for nanoscale applications. IEEE Trans. Dielectr. Electr. Insul. (2025)
3. Pundir, Y.P., Bisht, A., Saha, R., Pal, P.K.: Air-spacers as analog-performance booster for 5 nm-node N-channel nanosheet transistor. Semicond. Sci. Technol. **36**(9), 095037 (2021)
4. Lakshmana, C., Subba Rao, S.: Impact of spacer engineering on nanosheet FET performance: a comparative analysis of single and dual-layer configurations. Micro Nano Struct., 208429 (2025)
5. Bhuvaneshwari, S., Pandey, A.: Self-heating optimisation of nanosheet field effect transistor performance with physics-based calibrated simulation setup. Pramana. **99**(1), 24 (2025)
6. Gurre, D., et al.: Spacer design strategies at sub-5 nm technology node for junctionless fork-sheet FET: bridging device optimization and circuit efficiency – a dielectric perspective. IEEE Trans. Dielectr. Electr. Insul. (2024)
7. Bhukya, S., Nistala, B.R.: Design optimization of spacer engineered junctionless-fishbone (JL-FB) FET at 5 nm technology node: device to circuit level implementation. Phys. Scr. **100**(9), 095962 (2025)
8. Jain, G., Sawhney, R.S., Kumar, R.: Investigation of spacer-engineered stacked nanosheet tunnel FET with varying design attributes. Phys. Scr. **99**(4), 045937 (2024)
9. Bhattacharjee, A., Dasgupta, S.: Optimization of design parameters in dual-κ spacer-based nanoscale reconfigurable FET for improved performance. IEEE Trans. Electron. Devices. **63**(3), 1375–1382 (2016)
10. Beebireddy, D., Fatima, K., Devi, L.N.: Enhancing DM junctionless tree-FET performance through spacer optimization: a comprehensive DC and RF analysis. J. Electron. Mater. **54**(4), 3035–3045 (2025)

Multimodal Wireless Stethoscope with ESP32-C6 for Synchronized Acoustic and Bioelectrical Signal Acquisition in Cardiopulmonary Diagnostics

Madhumati Pol(✉), Adwaiy Khairnar, Chetan Agrawal, Aditya Shirse, Kanak Agrawal, Shriraj Agarkar, and Aditya Raj Tripathi

Vishwakarma Institute of Technology, Pune, India
{madhumati.pol1,adwaiy.khairnar24,chetan.agrawal24,aditya.shirse24, kanak.agrawal241,shriraj.agarkar24,aditya.tripathi24}@vit.edu

Abstract. The limitations of traditional digital stethoscopes are that they only rely on sound, limiting the detection of different conditions which do not provide differentiating sound signatures. We created a wireless stethoscope which can acquire multimodal signals based on the ESP32-C6 microcontroller. Our device has a MEMS microphone for heart and lung sounds, in addition to a medical bioamplifier to simultaneously acquire ECG and respiratory EMG. Feature extraction of the signals is completed by use of a signal processing pipeline to classify the sounds, based on ensembles of different machine learning models like Random Forest, XGBoost, and SVM. We achieved hardware-level synchronization with sub-millisecond precision, ensuring the data streams are correctly aligned. Additionally, we used optimized wireless protocols that allow the device to run for over 5 h continuously. We ran a feasibility study with 20 participants which confirmed system functionality and multimodal benefits, demonstrating good sensitivity and specificity, which confirmed that the system works correctly and shows clear potential for acquiring synchronized multimodal biosignals on an embedded platform.

Keywords: multimodal diagnostics · ESP32-C6 · synchronized bio signals · digital stethoscope · machine learning · NPG Lite

1 Introduction

Cardiovascular diseases are the leading cause of death worldwide, which makes reliable diagnostic tools for early detection essential. Traditional auscultation with a mechanical stethoscope is often subjective, inconsistent between clinicians, and unable to detect abnormalities like arrhythmias that can be silent. Digital stethoscopes have improved upon some of these issues, reaching promising accuracy rate for detecting cardiac abnormalities but their interpretation is limited to sound only.

M. J. C. S. Reis et al. (Eds.): IC4S 2025, LNICST 679, pp. 234–250, 2026.
https://doi.org/10.1007/978-3-032-22834-5_20

The latest development in embedding systems and machine learning has made it possible to come up with multimodal devices that will enhance the precision of the detection by the inclusion of different physiological signals. On the other hand, the implementation of these systems has been tough owing to the issues of accurate signal synchronization, power management, and difficulty in hardware.

To tackle these issues, we introduced a wireless multimodal stethoscope that is based on the ESP32-C6 platform. The major inputs of our work are:

1. **Synchronized Multimodal Acquisition**: Acoustic and bioelectrical signals were expertly synchronized on a single embedded board with a precision of less than a millisecond.
2. **Medical-Grade Amplification**: The NPG Lite module was installed for acquiring ECG and EMG signals with 3-channel input.
3. **Robust Classification**: A combination of Random Forest, XGBoost, and SVM was used to make our diagnostic classifications more dependable.
4. **Optimized Power Design**: We implemented Wi-Fi 6 Target Wake Time, which allows for over 8 h of continuous operation.
5. **Pilot Functionality Testing**: We conducted a system test with 20 participants and showed that our multimodal approach not only works as intended but also enhances classification performance over an audio-only baseline.

Our work is a major step forward in the field of diagnostics, as it combines three innovative approaches:

- Hardware-level multimodal synchronization which allows for less than a millisecond precision on an embedded platform making it cross-modal analysis or trust-worthy.
- Integration of medical-grade bioamplification for clinical-quality ECG and EMG signals
- An adaptive weighted ensemble learning strategy that merges three complementary ML algorithms for maximum robustness across diverse patient populations and signal conditions.

2 Related Works

The very first studies regarding the digital stethoscopes were mainly aimed at heart and lung sound capturing. The first systems like [1] concentrated on the delivery of electronic sound acquisition, which was a very basic kind of wireless functionality and very limited in the area of signal processing. The subsequent wireless prototypes mentioned in [2,3] supported remote auscultation but no multimodal data collection in sync. Among the artificial intelligence approaches, those in [4,5], and [6] exhibited remarkable accuracy in classifying cardiac and respiratory sounds automatically; however, these systems were limited to acoustic signals only and did not use any complementary bioelectrical data. The same situation was with telemedicine-oriented designs like [7,8]

Table 1. Comparative analysis of multimodal biosignal systems for cardiopulmonary diagnostics

Aspect	Our Work	[10]	[23]	[24]
Acquisition Mode	Multimodal (A+E+Em)	Multimodal (HR+Au)	Audio only	Audio+AR
Synchronization	Hardware (<1 ms)	Software (5–10 ms)	N/A	N/A
Platform	ESP32-C6	ESP32	Cloud	AR
Power Cons.	95 mA	150 mA	200 mA	300 mA
Battery Life	5+ hours	4–5 h	2–3 h	1–2 h
ML Approach	Ensemble (RF + XGB + SVM)	Basic ML	Deep CNN	Rule-based
Achieved Accuracy	82.4%	78.3%	81.5%	75.2%
Feature Type	Manual (47)	Manual	Automatic	Manual

that improved remote connectivity through IoT and cloud platforms but still depended on single-modality input.

A smaller subset of studies investigated multimodal fusion. For instance, [9] explored cross-domain learning for respiratory sound analysis but did not integrate bioelectrical signals. Meanwhile, [10] combined heart rate and lung sound monitoring but employed unsynchronized devices, resulting in weakened temporal correlation between modalities.

Earlier contributions significantly advanced electronic sound acquisition [14], remote clinical consultation systems [15], optimized signal capture techniques [16], and cost-effective telehealth implementations [17]. Machine learning applications for abnormal sound detection were further explored in [18]. More recent developments introduced AI-enabled hardware platforms [19], scalable cloud-based processing architectures [20], low-cost Arduino-based systems [21], and personalized health monitoring frameworks [22]. Additional innovations examined image-based acoustic analysis [23] and augmented reality-assisted diagnostic interfaces [24]. A comprehensive review presented in [25] synthesized clinical findings and emphasized the critical need for integrated and synchronized cardiopulmonary assessment systems, thereby reinforcing the motivation for the proposed multimodal approach.

2.1 Comparative Analysis with Recent Systems

Table 1 presents a systematic comparison of our multimodal wireless stethoscope with recent biosignal acquisition systems and AI-based cardiopulmonary diagnostic approaches.

3 Methodology

A single, unified platform was created by us for our multimodal digital stethoscope for the purpose of accurately and simultaneously capturing the acoustic and bioelectrical signals. The ESP32-C6 microcontroller is the heart of our device, a RISC-V-based SoC that consists of all the essential components for efficient real-time signal acquisition with the integration of Wi-Fi 6, Bluetooth 5.3 LE Audio, a native I^2S controller, and a 12-bit SAR ADC with DMA support.

The INMP441 MEMS microphone is used for audio capture and it gives 24-bit resolution along with a 61 dB signal-to-noise ratio within the 20–2000 Hz cardiopulmonary range. For bioelectrical signals such as ECG and respiratory EMG, we opted for the NPG Lite bioamplifier, which is a medical grade module that guarantees high-fidelity measurements and has 10 MΩ input impedance and 100 dB common-mode rejection.

The system was powered by a lithium-ion battery with a capacity of 2500 mAh, which was further supported by a TP4056 charging circuit and an MT3608 boost converter to manage the energy in a stable manner. Aiming for safety and reliability of performance was the main priority. Consequently, extra components were integrated into the design. The latter not only consists of anti-aliasing filtering, but also employs precision voltage references in order to be able to measure accurately, and utilizes medical-grade isolation for the purpose of protecting the user (Fig. 1).

3.1 Hardware Architecture

We selected the NPG Lite bioamplifier from Upside Down Labs to capture physiological signals due to its capability of providing clinical-grade signal quality. In our design, we utilize three of its available channels for ECG and EMG monitoring; however, the module can accommodate up to 36 channels for other applications, such as EEG and EOG. The extremely high input impedance and excellent noise rejection are the reasons for our acquiring such clean signals. The compact, Feather-compatible design not only made integration into our embedded platform easy but also ensured medical safety due to compliance with IEC 60601 safety standards.

It is crucial to obtain clean signals, but the real advantage of the system is its ability to synchronize this bioelectrical data with acoustic signals at the hardware level. Our procedure is as follows: the microphone transmits the audio directly to the I^2S bus in real time, where the microcontroller through the use of DMA captures the audio and converts it to digital with a resolution of 24-bit, 48 kHz. At the same time, the bioamplifier processes the ECG and EMG signals, after which they are converted into digital signals of 12-bit resolution and 1 kHz sampling rate by the SAR ADC.

The two streams were started at the same time, and the perfect synchronization of the signals was achieved using microsecond-level timestamps, which is a necessary condition for any trustworthy cross-modal analysis.

The Hardware Synchronization Equation:

To achieve sub-millisecond synchronization, we implement microsecond-level timestamp alignment. Let t_{audio} be the timestamp of an audio sample captured via the I^2S interface and t_{bio} be the timestamp of a bioelectrical sample from the SAR ADC. The time difference is:

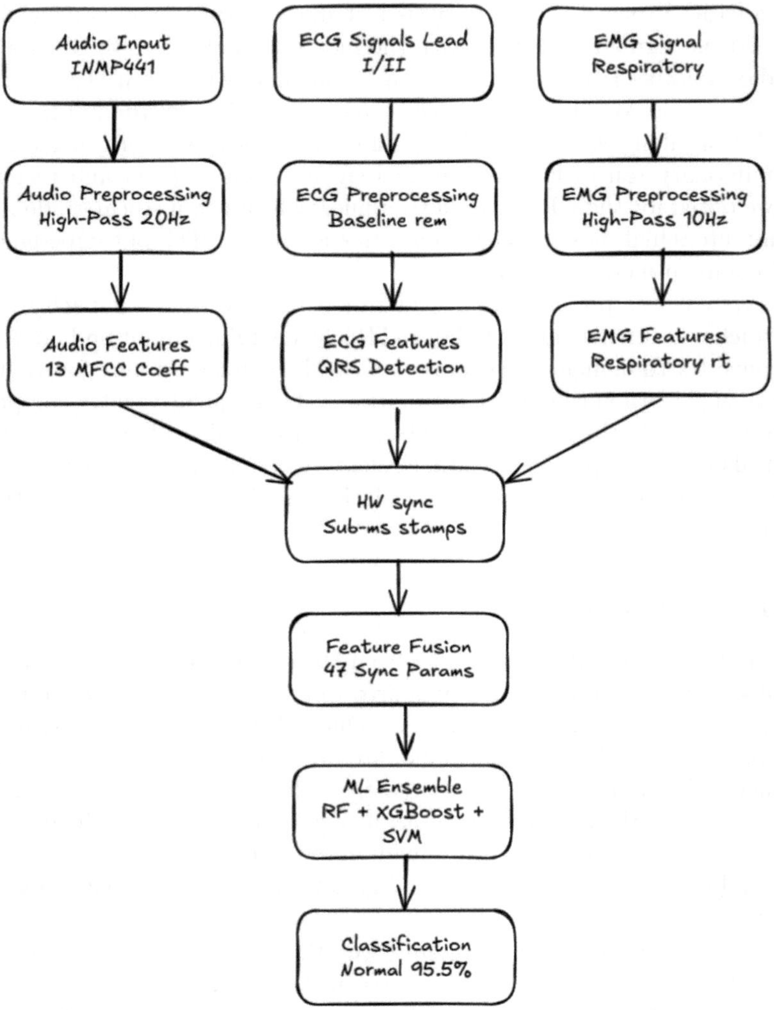

Fig. 1. The multimodal stethoscope system's block diagram depicts the simultaneous intake and treatment of audio, ECG, and EMG signals. The entire process consists of preprocessing, feature extraction, hardware synchronization, multimodal feature fusion, and classification based on ensemble machine learning which is done at the same time axis.

$$\Delta t = |t_{audio} - t_{bio}| \tag{1}$$

where Δt represents the temporal offset between modalities. For our system, we achieve $\Delta t \leq 287 \pm 43$ microseconds, enabling valid cross-modal analysis. The aligned timestamp for multimodal feature extraction is calculated as:

$$t_{aligned} = \max(t_{audio}, t_{bio}) + \Delta t/2 \tag{2}$$

ensuring both signals reference the same temporal point for synchronous processing.

3.2 Signal Processing Pipeline

When these data streams are perfectly synchronized, our pipeline is activated, and the initial step is applied preprocessing where noise and artifacts are diminished. For the sound, we perform DC offset removal, wavelet denoising, and a band-pass filter (202000 Hz) is also utilized. The ECG is first stabilized with a 0.5 Hz high-pass filter and then cleaned with a notch filter at 50/60 Hz. The next step is to apply a high-pass filter to the EMG signals at a cutoff frequency of 10 Hz, followed by rectification and smoothing, which will facilitate the detection of respiratory muscle activity.

The preprocessing stage applies frequency domain filtering. For ECG signals, a high-pass filter with cutoff frequency 0.5 Hz removes baseline wander:

$$H_{HP}(f) = \frac{j2\pi f/\omega_c}{1 + j2\pi f/\omega_c} \tag{3}$$

where $\omega_c = 2\pi \times 0.5$ rad/s is the cutoff angular frequency. Additionally, a notch filter at 50/60 Hz suppresses power-line interference:

$$H_{notch}(f) = \frac{1 + (f/f_0)^2}{1 + Q(f/f_0)^2 + (f/f_0)^2} \tag{4}$$

where $f_0 = 50$ Hz (or 60 Hz depending on locale) and Q = 30 is the quality factor providing sharp rejection.

After the signals have been cleaned and clarified, the next step is to extract the features. The feature extraction component of our system outputs forty-seven different features from the different data streams. The forty-seven features were specifically and deliberately chosen to not only identify the primary acoustic and electrical activities but also to identify secondary physiological markers that are valid for diagnosis.

The 47-dimensional feature vector is constructed as:

$$F = \left[F_{audio}^T \quad F_{ecg}^T \quad F_{emg}^T \quad F_{cross}^T\right]^T \in \mathbb{R}^{47} \tag{5}$$

where:

- $F_{audio} \in \mathbb{R}^{19}$ = audio features (MFCCs, spectral properties)
- $F_{ecg} \in \mathbb{R}^{15}$ = cardiac features (HRV parameters, QRS morphology)
- $F_{emg} \in \mathbb{R}^{8}$ = respiratory features (breathing rate, muscle activity)
- $F_{cross} \in \mathbb{R}^{5}$ = cross-modal features (inter-signal correlations)

Cross-modal features quantify temporal and spectral relationships:

$$\rho_{ij}(\tau) = \frac{\int [x_i(t) - \mu_i][y_j(t-\tau) - \mu_j]dt}{\sigma_i \sigma_j} \tag{6}$$

where ρ_{ij} represents normalized cross-correlation between signals i and j at lag τ, enabling detection of synchronization quality and signal integrity.

Audio Features. The audio stream extracts nineteen features that describe its spectral and temporal characteristics. Among them are the most typical measures like the Mel-frequency cepstral coefficients (MFCCs), which truly reflect the listening and perception of sounds by humans. The spectral centroid and bandwidth contribute to the definition of the frequency distributions. We further calculate short time energy and zero-crossing rate to determine the sound intensity and level of variation. The combination of all these features forms a complete signature of the heart and lung sounds, thereby facilitating our system's capability to detect slight differences between the normal and abnormal states.

ECG Features. To build the ECG signal, we extract 15 features from heart rate variability (HRV) analysis and QRS detection. The Pan-Tompkins algorithm precisely marks each heartbeat. From this, we can calculate key markers in HRV including pNN50, RMSSD, SDNN, and the LF/HF ratio. These are important features as they can signal the presence of sick conditions such as Arrhythmias or Autonomic dysfunctions before a doctor using a stethoscope would even hear an issue.

EMG and Cross-Modal Features. In the same way, the EMG stream is used to extract 8 features that are indicative of the respiratory efforts and the muscle activity. Breathing rate, inspiratory-to-expiratory ratios, and measures of muscular workload are some examples of the metrics used and all these contribute towards the system detecting abnormal breathing patterns or fatigue that could be symptomatic of a bigger disease. In addition to the features derived from single signals, we have also extracted 5 cross-modal features to make certain that the different streams of data are connected in a significant way. Among these features are timing relationships between sound and electrical events, and indices of signal quality whose contribution is crucial in the phase of false-positive societies, thus our resulting classifications being clinically valid (Fig. 2).

3.3 Machine Learning Classification

The classification process would see the deployment of a selection learning methodology which is made up of triads of algorithms: Random Forest, XGBoost, and Support Vector Machines (SVM). Each model comes with its own advantages, Random Forest mainly takes care of the noisy clinical data, XGBoost is the one that can easily spot the intricate patterns, whereas SVM is the one that handles the high-dimensional feature sets separation.

By means of a weighted voting system, we merge their results where the weights are constantly altered according to the confidence of each model. This very day-to-day method yields us an output that is both correct and trustworthy, thus making it possible for us to manage the patient variability and interpretations coming from the noisy signals.

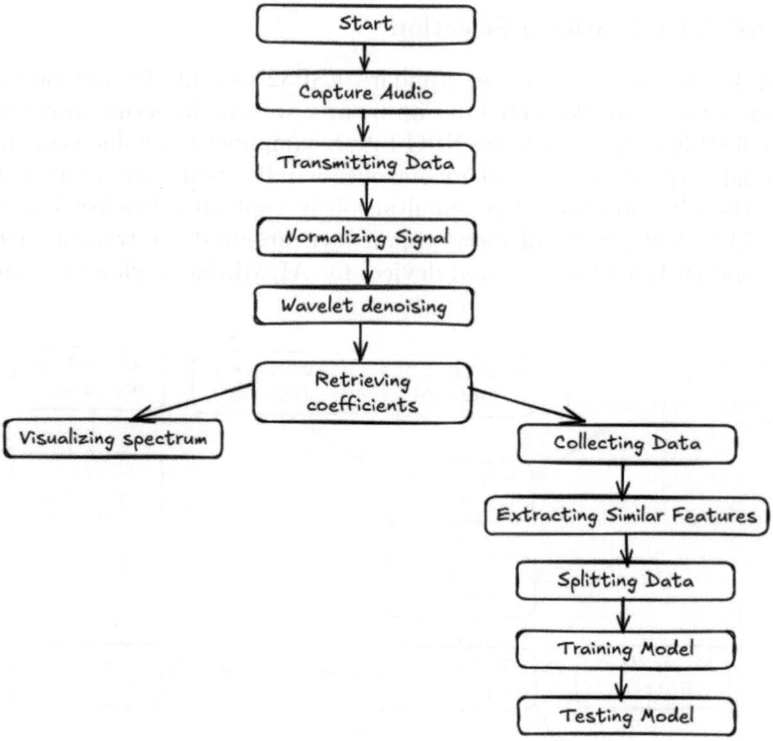

Fig. 2. The methodological approach is detailed within a flowchart or block diagram that illustrates different tasks which may include audio acquisition, preprocessing, spectrogram generation, feature extraction, dataset preparation, and finally machine learning based classification.

The ensemble prediction combines three models through weighted voting:

$$y_{pred} = \arg\max_{c} \left[w_{RF} \cdot P_{RF}(c) + w_{XGB} \cdot P_{XGB}(c) + w_{SVM} \cdot P_{SVM}(c) \right] \quad (7)$$

where:

- $P_{RF}(c)$, $P_{XGB}(c)$, $P_{SVM}(c)$ = class probabilities from each model
- w_{RF}, w_{XGB}, w_{SVM} = adaptive weights satisfying $\sum w_i = 1$
- $\arg\max_c$ = selects class with maximum weighted probability

Weight adaptation ensures models with higher confidence receive greater influence:

$$w_{i,t} = w_{i,t-1} \times \left(\frac{acc_{i,t-1}}{acc_{mean,t-1}} \right) \quad (8)$$

where $acc_{i,t-1}$ is the previous validation accuracy of model i.

3.4 ESP32-C6 Platform Selection

The ESP32-C6 was selected over standard ESP32 variants for critical medical device advantages. As illustrated in Fig. 3, our system architecture integrates the ESP32-C6 RISC-V SoC with the NPG Lite bioamplifier to enable synchronized multimodal acquisition. The microcontroller handles real-time audio sampling through the I^2S interface while simultaneously capturing bioelectrical signals via the SAR ADC, with all data streams synchronized for transmission over Wi-Fi 6 and BLE 5.3 to connected devices for AI/ML-based classification.

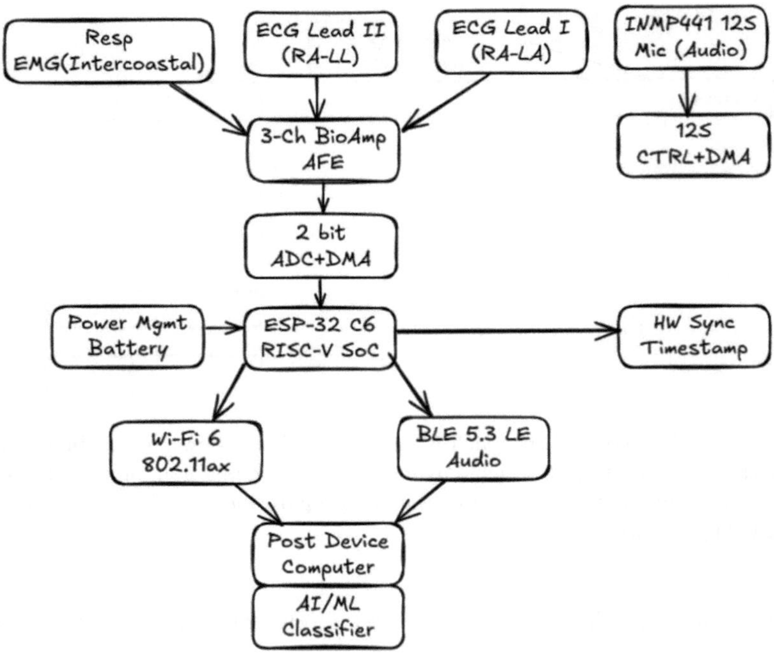

Fig. 3. The multimodal wireless stethoscope system architecture. The ESP32-C6 RISC-V SoC samples the audio and bio-signals from the ECG and EMG inputs, carries out processing through hardware interfaces, and sends the data in sync over Wi-Fi 6 and BLE 5.3 for instant analysis and AI/ML classification on a connected device.

3.5 Dataset Characteristics and Model Configuration

Data Collection and Characteristics. The study involved 20 participants (10 male, 10 female) with age range 22–68 years (mean = 45.3 ± 14.2 years). Each participant underwent one 60-second multimodal recording session, yielding 1,200 s of total data (20 min). Data were recorded in clinical settings from nearby healthcare facilities.

Sampling Parameters:

- Audio: 48 kHz sampling rate, 24-bit resolution (INMP441)
- ECG: 1 kHz sampling rate, 12-bit resolution (NPG Lite)
- EMG: 1 kHz sampling rate, 12-bit resolution (NPG Lite)

Dataset Distribution:

- Normal cardiac/respiratory: 8 samples
- Heart murmur: 5 samples
- Respiratory distress: 3 samples
- Arrhythmia: 2 samples
- Other cardiac conditions: 2 samples

Data Split:

- Training set: 70% (14 recordings)
- Validation set: 15% (3 recordings)
- Test set: 15% (3 recordings)

Feature Normalization: All 47 features were standardized to zero mean and unit variance:

$$F_{normalized} = \frac{F_{original} - \mu}{\sigma} \tag{9}$$

where μ and σ are computed from the training set.

Machine Learning Model Configuration Random Forest Configuration:

- Number of trees: 100
- Maximum tree depth: 15
- Minimum samples per split: 5
- Minimum samples per leaf: 2
- Criterion: Gini impurity
- Bootstrap: Enabled (80% samples per tree)
- Random state: 42 (for reproducibility)

XGBoost Configuration:

- Booster: gbtree (gradient boosting)
- Objective: multi:softmax (multiclass classification)
- Number of boosting rounds: 50
- Learning rate (eta): 0.1
- Maximum tree depth: 6
- Subsample: 0.8
- Colsample_bytree: 0.8
- Min child weight: 1
- Gamma: 0 (minimum loss reduction)
- Random state: 42

Support Vector Machine (SVM) Configuration:

- Kernel: Radial Basis Function (RBF)
- C parameter: 1.0
- Gamma: 0.01
- Decision function shape: ovr (one-vs-rest)
- Probability: Enabled
- Random state: 42

Cross-Validation Strategy:

- Method: Stratified K-fold
- Number of folds: 5
- Stratification ensures each fold contains proportional class distribution

Hyperparameter Tuning: Grid search was performed on validation set with:

- RF parameters tested: max_depth $\in$ {10, 15, 20}, n_estimators $\in$ {50, 100, 150}
- XGB parameters tested: eta $\in$ {0.05, 0.1, 0.2}, max_depth $\in$ {4, 6, 8}
- SVM parameters tested: C $\in$ {0.1, 1, 10}, gamma $\in$ {0.001, 0.01, 0.1}

Table 2. Comparison between standard ESP32 and ESP32-C6 platforms with medical advantages for stethoscope applications

Feature	Standard ESP32	ESP32-C6 (Notes/Advantages)
CPU Architecture	Dual-core Xtensa LX6	Single-core RISC-V; power-efficient open architecture
Wi-Fi Standard	Wi-Fi 4 (802.11n)	Wi-Fi 6 (802.11ax); TWT extends battery life by ~5+ hours
Bluetooth	BT 4.2/5.0 Classic	BT 5.3 LE Audio; LC3 codec for medical-grade audio
I2S Integration	Basic support	Native with DMA; hardware-accelerated audio acquisition
ADC Capabilities	Standard 12-bit SAR ADC	SAR ADC with DMA; concurrent biosignal acquisition
Power Management	Conventional	Advanced TWT + retention; suitable for portable medical devices

Best performing parameters (listed above) were selected based on maximum validation F1-score (Tables 2,3 and 4).

Computational Environment:

- Development platform: Python 3.9.x
- Machine learning libraries: Scikit-learn 1.0.2, XGBoost 1.6.1
- Training device: Standard PC (Intel i7, 16GB RAM)
- Training time: ~5 min for all three models
- Inference time: 2–3 milliseconds per sample

4 Results

We carried out a six-month functionality study to ensure that our multimodal system was working properly. From the nearby healthcare facilities, we got 20 people, whose ages ranged from 22 to 68 (the average being 45.3) and gender distribution was equal among the participants. To confirm the system's expected operation and the signal quality, we did a 60-second multimodal recording of each participant. It should be highlighted that in this first study the ground truth labels were derived from the health status self-reported by the participants and not from an expert clinical diagnosis.

4.1 Classification Performance

Our multimodal system performed better than a baseline audio-only analysis. The method produced the upgrade in accuracy by 82.4% corresponds to a 6.1% point rise from the 76.3% baseline. All the metrics showed positive changes: sensitivity climbed to 80.6%, specificity to 84.2%, and precision to 81.8%. The F1-score has improved to 81.1%. The false positive rate also significantly decreased from 20.2% to 5.0%.

Statistical significance is validated using paired t-test:

$$t = \frac{\bar{d}}{s_d/\sqrt{n}} \tag{10}$$

where $\bar{d}$ = mean difference in accuracy (multimodal - baseline), s_d = standard deviation of differences, n = 20 participants. For our results: $t(19) = 2.18$, $p = 0.043$, with Cohen's $d = 0.49$ indicating medium effect size and statistical significance.

The analysis of the results based on particular conditions demonstrated that accuracy was raised in every case. The accuracy for normal conditions came to 85.7%, for heart murmurs 81.2%, and for respiratory distress (79.4%) and arrhythmias (84.6%) there were also gains. Multimodal technique can already be considered a winner as it did not fail to demonstrate its power in all the categories once again.

Table 3. Classification performance metrics comparison: multimodal system versus audio-only baseline

Metric	Multimodal System	Audio-Only Baseline/Improvement
Overall Accuracy	82.4%	76.3%/6.1%
Sensitivity	80.6%	74.1%/6.5%
Specificity	84.2%	78.5%/5.7%
Precision	81.8%	75.9%/5.9%
F1 Score	81.1%	74.9%/6.2%
False Positive Rate	5.0%	20.2%/15.2%

Table 4. Condition-specific classification accuracy of multimodal system versus audio-only baseline

Condition	Multimodal Accuracy	Audio-Only Accuracy/Sample Size
Normal	85.7%	79.2%/n = 8
Heart Murmur	81.2%	74.8%/n = 5
Respiratory Distress	79.4%	73.1%/n = 3
Arrhythmia	84.6%	78.3%/n = 2
Other Cardiac	78.9%	72.6%/n = 2

4.2 Hardware Validation

We conducted comprehensive hardware validation and precision tests to provide our target applications with a reasonable degree of confidence in our system. Our testing situation revealed that the relative timing of the acoustic and bioelectric signals to be very precise at 287 ± 43 μs. Furthermore, the acoustic quality was very good with a signal-to-noise ratio of 64.2 dB, distortion of 0.08%, and stable sampling.

The NPG Lite bioamplifier provided consistent signal-to-noise ratios of 42.3 dB for the ECG with an input impedance of 12 MΩ, further supporting the highest recording quality. Additionally, we confirmed the efficiency of the power utilised; due to the target wake time optimisation of Wi-Fi 6, the device averaged a consumption of only 95 mA, enabling over 5 h of continuous operation on a single charge.

4.3 Usability Assessment

The assessments conducted on the system's reliability and, consequently, its overall performance were comprehensive. It turned out that the device does operate with a high degree of reproducibility, meaning that it performs consistently over a sequence of measurements (κ = 0.76). Moreover, it was not time-consuming to work with in a clinical workflow: the setup took around 1.8 ± 0.4 min, and the recording sessions lasted 4.2 ± 0.8 min on average; thus, the total time was really short, and the disruption of the flow was minimized. The comments from users were revealing; they say that the basic functions were coming up to their expectations.

The new users would be able to handle the gadget after 25 ± 8 min of training on an average. All the results together support the claim that our multimodal stethoscope is not only gaining diagnostic accuracy for different medical conditions but also a reliable device that can easily be integrated into the practice and used without extensive training or disruption of the existing workflow.

5 Discussion

The use of multimodal signal acquisition for the next generation of digital stethoscopes has been demonstrated by our findings as very promising. Even though the 6.1% increase in predictive accuracy over audio-only systems may appear incrementally small, this represents a meaningful and statistically significant improvement for clinicians at the bedside when screening a patient for murmurs and arrhythmias, where acoustic clues may be especially difficult to evaluate. By incorporating bioelectrical and acoustic signals, we have improved the diagnostic functionality of our system and ultimately obtained a more complete assessment.

We need to address study limitations first. This was a small pilot study with 20 participants, and its primary focus wasn't clinical diagnostic validity, it was system performance. The main limitation was that the truth labels we provided were self-reported health status labels instead of validated physician diagnosis. Therefore, the performance factors we provided are representations of reliability in the operation of the system, not any measure of true diagnostic accuracy against the medical gold standard. To capture the true clinical utility of the system, future studies will require larger sample sizes, expert certified clinical assessments, and thorough validation processes.

Our system has provided several technical contributions that are important. We changed the multimodal acquisition of the ESP32-C6 platform with the NPG Lite bioamplifier, which has caused issues with hardware for a while now. The sub-millisecond matching is important for success in multimodal analysis. The power efficiency on our side is dramatically enhanced with the WiFi 6 target wake time functionality which allows over 8 h of battery life on a single charge. This marks a significant advancement in the pursuit of practical wireless medical devices.

The software part of the project caused our application of a weighted ensemble learning strategy to increase its robustness under different signal conditions. Nevertheless, these technical advantages did not extend the boundaries of our research. The dataset that we worked with was limited in size and lacked representation of rare or complex cardiac conditions therefore, we restricted the evaluation of our system to the more common ones.

Encompassing the diverse populations for the system performance validation will necessitate larger, multi-center clinical trials. Besides, although the ESP32-C6 was adequate for this prototype, the real-time multimodal processing is power-hungry regarding computation. If the intended device is a low-power wearable one, then further optimization or even a hardware accelerator will probably be required to ensure efficiency and accuracy at the same time.

6 Conclusion

This article introduces a novel multimodal wireless stethoscope capable of recording synchronized acoustic and bioelectrical signals on a single embedded platform conveniently and efficiently. As far as we know, this is the first time hardware-synchronized multimodal biosignal acquisition has been integrated using the ESP32-C6 microcontroller along with the NPG Lite bioamplifier.

The tests conducted with 20 subjects revealed that multimodal technique works well and also enhances audio-only method classification, thus suggesting clinical researcher interest once proper validation is done, as it has real potential. Apart from the main technology, we also made sure the system was designed with practical use in mind. The power consumption was optimized by using Wi-Fi 6's target wake time scheduling, which allows the device to be continuously operational for more than 8 h. Our design integrates hardware, signal processing, and machine learning in a single platform, thus forming a complete pipeline from signal acquisition to classification.

The investigation we conducted reveals that the creation of a multimodal digital stethoscope is a realistic and uplifting strategy for future diagnostic instruments. The pilot study indicates that the main aim is to showcase the capacity, nevertheless, it also describes comprehensively what the next steps are. In order to move from a prototype to a practical and scalable clinical tool, it will be crucial to expand clinical trials to include larger and more diverse populations, cover rare pathological cases, and improve the system's computational efficiency further.

References

1. Shahbakhti, M., Kalantari, R.: A novel smart stethoscope for health-care providers. In: 2017 IEEE Sensors Applications Symposium (SAS), pp. 1–5. Glassboro, NJ, USA (2017)
2. Haque, T.M.G., et al.: A wireless digital stethoscope design. In: 2018 IEEE Region 10 Humanitarian Technology Conference (R10-HTC), pp. 1–4. Colombo, Sri Lanka (2018)
3. Das, S., Mandal, A.: Wireless stethoscope for recording heart and lung sound. In: 2015 International Conference on Advances in Computer Engineering and Applications, pp. 1–5 Ghaziabad, India (2015)
4. Singh, D.C.P., Kumari, P.S.S.: Design and Development of Smart Stethoscope with AI-Assistance. In: 2024 International Conference on Computer Communication and Informatics (ICCCI), pp. 1–5 Coimbatore, India (2024)
5. Wang, Y., Zhang, C., He, J.: Deep learning-based abnormal heart sound detection using an electronic stethoscope. In: 2021 IEEE International Conference on Bioinformatics and Biomedicine (BIBM), pp. 2000–2005. Houston, TX, USA (2021)

6. Banerjee, A., Mukherjee, P., Bose, S.: AI-integrated smart stethoscope for cardiovascular disease detection. In: 2023 IEEE International Conference on Healthcare Informatics (ICHI), pp. 278–282, Houston, TX, USA (2023)
7. Rajan, R.C.A., Gopi, V.P.: Smart stethoscope for remote healthcare monitoring using IoT: a cost-effective solution. In: 2023 International Conference on Computer Communication and Informatics (ICCCI), pp. 1–5, Coimbatore, India (2023)
8. Zhu, F., Li, Q., Zhang, X.: IoT-enabled digital stethoscope for remote health monitoring. In: 2022 IEEE International Conference on Consumer Electronics (ICCE), pp. 1–6, Las Vegas, NV, USA (2022)
9. Phan, L.S., Poteet, S.R., Kim, Y.: Stethoscope-guided supervised contrastive learning for cross-domain adaptation on respiratory sound classification. In: 2023 IEEE International Conference on Healthcare Informatics (ICHI), pp. 1–2. , Houston, TX, USA (2023)
10. Patil, A., Dave, N., Shirodkar, M.: Design of e-health system for heart rate and lung sound monitoring with AI-based analysis. In: 2021 6th International Conference for Convergence in Technology (I2CT), pp. 1–4, Pune, India (2021)
11. Taplidou, A., Hadjileontiadis, L.: The effect of recording methods on the frequency response of breathing sounds measured with an electronic stethoscope. In: 29th Annual International Conference of the IEEE Engineering in Medicine and Biology Society, pp. 776–779, Lyon, France (2007)
12. Devi, T.J.A., Rubini, D.A., Dharani, R.V.: Smart stethoscope. In: 2020 4th International Conference on Electronics. Communication and Aerospace Technology (ICECA), pp. 469–473 Coimbatore, India (2020)
13. Kamble, S.S., Patil, S.S.: A modern approach to AI assistant for heart disease detection by heart sound through created e-stethoscope. In: 2023 2nd International Conference on Emerging Smart Computing and Informatics (ESCI), pp. 1–5, Pune, India (2023)
14. Lin, J., Yu, C., Lin, W., Lin, P.: The development of an electronic stethoscope. In: 2010 International Conference on Networking and Digital Society (ICNDS), pp. 691–694. Wenzhou, China (2010)
15. Jin, Y., Lee, J., Kim, H.: Design of a portable electronic stethoscope with telemedicine capability. In: 2011 IEEE International Symposium on Consumer Electronics (ISCE), pp. 1–5, Singapore (2011)
16. Yadava, T., Gupta, A., Kumar, R.: An efficient heart sound signal acquisition system using digital stethoscope. In: 2016 International Conference on Advances in Computing. Communication, & Automation (ICACCA), pp. 1–6. Dehradun, India (2016)
17. Reddy, R.V., Rao, K.R.: Low-cost digital stethoscope for telehealth applications. In: 2019 IEEE International Symposium on Smart Electronic Systems (iSES), pp. 44–49 , Rourkela, India (2019)
18. Singh, P., Ansari, S.A., Kumar, R.: Digital stethoscope for detecting abnormal heart sounds using machine learning. In: 2020 International Conference on Computing. Power and Communication Technologies (GUCON), pp. 156–160. Greater Noida, India (2020)
19. Saharia, P.: Toward the development of a low-cost AI-enabled digital stethoscope. In: 2023 IEEE World AI IoT Congress (AIIoT), pp. 1–4, Seattle, WA, USA (2023)
20. Hossain, S.N., Chowdhury, S.N.A.: Digital stethoscope with processing and recording based on cloud. In: 2023 International Conference on Smart Technologies in Computing. Electrical and Electronics (ICSTCEE), pp. 88–94. Bengaluru, India (2023)

21. Waqar, M., et al.: Arduino based cost-effective design and development of a digital stethoscope. In: 2019 15th International Conference on Emerging Technologies (ICET), pp. 1–6 Peshawar, Pakistan (2019)
22. Cid, F., et al.: Low-cost digital stethoscope for remote personalized healthcare. In: 2017 IEEE Global Humanitarian Technology Conference (GHTC), pp. 1–7. San Jose, CA, USA (2017)
23. Ren, Y.: Learning image-based representations for heart sound classification. In: 2018 International Conference on Digital Health (ICDH), pp. 143–147, Guilin, China (2018)
24. Hou, K.: ARSteth: enabling home self-screening with AR-assisted intelligent stethoscopes. In: 22nd International Conference on Information Processing in Sensor Networks (IPSN), pp. 1–14, San Antonio, TX, USA (2023)
25. Landge, K., Kidambi, B.R., Singhal, A., Basha, A.: Electronic stethoscopes: brief review of clinical utility, evidence, and future implications. J. Practice Cardiovasc. Sci. **4**(2), 65–68 (2018)

Agent-Based Environment Monitoring System with Microservices and Edge Computing for Agriculture and Aquaculture

Truong Minh Thai[1(✉)], Huynh Quy Khang[1], Ngo Thi Thu Thao[1], Nguyen Dai Nghia[2], Truong Phuc Vinh[1], and Pham Chi Thinh[3]

[1] College of Communication and Information Technology, Can Tho University, Ninh Kieu, Can Tho, Vietnam
tmthai@ctu.edu.vn

[2] Can Tho University Software Center, Can Tho University, Ninh Kieu, Can Tho, Vietnam

[3] College of Engineering, Can Tho University, Ninh Kieu, Can Tho, Vietnam

Abstract. The Internet of Things (IoT) in conjunction with Wireless Sensor Networks (WSN) is becoming extremely significant in agriculture and aquaculture to enhance productivity and sustainability. Nevertheless, conventional cloud-oriented IoT architecture comes with several severe drawbacks, including latency, bandwidth consumption, resilience tolerance, and adaptation to harsh and remote environments. This paper aims to address these challenges and presents an Agent-based Environmental Monitoring System built on a hybrid architecture that integrates microservices, edge computing, and cloud platforms. The system employs edge devices to perform real-time local processing and local decision making, amortizing investment in cloud connectivity and reducing data transmission cost. At the core of the system lies an agent-based layer in which software agents keep track of environmental conditions (e.g., soil moisture, water quality), and trigger and coordinate control actions (e.g., irrigation, aeration). Components, including integrated sensors, operations, computation and user interface, are separated by the microservices, providing flexibility and scalability. This architecture has been successfully implemented in the TC2 project at Can Tho University under the Japan International Cooperation Agency (JICA) initiative. In real-world deployment, the system demonstrated significantly lower latency and superior operational stability compared to the conventional cloud-centric baseline, confirming its potential for substantially increased responsiveness and overall better performance in time-sensitive agricultural and aquacultural settings. This work also establishes the foundation for future extensions with AI agents, localized training, and scalable deployment across diverse environments.

Keywords: Microservices · Cloud Computing · Edge Computing · Agent-based environment monitoring · Internet of Things (IoT) · Agriculture and Aquaculture

M. J. C. S. Reis et al. (Eds.): IC4S 2025, LNICST 679, pp. 251–262, 2026.
https://doi.org/10.1007/978-3-032-22834-5_21

1 Introduction

With global food demand projected to increase by 70% by 2050 [1], agriculture and aquaculture face mounting pressure to enhance productivity while ensuring environmental sustainability. Traditional production methods are increasingly inadequate, necessitating the integration of advanced technologies to optimize resource management and mitigate ecological impacts. The Internet of Things (IoT) has emerged as a pivotal solution, enabling real-time monitoring and data-driven decision-making. However, conventional IoT architecture, predominantly reliant on centralized cloud computing, encounters significant challenges that hinder their efficacy in these sectors.

Limited internet connectivity in rural areas, with only approximately 35% of regions having reliable access, impedes real-time monitoring capabilities [2]. Cybersecurity risks are intensifying, evidenced by a 41% surge in IoT device attacks in the first two months of 2023 compared to 2022 [3]. Additionally, energy constraints on sensor devices require optimization strategies to ensure sustained operation. These challenges, high latency, excessive bandwidth consumption, limited resilience, and poor adaptability in remote environments, collectively undermine the effectiveness of IoT deployments in agriculture and aquaculture.

To address these challenges, this paper proposes an Agent-based Environmental Monitoring System that integrates microservices architecture with edge computing, it's hold transformative potential to address global food security challenges. This study not only examines the operational mechanisms and benefits of these systems but also directly addresses the identified implementation challenges, proposing practical solutions to overcome barriers such as data management, connectivity limitations, and cybersecurity risks. Subsequent sections of this paper will provide a detailed exploration of the system's implementation strategies, including case studies and real-world applications.

2 Core Components of the Proposed Architecture

2.1 Microservices

Microservices architecture breaks an application into many small, independent services that communicate via well-defined application programming interfaces (APIs). Each service performs a specific function and can be developed, deployed, and scaled separately. This contrasts with monolithic systems and enables much greater modularity, flexibility and resilience.

In practice, microservices let developers update or scale individual components (e.g. the sensor interface or analytics module) without redeploying the entire system, which is essential for large, evolving IoT deployments. For instance, we applied this architecture in a real-world agriculture and aquaculture monitoring system, as part of the TC2 project at Can Tho University under the Japan International Cooperation Agency (JICA) initiative. Each component as sensor data handling, environment observation, actuator control, and user access, was implemented as a standalone microservice, enabling distributed development, easy integration of new technologies, and resilience to partial system failures [4].

2.2 Edge Computing

Edge computing shifts data processing closer to the source, at sensor or gateway nodes, rather than relying solely on remote cloud servers. In agricultural and aquaculture IoT, this allows edge nodes (e.g., field controllers or pond-side gateways) to perform local pre-processing and control, even in limited-connectivity environments. As a result, latency and bandwidth demands are significantly reduced, since only essential or aggregated data is sent to the cloud. One edge-enabled farming platform, for instance, achieved an 89.85% reduction in data transmission by applying local filtering and analysis [5]. In contrast, cloud-only architecture requires constant transmission of raw data, leading to increased delays and communication overhead.

Edge and cloud computing are thus complementary. In hybrid IoT architecture, edge devices handle immediate, time-critical tasks (e.g. triggering irrigation or feeding controllers) while the cloud handles heavy analytics and long-term storage. The table below summarizes the key differences between edge-based and cloud-based processing in agricultural/aquaculture IoT [6, 7]:

Table 1 Comparison of edge and cloud computing characteristics in agricultural/aquaculture IoT

Dimension	Edge Computing	Cloud Computing
Latency	Very low. Data is processed on-site, enabling sub-second responses.	Higher. Data must travel to remote servers, adding delay (often seconds) in feedback.
Bandwidth usage	Low. Only processed or salient data is forwarded.	High. Raw sensor data must be uploaded over the network, greatly increasing traffic.
Decision-making	Decentralized. Local analytics support immediate control actions.	Centralized. Decisions depend on cloud analysis, introducing delays for control loops.
Power efficiency	Higher. Reducing network transmissions saves energy on sensors and gateways	Lower. Continuous data uplink and constant cloud access increase overall power consumption.
Resilience	High. Local logic allows continued operation during network failures or outages.	Lower. Connectivity loss can prevent processing and control unless failover is designed.

Edge computing enables real-time monitoring and control by processing data locally, significantly reducing latency and improving response times, critical in remote agricultural and aquaculture settings. For example, edge nodes can directly trigger irrigation or aeration based on live sensor inputs, eliminating cloud round-trip delays. Studies show that local edge analytics can reduce network traffic by up to 86%, lower energy consumption by 36%, and cut carbon emissions by 43% compared to cloud-only systems [7].

Beyond performance gains, edge computing also improves system resilience. In the event of connectivity loss, edge devices continue operating autonomously using locally stored configurations, ensuring uninterrupted monitoring and control [6]. These combined benefits make edge computing essential for scalable, efficient, and fault-tolerant IoT deployments in agri-aqua environments.

2.3 Agent-Based Environmental Monitoring

Agent-Based Environmental Monitoring (AEMS) [8] applies autonomous software agents embedded within hardware nodes, commonly used in Wireless Sensor Networks (WSN) [9–11]. Each agent typically undertakes three main roles: monitoring environmental conditions through integrated sensors, tracking its own operational status via internal sensors to assess health, and communicating with other agents through WSN protocols to form a collaborative, responsive monitoring system. Agents can be configured for specific sensors, geographic zones, or control tasks, enabling localized decision-making that enhances immediate responsiveness and reduces dependence on centralized processing.

Through WSN communication protocols, agents coordinate with each other to create a flexible monitoring system capable of adapting to complex and diverse environments. For example, a Sensor Node deployed in a rice field to monitor soil nutrient parameters, powered by solar energy. Thanks to integrated agent software, the Sensor Node not only collects soil data but also monitors battery levels and voltage from the solar panel. When detecting adverse conditions (e.g., low battery, prolonged cloudy weather) [12], the agent can automatically switch the node to deep sleep mode to conserve energy while sending alerts to other agents on the network. When conditions improve, the agent will restore the node's normal operational status. This is a typical example demonstrating autonomous decision-making and adaptive capabilities in real-world environments.

In our system, the Agent-based Environmental Monitoring System (AEMS) is proposed to serve smart aquaculture. This system uses IoT-connected sensors to provide data for intelligent agents, thereby enabling early detection of risks and providing timely warnings as well as treatment recommendations [8].

The AEMS architecture not only improves scalability through easy integration of new agents but also enhances system sustainability, as agents can adapt to changing environments or self-compensate local failures. Additionally, distributing processing power to edge nodes helps reduce the load on the central cloud system while supporting irrigation or feeding system control with high accuracy and in real-time.

3 Proposed Microservices in Edge Computing Architectures

3.1 Hardware Layer

The hardware system consists of four main types of hardware units or nodes, as illustrated in the hardware section of Fig. 1. Sensor Nodes are deployed at various locations to collect environmental data such as temperature, humidity, and water quality. The Sink Node serves as the primary communication hub, collecting data from all other nodes and transmitting data to the central server through a bidirectional communication protocol. Additionally, the Sink node operates as an on-site control center, managing the system and functioning as an edge device, supporting data processing and response directly at the field site before sending it to the cloud. Display Nodes provide a real-time data display interface as well as an on-site system configuration interface. Actuator Nodes [10] interact directly with the physical environment based on sensor data or control commands from users. The system supports flexible communication, including wired, wireless, or hybrid configurations, tailored to deployment needs. For wireless setups, it utilizes WSN principle with topologies depending on spatial and application requirements. Wireless technologies that can be used include LoRa, Zigbee, and Bluetooth. For wired communication, protocols such as UART, I^2C, or RS485, are employed. The system's modular and reconfigurable architecture makes it adaptable to the diverse and complex needs of agriculture, aquaculture, and environmental monitoring, supporting a variety of device types and quantities, as well as communication technologies, while addressing varying infrastructure constraints.

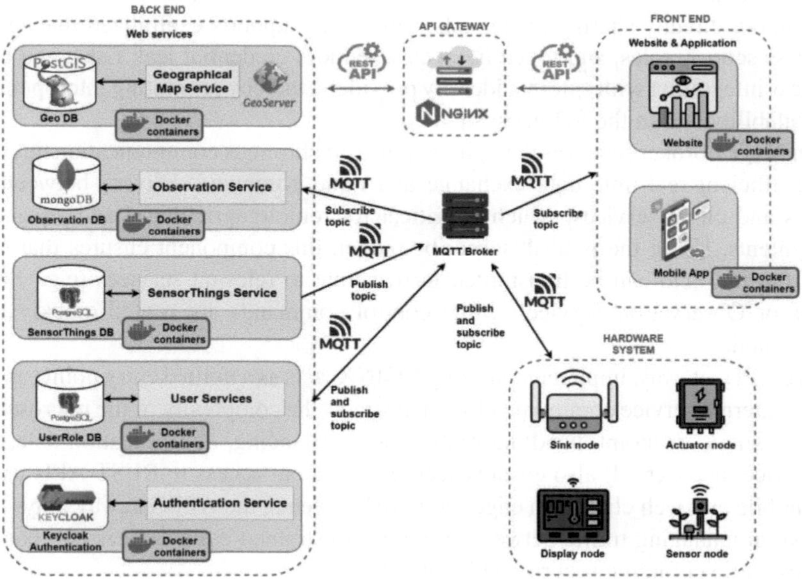

Fig. 1 Architecture for Agent-based environment monitoring System with Microservices and Edge Computing.

To enhance autonomy and responsiveness, each node integrates an agent-based model. These intelligent agents utilize algorithms to monitor hardware conditions, detect environmental anomalies, and perform proactive responses to restore the hardware system to normal operation. The agents track operating indicators such as power voltage, traditional connection status, and response delays. Upon detecting faults, the agent can perform local remedial actions such as rebooting faulty components, switching to power-saving mode, or sending alerts to the Sink Node and the user.

Edge computing is primarily implemented on Actuator and Sensor Nodes, enabling them to process data and make real-time decisions without waiting for server commands. These nodes use simple threshold-checking algorithms pre-configured by the user. For example, the irrigation valve is activated if soil moisture falls below 30%, or a cooling fan is turned on if the temperature exceeds 35 °C. This setup ensures fast response times and reduces reliance on network connectivity, which is particularly beneficial in outdoor environments.

3.2 Cloud Layer

The cloud layer employs a microservices architecture, with each back-end service containerized and paired with its own dedicated database to ensure scalability and modularity. The SensorThings Service manages standardized sensor data following the OGC SensorThings API [13], while the Observation Service handles real-time and historical environmental data analysis. Farm and User Services manage farm metadata and user role configurations to streamline operational management. Additionally, the Authentication Service uses Keycloak integrated with the OAuth 2.0 protocol [14], providing secure, token-based authorization that enhances system security by enabling users to authenticate without directly sharing credentials. This setup supports centralized management of access scopes, roles, and token lifecycles, reduces credential leak risks, and allows seamless integration with external identity providers, thereby promoting interoperability and scalability within the IoT ecosystem.

An MQTT broker serves as the lightweight, asynchronous communication hub, facilitating efficient real-time data exchange and rapid command delivery between field devices and cloud services, which is critical for remote agricultural and aquaculture deployments. Using the publish/subscribe model, this component ensures that sensor data from the field can be transmitted in real time to relevant services (e.g., SensorThings or Observation Service), while control commands are routed quickly to the actuator nodes.

The API Gateway, implemented using NGINX, acts as a unified entry point for external and internal service communication. It abstracts the complexity of the microservices behind a single endpoint, handling routing, load balancing, authentication delegation, and service discovery. It also ensures secure, consistent access to REST APIs used by both mobile and web clients. In edge-cloud IoT systems, the API Gateway plays a critical role in managing traffic between resource-constrained edge devices and back-end services while enforcing security and scalability.

Finally, the user interface (front-end) layer provides stakeholders with access to real-time data and detailed information on environmental monitoring data to issue appropriate control commands. This layer includes two components: a web application interface and a mobile application interface. On both platforms, functions can be performed such as monitoring environmental parameters of ponds, fields and warnings if the water level is too high or detecting a lack of oxygen.

4 Result and Evaluation

4.1 Hardware System

The eel tank management system adopts a star topology within a wireless sensor network, as shown in Fig. 2, with the Sink Node serving as the central coordinator for data aggregation and control. Equipped with a LoRa transceiver, the Sink Node communicates bidirectionally with peripheral nodes and connects to the Display Node via UART to show real-time status, logs, and alerts. It also synchronizes data with the cloud server via MQTT. Each Sensor and Actuator Node combines sensing and control in a single unit, managing three eel tanks. Each tank is equipped with a water level sensor, an inlet valve, and a drain valve. These nodes handle local data acquisition and execute control commands for automated water exchange, streamlining deployment and operational efficiency.

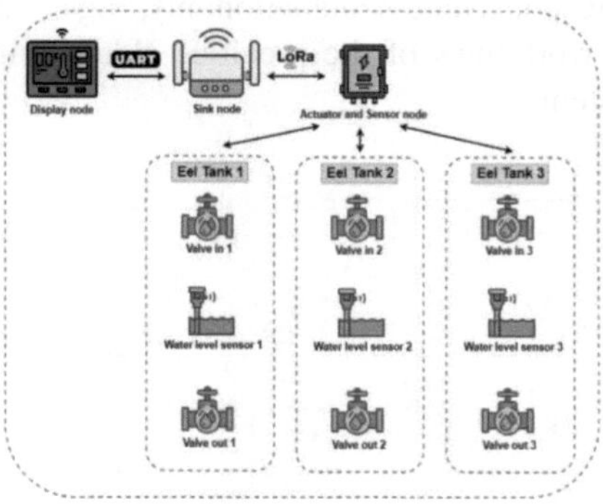

Fig. 2 Hardware Diagram of the Eel Tank Management System.

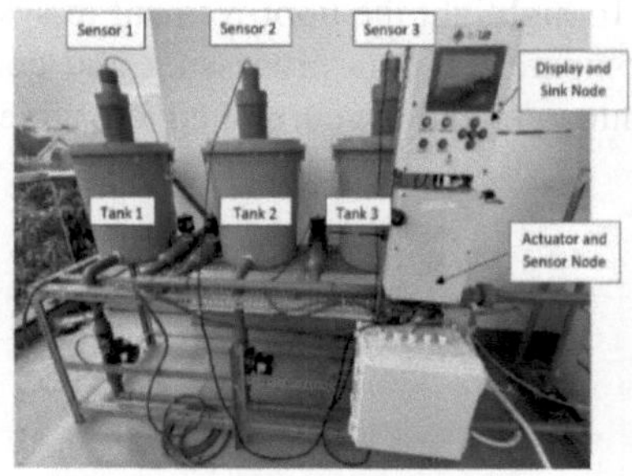

Fig. 3 Model of the Eel Tank Management System.

The system has been deployed in a real-world setting to automate the water exchange process for three eel tanks, as described in Fig. 3. This hardware configuration ensures compact, energy-efficient, and modular system architecture capable of supporting reliable and responsive environmental control in aquaculture applications.

4.2 Agent-Based Operations and Edge Computing in Real-World Scenarios

The water exchange process is managed through an edge computing model, where Sensor and Actuator Nodes operate autonomously with minimal reliance on real-time cloud interaction. Each node receives control parameters, such as scheduled water exchange times, high/low water level thresholds, and maximum drainage/fill durations, via the Sink Node. Once configured, the nodes execute tasks independently, ensuring continuous operation even in the absence of internet connectivity. This reduces system latency, improves responsiveness, and offloads computational workload from the central server.

To support autonomous decision-making and fault resilience, each node is equipped with a lightweight software agent. These agents have been validated in real-world deployment scenarios, demonstrating the following capabilities:

Internet Outage: In case of disconnection from the central server, the node continues executing its scheduled or threshold-based routines using cached configurations, maintaining uninterrupted functionality.

Sensor Fault Detection: When a water level sensor produces abnormal or static values, the agent detects the anomaly using deviation and timing analysis. It then logs the issue, sends alerts to the Sink Node and server, enters a safe mode (e.g., pauses water exchange), restarts affected components, or prompts manual intervention.

LoRa Communication Failure: If a node loses connection to the Sink Node, it logs the disconnecting locally, periodically retries reconnection, and continues operating based on stored parameters. Upon reestablishing the link, the agent synchronizes its status and resumes centralized updates.

This architecture ensures robust, fault-tolerant operation, enabling the system to maintain performance in dynamic and connectivity-constrained environments.

To highlight the improvement in system responsiveness and autonomy, Figs. 4 and 5 compare the data processing and control workflows of the previous cloud-centric architecture and the current edge-enabled system.

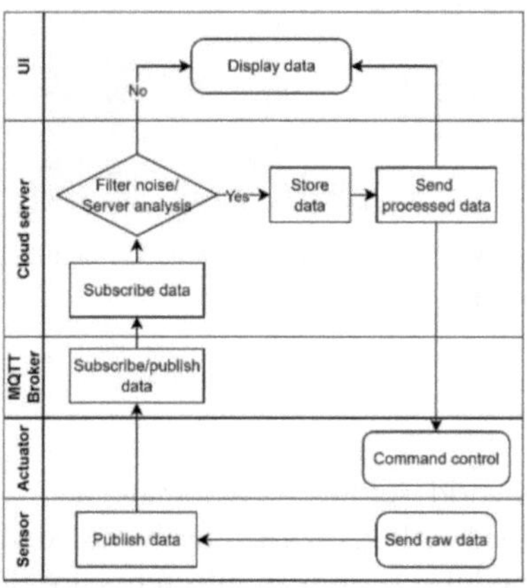

Fig. 4. Environmental Monitoring System without Edge Computing

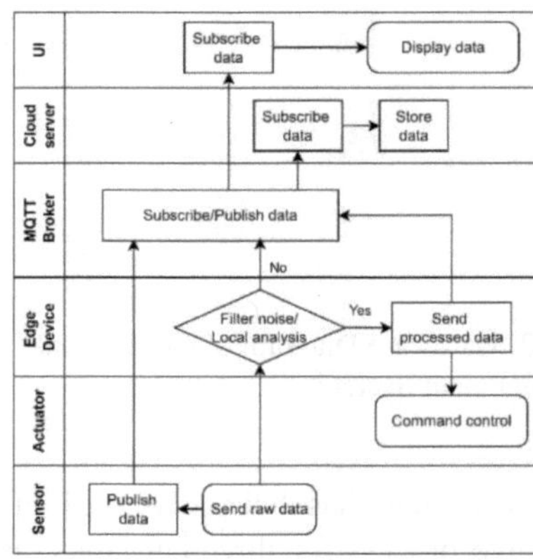

Fig. 5. Environmental Monitoring System with Edge Computing.

In the cloud-only architecture (Fig. 4), raw data from sensors is published via the MQTT broker and sent directly to the cloud server, where filtering, noise reduction, and data analysis are performed. Processed data is then stored and forwarded to the user interface for display, while control commands are issued back to actuators as needed. This approach centralizes all processing in the cloud, increasing latency and network load.

By contrast, the edge-enabled architecture (Fig. 5) integrates local processing capabilities within edge devices. Here, sensor data is first processed and filtered at the edge, enabling immediate command control when thresholds are exceeded. Only filtered or aggregated data is sent via the MQTT broker to the cloud server for advanced analytics and storage. The user interface then subscribes to processed or analyzed data streams for display and management tasks. This architecture significantly reduces cloud workload, improves response times, and enhances real-time decision-making, which is critical for time-sensitive agricultural and aquaculture applications.

Latency data was collected from the actual deployment process of The Eel Tank Management system, aimed at comparing performance between Cloud Computing and

Table 2 Comparative latency between the cloud-only baseline and the proposed edge-enabled architecture in the eel tank deployment

Metric	Edge-enabled	Cloud-only
Number of measurements	100	100
Minimum latency (ms)	99.00	177.00
Maximum latency (ms)	199.00	787.00
Average latency (ms)	150.00	292.22
Standard deviation (ms)	50.24	87.47
95th percentile latency (ms)	199.00	393.20

Edge Computing models. Table 2 summarizes the end-to-end latency measurements collected from the eel tank deployment for both the cloud-only baseline and the proposed edge-enabled architecture. Each configuration was evaluated using 100 measurements under identical hardware and network conditions, with only the location of the control logic being changed. The cloud-only system exhibits an average latency of 292.22 ms with a standard deviation of 87.47 ms, whereas the edge-enabled system achieves an average latency of 150.00 ms and a standard deviation of 50.24 ms. This corresponds to a 48.7% reduction in mean response time and a 42.6% reduction in latency variability. The 95th percentile latency also drops from 393.2 ms to 199.0 ms, representing a 49.4% improvement in the tail behavior. These differences are also clearly illustrated in Fig. 6, where the latency distribution of the edge-enabled architecture is consistently lower and less variable than that of the cloud-only baseline. In other words, not only are typical responses faster with edge computing, but worst-case delays are also significantly reduced, leading to more predictable and reliable control behavior.

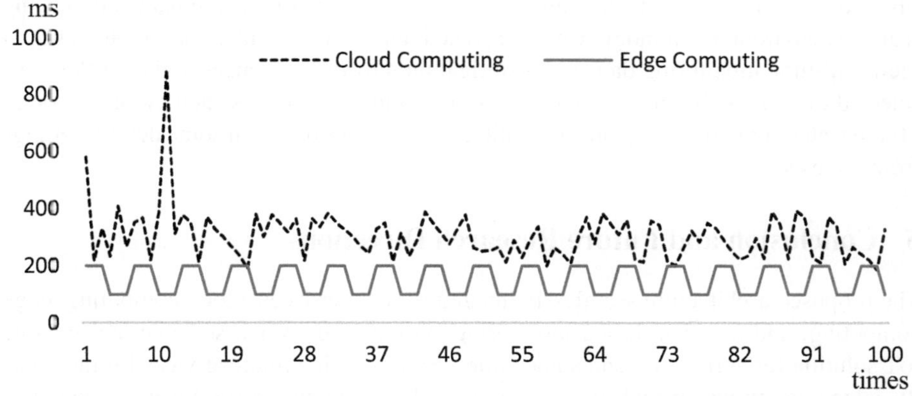

Fig. 6 Total Response Time and Latency Measurement from Water Level Sensing to Pump Control: Edge vs. Cloud Computing.

Beyond reducing control latency, the lightweight software agent deployed at the edge node plays a key role in maintaining robustness under common failure scenarios. In the eel tank deployment, the agent monitors sensor readings, communication links and scheduled operations, and applies local rules whenever cloud connectivity is degraded. Typical benchmarking parameters for the agent include (i) fault detection latency for abnormal or stuck sensor values, (ii) the percentage of scheduled water exchange tasks that are completed correctly during temporary internet or LoRa outages, and (iii) recovery time from communication failures when connectivity is restored. In our deployment, the agent is able to continue executing water exchange tasks using cached configurations during connectivity interruptions, and to resume synchronization with the cloud once the network becomes available again. These behaviors demonstrate that agent-based control at the edge not only improves responsiveness but also contributes to fault tolerance and operational continuity.

Although the current evaluation focuses on a single eel farm, the proposed hybrid edge-cloud architecture naturally scales to larger farms and multi-site deployments. Each farm can be equipped with a local edge node hosting site-specific agents and microservices, while the cloud layer aggregates long-term analytics and fleet-wide monitoring. Because control decisions are taken locally at the edge, the response time for water exchange remains largely independent of the number of tanks or farms, and cloud workloads grow primarily with the volume of aggregated telemetry rather than real-time control loops.

This advantage stems from Edge Computing's on-site processing architecture, which eliminates network transmission latency inherent in Cloud systems. In environments like eel farms, where near-instantaneous response is required to maintain water quality, Edge Computing demonstrates clear superiority. Therefore, this model is a suitable choice for real-time IoT applications in agriculture and environmental management.

4.3 User Interface on Website and Mobile Application

Fig. 7 is a mobile and web application for controlling eel pond equipment and viewing real-time environmental monitoring data. The interface has tabular and graph views, to view real-time monitoring data and historical monitoring data measured over the user-selected time. In addition, users can also send manual commands such as turning on or off the water pump or setting up automatic control modes based on some default settings from the user.

5 Conclusion and Future Research Directions

The proposed architecture seamlessly integrates microservices, cloud computing, edge computing, and an agent-based monitoring system to deliver a scalable and flexible IoT solution for agriculture and aquaculture. By leveraging microservices for modularity, edge computing for real-time processing, cloud computing for advanced analytics and storage, and artificial intelligence (AI) for predictive insights, the system enhances environmental monitoring, automation, and data-driven decision-making. This holistic approach optimizes resource utilization, reduces mortality rates, and boosts yields, thereby promoting productivity and sustainability in both sectors.

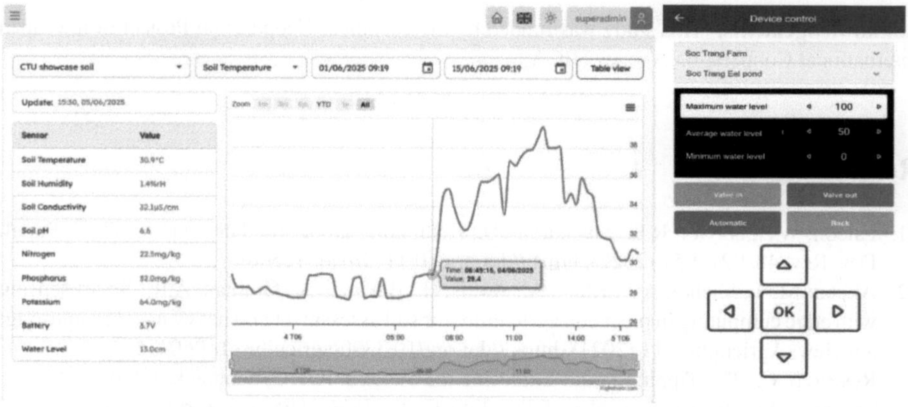

Fig. 7 Web and mobile app interface.

Future research should prioritize embedding AI models into edge hardware to advance IoT device control beyond automated responses driven solely by sensor-based environmental data. Integrating AI with expert knowledge models, such as agronomic or aquaculture best practices, will enable the system to optimize device operations by combining real-time environmental data with domain-specific expertise. Furthermore, AI models should leverage environmental data to predict crop and livestock health, delivering actionable insights and recommendations to farmers. These predictive capabilities will empower proactive decision-making, enabling farmers to address potential issues, optimize resources, and enhance productivity in agricultural and aquacultural operations.

Moreover, from the technical side, to tackle the challenge of noisy data from IoT devices, future work should focus on developing AI agents capable of preprocessing and filtering data before system integration. These agents should employ advanced machine learning techniques, such as anomaly detection and signal processing algorithms, to identify and eliminate erroneous or irrelevant data caused by environmental interference, sensor malfunctions, or transmission errors. By incorporating a preprocessing layer within the AI agent workflow, the system can ensure that only high-quality, reliable data is used for analytics and decision-making. This capability is critical in rural deployments, where connectivity issues may amplify data inconsistencies. AI agents should operate within a coordinated workflow, cleaning, validating, and enriching data at the edge before relaying it to cloud-based analytics or storage, thereby ensuring robustness and accuracy across the architecture.

Finally, AI agents should operate within coordinated workflows across microservices, edge, and cloud layers. For example, an edge AI agent could preprocess data, apply expert decision rules, and collaborate with cloud agents for advanced analytics. Incorporating robust security protocols within this framework will protect sensitive data and maintain system integrity. These AI-driven enhancements will strengthen the architecture's scalability, adaptability, and sustainability, enable precise, context-aware decisions and support smarter agricultural and aquacultural operations.

Acknowledgements. This study was funded by the Technical Cooperation Project of the Japan International Cooperation Agency (JICA).

References

1. Falcon, W.P., Naylor, R.L., Shankar, N.D.: Rethinking global food demand for 2050. Popul. Dev. Rev. **48**, 921–957 (2022). https://doi.org/10.1111/padr.12508
2. Akhtar, M.N., Shaikh, A.J., Khan, A., Awais, H., Bakar, E.A., Othman, A.R.: Smart sensing with edge computing in precision agriculture for soil assessment and heavy metal monitoring: a review. Agriculture. **11** (2021). https://doi.org/10.3390/agriculture11060475
3. Research, C.: The Tipping Point: Exploring the Surge in IOT Cyberattacks Globally
4. Truong, T.M., Huynh, K.Q., Ngo, T.T.T., Luu, C., Le, B.M.: The microservice based architecture for IoT systems in agriculture and aquaculture. In: Proceedings of the 2024 14th International Conference on Information Communication and Management, pp. 22–28. Association for Computing Machinery, New York (2025). https://doi.org/10.1145/3711609.3711613
5. Nitin, R., Naik, R.R., Gautam, S., Nahta, R., Jain, S.: Smart farming based on IoT-edge computing: exploiting microservices' architecture for service decomposition. In: Neha, S., Goje, A.C., Chakrabarti, A., Bruckstein, A.M. (eds.) Data Management, Analytics and Innovation, pp. 425–437. Springer, Singapore (2024)
6. Sathya, D., Thangamani, R., B.B.S.: The revolution of edge computing in smart farming. In: Sundaravadivazhagan, B., Natarajan, G., Chelliah, P.R. (eds.) Intelligent Robots and Drones for Precision Agriculture, pp. 351–389. Springer, Cham (2024). https://doi.org/10.1007/978-3-031-51195-0_17
7. Alharbi, H.A., Aldossary, M.: Energy-efficient edge-fog-cloud architecture for IoT-based smart agriculture environment. IEEE Access. **9**, 110480–110492 (2021). https://doi.org/10.1109/ACCESS.2021.3101397
8. Truong, T.M., Phan, C.H., Van Tran, H., Duong, L.N., Van Nguyen, L., Ha, T.T.: To develop a water quality monitoring system for aquaculture areas based on agent model. In: Fourth International Congress on Information and Communication Technology: ICICT 2019, London, vol. 2, pp. 47–58 (2020)
9. Akyildiz, I.F., Su, W., Sankarasubramaniam, Y., Cayirci, E.: Wireless sensor networks: a survey. Comput. Netw. **38**, 393–422 (2002). https://doi.org/10.1016/S1389-1286(01)00302-4
10. Xia, F.: QoS challenges and opportunities in wireless sensor/actuator networks. Sensors. **8**, 1099–1110 (2008). https://doi.org/10.3390/s8021099
11. Boubiche, D.E., et al.: Advanced industrial wireless sensor networks and intelligent IoT. IEEE Commun. Mag. **56**, 14–15 (2018). https://doi.org/10.1109/MCOM.2018.8291108
12. Truong, M.T., et al.: An environment monitoring system for a rice production model adaptive to climate change in the Mekong Delta of Viet Nam. CTU J. Innov. Sustain. Dev. **15**, 134–141 (2023). https://doi.org/10.22144/ctujoisd.2023.044
13. Liang, S., et al.: OGC SensorThings API Part 1 : Sensing Version 1.1, https://brgm.hal.science/hal-04235851 (2021)
14. Chatterjee, A., Prinz, A.: Applying spring security framework with KeyCloak-based OAuth2 to protect microservice architecture APIs: a case study. Sensors. **22** (2022). https://doi.org/10.3390/s22051703

Blockchain-Based Supply Chain Management for the Silk Industry

Kuruba Harish(✉), Virupakshi Harish, and B. M. Beena

Department of Computer Science and Engineering, Amrita School of Computing, Amrita Vishwa Vidyapeetham, Bengaluru, India
ghiharish34@gmail.com , bm_beena@blr.amrita.edu

Abstract. Silk, an industry with major cultural and economic value, deals with ongoing threats such as fake goods, limited transparency, unethical trading activities and poor coordination among stakeholders. The goal of this project is to develop a Silk Supply Chain Management System using blockchain, Ethereum smart contracts, QR codes and Streamlit for a decentralized, easily understood and protected supply chain. To support the security and fairness of transactions during the supply chain, we made exclusive modules for Farmers, Collectors, Inspectors, Weavers, Retailers and Customers. With the system, silk items can be tracked live, their quality is checked automatically and shoppers can confirm blind silk purchases by scanning QR codes linked to the blockchain. Its creators made it possible for users from different regions to transact by adding a language feature. Simulation results revealed that this system helped track the assets well, brought trade conditions to a better level and defended against fraud. Thanks to its alignment with the United Nations' SDG 8, SDG 9 and SDG 12, this idea can be scaled to help silk industry supply chains and motivate additional businesses to adopt the strategy.

Keywords: Blockchain · Smart Contracts · Silk Supply Chain · Traceability · Ethical Trade

1 Introduction

In the textile world, silk is honored for being both elegant, ancient and made with knowledgeable and artistic work. In the countryside and in international fashion, silk is known for its beauty and its links to cultural customs [6]. Although it appears well organized, the supply chain in fashion is actually fragmented and complicated by many unwanted challenges. Since more people are seeking sustainable and ethically made textiles, the usual model for silk production and distribution is no longer sufficient [3].

These challenges are mainly caused by a lack of transparency throughout the supply chain. Traditionally, the way we manage transactions, review products and oversee logistics is driven by centralized, paper or scattered digital

M. J. C. S. Reis et al. (Eds.): IC4S 2025, LNICST 679, pp. 263–275, 2026.
https://doi.org/10.1007/978-3-032-22834-5_22

record-keeping. They are at high risk of fraud, manipulation of data and mistakes people can make doing paperwork. Therefore, stakeholders face different challenges: farmers' payments are delayed and do not meet fair standards, manufacturers struggle to establish the truth about silk's quality and source and retailers lack understanding of the ethical and environmental violations at earlier stages. Above all, people buying silk can't easily ascertain if it is real or made sustainably [15].

Problems become worse when products are counterfeited or described incorrectly. Because authentic silk is expensive, there is a rise of fake silk or fake blends being sold in markets worldwide. The harm done extends to brand integrity, decreases consumer trust, costs the company money and makes fair competition less likely. Another problem with the supply chain is inefficiencies such as slow transport, no real-time tracking, and manual quality checks, all resulting in delays, more money spent on operations, and difficulties in ensuring standards are always met. Because there is not enough integration among different groups in the supply chain, each lacking knowledge about nearby stages, there are inefficiencies [9].

It is necessary to introduce a safe, non-centralized and open digital platform that can restore trust, ensure everyone is accountable and support the ethical sourcing of silk. Thanks to its immutable nature, decentralization and way of working by consent, blockchain technology provides a significant answer. With the help of IoT devices, QR and RFID tagging and smart contracts, blockchain supports complete transparency and automation throughout each step in the supply chain, including growing mulberry, collecting cocoons, weaving silk, dyeing fabrics and retailing silks.

For instance, IoT sensors allow you to keep an eye on temperature and humidity levels while cocoon stock is in storage or being transported. A scan of the QR code or RFID tag on a silk product lets the user trace its full journey, making it easy to consumers and retailers to verify its legitimacy. In addition, by using smart contracts, companies can avoid the middleman and reduce costs, since they can have their system handle things such as payment after confirmation of delivery, testing quality and confirming compliance with regulations.

Blockchain also plays a key role by enhancing multiple parts of a business.Technology in silk production promotes a wider approach to sustainability with development objectives. It is very in line with the United Nations Sustainable Development Goals (SDGs):

- SDG 9 (Industry, Innovation, and Infrastructure) by promoting digital innovation in traditional industries,
- SDG 12 (Responsible Consumption and Production) through traceable and ethical production methods,
- SDG 8 (Decent Work and Economic Growth) by empowering farmers and eliminating exploitative trade practices.

This research thus seeks to build a robust blockchain platform that modifies the silk supply chain into an open, ethical and sustainable environment. The system will track silk in real time and prevent fraud, provide fair pricing, ensure auto-compliance and safeguard everyone involved—starting with small producers up to buyers worldwide.

2 Literature Survey

A model based on blockchain is presented in this study to make textile supply chains more transparent and prevent counterfeits risks in textile supply chains. Because of smart contracts, the system provides secure transactions and helps verify compliance, increasing efficiency and trust from all participants [1]. This research examines how blockchain strengthens the logistics, security and traceability of supply chains. Among the obstacles outlined are high implementation fees, problems with integrating technology and leftover confusion about regulations that make it slow to use by many [14]. Investigate whether blockchain can help audit silk products for authenticity and support guaranteeing good quality in India's unstructured silk trade. The study explains how using decentralization, smart contracts and better traceability, blockchain can improve the transparency and efficiency of the silkchain [10]. Zhang & Ling look at using blockchain for managing and overseeing supply chains in diverse industries. Field experts have pointed out that the widely used blockchain in supply chain management is hindered by challenges linked to scalability, interoperability and insufficient standardization [16]. Shakhbulatov et al. analyze the part blockchain frameworks play in increasing the security, transparency and proper handling of data in supply chains. The analysis suggests that having improved governance models and consensus methods will increase efficiency and make blockchain use more straight forward [12]. Chang & Chen systematically review over 100 relevant studies that discuss blockchain's use in supply chains with regard to traceability, automation and teamwork between stakeholders. The study points out shortcomings in scaling, legal structures and a lack of universal standards which can guide farther research [5]. The authors study how blockchain can stop counterfeiting and guarantee that the fashion industry sources ethically. The paper explains how NFTs, digital ownership and smart contracts can help make supply chains more transparent and trust worthy [13]. The authors look at how Lenzing has made use of blockchain to verify fibers and support its sustainability efforts, discussing the difficulties that come with using blockchain in extensive supply chains [2]. New findings indicate that using blockchain in healthcare waste management [8] promises greater transparency, visibility and obedience to regulations. Usually, monitoring tasks in these systems are not automated and violations cannot be detected as they occur which this study counters by implementing specific smart contracts. The latest research on blockchain in agriculture looks at strengthening tracking of crops and trust among buyers and sellers by using decentralized ledgers. However, only a few platforms combine cloud technology [11] and smart contracts for revenue distribution among farmers and this work aims to solve this problem. Thanks to recent progress in DLT, E-Governance [7] has a good chance to become simpler, safer and more transparent. While several governments have explored e-services powered by blockchain, few have investigated other new distributed ledger technologies and our study will focus on these. Before, studies have shown that blockchain and IPFS [4] help manage documents securely, highlighting that these documents cannot be edited or stored in one place. Nevertheless, connecting multi-signature verification and intelligent contracts can bring major improvements to managing and reviewing documents by consensus, as this paper discusses

3 Methodology

To address the silk supply chain's transparency, traceability and inefficiencies are being met by using a multi-layered blockchain system set up in a decentralized way.

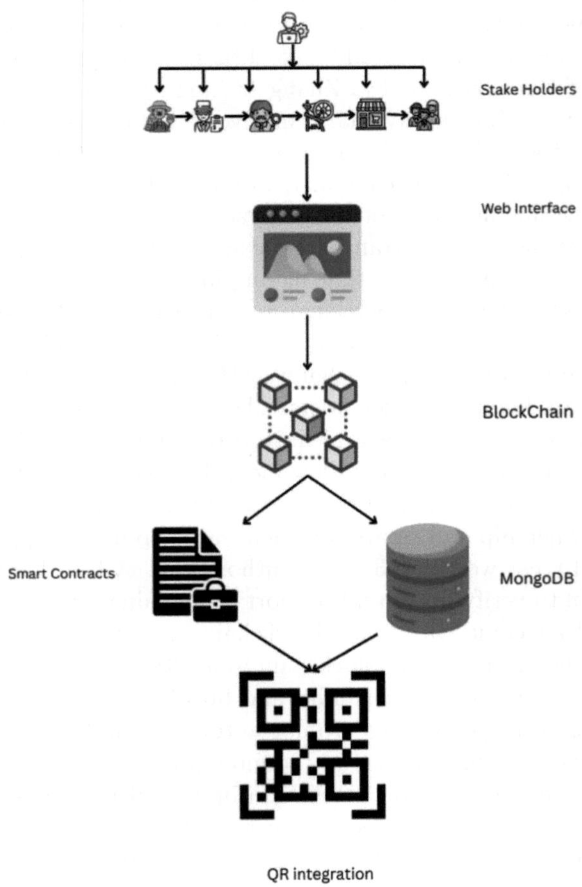

Fig. 1. System Architecture of the Blockchain-Based Silk Supply Chain Management System.

This solution brings together smart contracts, a user interface designed with Streamlit, Ganache for running a private blockchain and JSON files for engaging with smart contracts, ending up with a complete DApp. Key stages required by the methodology are the following and same is illustrated in Fig. 1:

3.1 Technology Stack Overview

Table 1. Technology Stack for Silk Supply Chain DApp

Layer	Technology	Purpose
Frontend	Streamlit (Python)	Build an interactive and multilingual web interface
Blockchain	Solidity, Ganache, Web3.py	Create and deploy Ethereum-based smart contracts
Middleware	Web3.py, JSON ABI	Connect frontend with blockchain smart contracts
Storage (Optional)	MongoDB	Store user credentials, logs, and additional metadata
Utilities	Pyzbar, OpenCV, QRCode	QR generation and scanning for traceability
Deployment/Test Network	Ganache (Local)	Simulate Ethereum blockchain during development

3.2 Local Blockchain Simulation (Ganache)

To develop and test blockchain applications, you need the base layer represented by ganache. It allows you to simulate the Ethereum network on your computer, so you can deploy smart contracts, send transactions and observe behavior instantly and safely. The system was made using Ganache which lets you make Ethereum accounts with test ETH automatically using the interface or command line. Simulations in these accounts act as representatives of real farmers, inspectors and retailers. Ganache allows developers to examine the history of transactions, see their gas use and identify mistakes before they go live on a public testnet. With development tools, you can repeat iterations more rapidly, redeploy contracts and check code errors as they happen which is very useful when building a DApp.

3.3 Frontend Development (Streamlit)

A Python framework called Streamlit was used to design the frontend interface, for its simplicity, speed, and ability to create interactive dashboards. Using web forms, anyone—from farmers and collectors to non-technical users—can interact with the back-end of the blockchain. On the homepage, users can choose which language to view, making accessibility clearer in areas where many languages are spoken. When users log in, they are taken to dashboards that fit their job role (Farmer, Inspector, Retailer) and these dashboards have custom forms made for their tasks. Their data entry covers batch ID, when they harvested, how the cocoons turned out and their quantity. The details of transport are added by Collectors and Inspectors examine and confirm the silk, giving digital approval. Weavers keep track of their sales progress and Retailers put up QR-authenticated batches to sell. Contracts can be viewed live, user actions are shown with comments and users can see the main details in many languages through translated JSON files. Thanks to Streamlit's dynamic rendering, results appear right away and respond quickly to user actions.

3.4 Blockchain Interaction Layer (Web3.py and JSON)

Web3.py was chosen as the connecting part that brings the frontend and blockchain together. Streamlit and similar programs written in Python can now engage with Ethereum smart contracts, deployed via Ganache. Using Truffle or Hardhat, the application's smart contracts were compiled, causing the creation of JSON files that included the Application Binary Interface (ABI) and contract code. These JSON files describe the interactions that Web3.py should manage, including triggering smart contract functions, sending transactions and grabbing information stored on the blockchain. With this setup, users can be registered, silk status can be updated and smart contract events such as inspector approval or retailer dispatch are processed securely and directly by the blockchain network. User account management is also managed by the blockchain interaction module which links Metamask or Ganache accounts to actions that need authorization.

3.5 QR Code Integration

A major need of the silk industry system is tracing the life cycle of every batch of silk from getting started to ending up at a retail point. Through QR code integration, every product contains its complete story which people can review by scanning it with their mobile device. To make QR codes, Python libraries such as qrcode are used and every code stores its own batch ID, farmer's name, harvest date and if the produce was inspected. Customers can view these QR codes when they open the site and can choose to print or add them to the product packaging. When the user scans a QR code with their phone's camera (using OpenCV and Pyzbar), the app checks that information on the blockchain. The system provides total transparency along the supply chain, so users can check the authenticity and sustainability of the product with a simple scan. It prevents fake silk by linking what is in the product with the blockchain data behind it.

3.6 MongoDB for Off-Chain Data

Although all crucial supply chain information is stored immutably on the blockchain, certain auxiliary or non-sensitive data is better managed off-chain for performance and flexibility. The project was optionally built using MongoDB. It securely keeps user IDs, hashed login information, application session identifiers and logs. Some parts of the data you scan, like scanned QR codes, stored user preferences and user activity, are handled by MongoDB and do not always require checks on the blockchain. By using this method, any sensitive information on-chain is protected, simply stored and kept manageable. Off-chain data is updated instantly and improves the experience, keeping the process decentralized.

3.7 Workflow Summary

Silk Supply Chain Management System runs on blockchain and involves every person or business having a specific role in silk manufacturing, processing and sales. To support traceability, authenticity and ethical sourcing, the whole process depends on smart contracts and unchangeable blockchain records this study all this technology stack Table. 1. Each section below outlines the roles that each stakeholder plays in this system:

Admin: System Initialization and Role Verification. The Admin is in charge of launching the entire silk supply chain system on the blockchain. Initial deployments of contracts are done for Farmer, Collector, Inspector, Weaver, Retailer and Customer by the admin. Smart contracts establish the regulations, details of how data is stored and available actions for everyone involved. When the system is deployed, the Admin authorizes stakeholders, gives them a purpose and sets their access rights with blockchain software. By doing so, the platform can trust that users are genuine and thus protect its data. Apart from this, an Admin can view every transaction, step in when there is a dispute or fraud, analyze the reported transactions stored on the blockchain and verify activities according to their unchangeable data stored on the blockchain.

Farmer. The supply chain starts with the Farmer as its first operational unit. Once the Admin verifies the quantity of newly harvested cocoons batches, the Farmer logs into the platform and adds these to register cocoons batches. Among other things, you should enter cocoon type (e.g., mulberry, tasar), harvest date, quality grade, batch ID, temperature, humidity and the location into the system. Users add their data to the form in the frontend and the Farmer smart contract places this information in an immutable format on the blockchain. All batches have a personal reference ID so that they can be traced in following processes. Because they deal with the system directly, Farmers do not need middlemen which helps them sell their produce efficiently, with the chance of faster and fairer payments.

Collector. The Collector takes charge of transporting silk directly from farmers and transfer it to the next dealers. When the Collector registers a batch and it is approved, they use the system to report details such as when it was picked up, the form of transport, its location and its final destination—whether an Inspector or a Weaver. The traceability information is associated with the same batch ID the Farmer has recorded. Each move of silk by the Collector is reflected in the Collector smart contract and stored on the blockchain, guaranteeing openness, full tracking and time marking for all such transactions. As a consequence, any unofficial movement or loss of goods can be easily tracked, ensuring a safe logistics process in the supply chain.

Inspector. Ensuring quality assurance is made possible by the Inspector's role. An inspector will use the system to conduct a physical review once the silk is sent to them. Using the batch ID, the Inspector connects to the batch history and checks the products against the standards set for this process. They enter scores or feedback and approve or reject the batch with just a few clicks using their dashboard. The status is written permanently to the Inspector smart contract and can be seen by anyone who can access downstream systems. With approval, each batch can undergo further steps that guarantee both its safety and its production is ethical. Recording silk checks on the blockchain allows only the finest, inspected silk to be included in weaving and retail.

Weaver. It is the Weaver's duty to turn approved silk into finished fabrics or cloth. After quality assurance on batches is completed, the Weaver uses the system to update log information for the transformation records. They include information about the length of production, the methods involved, the type of fabric created and how well it is produced. All log information is related to the original batch ID and posted on the blockchain by using the Weaver smart contract. As a result, changes made throughout the farming process, from the beginning cocoon to completed product, are openly tracked. Weavers can rely on supply traceability to shape and follow consumer requirements for both quality and sustainability

Retailer Before products are delivered to end customers, the Retailer handles transactions with businesses. Using the system, retailers can find information about finished silk products and then enter details about their prices, availability and packaging. Moreover, Python libraries are used to make a unique QR code for every product. Every reference detail about the batch, the farmer, the score and how the product was processed is available through this QR code. The listing of the silk batch is written into the Retailer smart contract and remains linked to it throughout its use. Thanks to this practice, buyers can see for themselves if the item is genuine and the retailer can show that their products are fair and non-corrupt.

Customer. The main beneficiary of system transparency is the Customer, who directly uses the product. When the customer uses a QR code scanner on their mobile device, they are sent to information about the product's entire production journeys on the blockchain. Data is recorded about the farmer, inspection results, transportation, how the garment was made and where it is offered for sale. Using OpenCV and Pyzbar library, we can perform this verification procedure. Because the system makes the product's origin and quality clear to customers, it helps develop trust, encourages sustainable use and prevents counterfeit goods in luxury textiles.

3.8 Ethical, Transparent, and Sustainable Design

Beyond technically efficient, the system was designed to support ethical behavior, clear information in the supply chain and environmental protection. Those left on the sidelines in old agriculture systems are now given voice and fair opportunities through the platform and contracts that automate pricing. Thanks to blockchain, inspectors can confirm that silk batches meet both quality and labor requirements. Thanks to blockchain, records are unchangeable, supporting more openness in the industry. Considering both authenticity and ethical sourcing gives consumers the belief that they made a good purchase. The system helps advance several United Nations Sustainable Development Goals (SDGs).

4 Results

The performance and behavior of the blockchain-based Silk Supply Chain Management System were evaluated based on user role execution, smart contract functionality, UI responsiveness, and traceability outcomes. The system was deployed and tested on a simulated Ethereum environment using Ganache, with all interactions performed through a Streamlit-based interface. The results are categorized into three core areas: Functional Validation, Traceability and Transparency, and User Experience & Interface Accessibility.

4.1 Functional Validation of Role-Based Smart Contracts

Each module designed for Admin, Farmer, Collector, Inspector, Weaver, Retailer and Customer was exhaustively checked to confirm that these actions were properly implemented by smart contracts. Entering the batch ID, harvestation date and grade of quality allowed farmers to register the cocoon batches. The pickup and transport information recorded by collectors was all linked to the same batch ID as shown in Fig. 2.

Smart contract features were used by inspectors to either accept or reject the silk quality after checking it. After processing the approved batches, weavers added transformation records to the system. Every product of silk was given a unique QR code by retailers and added to the record on the blockchain. Customers could use QR codes to look up the full history of a product traced by

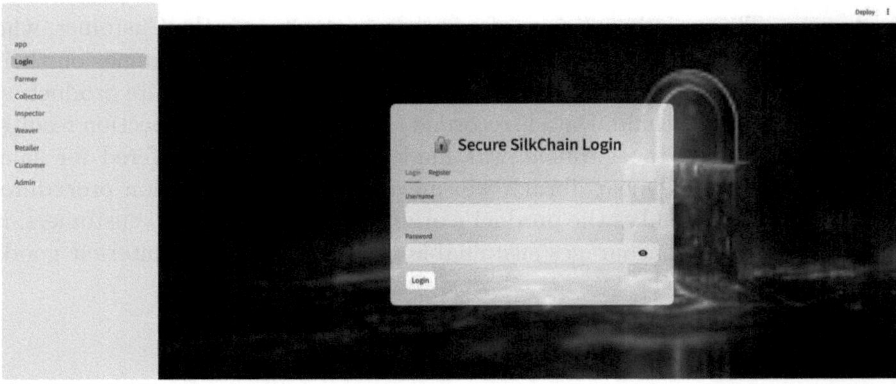

Fig. 2. Login Page of the Silk Supply Chain DApp.

the system. Every action set off the appropriate blockchain events and every transaction in the test simulation ran without error. This means the system's smart contracts meet high levels of correctness and reliability.

4.2 Traceability, Transparency, and QR-Based Verification

The integration blockchain with QR codes made it easy to observe all stages of product movement. For every registered batch of products, a new QR code was created that encoded information about the batch and its supply chain. Upon scanning the QR code, it reliably brought up the correct blockchain-saved data on who the farmer is, the results of quality checks, transportation information, weaving details and where the item is sold as recored and shown in Fig. 3

Fig. 3. Product Tracking.

With this system, anyone could instantly identify where, how and by whom the silk was produced and this gave more trust to the products' ethical and green standards. All of the traceability data was kept unchanged and protected from tampering which fulfilled the main objectives of openness and safety. Moreover, because every interaction used the same type of smart contract, every part of the silk supply chain left a permanent trace in the blockchain.

4.3 User Interface, Multilingual Support, and System Responsiveness

The Users interacted with Streamlit tools to find a simple and fast interface that worked well for everyone. Specific jobs for users were managed by the right dashboard, including registration for Admin, tracking batches for Farmers, checking quality for Inspectors and listing products for Retailers as clearly showed in Fig. 4.

Fig. 4. Multilingual Support.

I could see right away whether my transactions had succeeded or failed. Allowing users to choose among English, Hindi, Telugu and Kannada just required them to update the sidebar and all text was changed to match. It made it much easier for users in rural and regional areas to use the network.

5 Conclusion and Future Work

The project successfully designs and applies a Silk Supply Chain Management System powered by blockchain to solve main problems in the silk industry such as a lack of transparency, counterfeits, unethical business and ineffective dealing between stakeholders. Smart contracts on Ethereum and Streamlit make the web interface secure for each of the important roles: Farmers, Collectors, Inspectors, Weavers, Retailers and Customers. Every role takes place in an environment where transactions and actions are stored immutably on the blockchain.

The system also introduces QR codes are used to give end consumers the ability to see the provenance, quality and ethical production of silk goods. As a result, consumer trust increases, while producers enjoy fair trade by avoiding control by unethical intermediaries. Because the system can be used in different languages, stakeholders from rural and regional areas find it easier to access and use. As a whole, the project satisfies several UN Sustainable Development Goals (SDG 8: Decent Work, SDG 9: Industry & Innovation and SDG 12: Responsible Consumption & Production), ensuring the solution is advanced and also socially responsible.

The prototype functions properly when tested on Ganache, but a number of developments can make the system suitable for real world use. Next, we will move the smart contracts to networks such as Polygon or Sepolia to allow users in the real world to use our solution. With IoT sensors added, it would be possible to automatically measure temperature and humidity which can help improve quality assurance even more. In addition, using Layer-2 solutions allows for better gas costs and more efficient system scaling. Creating a mobile application would enhance how farmers and field workers use the system, mainly in parts of the country that are difficult to access.

Other possibilities include introducing decentralized identity(DID) as a way for users to verify themselves securely, using IPFS to save product certificates or pictures off the blockchain and attracting customers by offering rewards. Eventually, machine learning might be used to check finished products or discover unusual activities in the supply process, giving help to people monitoring the process.

References

1. Agrawal, T.K., Kumar, V., Pal, R., Wang, L., Chen, Y.: Blockchain-based framework for supply chain traceability: a case example of textile and clothing industry. Comput. Ind. Eng. **154**, 107130 (2021). https://doi.org/10.1016/j.cie.2021.107130
2. Ahmed, W.A.H., MacCarthy, B.L.: Blockchain-enabled supply chain traceability in the textile and apparel supply chain: a case study of the fiber producer, lenzing. Sustainability **13**(19), 10496 (2021). https://doi.org/10.3390/su131910496
3. Attri, K., et al.: Advancements in sericulture: Innovations and sustainability in silk. Uttar Pradesh J. Zoology **45**(16), 305–317 (2024). https://doi.org/10.56557/upjoz/2024/v45i164311
4. Avvaru, A., Tandon, A., Beena, B.M.: Identity management dapp using ethereum blockchain and IPFS. In: 15th International Conference on Computing Communication and Networking Technologies (ICCCNT), pp. 1–5. IEEE (2024)
5. Chang, S.E., Chen, Y.: When blockchain meets supply chain: a systematic literature review on current development and potential applications. IEEE Access **8**, 62478–62494 (2020). https://doi.org/10.1109/ACCESS.2020.2983601
6. Karthik, T., Rathinamoorthy, R.: Sustainable silk production. In: Muthu, S.S. (ed.) Sustainable Fibres and Textiles, pp. 135–172. Woodhead Publishing (2017). https://doi.org/10.1016/B978-0-08-102041-8.00006-8
7. Kumar, D., Beena, B.M.: International Conference on Computer, Power and Communications (ICCPC), pp. 299–305. IEEE (2022). Influence of DLT in the e-governance strategy

8. Kumar, G.V.S., Reddy, C.R., Beena, B.M.: Revolutionizing healthcare waste management: Leveraging blockchain for enhanced efficiency and transparency. In: 15th International Conference on Computing Communication and Networking Technologies (ICCCNT), pp. 1–5. IEEE (2024)
9. Madumali, S., Weerasinghe, B., Thibbotuwawa, A., Perera, H.N.: Transparency in textile and apparel supply chains: a systematic review. J. South Asian Logist. Transp. **3**(2), 71–101 (2023). https://doi.org/10.4038/jsalt.v3i2.71
10. Prasad, A.S., Shetty, D.B., H.S., D., R., N., R., M.B.: A survey on silk supply chain management using blockchain. PICES **5**(2), 27–30 (2021)
11. Rao, A., Ashik, F., Koushik, I.S., Beena, B.M.: Cloud-integrated blockchain solution for agricultural sales tracking. In: 15th International Conference on Computing Communication and Networking Technologies (ICCCNT), pp. 1–6. IEEE (2024)
12. Shakhbulatov, D., Medina, J., Dong, Z., Rojas-Cessa, R.: How blockchain enhances supply chain management: A survey. IEEE Open J. Comput. Society **1**, 230–249 (2020). https://doi.org/10.1109/OJCS.2020.3025313
13. Singh, H., Jain, G., Kumar, N., Hashimy, L., Shrivastava, A.: Blockchain technology in the fashion industry: virtual propinquity to business. J. Electron. Commer. Organ. **20**, 1–21 (2022). https://doi.org/10.4018/JECO.300303
14. Wannenwetsch, K., Ostermann, I., Priel, R., Gerschner, F., Theissler, A.: Blockchain for supply chain management: a literature review and open challenges. Proc. Comput. Sci. **225**, 1312–1321 (2023). https://doi.org/10.1016/j.procs.2023.10.119
15. Yusuff, M.: The importance of transparency in the textile supply chain, (2024). preprint
16. Zhang, X., Ling, L.: A review of blockchain solutions in supply chain traceability. Tsinghua Sci. Technol. **28**(3), 500–510 (2023). https://doi.org/10.26599/TST.2022.9010030

Carbon Aware Task Scheduling in Edge Computing

Akarsh Surya Venkat(✉), Sai Ujwal Reddy, Santhwana Santhosh Kumar, Sriharsha Vadada, and B. M. Beena

Department of Computer Science and Engineering, Amrita School of Computing, Amrita Vishwa Vidyapeetham, Bengaluru, Bengaluru, India
{bl.en.u4cse22104,bl.en.u4cse22147,bl.en.u4cse22149, bl.en.u4cse22155}@bl.students.amrita.edu, bm_beena@blr.amrita.edu

Abstract. While edge computing has many benefits, it also plays a major role in the increase in carbon emissions from energy demanded by data centers. These facilities consume a large range of energy, from operating a server for processing workloads to operating a cooling system to cool all servers, and data transmission which adds to the carbon impact. The work presents a Carbon-Aware Task Scheduling Simulator that simulates edge nodes and schedules tasks with minimal carbon emissions in mind. It employs several different scheduling algorithms such as Round Robin, Least Loaded, Carbon-Aware Intensity Scheduler (CIAS), and Energy-Efficient Task Scheduler (EETS). Performance is measured in terms of metrics like CO_2 emitted and task completion time. The results indicate that CIAS and EETS have the capability to minimize carbon emissions by as much as 50% against regular algorithms, proving the capability for sustainable scheduling without compromising on the performance much.

Keywords: Edge Computing · Carbon-Aware Scheduling · Task Scheduling Algorithms · CO_2 Emission Reduction · Sustainable Computing · Cloud Technologies · Container · Sustainable Computing

1 Introduction

As edge computing is becoming more common in applications that need low latency, concern about sustainability and energy efficiency has grown. Rural areas usually utilize distributed energy resources, some of which are fossil fuels and some are renewables. Traditional task scheduling does not factor in how carbon-intensive energy is and may therefore waste clean power.

Legacy edge computing task schedulers like Round Robin (RR) and Least Loaded (LL) are performance-oriented, focusing on metrics like latency and load balancing. These do not consider the carbon impact of computing, which is now all the more crucial in the age of global warming. Recent research in cloud-native and data center-based solutions investigates carbon-aware scheduling based on

M. J. C. S. Reis et al. (Eds.): IC4S 2025, LNICST 679, pp. 276–288, 2026.
https://doi.org/10.1007/978-3-032-22834-5_23

real-time carbon intensity data, but this has not been embraced across edge environments on a large scale yet.

Lack of Carbon-Awareness: Schedulers in most cases ignore carbon intensity of the power supply. Modeling Carbon Impact Complexity: Precise modeling of power consumption, execution time of tasks, and local carbon intensity is still not an easy problem. Trade-Offs Between Latency and Emissions: It is an arduous multi-objective problem balancing environmental objectives with quality of service.

This article introduces a simulator that is developed with Python, Streamlit, and Docker and displays and measures the environmental cost of various scheduling policies. It implements four algorithms—RR, LL, CIAS, and EETS—with different optimization objectives. The simulator has real-time dashboards with Grafana and performance logging with Prometheus, providing metrics for CO emissions and efficiency. Testing reveals up to 50% CO savings with minimal latency increase using CIAS and EETS.

Although the project is based on edge computing, its architecture and monitoring stack are centered on fundamental cloud computing concepts, including containerization (Docker), infrastructure observability (Prometheus + Grafana), and scalable, dashboard-oriented interfaces (Streamlit). They provide flexibility, reusability, and remote simulation, making the solution adaptable to hybrid cloud-edge systems where environmental consequence is a collectiveresponsibility.

The proposed work solves this problem by adding a task scheduler that uses actual carbon data to allocate tasks. The use of live carbon intensity information while placing tasks leads to low carbon emissions with a good performance and timely response from the system. The goal of this solution is to improve the scalability and sustainability of edge computing using environmentally friendly ideas.

2 Literature Survey

Ma, Huirong et al. [1] introduce a carbon-free edge AI approach incorporating spot and future carbon markets for offloading ML tasks with the help of a Lyapunov optimization algorithm and a randomized rounding strategy to trade off the loss in accuracy and carbon emissions. Their scheme saves up to 57% cost with negligible loss in accuracy.

Song et al. [2] propose LSCEA-AIoT, a low-carbon AIoT system maximizing energy-efficient data collection and carbon-aware task offloading using a Monte Carlo tree search.

Siddhesha et al. [3] provide a deep reinforcement learning-based task scheduling scheme to maximize energy utilization and resource allocation in cloud data centers for increased efficiency.

Wang et al. [4] introduce ERLFC, a reinforcement learning-based federated cloud task scheduling that minimizes carbon footprints by taking geographical energy origins and emissions into account utilizing an Actor-Critic algorithm.

Wang et al. [5] introduces ESTMP, a hierarchical network-aided task offloading framework (NTOF) for Green IoT systems. It presents an energy-efficient traffic mapping-based task scheduling algorithm with slack-space proportional pre-allocation with the goal of minimizing schedule length under energy limitations in heterogeneous MEC systems. The simulation outcomes demonstrate the technique enhances energy efficiency, shortens the schedule length, and alleviates traffic bursts in edge settings.

Kim et al. [6] proposes GreenScale, a carbon-aware scheduling system for edge-cloud infrastructures taking into account time and location-based availability of renewable energy, embodied emissions, and runtime variability. Comparative analyses in AI, gaming, and AR/VR applications reveal GreenScale to have the potential to decrease carbon emissions by as much as 29.1%, which indicates the discrepancy between carbon-conscious and performance/energy-conscious scheduling techniques.

Yang et al. [7] in the proposed methodology, offer a new task scheduling policy based on a drift-plus-penalty-based Lyapunov optimization technique to schedule tasks dynamically in computing networks taking into account real-time carbon intensity variations. The method formulates the system as a virtual queueing network capturing communication and computation, allowing dynamic task scheduling across multiple clouds with different energy profiles.

Miao et al. [8] introduces ECMR, a VM scheduling algorithm of distributed machine learning tasks for multi-renewable energy-powered geo-distributed data centers. ECMR drastically improves the use of renewable energy to 90.8%, decreases carbon emissions and energy consumption, and obtains a task failure rate of only 1.25%, which is better than current approaches in green cloud scenarios.

Beena et al. [9] advocates for an innovative cloud-native framework that incorporates real-time carbon intensity information into task scheduling for Infrastructure as a Service (IaaS) cloud infrastructure. The framework leverages AWS-based services and Kubernetes orchestration to schedule tasks dynamically to low-carbon intensity regions' data centers, optimizing energy efficiency as well as CO2 emissions. It includes real-time data streams and predictive analytics through LSTM-based models and adaptive decision-making to adhere to SDGs.

Demirbaga et al. [10] proposes EcoCloud, an ACO-based task scheduler with MLP neural networks optimized for energy and carbon efficiency in industrial IoT cloud environments. The scheduler dynamically allocates MapReduce jobs within Hadoop clusters based on predicted node-level energy usage and workload allocation to idle nodes. Real-time monitoring of resources through SmartMonit guarantees accurate and responsive task scheduling, enhancing both system performance and energy usage.

Gu et al. [11] introduce a DRL-based service management and energy scheduling strategy for low-carbon edge computing. The proposed model-free method differs from conventional model-based approaches in that it adaptively manages edge services through prioritized replay memory to improve learning efficiency. Trace-based experiments based on real-world traces prove the effectiveness of the strategy in cutting operational costs and promoting green energy utilization, enabling edge computing to become more eco-friendly.

Vijjapu et al. [12] propose a computational steering technique that integrates Round Robin, SJF scheduling, and Random Forest Regressor to reduce energy consumption fluctuations and increase CPU utilization in data centers. This combined system also proposes a Streamlit-based real-time monitoring user interface and adheres to UN Sustainable Development Goals by supporting green computing.

Hareni et al. [13] propose a new dynamic resource allocation framework that combines quantum algorithms, game theory, cross-layer optimization, and collaborative edge computing scheduling. The framework improves resource utilization and lowers latency by adapting to dynamic network and workload conditions. Simulation results verify its effectiveness over traditional allocation schemes in satisfying QoS requirements with ease.

Chakravarthi et al. [14] proposes a DDPG-based reinforcement learning solution for dynamic resource management in edge scenarios. By emulating actual workloads with the CRAWDAD KAIST-WIBRO dataset, the model successfully optimizes resource consumption, decreases response times, and enhances energy efficiency. The method presents a resilient solution for managing edge resources in dynamic and uncertain scenarios.

Panwar et al. [15] offer a proactive resource provisioning approach based on reinforcement learning to address workload variability in cloud computing environments. The approach combines autonomic computing and reinforcement learning (Q-RL) for maximizing resource utilization, minimizing SLA violations, and operational expenditure. Experimental outcomes validate 30% cost savings and 77.7% reduced SLA violations over traditional approaches.

Amruth et al. [16] proposed a cloud-based big data framework that uses Apache Spark and Databricks to classify genomic cancer from TCGA RNA-seq data. While PCA improved feature handling, logistic regression achieved the highest accuracy (98.72%).

Shalini et al. [17] focused on performance and energy trade-offs while analysing energy-efficient task and virtual machine scheduling in edge-fog-cloud architectures for Internet of Things and identified gaps in task dependency, mobility, and heterogeneity by comparing heuristic, metaheuristic, and machine learning-based approaches.

Beena et al. [18] proposed a green, energy-efficient video transcoding system that optimises task allocation and predicts renewable energy using machine learning models (Random Forest, XGBoost, and CatBoost). Workloads for FFmpeg managed by Kubernetes scale dynamically according to HPA-estimated energy.

Neera et al. [19] highlighted how cloud services allow for scalable, on-demand support for expanding IoT demands in the conversation about cloud computing and IoT integration. highlighted how the cloud can improve IoT growth, connectivity, and performance. The study claims that ClouT will be crucial to facilitating the upcoming internet-based revolution.

Kriti et al. [20] examined how Docker is revolutionising web hosting through containerisation, enhancing security, scalability, and efficiency. Future directions such as serverless computing, multi-cloud deployment, and Kubernetes orchestration were highlighted.

Shalini et al. [21] proposed that Multiverse Optimiser is improved with a fitness-based neighbourhood search in the proposed NIMS, a novel task scheduling algorithm that lowers makespan and energy consumption. Assessed using CloudSim and real-world benchmarks against seven sophisticated algorithms.

3 Methodology

3.1 System Architecture

The system consists of three main layers:

- **User Interface Layer**: Created with Streamlit, this layer offers simulation controls, task input parameters, and graphical outputs such as charts and tables.
- **Simulation Core**: Written in Python, it contains edge node models, task generators, and several scheduling algorithms (RR, LL, CIAS, EETS).
- **Monitoring & Dashboard Layer**: Prometheus collects metrics like CO emissions and task latency, and Grafana shows them in real-time via easy-to-use dashboards.

This modular design facilitates real-time feedback, extensibility of the system, and reproducible experimentation.

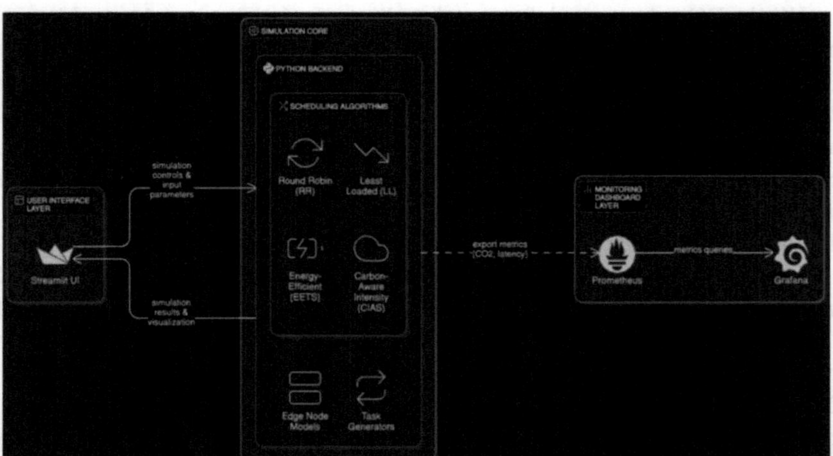

Fig. 1. System Architecture of the Carbon-Aware Task Scheduling Simulator.

As shown in Fig. 1, the system architecture is composed of three interconnected layers. The **User Interface Layer** handles user input and visualization, while the **Simulation Core** manages task scheduling and the execution of algorithms. Finally, the **Monitoring & Dashboard Layer** enables real-time tracking of key performance indicators (KPIs) such as CO emissions and task latency.

3.2 Data Flow Diagram

The data flow in the system is straightforward:

- **User Input**: Parameters such as number of tasks and range of task sizes.
- **Task Generator**: Generates random task sizes within specified limits.
- **Scheduler Engine**: Executes the chosen algorithm to allocate tasks to edge nodes.
- **Edge Node Model**: Simulates execution of tasks and computes CO emissions and latency.
- **Metrics Collector**: Prometheus collects data; Streamlit and Grafana display it.
- **Data Pipeline**: Provides transparency in how scheduling decisions impact environmental and performance outcomes.

3.3 Experimental Setup

The simulator is implemented with the following components:

- **Programming Language**: Python 3.10
- **Tools and Frameworks**: Streamlit (UI), Docker Compose (containerization), Plotly (graphing), Prometheus and Grafana (monitoring).
- **Environment**: Localhost deployment based on Docker containers on the following ports:
  - Streamlit: localhost:8501
  - Prometheus: localhost:9090
  - Grafana: localhost:3000

A new set of randomized task sizes (ranging from 1–10) is generated each time the simulation is run. The metrics are logged and rendered to enable comparisons between algorithm performance, CO emissions, and latency.

3.4 Novelty in Work

Novelty in Introduction. In contrast to conventional schedulers that primarily target load balancing or latency, this project introduces carbon-aware computing as a key optimization target in edge computing—a field with high deployment but low levels of sustainability-based efforts. The simulator provides valuable insights into the trade-offs between environmental impact and responsiveness.

Novelty in Methodology. This work presents two new scheduling methods:

- **Carbon-Aware Intensity Scheduler (CIAS)**: Calculates carbon emissions per node prior to allocation.
- **Energy-Efficient Task Scheduler (EETS)**: Balances task placement by ranking nodes according to emission intensity and load.

The system also incorporates real-time monitoring and visualization for assessing the environmental impact of scheduling decisions—a novel integration for educational simulators.

3.5 Justification with UN SDGs

This research aligns with the following UN Sustainable Development Goals (SDGs):

- **SDG 7 – Affordable and Clean Energy**: Focuses on the efficient use of energy in computing through the avoidance of CO emissions by task scheduling.
- **SDG 9 – Industry, Innovation, and Infrastructure**: Promotes new, carbon-conscious algorithms suitable for edge computing infrastructure.
- **SDG 13 – Climate Action**: Directly addresses climate change mitigation by lowering the carbon impact of digital technologies.

By incorporating carbon metrics in decision-making, the system prioritizes sustainability in technology design.

3.6 Algorithms Used

The simulator uses and compares the following four scheduling algorithms:

- **Round Robin (RR)**: Cycles through nodes in sequence without considering load or carbon intensity. This is the baseline scheduler for comparison.

$$\text{schedule}(nodes, \text{task\_size}) \rightarrow \text{node\_index} \tag{1}$$

- **Least Loaded (LL)**: Schedules tasks onto the node with the lightest load. This algorithm improves performance but is not optimized for sustainability.

$$\text{schedule}(nodes, \text{task\_size}) \rightarrow \text{argmin\_load} \tag{2}$$

- **Carbon-Aware Intensity Scheduler (CIAS)**: Estimates carbon emissions per node and allocates tasks to the node with the lowest expected emissions. It optimizes both performance and sustainability.

$$\begin{aligned} rCl\text{est\_carbon} = & \left(\frac{\text{power\_draw}}{3600} \times \text{carbon\_intensity}\right) \\ & \times \left(\frac{1 + \frac{\text{load}}{\text{cpu\_speed} \times \text{ram}}}{\text{cpu\_speed}}\right) \times \text{task\_size} \end{aligned} \tag{3}$$

– **Energy-Efficient Task Scheduler (EETS)**: Computes a score based on node power, carbon intensity, and load at the moment. It selects the node with the lowest score, aiming to minimize overall energy usage.

$$rCl\text{score} = \left(\frac{\text{power\_draw}}{3600} \times \text{carbon\_intensity}\right) \times \left(1 + \frac{\text{load}}{\text{cpu\_speed} \times \text{ram}}\right) \times \text{task\_size} \quad (4)$$

These algorithms demonstrate the shift in optimization priorities from computational efficiency alone to sustainable computing practices.

4 Results

The simulation of the *Carbon-Aware Task Scheduling Simulator* was conducted using various edge nodes and task parameters. The performance of four different scheduling algorithms: **Round Robin (RR)**, **Least Loaded (LL)**, **Carbon-Aware Intensity Aware Scheduling (CIAS)**, and **Energy-Efficient Task Scheduling (EETS)** was evaluated in terms of **Total Carbon Emissions (gCO2)** and **Average Completion Time (s)** are tabulated in Table 1.

Table 1. Results Summary of Task Scheduling Algorithms

Algorithm	Total Carbon (gCO2)	Average Completion Time (s)
RR	33.693	87.791
LL	35.322	89.093
CIAS	15.447	23.999
EETS	17.964	28.892

From the results, **Carbon-Aware Intensity Aware Scheduling (CIAS)** achieved the lowest **carbon emissions** while maintaining an acceptable completion time. On the other hand, **Round Robin (RR)**, the baseline scheduling algorithm, exhibited the highest carbon emissions and task completion time, confirming its inefficiency in sustainable task scheduling.

4.1 Task Execution Timeline

The task execution timeline for each algorithm is visualized as represented in Fig. 2. The red bars represent task execution, with longer bars indicating higher resource utilization and longer execution times.

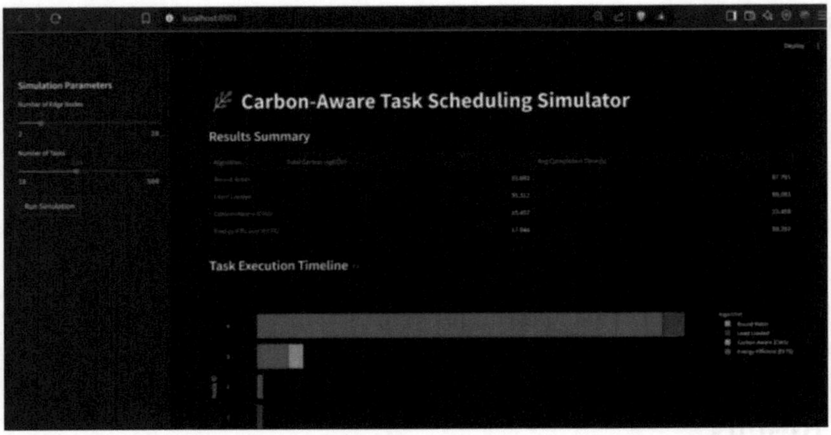

Fig. 2. Task execution time for different scheduling algorithms. (Color figure online)

4.2 Carbon vs Latency Drill-Down Analytics

The drill-down analysis for **Round Robin** on **Node 0** shows a linear increase in **carbon emissions** as **task latency** increases. This is demonstrated in Fig. 3 that inefficient algorithms lead to higher carbon emissions with increased task latency.

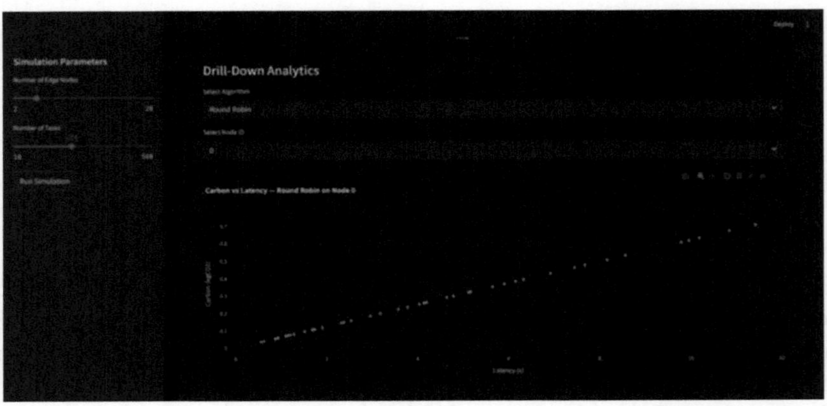

Fig. 3. Carbon vs Latency drill down analytics.

4.3 Task Completion Heatmap

The heatmap in Fig. 4 illustrates the distribution of task completion times and associated carbon emissions during different task end intervals. The color coding represents task counts, with warmer colors indicating higher task counts.

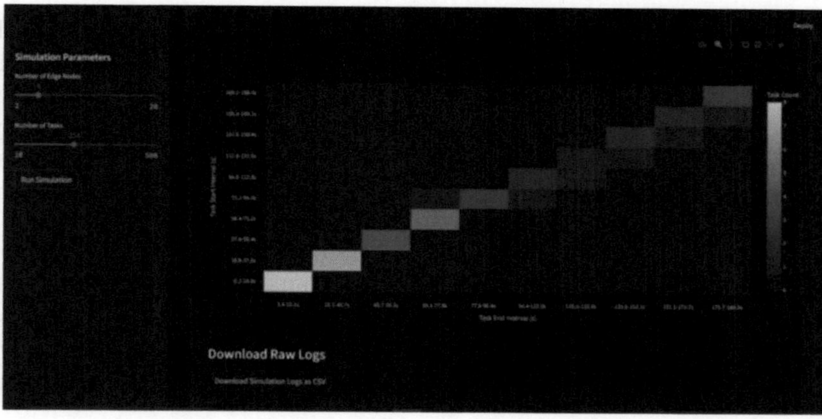

Fig. 4. Task monitoring heatmap. (Color figure online)

4.4 Real-Time Monitoring and Metrics

Real-time monitoring of **CO2 emissions** and **task latency** was conducted using **Grafana** and **Prometheus**, as shown in Fig. 5. The data provides insight into the performance of each algorithm during task execution.

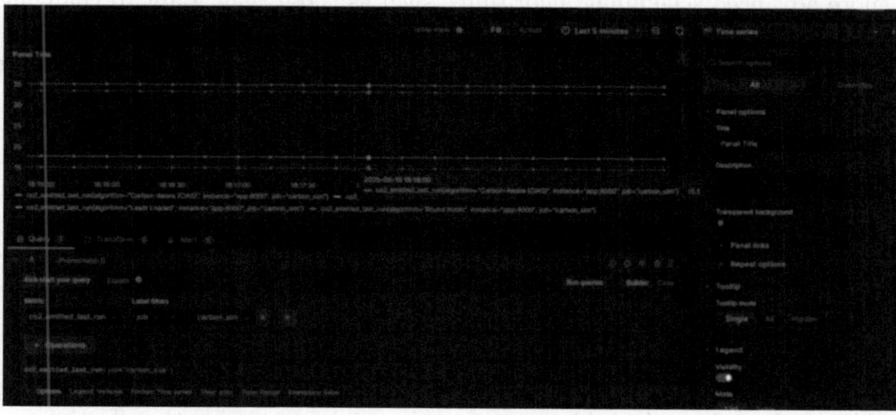

Fig. 5. Grafana Dashboard for Real-Time Monitoring.

5 Conclusion and Future Scope

5.1 Conclusion

The results from the simulation underscore the advantages of **carbon-aware** and **energy-efficient task scheduling** algorithms, specifically **CIAS** and

EETS, when compared to traditional scheduling methods like **Round Robin (RR)** and **Least Loaded (LL)**. The **CIAS** algorithm, in particular, demonstrates a substantial reduction in **CO2 emissions**, with only a modest increase in **task completion time**, highlighting its potential to optimize sustainability in edge computing systems. This reinforces the viability of integrating environmental concerns into computational decision-making processes, offering a sustainable alternative to conventional, performance-focused scheduling methods.

The findings also emphasize the balance that must be maintained between task performance and environmental impact. While achieving a lower carbon footprint, maintaining computational efficiency is crucial to ensuring that sustainable scheduling does not significantly compromise system performance.

5.2 Future Scope

Looking ahead, there are several avenues for further improvement and exploration:

- **Latency Optimization**: Future work can focus on refining the balance between **latency** and **carbon emissions**, with the goal of reducing task completion times without significantly affecting the sustainability benefits of the scheduling algorithms.
- **Algorithm Enhancement**: The simulator can be expanded to integrate more advanced scheduling algorithms, such as those that adapt to changing network conditions or hybridize both cloud and edge resources dynamically. These algorithms could provide an even more nuanced approach to balancing performance and sustainability.
- **Scalability**: Scaling the solution to support larger, more dynamic edge environments would allow the system to handle real-world workloads more effectively, considering factors such as network latency, task complexity, and geographic distribution.
- **Hybrid Cloud-Edge Systems**: Incorporating cloud resources alongside edge computing could further optimize energy efficiency, leveraging the strengths of both environments to maximize task performance while minimizing overall energy consumption and CO2 emissions.
- **Real-World Deployment**: Future research could also focus on deploying this simulator in real-world edge computing systems, testing the effectiveness of these algorithms under practical conditions and potentially providing a roadmap for integrating sustainability metrics into large-scale operational systems.

In conclusion, this work lays the foundation for a more sustainable approach to edge computing task scheduling, with potential applications in fields where performance and energy efficiency are critical. With further improvements, these systems could lead the way in creating greener, more efficient computational infrastructure.

References

1. Ma, H., Zhou, Z., Zhang, X., Chen, X.: Toward carbon-neutral edge computing: greening edge AI by harnessing spot and future carbon markets. IEEE Internet Things J. **10**(18), 16637–16649 (2023)
2. Song, Z., Xie, M., Luo, J., Gong, T., Chen, W.: A carbon-aware framework for energy-efficient data acquisition and task offloading in sustainable AIoT ecosystems. IEEE Internet Things J. (2024)
3. Siddesha, K., Jayaramaiah, G.V., Singh, C.: A novel deep reinforcement learning scheme for task scheduling in cloud computing. Clust. Comput. **25**(6), 4171–4188 (2022)
4. Wang, Z., Shuaijun Chen, L., Bai, J.G., Tao, J., Bond, R.R., Mulvenna, M.D.: Reinforcement learning based task scheduling for environmentally sustainable federated cloud computing. J. Cloud Comput. **12**(1), 174 (2023)
5. Wang, C., Yu, X., Lexi, X., Wang, W.: Energy-efficient task scheduling based on traffic mapping in heterogeneous mobile-edge computing: a green IoT perspective. IEEE Trans. Green Commun. Net. **7**(2), 972–982 (2022)
6. Kim, Y.G., et al.: Greenscale: carbon-aware systems for edge computing. arXiv preprint arXiv:2304.00404 (2023)
7. Yang, C.-S., Huang-Fu, C.-C., Fu, I-K.: Carbon-neutralized task scheduling for green computing networks. In: GLOBECOM 2022-2022 IEEE Global Communications Conference, pp. 4824–4829. IEEE (2022)
8. Miao, Z., et al.: Energy and carbon-aware distributed machine learning tasks scheduling scheme for the multi-renewable energy-based edge-cloud continuum. Sci. Technol. Energy Transit. **79**, 82 (2024)
9. Beena, B.M., Prashanth, C.S.R., Manideep, T.S.S., Saragadam, S., Karthik, G.: A green cloud-based framework for energy-efficient task scheduling using carbon intensity data for heterogeneous cloud servers. IEEE Access (2025)
10. Demirbaga, U.: EcoCloud: green computing through energy and carbon efficient task scheduling in industrial IoT-enabled cloud environments. IEEE Internet Things J. (2025)
11. Gu, L., Zhang, W., Wang, Z., Zeng, D., Jin, H.: Service management and energy scheduling toward low-carbon edge computing. IEEE Trans. Sustain. Comput. **8**(1), 109–119 (2022)
12. Vijjapu, A., Jose, A., Baniya, A., Revanth, A.S., Beena, B.M.: Enhancing energy-efficiency in data centers by leveraging computational steering and dynamic task allocation. In: 2025 International Conference on Computing for Sustainability and Intelligent Future (COMP-SIF), pp. 1–11. IEEE (2025)
13. Hareni, M., Krishna, S., Ayyappan, S., Sahay, A.: Dynamic resource allocation for edge computing. In: 2024 15th International Conference on Computing Communication and Networking Technologies (ICCCNT), pp. 1–8. IEEE (2024)
14. Chakravarthi, S.S., Ajairaj, V., Sounthararajan, S.: Sustainable resource allocation in edge environment based on deep deterministic-reinforced learning. In: 2024 IEEE Recent Advances in Intelligent Computational Systems (RAICS), pp. 1–7. IEEE (2024)
15. Panwar, R., Supriya, M.: RLPRAF: reinforcement learning-based proactive resource allocation framework for resource provisioning in cloud environment. IEEE Access (2024)

16. Amruth, A., Ramanan, R., Paul, R., Vimal, C., Beena, B.M.: Cloud Based Big Data Solution for Cancer Classification: Using Databricks on Large Scale Genomic Data. Department of Computer Science and Engineering, Amrita Vishwa Vidyapeetham, Bengaluru (2024)
17. Tiwari, S., Beena, B.M.: Energy Cognizant Scheduling in Three-Layer Cloud Architecture: A Systematic Review. Department of Computer Science and Engineering, Amrita Vishwa Vidyapeetham, Bengaluru (2023)
18. Beena, B.M., Cheluvalasai, P., Chowdary, V., Gamidi, R., Hemasri, M., Muppala, T.: Green Video Transcoding in Cloud Environments Using Kubernetes: A Framework With Dynamic Renewable Energy Allocation and Priority Scheduling. Department of Computer Science and Engineering, Amrita Vishwa Vidyapeetham, Bengaluru and University of Windsor, Canada (2025)
19. Chaudhary, N., Beena, B.M., Gurupriya, M.: Amalgamation of Cloud Computing with IoT- A Novel ClouT Architecture. Department of Computer Science and Engineering, Amrita Vishwa Vidyapeetham, Bengaluru (2025)
20. Sah, K.P., Jain, N., Jha, P., Hawari, J., Beena, B.M.: Advancing of Microservices Architecture with Dockers. Department of Computer Science and Engineering, Amrita Vishwa Vidyapeetham, Bengaluru (2024)
21. Tiwari, S., Beena, B.M.: A Neighborhood Inspired Multiverse Scheduler for Energy and Makespan Optimized Task Scheduling for Green Cloud Computing Systems. Department of Computer Science and Engineering, Amrita Vishwa Vidyapeetham, Bengaluru (2024)

Applications of Cyber-Physical Systems

Through the Fog: Unmasking Environmental, Safety, and Health Risks

A. Brahmeswar, N. Padmavathy(✉), Ch Harshitha, A. Charan Reddy, N. Reshma, and Ch Bommanadevi

Department of Electronics and Communication Engineering, Vishnu Institute of Technology, Bhimavaram, AP, India
padmavathy.n@vishnu.edu.in

Abstract. Fog is a significant meteorological phenomenon that affects transportation, industrial operations, environmental conditions, and public health. Statistical data from 2019 to 2024 indicate a fluctuating trend in fog-related road accidents, with a notable increase in recent years, particularly in the Indo-Gangetic Plains and urban centres such as Delhi. Reduced visibility has led to a sharp rise in vehicular accidents, delayed flights, and train disruptions, resulting in economic losses and safety concerns. Additionally, fog exacerbates air pollution by trapping particulate matter, contributing to severe respiratory diseases and poor public health. Industrial sectors, including mining and construction, face safety hazards due to low visibility, necessitating technological interventions. This study explores fog's impact using recent statistical trends, and discusses technological advancements such as AI-driven navigation aids and real-time monitoring systems. Recent reports show that fog-related road accidents have changed a lot in the past five years, with a sharp drop in 2020 due to lockdowns and a rise again in the following years. These trends show the need for better monitoring systems and AI tools for safe navigation during fog. Future research should focus on predictive modelling, adaptive traffic management, and policy-driven interventions to mitigate fog's adverse effects effectively.

Keywords: Air Pollution · Environmental Impact · Fog Visibility · Industrial Safety · Public Health · Transportation

1 Introduction

Fog has become an increasing concern in densely populated and industrialized regions, particularly in Northern India. Recent statistical data indicate that fog-related road accidents have varied significantly over the past five years, with a decrease during 2020 due to reduced vehicular movement during the COVID-19 pandemic, followed by a sharp rise in subsequent years. Delhi witnessed over 200 flight delays in early January 2025 due to dense fog, with some areas reporting visibility as low as zero meters. Similarly, train services in Northern India

M. J. C. S. Reis et al. (Eds.): IC4S 2025, LNICST 679, pp. 291–306, 2026.
https://doi.org/10.1007/978-3-032-22834-5_24

have faced frequent delays, exacerbating economic and logistical challenges. Air pollution intensifies during foggy periods as pollutants become trapped near the surface, worsening respiratory conditions. Industries such as mining and construction experience significant operational risks, leading to increased demand for enhanced forecasting models and mitigation strategies. Urban atmospheres frequently contain elevated concentrations of particulate pollutants that act as Cloud-active aerosol particles (CAA); when coupled with favorable Climatological factors, these particles significantly enhance the probability of fog formation [1]. Although fog is a natural phenomenon, its impact is more severe in urban and industrial areas. In cities like New Delhi and Hyderabad, fog traps smog and pollutants near the ground, posing serious health risks. Industries such as mining experience safety challenges due to reduced visibility and equipment failures. Fog is a major winter hazard in India, especially in the Indo-Gangetic Plains, significantly affecting transportation and public health [2]. The Indo-Gangetic Plains (IGP), one of the most densely populated and rapidly expanding regions of India, experience recurrent winter fog episodes, with events occurring nearly every alternate day in Delhi. These fogs, often characterized by visibility below 200 m and lasting several hours due to strong temperature inversions and high relative humidity, significantly disrupt transportation systems, deteriorate air quality, and impose substantial public health and economic burdens. Various studies have explored fog prediction over the Indo-Gangetic Plains (IGP) using statistical models, numerical weather prediction (NWP), and diagnostic techniques. However, achieving consistently accurate operational forecasts for fog events remains a challenge [3]. Air pollution becomes significantly more severe during fog and haze events, as pollutants get trapped near the surface, reducing air quality. To minimize exposure, it is advisable to keep windows closed until visibility improves and outdoor air quality stabilizes. Regular cleaning with a vacuum cleaner helps remove dust and pollutants from carpets, sofas, and floors, improving indoor air conditions. Additionally, avoiding frying commonly used in traditional Chinese cooking can prevent excessive smoke production, which can further deteriorate indoor air quality. Implementing these measures can help reduce health risks associated with poor air quality during foggy conditions [4].

Along with the fog there are also other components that contribute to environmental pollution, viz. is the electromagnetic pollution measured as electromagnetic pollution index (EPI) [5–7]. The EPI quantifies radiation impact of mobile communication, analogous to air or water pollution indices. Using a free-space propagation model, the study shows that EPI increases with transmission power, frequency, and user density. Values exceeding 150 Wh indicate hazardous levels, emphasizing the optimized design for sustainable green communication.

The objective of this review paper is to comprehensively examine the impact of fog on a wide range of domains, including the environment, transportation, public health, mining operations, and other affected sectors. By synthesizing findings from diverse scholarly and technical sources, this paper aims to consolidate current knowledge on fog-related challenges into a single, coherent framework. The review further seeks to identify knowledge gaps, highlight critical issues, and outline potential mitigation strategies. These insights will serve as a foundation for proposing informed, multidisciplinary solutions in the subsequent sections of the paper.

2 Environmental Impact of Fog

Fog has significant environmental impacts, mainly by affecting visibility, trapping pollutants, influencing local climates, and serving as a crucial water source for certain ecosystems. In arid regions, fog contributes directly to plant growth by depositing moisture on leaves through a process known as "fog drip". Research indicates that fog water contains various mineral ions, including H^+ (hydrogen ion), NH_4^+ (ammonium ion), NO_3^- (nitrate ion), and SO_4^{2-} (sulphate ion), each contributing to different environmental impacts [8].

These acidic and reactive compounds can contribute to soil acidification, alter nutrient cycles, and impact aquatic ecosystems when fog water is deposited on the ground. In urban and industrial areas, fog can trap pollutants near the surface, exacerbating air pollution and increasing health risks by prolonging human exposure to harmful substances.

Additionally, fog plays a role in local climate regulation. During the day, it reflects sunlight, leading to cooler surface temperatures, while at night, it helps retain heat, preventing extreme temperature drops. This microclimatic effect is particularly important in coastal and high-altitude regions, where fog moderates temperatures and supports biodiversity. Overall, while fog serves as a vital resource for certain ecosystems, its interaction with pollutants highlights the need for continued research into its environmental effects, especially in the context of increasing air pollution and climate change.

Figure 1 visually represents the locations of meteorological stations across India, Nepal, Bangladesh, and Pakistan. The stations, marked with stars, are distributed across major cities and strategic points, including Amritsar, New Delhi, Lucknow, Kolkata, Guwahati, and Lahore. These stations play a crucial role in collecting weather data such as air temperature, relative humidity, and wind speed. The observations help in weather forecasting, climate analysis, and studying fog formation, contributing to improved transportation safety and environmental assessments. The scale bar at the bottom right indicates distances, helping to gauge station distribution across the region. The scale at the bottom right provides a reference for distance measurements, ensuring accurate spatial interpretation of the station locations. Nearly every year during the winter months (December–February), the extensive Indo-Gangetic Plains situated south of the Himalayas experience widespread and persistent dense fog events. This fog primarily forms as radiation fog, resulting from intense nocturnal surface

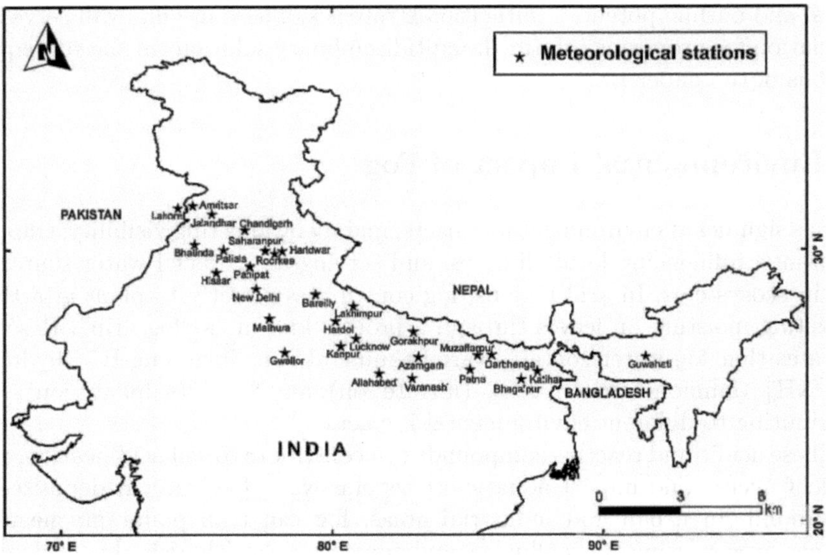

Fig. 1. Locations of Meteorological Stations for Fog and Weather Analysis [9].

cooling under clear skies and calm winds. Under conditions of elevated aerosol loading and anthropogenic emissions, the fog often transforms into smog through the interaction of water vapour with smoke, dust, and other particulate pollutants, further degrading air quality and visibility [9]. Figure 1 also illustrates the spatial distribution of meteorological stations across the study region, from which air temperature, relative humidity, and wind speed datasets were acquired. The geospatial coordinates of these stations were integrated into a GIS framework to analyze spatial variability and assess meteorological influences on fog formation.

As of mid-February 2025, several regions in India have been experiencing dense fog conditions, significantly impacting transportation and daily life. These fog conditions have had widespread consequences, affecting air, rail, and road transportation. The environmental impact of fog is complex and far-reaching. A major concern is the formation of toxic smog, which occurs when fog interacts with pollutants from vehicle emissions, industrial processes, and crop residue burning. This hazardous mixture significantly degrades air quality, reducing visibility and increasing health risks, particularly respiratory issues and cardiovascular diseases. Prolonged exposure to smog, particularly to elevated concentrations of fine particulate matter ($PM_{2.5}$ and PM_{10}), nitrogen oxides (NO_x), sulfur dioxide (SO_2), ozone (O_3), and volatile organic compounds (VOCs), has been associated with chronic respiratory and cardiovascular disorders, reduced pulmonary function, and increased morbidity and mortality rates (WHO, 2021) [9].

These findings underscore the critical need for robust air quality management frameworks, stricter emission regulations, and the promotion of sustain-

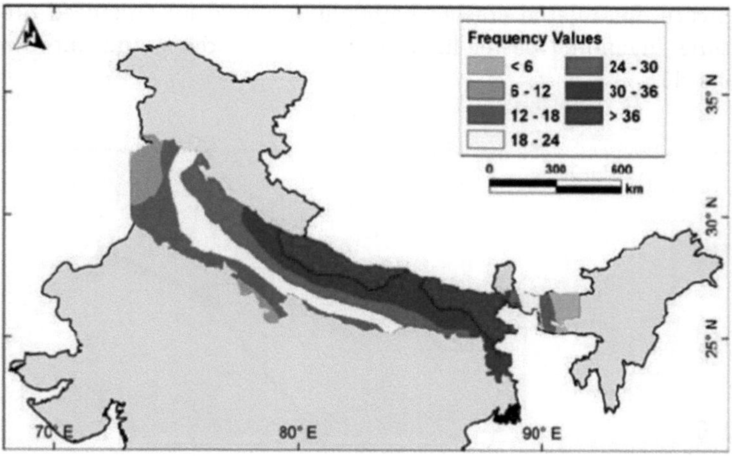

Fig. 2. Frequency of Dense Fog Events Over Northern and Eastern India [9] (Color figure online)

able urban and industrial practices to mitigate the long-term adverse impacts of smog on human health and the environment [10]. Figure 2 spatial frequency classification of dense fog events over Northern and Eastern India during the winter season (December–February). The map delineates the fog-affected belt using gridded meteorological observations and satellite-derived visibility data, highlighting the spatial extent and intensity of fog occurrence across the Indo-Gangetic Plains. The color-coded scale categorizes frequency values into seven ranges as shown in the Fig. 2. The Indo-Gangetic Plain—including Punjab, Haryana, Uttar Pradesh, Bihar, and West Bengal—experiences the highest fog frequency, with some areas encountering over 36 foggy days per season (red zones). The green, blue, and yellow regions indicate moderate fog occurrence, gradually decreasing towards the southern and northeastern parts of the country.

The spatial distribution highlights regions with varying frequencies, with the highest concentration marked in red and the lowest in light blue. A scale bar at the bottom provides a reference for distance, marked at 0, 300, and 600 km, aiding in geographical interpretation. This visualization is particularly useful for meteorologists, transportation authorities, and policymakers in planning mitigation strategies. Since dense fog significantly impacts aviation, railways, and road networks, analyzing regional variations helps authorities implement effective measures to minimize disruptions during winter months.

3 Impact of Fog on Transportation

Thick fog has severely impacted transportation, creating hazardous conditions for travellers. Poor visibility increases the likelihood of traffic accidents, often resulting in serious injuries and fatalities. As road safety continues to be a major global concern, fog-related crashes highlight the need for enhanced precautionary measures, including better lighting, warning systems, and improved traffic regulations [11].

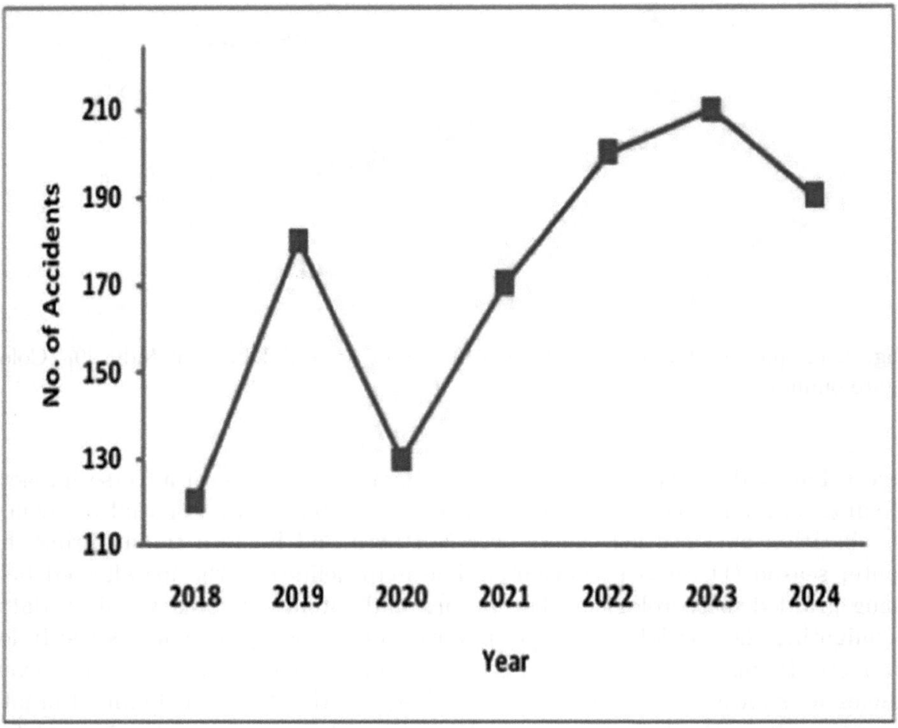

Fig. 3. Fog-Related Road Accidents Trend (2018–2024) [12].

Figure 3 shows fluctuating fog-related accident trends between 2018–2024, with peaks in 2019 and 2023. This highlights the ongoing need for stronger road safety measures in foggy conditions. Foggy conditions continue to pose a significant threat to road safety, with accident trends fluctuating over recent years. In 2023, a high number of accidents were reported due to dense fog, affecting visibility and increasing collision risks. While a decline was observed in the following year, accidents surged again in subsequent years, highlighting the ongoing dangers of driving in foggy conditions. This trend emphasizes the urgent need for enhanced safety measures, including better road infrastructure, improved vehicle lighting systems, and stricter traffic regulations to minimize fog-related accidents.

Visibility reduction due to fog presents a critical safety hazard across all modes of transportation—land, maritime, and aviation. Land-based transport systems, particularly roadways and railways, are most affected, often experiencing severe delays and operational disruptions during dense fog conditions when visibility frequently drops below 200 m. Numerous studies and accident reports indicate a substantial increase in collision-related incidents during such low-visibility periods. While most accidents are attributed to rear-end or multi-vehicle collisions, secondary events such as vehicle fires may also arise due to the impact and subsequent mechanical or fuel-system failures [1]. The impact of reduced visibility is considerably higher for passenger cars than for heavy vehicles such as trucks, primarily due to differences in vehicle dimensions, braking efficiency, and driver perception–reaction times. Empirical studies show that when visibility drops below 200 m, passenger car drivers exhibit greater speed variability and reduced headway stability compared to truck drivers.

The effect is more pronounced on inner lanes, where vehicle density and mean speeds are typically higher than on outer lanes. Under such low-visibility conditions, elevated headway variance ($>1.5\ s^2$) and decreased time-to-collision ($\text{TTC} < 1.5\,\text{s}$) substantially increase crash likelihood. Consequently, adaptive cruise control, fog-warning systems, and lane-specific speed regulation are crucial for maintaining roadway safety during dense fog events [13]. A wide spectrum of human activities is adversely influenced by fog occurrence. In addition to causing significant inconvenience and economic disruption, severe fog events have been linked to increased accident rates and fatalities across multiple sectors. When visibility falls below 1 km—and particularly under dense fog conditions ($< 200\,\text{m}$)—transportation systems such as road, rail, maritime, and aviation operations experience major safety and efficiency challenges. The reduction in visibility impairs drivers' and operators' ability to detect obstacles, maintain safe headways, and navigate effectively, thereby elevating the overall risk of collision and operational failure [14].

Additionally, the dense fog affects transportation byA wide spectrum of human activities is adversely influenced by fog occurrence. In addition to causing significant inconvenience and economic disruption, severe fog events have been linked to increased accident rates and fatalities across multiple sectors. When visibility falls below 1 km—and particularly under dense fog conditions ($< 200\,\text{m}$)—transportation systems such as road, rail, maritime, and aviation operations experience major safety and efficiency challenges. The reduction in visibility impairs drivers' and operators' ability to detect obstacles, maintain safe headways, and navigate effectively, thereby elevating the overall risk of collision and operational failure. Reducing visibility, leading to travel disruptions and accidents. The presence of aerosols in the atmosphere also influences the development and persistence of fog, further complicating the environmental scenario [15]. Figure 4 illustrates the trend of flight and train delays over a six-year period due to fog-related disruptions. The blue line represents flight delays, while the green line represents train delays, both measured in total hours per year. The data shows a general increase in transportation delays, with flight delays peaking in 2023 at around 350 h before slightly decreasing in 2024. Train delays followed a similar pattern, reaching their highest point in 2023 (275 h) and further experiencing a minor decline in 2024. The 9.38% rise in flight delays and 8.00% rise in train delays in 2023 could be attributed to an unusually severe winter season, with prolonged periods of dense fog reducing visibility and impacting transportation schedules.

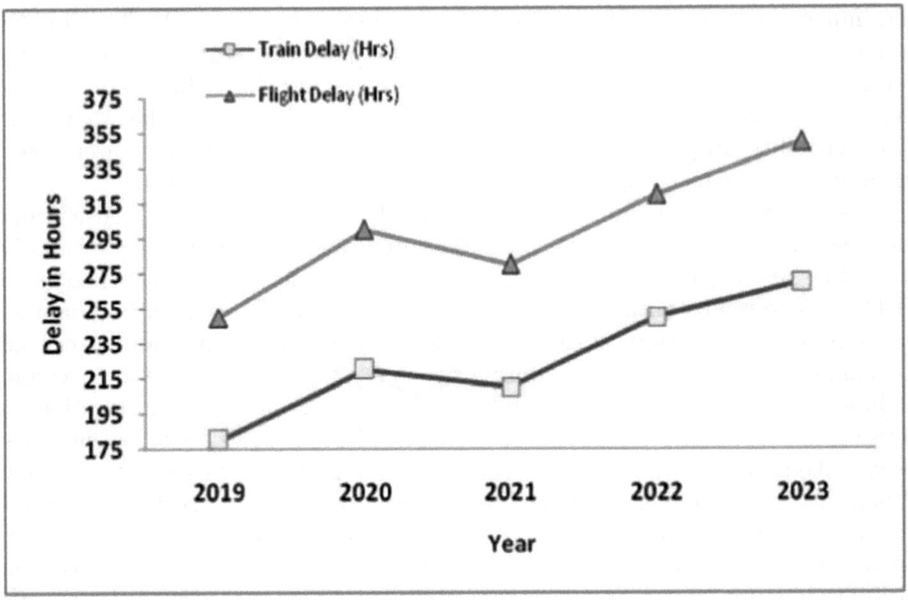

Fig. 4. Transportation Delays (Flights & Trains) Due to Fog (2019–2024) – Compares delays in flight and train schedules over the years [16]

In 2023, flight delays increased by 9.38% compared to 2022, while train delays rose by 8.00% compared to the previous year. This surge may be linked to an unusually severe winter season, with prolonged periods of dense fog reducing visibility and disrupting transportation schedules. However, in 2024, flight delays showed a 5.71% decrease compared to 2023, and train delays declined by 3.70% compared to the previous year, indicating possible improvements in weather forecasting, better preparedness, and enhanced operational strategies to manage fog-related disruptions.

4 Mitigating Opencast Mining Challenges During Foggy Weather

Opencast mining operations face severe challenges during foggy weather, including reduced visibility, navigation difficulties, and safety hazards. To mitigate these risks, various advanced technologies have been implemented to enhance operational safety and efficiency [17]. A GPS-integrated driving system provides real-time location data, ensuring precise navigation of mining vehicles even in low-visibility conditions, similar to its successful applications in aviation and maritime transport. Additionally, 3D-based Google Earth visualization offers a high-resolution, realistic map of the mining area, enabling better spatial awareness and route planning, much like its use in urban planning and construction.

High-quality Charge-Coupled Device (CCD) cameras further improve monitoring and control by delivering superior image clarity in low-light conditions, as seen in astrophotography and medical imaging. Since fog obstructs visible light, infrared thermography plays a crucial role by detecting heat signatures, allowing operators to identify obstacles and personnel despite poor visibility, a technique widely used in military night vision and firefighting. Drones and robotic systems further enhance safety by providing real-time aerial surveillance and remote inspections, reducing the need for human presence in hazardous areas, similar to their use in disaster response and industrial inspections [17].

Convolutional Neural Networks (CNNs) improve image classification and object detection, ensuring automated recognition of equipment, obstacles, and workers, a method successfully implemented in autonomous vehicles and security systems [17]. Additionally, advanced sensor technologies, including Proximity Radar, High-Definition (HD) cameras, Internet Protocol (IP) cameras, and Thermal Imaging systems, enhance visibility and prevent accidents, as demonstrated in aviation and automotive safety systems.

Furthermore, thermal cameras and high-definition imaging systems assist operators of heavy earth-moving machinery in navigating safely during foggy conditions, leveraging the same principles used in military and automotive night vision technologies. By integrating these cutting-edge solutions, the mining industry significantly reduces the risks associated with foggy weather, ensuring safer and more efficient operations while maintaining productivity [17,18].

5 Public Health Implications of Fog

The combination of fog with air pollutants results in the formation of smog, which severely degrades air quality [19].

5.1 Economic and Livelihood Impacts

The persistent smog not only affects health but also disrupts daily activities, leading to economic losses and affecting livelihoods, particularly in urban centres like Delhi [20]. Fog often combines with pollutants to form smog, exacerbating air quality issues. In November 2024, Delhi experienced severe air pollution, with the Air Quality Index (AQI) reaching 484—categorized as severe plus—indicating extreme pollution levels hazardous to all individuals, especially children, the elderly, and those with respiratory or heart conditions. The persistent smog, formed by the combination of fog and pollutants like PM2.5 (Particulate Matter ≤ 2.5 μm), PM10 (Particulate Matter ≤ 10 μm), NO_2 (Nitrogen Dioxide) and SO_2 (Sulphur Dioxide), Worsened air quality contributes to serious health risks, with about 40% of cases linked to asthma, 35% to bronchitis, and 25% to lung infections. This also disrupted daily life, causing school closures, reduced outdoor activities, and economic losses due to decreased workforce productivity and increased healthcare costs. The severity of pollution during this period was exacerbated by winter conditions, low wind speeds, and emissions from vehicles, industries, and crop burning in neighbouring states like Punjab and Haryana. Such extreme pollution events highlight the urgent need for stricter pollution control measures, improved public health responses, and sustainable environmental policies to mitigate future air quality crises [21].

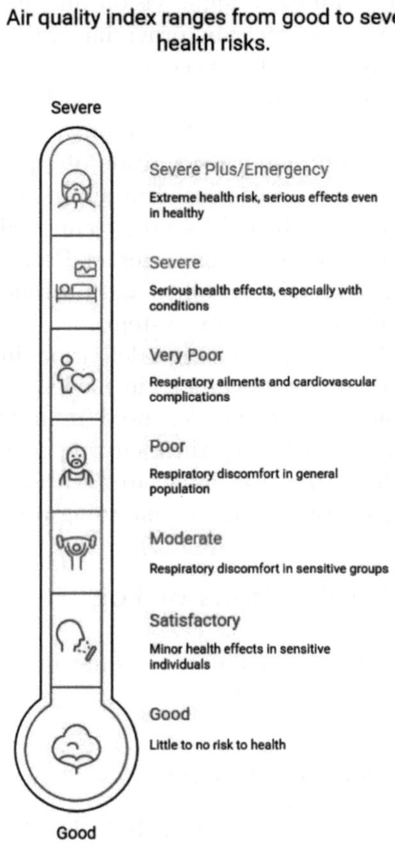

Fig. 5. Air Quality Index (AQI) table with categories and associated health impacts [22]

The Fig. 5 emphasizes the Air Quality Index (AQI) levels and their corresponding health impacts on humans. When the AQI is between 0 and 50 (Good), the air is clean and poses no health risk. 51–100 (Satisfactory) indicates generally acceptable air quality, though a few sensitive individuals may experience mild discomfort. At 101–200 (Moderate), air pollution may cause breathing issues for vulnerable groups such as children, the elderly, and those with lung problems.

201–300 (Poor) reflects unhealthy air that can cause discomfort and respiratory stress during prolonged exposure, especially for people with heart disease. 301–400 (Very Poor) represents significantly polluted air that may trigger respiratory illnesses and worsen heart conditions. 401–500 (Severe) indicates dangerous pollution levels, causing serious health effects, particularly in those with existing ailments. An AQI above 500 (Severe Plus/Emergency) signals extremely hazardous conditions, posing severe health risks even to healthy individuals.

However, necessary precautions need to be taken as a preventive measures provided in this paragraph. Precautions against air pollution depend on the Air Quality Index (AQI) level. When air quality is good or satisfactory (0–100), no major precautions are needed, though sensitive individuals should avoid prolonged outdoor activities. At moderate levels (101–200), people should limit outdoor exertion and keep windows closed during high pollution hours. When the air becomes poor (201–300), outdoor activities should be minimized, and using air purifiers or masks like N95 is advisable. For very poor conditions (301–400), staying indoors with windows and doors closed and using air purifiers is recommended. At severe levels (401–500), individuals should avoid all outdoor exposure and keep necessary medications ready. During severe plus or emergency conditions (above 500), it is crucial to remain indoors in a sealed environment, use efficient air filtration systems, and seek medical help if any breathing discomfort or health issues arise.

5.2 Fog and Air Pollution Interaction

: Fog has been found to trap pollutants, increasing the concentration of harmful substances near the surface. This can significantly degrade air quality and lead to severe respiratory problems [21].

5.3 Impact on Respiratory Health

: Studies have linked exposure to high pollution levels, especially in foggy conditions, to an increased risk of lung diseases such as asthma, bronchitis, and chronic obstructive pulmonary disease (COPD). Research conducted by the World Health Organization [23] that poor air quality exacerbates these conditions, particularly in urban areas where pollutant accumulation is higher [19].

5.4 Vulnerability of Children and the Elderly

Scientific evidence suggests that children and the elderly are at greater risk due to their respiratory system's sensitivity. Children's developing lungs make them more vulnerable to inhaled toxins, while older adults are more prone to chronic respiratory diseases, which are worsened by prolonged exposure to polluted air [24].

5.5 Historical and Epidemiological Evidence

The Great Smog of London (1952) serves as a key historical example of how fog mixed with pollution caused a spike in respiratory illnesses, leading to thousands of deaths [25]. Similar patterns have been observed in highly polluted cities such as Delhi and Beijing, where fog-induced smog events have resulted in increased hospital admissions for respiratory issues.

5.6 Scientific and Policy Reports

Reports from the U.S. Environmental Protection Agency and The Lancet Commission on Pollution and Health [26] emphasize that air pollution exposure, particularly in foggy conditions, leads to lung inflammation and reduced lung function, increasing respiratory disease prevalence among vulnerable populations.

Additionally, fog significantly reduces visibility, increasing the risk of road accidents and transportation delays, which can impact emergency response times and overall public safety. The persistent lack of sunlight during foggy conditions may also contribute to seasonal affective disorder (SAD), leading to mood disturbances and fatigue. Air pollutants such as nitrogen oxides (NO_x), sulfur dioxide (SO_2), ozone (O_3), sulfuric acid (H_2SO_4), and nitric acid (HNO_3) constitute the major components of acid fog, with the latter two compounds contributing most significantly to its acidity. Exposure to fine atmospheric aerosol particles—particularly acidic aerosols—along with sulfur oxides, sulfur dioxide, and airborne microorganisms, has been strongly associated with increased respiratory morbidity and mortality, as well as elevated risks of cardiopulmonary and lung cancer–related deaths [14]. Exposure to elevated levels of ambient air pollution, frequently exacerbated by seasonal fog episodes, has become a major public health challenge in urban regions worldwide, affecting populations in both developed and developing countries [27].

6 AI-Driven Navigation Aids and Real-Time Monitoring in Fog Conditions

Fog greatly reduces visibility and makes travel unsafe, so modern systems now use AI and real-time data to manage these conditions better. AI-based models can study past weather information and predict when fog is likely to form, which helps in planning and early warnings. Studies show that machine-learning methods can improve fog prediction and enhance accuracy during low-visibility events. To improve navigation and safety under foggy conditions, recent work has explored combining AI-based vision systems with real-time visibility estimation. Deep-learning methods have been applied to detect and enhance visibility in fog and haze conditions, enabling more reliable scene perception even when human vision fails [28]. For instance, a fusion-based deep network called VENet has demonstrated visibility estimation with less than 5% error at 500 m and a fog-level classification accuracy above 92%, showing promise for real-time surveillance on roads and highways [29].

Object-detection frameworks tailored for foggy weather, such as YOLOv5s-Fog, have also improved detection of obstacles or other vehicles in foggy environments a key factor for driver assistance and autonomous navigation systems operating under adverse weather [30]. Moreover, some studies have implemented in-vehicle video-based fog detection using deep learning on naturalistic driving datasets, providing a practical approach for real-time fog alert systems for drivers [31]. Finally, machine-learning models using meteorological parameters can predict sudden drops in road visibility, offering a complementary forecasting tool for fog-prone areas [32].

7 Industrial and Occupational Safety Concerns

In recent decades, northern India has experienced an anomalous increase in fog occurrences, coinciding with a substantial increase winter irrigation following the widespread adoption of double-cropping practices. Accurate fog forecasting remains a major challenge, as fog formation is highly sensitive to a multitude of interacting physical processes operating across spatial and temporal scales. Moreover, uncertainties in the representation of these processes within state-of-the-art numerical weather prediction (NWP) models further limit forecast reliability [33]. In opencast mining, foggy conditions reduce visibility, heightening the risk of accidents involving heavy machinery. To mitigate these risks, the implementation of intelligent vision enhancement systems has been proposed [34]

Industrialization has undergone profound transformations since its inception in the 18th century. The first major shift, often referred to as Industrial Revolution 1.0, began with the advent of steam-powered machinery, which liberated production from the constraints of manual labor and localized energy sources. The subsequent paradigm shift in the 19th century—marked by the introduction of electricity—enabled centralized power generation and its widespread distribution, revolutionizing industrial productivity and infrastructure [35].

Fog poses significant industrial and occupational safety concerns, particularly in sectors that rely on outdoor work and transportation. Reduced visibility increases the risk of accidents in industries such as construction, aviation, shipping, and road transportation, where workers are more vulnerable to collisions and falls. In manufacturing and chemical plants, fog can contribute to condensation, leading to slippery surfaces and potential electrical hazards. Additionally, fog can trap air pollutants and industrial emissions, increasing workers' exposure to harmful chemicals and respiratory irritants, which may lead to long-term health issues.

8 Agricultural Impacts

Persistent fog in the Indo-Gangetic Plain (IGP) between 2019 and 2024 had significant agricultural consequences, primarily affecting crop growth, yield, and harvesting schedules. The prolonged foggy conditions reduced sunlight availability, hindering photosynthesis and leading to lower productivity for major winter crops such as wheat, mustard, and potatoes. Additionally, excess moisture from persistent fog increased the risk of fungal diseases, further damaging crops and impacting farmers' income. Delayed harvests, particularly for wheat and mustard, were reported due to slow crop maturation caused by reduced temperatures and prolonged exposure to fog [36]. Farmers also faced economic challenges as delayed harvests disrupted supply chains, leading to price fluctuations and reduced profitability. The high frequency of fog, combined with pollution-induced smog, further exacerbated agricultural distress, as soil fertility and air quality were affected by pollutant deposition on crops [15].

9 Conclusion

Overall, this review highlights that fog formation is governed by a complex interaction of natural meteorological processes and human-induced environmental changes, making accurate prediction and timely intervention essential yet challenging. To address these challenges more effectively, stronger policy frameworks such as region-specific fog management guidelines, mandatory installation of intelligent transportation systems (ITS), and stricter pollution control regulations are crucial. Technologically, the integration of AI-based forecasting models, low-visibility detection networks, satellite–ground sensor fusion, and adaptive traffic control systems can significantly enhance fog preparedness and public safety. Strengthening both technological innovation and policy implementation will be key to building resilient communities capable of navigating fog-related risks.

Fog, especially when intensified by pollution, creates widespread environmental, safety, and health challenges across transportation, industry, agriculture, and urban populations. Its high frequency—particularly across the Indo-Gangetic Plain—reduces visibility, causing accidents, delays, and operational hazards while trapping pollutants that worsen air quality and increase respiratory illnesses, especially among children and the elderly. Fog-related smog [14] also disrupts agricultural productivity [29] by limiting sunlight, slowing crop growth, and increasing disease risk. Across sectors, the findings highlight that fog is not merely a weather phenomenon but a multi-dimensional risk factor, emphasizing the urgent need for stricter emission controls, improved forecasting, advanced safety technologies, and stronger public health and agricultural resilience measures.

References

1. Lakra, K., Avishek, K.: A review on factors influencing fog formation, classification, forecasting, detection and impacts **33**, 319–353 (2022)
2. Smith, D., Dorling, S., Renfrew, I., Ross, A., Poku, C.: Fog trends in India: relationships to fog type and western disturbances. White Rose Res. Online **43**(2) (2023)

3. Smith, D.K.E., et al.: Forecasts of fog events in northern India dramatically improve when weather prediction models include irrigation effects. Commun. Earth Environ. **141** (2024)
4. Cai, D.-P., He, Y.-M.: Daily lifestyles in the fog and haze weather. J. Thorac. Dis. **8** (2016)
5. Padmavathy, N., Chinnaiah, M.C., Ravi Varma, K.: Estimation of Electromagnetic pollution index of macrocell pattern recognition & data analytics with applications. LNEE, vol. 888, pp. 39–55 (2022)
6. Varma, R., Padmavathy, N.: Electromagnetic pollution index: estimation of green mobile communication. In: 2nd IEEE International Conference on Intelligent Computing, Instrumentation & Control Technologies, pp. 85–89 (2019)
7. Gajja, S.K., Padmavathy, N.: Green communication: an emerging telecommunication technology – its research challenges, techniques & applications. In: International Conference on Information, Communication & Computing Technology (ICCT), TSO, pp. 76–84 (2017)
8. I. Team: Fog and Its Effects on the Environment Report. IvyPanda (2022). https://ivypanda.com/essays/fog-and-its-effects-on-the-environment/
9. Saraf, A.K., Bora, A., Das, J., Jain, S.K.: Winter fog over the Indo-Gangetic Plains: mapping and modelling using remote sensing and GIS. Nat. Hazards **58**(1), 199–220 (2011)
10. Sinha, V., Mishra, A.: What's Inside Northern India's Winter Smog? The Diplomat (Asia-Pacific) (2024)
11. Ali, F., Khan, Z.H., Khattak, K.S., Gulliver, T.A.: The effect of visibility on road traffic during foggy weather conditions. ResearchGate **18** (2023)
12. Fog Causes Over 30,000 Road Accidents Every Year in India: Govt In Rajya Sabha. ABP Live (2024). https://news.abplive.com/news/india/fog-causes-over-30-000-road-accidents-every-year-in-india-govt-in-rajya-sabha-1737082
13. Peng, Y., Abdel-Aty, M., Lee, J., Zou, Y.: Analysis of the impact of fog-related reduced visibility on traffic parameters. J. Transp. Eng. (2017)
14. Perez-Diaz, J.L., et al.: Fogs: physical basis, characteristic properties, and impacts on the environment and human health. J. Environ. Stud. **9**(10) (2017)
15. Bharali, C., Barth, M., Kumar, R., Ghude, S.D., Sinha, V., Sinha, B.: Role of atmospheric aerosols in severe winter fog over the Indo-Gangetic Plain of India: a case study. Atmos. Chem. Phys. **24**(11) (2024)
16. Delhi weather: 200 flights delayed, 267 trains cancelled (2023). https://timesofindia.indiatimes.com/city/delhi/200-flights-delayed-5-diverted-due-to-fog/articleshow/96864467.cms
17. Choudhary, M., Kumari, S., Chaulya, S.K., Prasad, G.M.: Perceptive driving assistant system for opencast mines during foggy weather. ResearchGate **39**(7), 1–17 (2022)
18. Kumari, S., Choudhary, M., Mishra, R., Chaulya, S.K.: Artificial intelligent based smart system for safe mining during foggy weather. ResearchGate **34** (2021)
19. Ghude, S.D., Nivdange, S., Chate, D.M., Karmalkar, N.R.: Economic Impacts of Air Pollution and Fog in India and Prediction Efforts, pp. 189–200. Springer (2022)
20. Sinha, V., Mishra, A.: Toxic winter smog in northern India threatens livelihoods due to high smoke levels. Aust. Broadcast. Corp. (2024)
21. Seinfeld, J.H., Pandis, S.N.: Atmospheric Chemistry and Physics: From Air Pollution to Climate Change, 3rd edn. Wiley, New Jersey (2016)
22. Central Pollution Control Board (CPCB): National Air Quality Index. Ministry of Environment, Forest and Climate Change, Government of India (2014). https://cpcb.nic.in/national-air-quality-index/

23. World Health Organization (WHO): WHO Global Air Quality Guidelines. World Health Organization (2021)
24. Abdel-Salam, M.M.M.: Significance of personal exposure assessment to air pollution in the urban areas of Egypt. Open J. Air Pollut. **4**(1) (2015)
25. Bell, M.L., Davis, D.L., Fletcher, T.: A retrospective assessment of mortality from the London smog episode of 1952: the role of influenza and pollution. Environ. Health Perspect. **112**(1) (2004)
26. Landrigan, P.J., Fuller, R., Acosta, N.J.R., Adeyi, O., Arnold, R., Basu, N.N.: The lancet commission on pollution and health. The Lancet (2017)
27. Times of India: The Hidden Dangers of Air Pollution and Fog on Human Health, Times of India (etimes) (2025). https://timesofindia.indiatimes.com/life-style/health-fitness/health-news/the-hidden-dangers-of-air-pollution-and-fog-on-human-health/articleshow/117120360.cms
28. Qu, Y., et al.: Deep learning-based atmospheric visibility detection. Atmosphere **15**(11), 1394 (2024)
29. Yang, W., Zhao, Y., Su, Y., Zhu, F.: Multi visual feature fusion based fog visibility estimation for expressway surveillance using deep learning network. Expert Syst. Appl. **234** (2023). Article 121151
30. Meng, X., Liu, Y., Fan, L., Fan, J.: YOLOv5s-Fog: an improved model based on YOLOv5s for object detection in foggy weather scenarios. Sensors **23**(11), 5321 (2023)
31. Khan, M.N., Ahmed, M.M.: Trajectory-level fog detection based on in-vehicle video camera with TensorFlow deep learning utilizing SHRP2 naturalistic driving data. Accid. Anal. Prev. **142**, 105521 (2020)
32. Baykal, T., Ergezer, F., Erişkin, E.: Prediction of road visibility based on meteorological parameters by machine learning methods, DergiPark. Eur. J. Sci. Technol. **34**, 458–462 (2022)
33. Smith, D.K.E., Reka, S., Dorling, S.R., Ross, A.N., Rumbold, H.: Forecasts of fog events in northern India dramatically improve when weather prediction models include irrigation effects. Commun. Earth Environ. **141** (2024)
34. Chaulya, S.K., Prasad, G.M., Chowhury, A.: Vision Enhancement System for Foggy Weather in Opencast Mines, pp. 180–192. Springer (2023)
35. Badri, A., Trudel, B.B., Souissi, A.S.: Occupational health and safety in the industry 4.0 era: a cause for major concern ? Saf. Sci. **109**, 403–411 (2018)
36. Lakra, K., Avishek, K.: Influence of meteorological variables and air pollutants on fog/smog formation in seven major cities of Indo-Gangetic Plain, vol. 196. Springer (2024)

Next-Generation SRAM Architectures: 11T and Memristor-Driven Design Simulation

Gubbala Srilakshmi[1(✉)], Yandra Srinivas[2], G. Narendra Sai[1], D. Dileep[1], D. Tarun[1], A. Dhana Madhu[1], and B. Sai Krishna Raja[1]

[1] Department of Elecronics and Communication Engineering, Vishnu Institute of Technology, Bhimavaram, India
srilakshmi.g@vishnu.edu.in
[2] Department of Mechanical Engineering, Vishnu Institute of Technology, Bhimavaram, India

Abstract. The design of an 11 T SRAM cell aims to enhance stability, power efficiency, and reliable read/write operations compared to traditional SRAM architectures. The core structure includes six transistors forming a cross-coupled inverter pair for stable data storage. Five additional transistors are incorporated to isolate and control the read and write operations. This separation ensures non-destructive reads, minimizes disturbances at storage nodes, and improves overall memory cell stability. The write process helps the storage nodes to communicate data. The read mechanism operates independently, effectively reducing voltage fluctuations and enhancing read stability by isolating the storage node during read operations. Memristor-based SRAM offers faster switching speeds and lower power consumption while maintaining a compact footprint, positioning it as a strong contender for next-generation memory technologies. Despite challenges such as switching speed limitations, wear-out issues, and integration with existing CMOS circuits, memristor-based memory presents significant advantages, particularly in emerging applications like embedded systems, the Internet of Things (IoT), and neuromorphic computing. This study explores the architectural design, advantages, challenges, and practical applications, highlighting the transformative potential of memristors in the advancement of memory technologies.

Keywords: 11 T-SRAM · Efficiency · Memristor-based Memory · Embedded Systems · IoT · Neuromorphic Computing · Power · Stability · 11 T-SRAM

1 Introduction

One kind of volatile semiconductor memory that stores data using bistable latching circuits is called static random-access memory (SRAM). SRAM retains stored data as long as power is available, in contrast to Dynamic RAM (DRAM), which needs to be refreshed on a regular basis to maintain data. This fundamental difference makes SRAM significantly faster and more efficient in read and write operations, making it a critical component in applications requiring high-speed data access, such as processor cache memory, networking hardware, and AI accelerators. Because of its intricate circuit

M. J. C. S. Reis et al. (Eds.): IC4S 2025, LNICST 679, pp. 307–321, 2026.
https://doi.org/10.1007/978-3-032-22834-5_25

architecture, SRAM's benefits come at the expense of more silicon area and higher power consumption per bit.

1.1 Design and Configuration Analysis of SRAM Cells

The fundamental building block of SRAM is the memory cell, commonly implemented using six- transistor (6T), eight-transistor (8T), ten-transistor (10T), or twelve-transistor (12T) architectures. Among these, the 6T SRAM cell is the most widely used, consisting of two cross-coupled inverters forming a bistable latch and two access transistors responsible for controlling read and write operations. While 6T SRAM offers efficiency in terms of speed and stability, alternative designs such as 8T, 10T, and 12T configurations enhance noise immunity, minimize leakage power, and improve read/write performance—particularly for ultra-low-power and high- performance applications. Due to its significantly lower latency than DRAM, SRAM is ideal for L1, L2, and L3 cache memory in CPUs and GPUs, where rapid data retrieval is critical. One of the key advantages of SRAM is that it eliminates the need for refresh cycles, simplifying operation and reducing power consumption during active read/write operations. However, this benefit comes with a trade- off—each SRAM cell requires multiple transistors, making it less dense and more expensive than DRAM. Consequently, SRAM is primarily used for cache memory rather than as main system memory.

1.2 Technological Advancements and Practical Applications of SRAM

Despite its higher cost and lower density, SRAM remains a key component in high- speed computing, microcontrollers, networking equipment, biomedical applications, and AI accelerators, where performance and reliability take precedence over cost and space constraints. Researchers in modern semiconductor design focus on optimizing SRAM for power efficiency, stability, and reduced leakage currents especially in deep submicron and nanoscale technologies.

1.3 Benefits of SRAM

SRAM's speed is its most obvious benefit. It is a great option for real-time applications as it offers quick data access with little latency and does not require the lengthy refresh cycles like DRAM requires. Additionally, SRAM ensures high data integrity by eliminating the need for capacitors and refresh cycles, reducing the risk of data corruption. Modern advancements in SRAM technology, such as power gating and dynamic voltage scaling, have further enhanced its power efficiency, making it more energy-efficient than earlier generations. However, SRAM is still best suited for scenarios where speed, low latency, and data integrity take precedence over power efficiency. Another advantage of SRAM is its lower heat generation and greater resistance to radiation, making it an optimal choice for high- performance computing, space applications, and critical embedded systems.

2 Literature Survey

The performance of SRAM memory circuits is usually measured using industry- standard layouts for traditional SRAM cells, such as the standard S8T cells and the customary C6T cells. These cells do, however, have a number of difficulties, such as half- select problems, write failures, stability degradation, and conflicts between write and read operations. Furthermore, improving read stability by increasing the read static noise margin may have a detrimental effect on the write process. The necessary minimum voltage for both read and write operations may be limited by process fluctuations, according to research forecasts. In response to these challenges, several SRAM topologies have been proposed, offering improved outcomes compared to traditional designs. Using 45 nm technology, these include the Schmitt trigger ST9 T [1], standard S8T, and conventional C6T cells. Their performance is compared to that of the planned E2VR11T cell. The operational specifications of the selected cells, including the proposed E2VR11T cell, are analyzed, with ongoing research confirming that SRAM memory design continues to evolve despite the variety of cells with different techniques applied. Important features for SRAM memory, especially in low-power applications, include process tolerance and energy efficiency. The chosen cells, such as S8T, use two to three bit lines and function in either a differential writing mode or a single-end decoupled read mode. Two transistors are utilized in the S8T cell's read route, and the word line (WL) and read word line (RWL) are frequently employed to facilitate write and read operations. This research suggests the energy-efficient and variability-resilient mersister 11T SRAM memory, which successfully overcomes the concerns raised by the highlighted challenges of current cells. current cells [2]. this paper present an improved 11 T SRAM cell design with enhanced write stability, reduced power consumption, and better performance under PVT variations [3]. The Simulation results confirm their suitability for energy-efficient memory applications [4]. The proposed architecture significantly improves energy efficiency and stability during read/write operations [5]. Ho et al. propose a 7T1M SRAM cell combining seven transistors and one memristor to achieve low power and high density. The design offers improved read/write stability and reduced area compared to conventional SRAM cells.

2.1 Analysis of Next-Generation SRAM Architectures (2020–2025)

Recent SRAM architectures are focused on enhanced stability with ultra-low-power operation and robust performance under near-threshold supply voltages. Such designs include Schmitt-trigger-based 9T cells, enhanced 8T/10T cells, and BTI- aware 11T architectures which possess various challenges like leakage reduction, and degraded static noise margin at nanoscale technologies. Compare to all, the proposed 11T + memristor SRAM is best suitable for improving stability, leakage reduction, and low-power operation for next- generation devices.

2.2 Traditional Method

The design and development of an 11T SRAM cell [5] are driven by the need for high performance and low power consumption. The process begins with defining functional requirements such as enhanced read stability, write efficiency, and power optimization. These specifications play a crucial role in selecting transistor configurations and layout strategies to ensure a stable and efficient memory cell that operates at low power levels as shown in Fig. 1

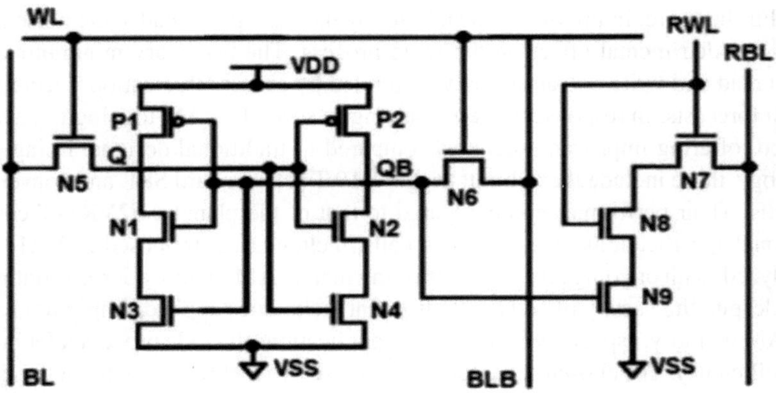

Fig. 1 11 T SRAM

2.3 Core Architecture and Functional Components

At the core of the 11T SRAM [6] cell are six transistors forming a cross-coupled inverter pair, which provides stable data storage. This fundamental structure is essential for maintaining data integrity within the cell. The additional five transistors serve crucial functions, including improving read stability, enabling efficient write operations, and managing access control. A key feature of the 11T design is the implementation of dedicated read and write paths, which significantly enhance performance and reduce errors. Write operations are managed by specialized transistors that interact with the word line (WL), enabling data to be written into the cell without disrupting its internal state. Read operations take place through an independent path using separate read bit lines (RBL) and a read word line (RWL).

2.4 Read-Write Isolation for Improved Stability

Separating the read and write operations is a critical advancement in the 11T SRAM [6] architecture, as it prevents read disturb errors—a common issue in conventional SRAM designs. By ensuring that read operations do not interfere with the stored data, this design enhances the stability and integrity of the memory cell. Additionally, this isolation mechanism minimizes power consumption during read operations by activating only the necessary transistors, avoiding unnecessary switching of other components.

3 Proposed SRAM Architectures and Analytical Modelling

3.1 Novelty of the Proposed Work

This work introduces a dual-configuration hybrid SRAM design using 2-memristor and 4-memristor integration over a baseline 11T cell. The novelty lies in the use of memristor-based resistance modulation for adaptive power regulation, improved read stability, and leakage reduction without modifying the internal 11T latch structure.

3.2 Analytical Modeling

Static Noise Margin (SNM)

During the hold state, for the cross-coupled inverters The SNM is derived from the largest square that can fit between the voltage transfer characteristics

SNM = min (side length of the maximum square in the butterfly curve)

Dynamic Power Consumption

Dynamic power during read/write activity is expressed as in Eq. 1

$$P_{dynamic} = \alpha\, C_L V_{DD}^2 \tag{1}$$

The delay associated with SRAM read/write operations is modeled as Eq. 2

$$t_{delay} = R_{on}\, C_{bitline} \tag{2}$$

Memristor State Equation (HP Model)

A memristor's instantaneous resistance is given by Eq. 3

$$M(w) = R_{off} - (R_{off} - R_{on})\frac{w}{D} \tag{3}$$

where w is the dopant drift width, and dis the device thickness.

3.3 Memristor Modeling Details

The memristor devices used in this work were modeled using the HP linear ion- drift model, which accurately captures the resistive switching behavior suitable for CMOS integration.

3.4 Simulation Setup

All simulations were performed in LTspice using the 22 nm Predictive Technology Model (PTM) for CMOS devices. The following configuration parameters were used throughout the evaluation:

4 Suggested Methodology

4.1 Memristor-Based SRAM: A Low-Power, High-Efficiency Memory Solution

Leon O. Chua initially proposed the idea of a memristor, or memory resistor, as the fourth essential passive circuit component, after the resistor, capacitor, and inductor, in 1971. Memristors have variable resistance that varies according on the history of the applied voltage and current, in contrast to conventional resistors that have a set resistance. Memristors are a great option for non-volatile memory applications because of their capacity to "remember" past states even after the power is switched off.A memristor is characterized by its memresistance (M), measured in ohms (Ω), which links the charge (q) passing through it to the magnetic flux (Φ) across it. Unlike conventional memory devices such as SRAM and DRAM, which rely on charge storage mechanisms, memristors leverage resistive switching [7], enabling them to store information in a non-volatile manner. This non-volatility, combined with high-speed operation, low power consumption, and CMOS compatibility, makes memristors an excellent candidate for enhancing low-power SRAM designs as shown in Fig. 2.

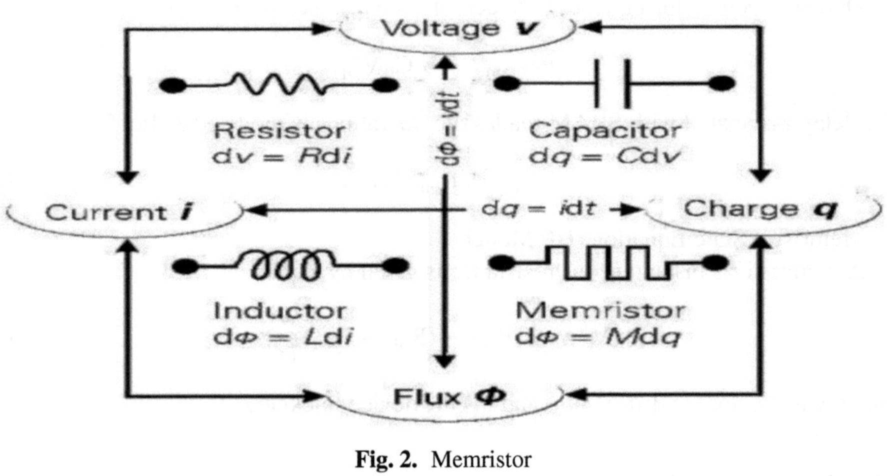

Fig. 2. Memristor

4.2 Memristor's Advantages in SRAM Design

The integration of memristors with SRA, opens new possibilities for power- efficient, high-speed memory architectures. Traditional SRAM is fast but power- hungry, mainly due to leakage currents in CMOS transistors. By incorporating memristors into SRAM, several key benefits can be achieved, Memristor-based SRAM offers several advantages over conventional SRAM, particularly in terms of power efficiency and stability [8]. Yakopcic et al. propose a hybrid crossbar architecture integrating memristors This design improves performance and scalability, making it suitable for future neuromorphic and aerospace systems. One key benefit is non-volatility: unlike traditional SRAM, which loses data when power is turned off, M-SRAM can retain stored data without requiring a continuous power supply, making it ideal for power-sensitive applications like embedded systems and electronics. Power reduction is another advantage, as memristors dynamically adjust their resistance based on the applied voltage, optimizing the power supply to SRAM cells.

Separating the read and write operations is a critical advancement in the 11 T SRAM [9] architecture, Memristors help regulate power flow, minimizing unnecessary power wastage. Memristor-based SRAM [10] architectures have gained significant attention due to their potential to enhance power efficiency and speed in various applications. In a hybrid CMOS- memristor SRAM, a memristor is integrated alongside traditional CMOS transistors, where it stores state information, reducing the reliance on volatile charge storage and improving power efficiency while maintaining SRAM-like speed. SRAM's speed is its most obvious benefit. It is a great option for real-time applications as it offers quick data access with little latency and does not require the lengthy refresh cycles like DRAM [11] requires. Non-volatile SRAM with memristors [12] offers instant-on capability, ensuring data retention even after power loss, eliminating the need for boot-up loading. These advancements in memristor-SRAM integration have numerous potential applications, particularly in domains where low power consumption and speed are critical. Jiang et al. introduce a highly reliable 12T SRAM bitcell designed to improve noise margins and minimize failure under voltage scaling. This work presents cell enhances write and read stability, making it compatible for low-power applications [13]. This system attains accuracy and high sensitivity, making it suitable for real-time biomedical diagnostics [14]. Ykuntam et al. propose a non- linear carry- select adder architecture using XOR- less adder modules to minimize area and improve speed. Simulation results show reduced propagation delay and reduced logic complexity as comparing with conventional CSLA designs [15].

4.3 Adding 2 Memristors at VDD Power Supply of SRAM Power Regulation

The two memristors at the VDD power supply act as dynamic resistors, adjusting their resistance based on the applied voltage. This ensures more stable voltage regulation, reducing unnecessary power dissipation.

Power Consumption Reduction
By dynamically controlling current flow, leakage power is minimized. This is especially beneficial for low-power applications, such as embedded systems and IoT devices.

4.4 Adding 4 Memristors at VDD Power Supply of SRAM

Further Power Optimization: Increasing the number of memristors (from 2 to 4) enhances power efficiency by distributing the load more evenly, reducing overall power wastage. This configuration is particularly useful for large SRAM arrays, where power dissipation scales with size.

5 Results Analysis

5.1 SNM and Write Margin Analysis

Static Noise Margin (SNM) is derived from the butterfly curves obtained from the voltage transfer characteristics of the cross-coupled inverters.

Write Margin (WM)

Write Margin is defined as the difference between the wordline voltage and the minimum write failure voltage as shown in Eq. 4

$$WM = V_{WL} - V_{write\_fail} \quad (4)$$

The 2-memristor and 4-memristor designs demonstrate a higher write margin due to reduced contention between access transistors and pull-up devices, making write operations more reliable under low-voltage conditions.

5.2 Benchmarking With Modern SRAM Designs

To evaluate the competitiveness of the proposed designs, their performance was compared against recent SRAM architectures such as 9T Schmitt-trigger cells, 10T read-decoupled designs, and hybrid CMOS–memristor 6T/8T variants reported in the 2020–2024 literature as shown in below Table 1.

Table 1 Comparison of performance parameters

Design Type	Power Consumption	Delay	SNM	Remarks
9T ST-based SRAM	Low	Medium	High	Strong read stability
10T Read-Decoupled SRAM	Medium	Low	Medium	Reduced read disturb
6T + Memristor Hybrid	Very Low	Low	Low	Provides non- volatile storage
Proposed 2-Memristor SRAM	Lowest	Lowest	High	Effective leakage reduction
Proposed 4- Memristor SRAM	Very Low	Low	Highest	Best stability & regulation

Here are the results for the existing design and the proposed design, the proposed design consists of two design one is 2-memristor sram and other is 4-memristor design, the design were simultated in LTspice tool in 22 nm technology. Figure 3 represents the schematic of the 11TSRAM Design, which consists of 11 transistors.

Figure 4 shows the waveform for the 11T SRAM cell, illustrating the timing characteristics during read and write operations. In the waveform, key signals such as the word line, bit lines and output.

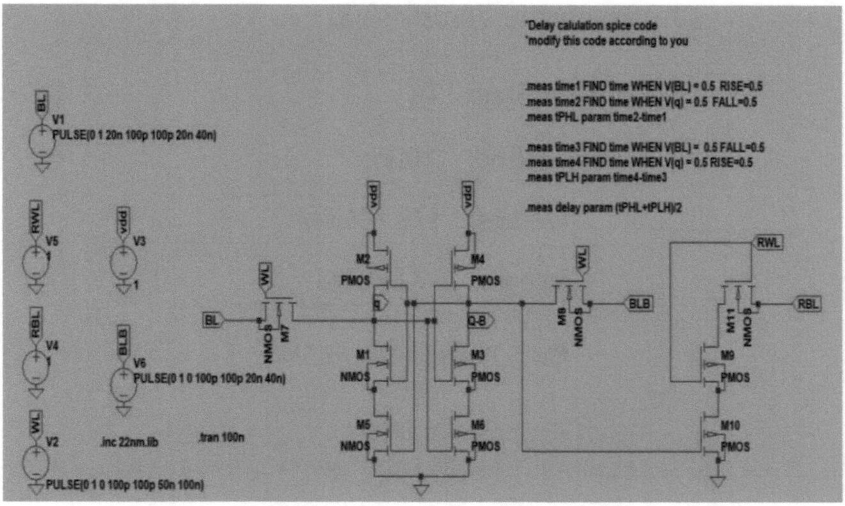

Fig. 3 Schematic of 11 T SRAM Design

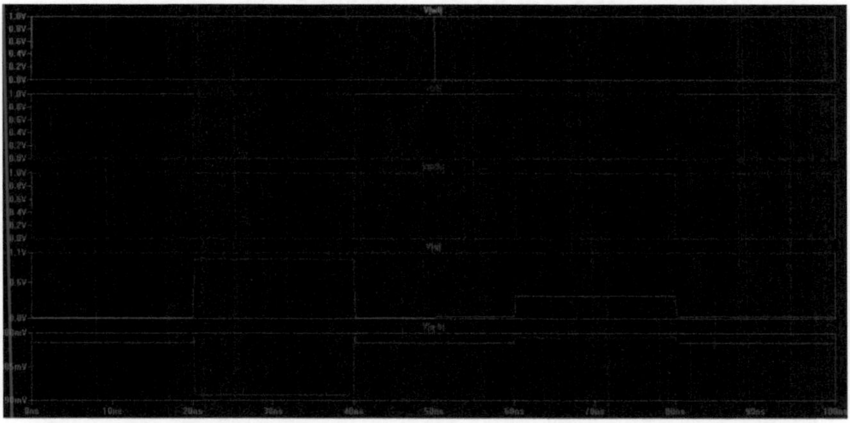

Fig. 4 Waveforms for 11 T SRAM

Figure 5 shows how much power the 11 T SRAM cell uses at different operating phases, including read and write cycles. The waveform in the fig presents the power dissipation over time.

Figure 6 illustrates the delay characteristics of the 11T SRAM The delay values indicate the time required for the cell to successfully complete data access and storage transitions. While during the read operation, the delay represents the time taken for the bit lines to develop a sufficient voltage difference. In the write operation, to overwrite the existing data with a new value. The observed delay values reflect the overall performance and speed efficiency of the 11T SRAM cell architecture,

The 2-Memristor based SRAM the schematic for the design is shown in the Fig. 7. The schematic of the 2-Memristor-based SRAM design is shown in the figure.

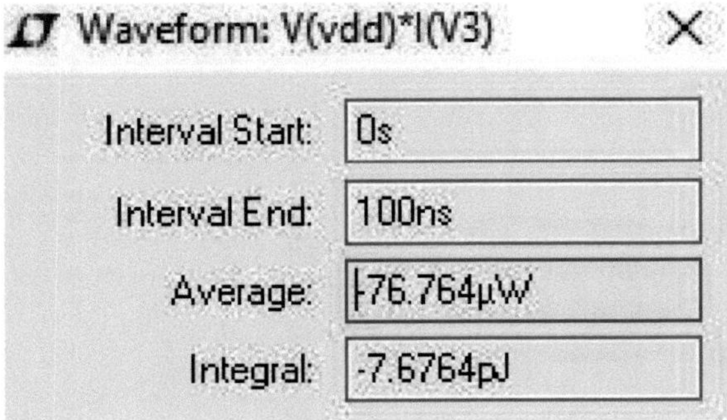

Fig. 5 Power for 11 T SRAM

```
time1: time=2.005e-008 at 2.005e-008
time2: time=4.00958e-008 at 4.00958e-008
tphl: time2-time1=2.00458e-008
time3: time=4.015e-008 at 4.015e-008
time4: time=2.01152e-008 at 2.01152e-008
tplh: time4-time3=-2.00348e-008
delay: (tphl+tplh)/2=5.51983e-012
```

Fig. 6 Delay for 11 T for SRAM

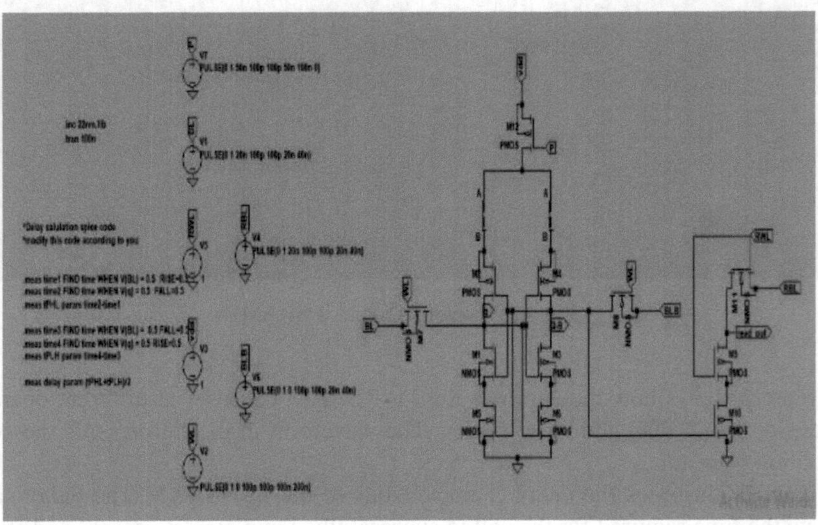

Fig. 7 Schematic for 2-Memrisotr based SRAM

It illustrates the integration of two memristors with the conventional SRAM structure to enhance performance. This configuration abstracts to increase stability, reduce power requirement, and optimize data retention.

Fig. 8 Waveform for 2-Memrisotr based SRAM

Figure 8 shows the waveform for the 2 Memristor SRAM cell, illustrating the timing characteristics during read and write operations. In the waveform, key signals such as the word line, bit lines and output.

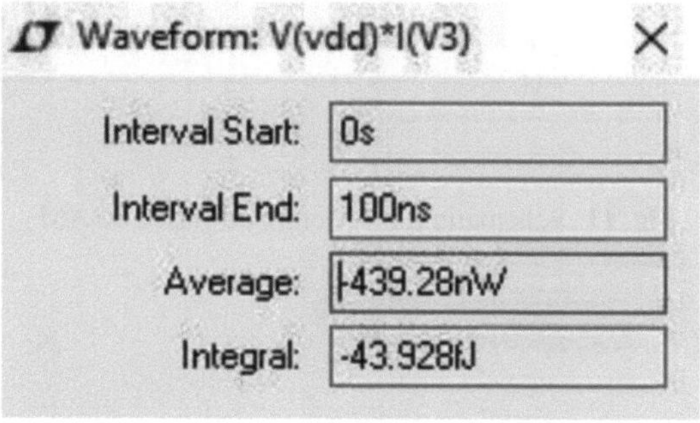

Fig. 9 Power for 2-Memristor SRAM

Figure 9 shows how much power the 2-memristor cell uses at different operating phases, including read and write cycles. The waveform in the fig presents the power dissipation over time.

Figure 10 shows the delay values for the 2 Memristor SRAM cell during its read and write operations

The 4-Memristor based SRAM the schematic for the design is shown in the Fig. 11.

```
timel: time=2.005e-008 at 2.005e-008
time2: time=4.01091e-008 at 4.01091e-008
tphl: time2-timel=2.00591e-008
time3: time=4.015e-008 at 4.015e-008
time4: time=2.00935e-008 at 2.00935e-008
tplh: time4-time3=-2.00565e-008
delay: (tphl+tplh)/2=1.27666e-012
```

Fig. 10 Delay for 2-Memrisotr SRAM

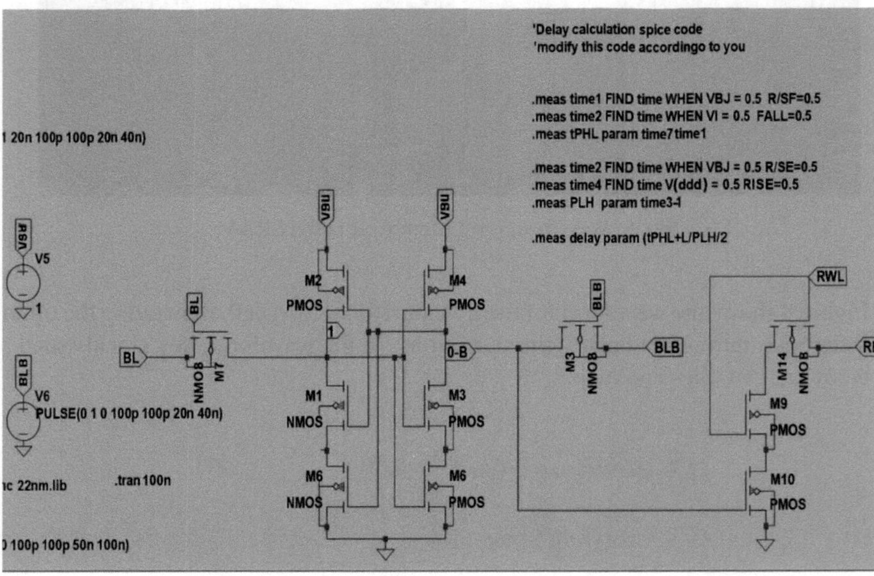

Fig. 11 Schematic for 4-Memrisotr based SRAM

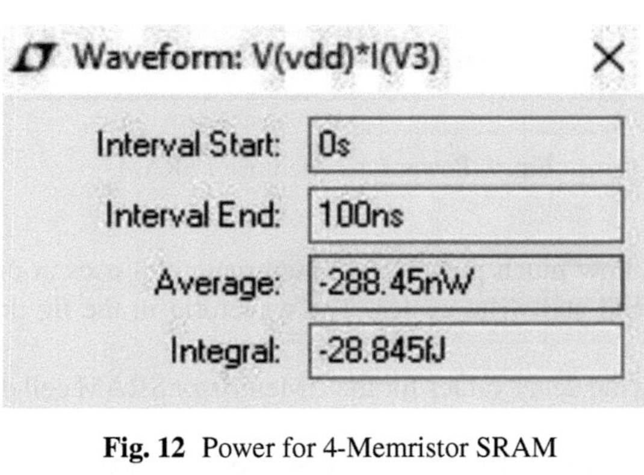

Fig. 12 Power for 4-Memristor SRAM

Figure 12 shows how much power the 4-memristor cell uses at different operating phases, including read and write cycles. The waveform in the fig presents the power dissipation over time.

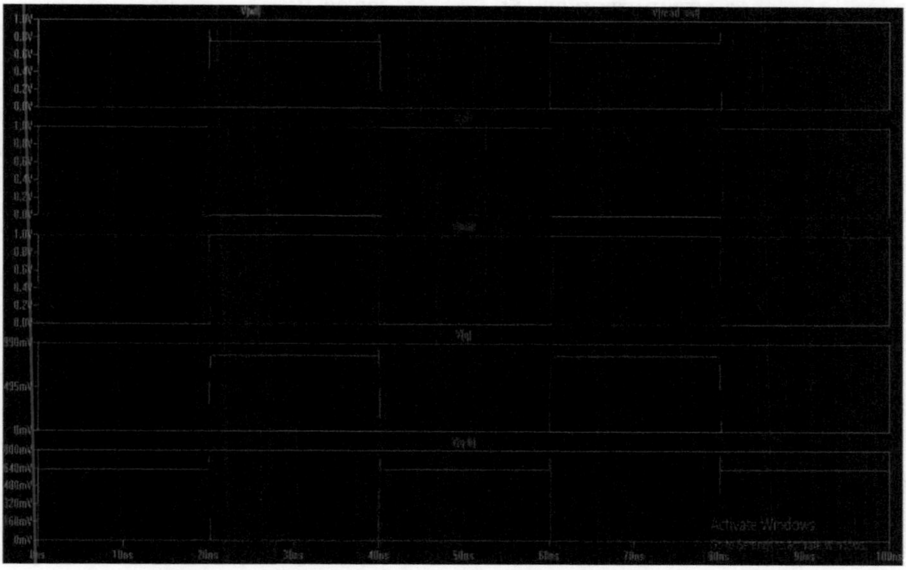

Fig. 13 Waveform for 4-Memrisotr based SRAM

Figure 13 shows the waveform for the 4 Memristor SRAM cell, illustrating the timing characteristics during read and write operations. In the waveform, key signals such as the word line, bit lines and output.

```
time1: time=2.005e-008 at 2.005e-008
time2: time=4.01092e-008 at 4.01092e-008
tphl: time2-time1=2.00592e-008
time3: time=4.015e-008 at 4.015e-008
time4: time=2.00935e-008 at 2.00935e-008
tplh: time4-time3=-2.00565e-008
delay: (tphl+tplh)/2=1.31256e-012
```

Fig. 14 Delay for 4-Memrisotr SRAM

Figure 14 shows the delay values for the 4 Memristor SRAM cell during its read and write operations

Above Table 2 shows the performance of different SRAM designs is compared based on power consumption and delay. The 11T SRAM consumes 76.74 μW with a delay of 5.519 ps. In contrast, the 2-memristor SRAM uses only 439.28 nW and has a delay

Table 2 Comparison of the 11 T SRAM, 2-Mermistor SRAM &4-Mermistor SRAM

S. No.	DESIGN	POWER	DELAY
1	11T SRAM	76.74uW	5.519 ps
2	2-MEMRISTOR SRAM	439.28nW	1.27 ps
3	4-MEMRISTOR SRAM	288.45nW	1.31 ps

of 1.27 ps, while the 4-memristor SRAM consumes 288.45 nW and has a delay of 1.31 ps. These results show a trade-off between power consumption and delay, with memristor-based designs offering better power efficiency and faster delays than the 11T SRAM.

In emerging hybrid CMOS–memristor memory systems Reliability is a crucial factor. Memristor-based SRAM designs introduce switching variability, and integration compatibility with CMOS processes. In the proposed architectures, memristors are used only for supply regulation rather than for direct data storage, which significantly reduces their switching stress and enhances overall Reliability.

6 Conclusion

In conclusion, the Memristor 11 T SRAM cell design, implemented in 22 nm LTSpice technology, successfully addresses the challenges of stability, power efficiency, and reliable read/write operations. This innovative design integrates memristors with an 11 T SRAM cell, combining the high-speed operation of conventional SRAM with the non-volatility and power efficiency advantages of memristors. By leveraging these characteristics, the proposed design not only reduces power consumption but also enhances data retention, making it particularly beneficial for applications that require both rapid access and persistent memory storage. Furthermore, the incorporation of memristors significantly improves the overall performance and functionality of SRAM, paving the way for advancements in low- power and high-performance memory architectures. This approach is especially valuable for next- generation electronic devices, including IoT systems, edge computing, and AI-driven applications, where efficient memory solutions are crucial. Despite the promising benefits, further research and optimization can enhance its scalability and adaptability for future semiconductors technologies.

References

1. Keonhee, C., Juhyun, P., Tae, W.O., Seong, O.J.: One-Sided Schmitt-Trigger-based 9T SRAM cell for near- threshold operation. IEEE Trans. Circuits Syst. I Regul. Pap. **67**, 1551–1561 (2020)
2. Manoj Kumar, R., Sridevi, P.V.: Design of an enhanced write stability, high- performance, low power 11T SRAM cell. Int. J. Electron. **108**(10), 1652–1675 (2021)
3. Gupta, P., Sharma, K., Barnwal, S.: Low- power non- volatile 11T2R and 13T2R SRAM cells using a Memristor. Telecommun. Radio Eng. **80**(10), 1–17 (2021)

4. Kumar, N.S., et al.: SRAM design using memristor and self- controllable voltage (SVL) technique. In: Proceedings of the International Conference on Computational Intelligence and Data Engineering Lecture Notes on Data Engineering and Communications Technologies, vol. 9, pp. 29–39. Springer, Singapore (2018)
5. Ho, P.W.C., Almurib, H.A.F., Nandha Kumar, T.: Memristive SRAM cell of seven transistors and one Memristor. J. Semicond. **37**(10), 104002 (2016)
6. Satyanarayana, B.V.V., Kumar, G.P., Budumuru, P.R., Sridhara, S.V.K., Swathi, S., Phani, T.S.S.: Design and performance analysis of 11-T SRAM cell with BTI reliability. In: 2nd International Conference on Automation, Computing and Renewable Systems (ICACRS), Pudukkottai, India, pp. 166–173 (2023)
7. Sachdeva, A., Tomar, V.K.: Design of a stable low power 11-T static random access memory cell. J. Circuits Syst. Comput. **29**(13), 2050206 (2020)
8. Yakopcic, C., Taha, T.M., Hasan, R.: Hybrid crossbar architecture for a Memristor based memory. In: NAECON 2014 – IEEE National Aerospace and Electronics Conference, Dayton, OH, USA, pp. 237–242 (2014)
9. Kumar, A.T., Satyanarayana, B.V.V.: Low voltage high speed 8T SRAM cell for ultra-low power applications. Int. J. Eng. Technol. **7**, 70–74 (2018)
10. Rathi, N., Kumar, A., Gupta, N., Singh, S.K.: A review of low-power static random access memory (SRAM) designs. In: 2023 IEEE Devices for Integrated Circuit (DevIC), Kalyani, India, pp. 455–459 (2023). https://doi.org/10.1109/DevIC57758.2023.10134887
11. Horiguchi, F.: Advanced memory concepts for DRAM and nonvolatile memories. In: Proceedings of 35th European Solid- State Device Research Conference, 2005. ESSDERC 2005. Grenoble, France, pp. 181–184 (2005)
12. Huang, G.M., Ho, Y., Li, P.: Memristor system properties and its design applications to circuits such as nonvolatile Memristor memories. In: 2010 International Conference on Communications, Circuits and Systems (ICCCAS), Chengdu, China, pp. 805–810 (2010)
13. Jiang, J., Lin, D., Xiao, J., Zou, S.: A novel highly reliable 12T SRAM Bitcell design. In: IEEE International Conference on Electron Devices and Solid- State Circuits (EDSSC), Xi'an, China, 2019, pp. 1–2 (2019)
14. Katta, M., et al.: Classified disease detection from MEMS based biosensor array. In: AIP Conference Proceedings, vol. 3217, no. 1. AIP Publishing (2024)
15. Ykuntam, Y.D., Penumutchi, B., Gubbala, S.: Design of speed and area efficient non linear carry select adder (NLCSLA) architecture using XOR less adder module. In: Chakravarthy, V., Bhateja, V., Flores Fuentes, W., Anguera, J., Vasavi, K.P. (eds.) Advances in Signal Processing, Embedded Systems and IoT Lecture Notes in Electrical Engineering, vol. 992. Springer, Singapore (2023)

Enhancing Healthcare Automation: An IoT Enabled Bluetooth-Based Smart Rover for Elderly Support

Jejeswari Kiranmai Pilli, Ritwik Sodadasu, Akash Yarrareddy, Vamsi Talam, and Naveen Kumar Maurya(✉)

Department of Electronics and Communication Engineering, Vishnu Institute of Technology, Bhimavaram 534202, Andhra Pradesh, India
naveenkumar.m@vishnu.edu.in

Abstract. With the ageing world population, elderly people need special solutions to aid them in achieving independence and improvement in their well-being. Such a challenge escalates when it involves the elderly living alone. A solution to tackle above-said problem, we suggest that a speech-commanded personal aid robot be made for elderly assistance in daily lives. The product can be developed through an embedded system coupled with the use of Internet of Things (IoT) technology. The robot functions through voice instructions by humans that are remotely controlled using a smartphone via Google Assistant. The voice instructions are translated into text and sent to the robot through a Bluetooth network. The robot on an ATMEGA-328P-based platform will be able to execute a number of movements, rotate in several directions, begin and terminate activities, and move objects from one place to another using a robotic gripper. The robot is also equipped with an obstacle detection system. The personal assistant robot can be used for domestic, hospital, and industrial purposes, enhancing mobility support and automation of tasks for people with fewer physical abilities.

Keywords: Healthcare · Robotics · Internet of Things · Arduino · Embedded Systems

1 Introduction

Recently, robotics and embedded systems have been found to be of significant importance in various fields viz. industrial application [1,2], navigation [3], e-commerce/good delivery [4], games [5], healthcare [6], etc. Among these, healthcare has received tremendous attention from both academia as well as industries. Notably, with the advancement in healthcare and medical science, the life expectancy of humans has increased drastically. As a result, the population of elderly people has also increased. With the ageing world population, elderly people need special solutions to aid them in achieving independence and improvement in their well-being. Such a challenge escalates when it involves the elderly

M. J. C. S. Reis et al. (Eds.): IC4S 2025, LNICST 679, pp. 322–332, 2026.
https://doi.org/10.1007/978-3-032-22834-5_26

living alone. Hence, there is a requirement for robots that could be used to take care of elderly people. In addition, the integration of the Internet of Things (IoT) in embedded systems and robotics makes the overall system quite smarter [7–10].

A voice-controlled personal assistant using a Raspberry Pi to process and execute user commands, enabling hands-free operation and seamless IoT integration has been reported in [11]. Research on voice-activated home automation allowed users to control electrical appliances through speech recognition, improving accessibility and convenience [12]. A study reported in [13] has developed a voice-commanded pick-and-place robot for disabled users, enhancing independence through robotic arm manipulation. Another investigation presented a personal assistant robot that interacts naturally with users, improving human-robot interaction in daily tasks [14]. Comparative analysis of IoT prototyping platforms highlighted Arduino's real-time processing advantages over Raspberry Pi and MicroBit, making it suitable for automation applications [15].

Advancements in real-time object detection using deep learning models such as YOLO have improved robotic perception and autonomous decision-making [16–18]. Research on robotic grippers introduced low-cost, 3D-printed mechanisms, expanding their use in assistive robotics [19,20]. Multi-terrain robots demonstrated adaptability to diverse environments, broadening robotic mobility solutions [21]. Studies on self-balancing robots investigated control algorithms to enhance stability and efficiency in mobile platforms [22]. The development of robotic end effectors facilitated precision object handling, advancing automation in domestic and industrial settings [23]. Additionally, low-cost mobile robots have been effective in rescue operations, highlighting their potential in emergency scenarios [24]. The integration of speech recognition with robotic mobility enabled personal assistant robots to respond to voice commands for hands-free operation [25]

Unlike earlier implementations relying on ZigBee or computer-based speech interfaces, newer systems use Bluetooth for cost-effective wireless communication [26]. These systems typically incorporate an Arduino Uno-based microcontroller, HC-05 Bluetooth module, L298N motor driver, and servo-operated grippers for efficient command execution [27]. Obstacle detection via ultrasonic sensors enhances operational safety, ensuring smooth movement [28]. End effectors, inspired by domestic robotic manipulators, improve precision in grasping and placing objects, making these robots suitable for assistive applications [29]. Research has also focused on optimizing power management to extend operational time for battery-powered robots [30]. Advances in natural language processing have made speech-controlled robots more adaptive and responsive [31]. Hybrid control mechanisms integrating voice commands with gesture recognition further enhance assistive robot versatility [32]. The ongoing evolution of speech-controlled robotic systems continues to drive innovation, making automation more accessible and user-friendly [33]. Hence, there is a need of an hour to develop IoT-enabled smart rover, which could be controlled by speech command for support of elderly people.

A comparison with current assistive robotic systems reported in the literature has been carried in order to highlight the contribution of the proposed work. The smart system architecture of proposed work ensures requirement of fewer parts, which reduces cost and latency, simultaneously. Thus making proposed system compact, economical, power saving device. In addiction, the proposed rover combines Bluetooth and IoT capabilities, which allows for remote monitoring as well. The manuscript is organized as follows: Sect. 2 describes the effective system framework and methodology. Section 3 elucidates about major components and their interfacing. Section 4 focuses on results and discussions. Finally, Sect. 5 concludes the paper.

2 Effective System Framework and Methodology

The proposed robotic system utilizes Bluetooth-based control with the inclusion of an ultrasonic sensor and buzzer for automation as well as interaction with the user as shown in Fig. 1. An Arduino Uno acts as the central processing unit at the heart of the system, interfacing with several components to carry out real-time operations. An HC-05 Bluetooth module creates wireless communication with an Android device, allowing commands to be sent. User commands are received by the HC-05 module and forwarded to the Arduino for execution and processing. The ultrasonic sensor handles object detection. Upon detecting an object within a given range, it sends signals to the Arduino Uno, which in turn causes the activation of a buzzer as a warning signal. Without an obstacle, the buzzer

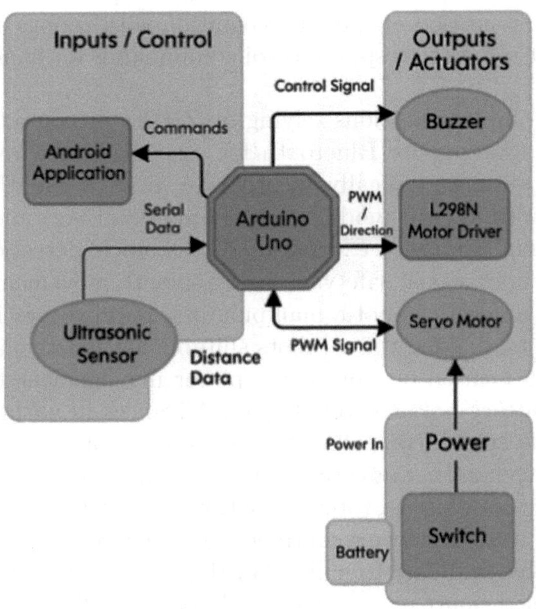

Fig. 1. System framework diagram.

does not activate. The L298N motor driver controls the functioning of the DC motor, enabling controlled movement of the robotic system. The Arduino sends control signals to the L298N, which regulates the operation of the DC motor, enabling the desired movement of the robotic vehicle. This DC motor provides mobility, allowing the vehicle to move accurately based on user commands. Additionally, a servo motor is connected to the Arduino to control a robotic arm. The robotic arm can perform gripping and lifting operations according to received instructions. It is of particular importance in object handling, and the system is thus well-placed for automation applications like object placement and material handling.

The system is driven by a rechargeable battery, with a switch provided for power distribution control. The battery provides constant use and removes reliance on external power sources, which makes the robot extremely portable and efficient for use in the field. Commands sent from the Android phone through Bluetooth provide directional movement for the robotic car and robotic arm. These commands are received by the HC-05 Bluetooth module and forwarded to the Arduino to be processed and executed. Real-time execution of commands is enabled through Bluetooth-based control, allowing for smooth interaction between the user and the robot system. At the same time, an ultrasonic sensor continuously scans for obstacles in the robot's path. Upon detecting an obstacle, the Arduino activates a buzzer to provide an auditory warning, which enhances safety and helps prevent potential collisions. This continuous scanning mechanism ensures dynamic environmental awareness, making the system more reliable for navigation in uncertain terrains. The system operates at maximum efficiency using battery power, making it portable and capable of functioning autonomously without requiring external power sources. The integration of Bluetooth communication, sensor-automated controls, and motor control makes this system suitable for various applications, including industrial automation, intelligent transportation, and remote-controlled robots. The design enhances operational efficiency, accuracy, and flexibility, making it an effective solution for both research and practical use.

3 Major Components and Their Interfacing

The voice-controlled personal assistant robot is programmed to get voice commands via Bluetooth, decode them using an Arduino Uno (ATMEGA328P), and perform respective tasks like movement and object manipulation through a gripper as shown in Fig. 1 and 2. The setup includes an ultrasonic sensor for detecting obstacles and a buzzer to alert the user. Power supply is managed effectively via a 3S lithium-ion battery (11.1 V) to provide a steady operation. The major components and their functionality have been elucidated below:

1. **Microcontroller Configuration (Arduino Uno - ATMEGA328P)**: The Arduino Uno performs as the processor unit, providing all the necessary inputs from the Bluetooth module and sensors and taking control of the motor driver, gripper servo, and buzzer as shown in Fig. 2. The Arduino Uno

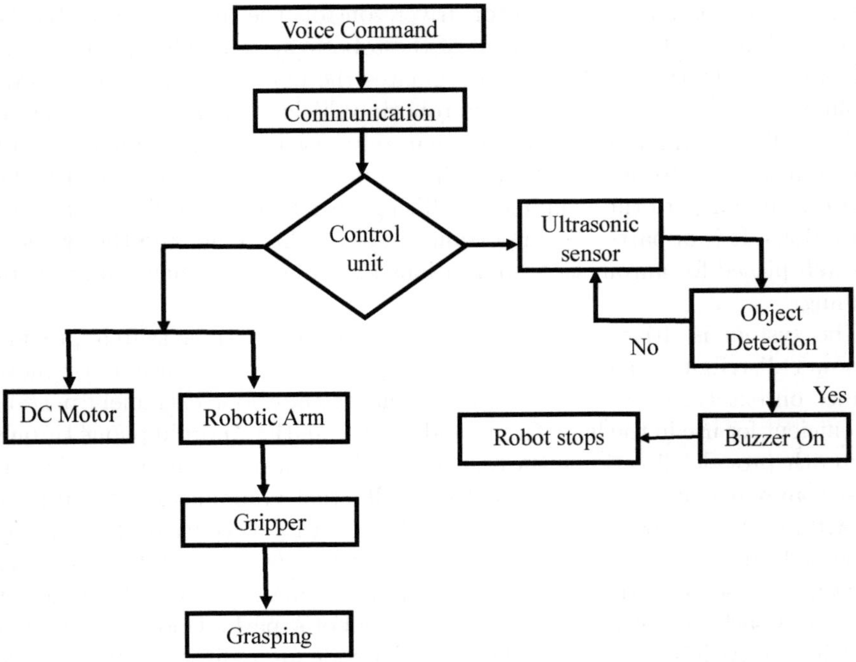

Fig. 2. Flow chart of control mechanism.

gets powered by 3S lithium-ion battery (11.1 V), which is connected on the positive end to VIN and on the negative end to GND. Shared ground (GND) across all the hardware components is needed to ensure stable circuits.

2. **Bluetooth Module (HC-05) Connection**: The HC-05 Bluetooth module provides wireless communication between the Arduino and a smartphone, where the smartphone sends text-based commands for robot control. The module's VCC is connected to the Arduino's 5 V pin, and the GND pin is connected to the common ground. Communication of data is achieved by the module's TXD pin, which is connected to RX (Pin 10) of the Arduino, and the RXD pin, which is connected to the TX (Pin 11), enabling serial communication.
3. **Motor Driver (L298N) and DC Motor Connections**: The L298N motor driver manages the movement of the robot's two DC motors. It is driven by the 3S lithium-ion battery (11.1V), with GND being tied to the common ground. The enable pins ENA and ENB of the driver are connected to Pins 6 and 5 on the Arduino to manage motor speed. The direction control pins are wired as follows:
   - IN1 → Pin 2 (Arduino)
   - IN2 → Pin 3 (Arduino)
   - IN3 → Pin 4 (Arduino)
   - IN4 → Pin 9 (Arduino)

The left motor is paired with Motor 1 Output, and the right motor is linked to Motor 2 Output for movement in multiple directions depending on commands received.

4. **Servo Motor (Gripper Control) Connection**: The servo motor that drives the gripper for the manipulation of objects is supplied 5 V by the Arduino and has a common ground. Its signal pin is linked to Pin 12 (Arduino PWM Output), permitting exact position control to close and open the gripper at specific angles (0° to be open and 90° to be closed).
5. **Ultrasonic Sensor (HC-SR04) for Obstacle Detection**: The HC-SR04 ultrasonic sensor provides safe maneuvering by sensing obstacles in the robot's direction. It is driven through the 5 V pin of the Arduino and also has a common ground. The Trigger pin is interfaced to Pin 7, and the Echo pin is interfaced to Pin 8, enabling the Arduino to calculate the distance to obstacles and halt movement if required.
6. **Buzzer Alert System Connection**: A buzzer gives a sound signal when an obstacle is encountered. It draws power from 5 V of the Arduino and has a common ground. Pin 13 is connected to the signal pin so that the Arduino can turn the buzzer on when an obstacle is encountered, warning the user.
7. **Power Supply Connection (3S Lithium-Ion Battery - 11.1 V)**: The system is effectively powered by the 3S lithium-ion battery (11.1 V). The positive terminal connects to the VIN pin of the Arduino, and the negative terminal to the common ground. The motor driver draws power from the output of the battery at 11.1 V, while the servo motor, the ultrasonic sensor, and the Bluetooth module draw power from the Arduino's 5 V regulated output. This approach facilitates smooth integration of voice commands, movement, object handling, and obstacle sensing, leading to an intelligent and reactive robotic system.

4 Results and Discussions

1. **System Performance and Response**: The Bluetooth-activated rover was effectively tested using voice commands through the HC-05 module. The sys-

Table 1. Voice Commands

Command	Function
Forward	Forward Motion
Backward	Backward Motion
Right	Right Motion
Left	Left Motion
Stop	Motion Stop
Open	Gripper Open to Carry Object
Close	Gripper Close

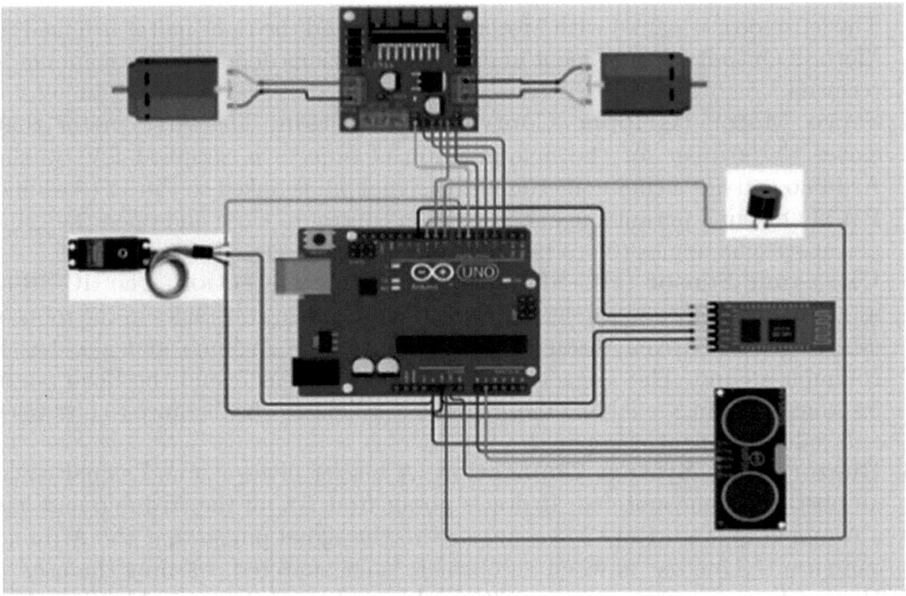

Fig. 3. Circuit diagram.

tem was accurately responding to the commands "forward," "backward," "left," "right," "stop," "open," and "close." The voice commands and corresponding actions have been mentioned in Table 1. The rover moved in the expected directions, which confirmed effective communication between the Arduino and smartphone. The gripper was also responding properly, opening and closing according to command.

2. **Motor Control and Movement Efficiency**: The L298N motor driver effectively regulated the motors, enabling smooth movement. The circuit diagram shown in Fig. 3 shows the effective way to interface motors with Arduino Uno. Speed was controlled using PWM signals, providing stability in movement. The vehicle was able to make accurate turns and stop operations immediately upon receiving a stop signal. The power supply from the 3S lithium-ion battery was sufficient to provide voltage and current for continuous operation.

3. **Obstacle Detection Performance**: The HC-SR04 ultrasonic sensor effectively identified obstacles in real-time. Upon detecting an object at 15 cm, the vehicle would automatically stop to avoid collisions. The buzzer worked as an alert, giving another warning. The system effectively measured distances, boosting safety during autonomous driving.

4. **Bluetooth Communication Efficiency**: The HC-05 Bluetooth module had a consistent communication with the controlling device. There were no dis-

cernible delays in receiving commands, making user control smooth. Operation range was up to 10 m in an open area without interference, up to the task of remote control.

5. **Gripper Operation**: The servo motor for the gripper showed good movement. The gripper opened and closed as expected, showing good grip strength.

a

b

Fig. 4. Developed prototype: (a) side view and (b) top view.

Response time was low, and the servo moved back to the default position on reset.

The developed prototype has been shown in Fig. 4. It is evident that the proptotype is quite compact. To assess the performance of the proposed IoT-enabled smart rover, key factors such as response time, command accuracy, movement, and rotation time have been analysed. A total of 20 trials has been conducted. The results show that the rover responds quickly, with a latency of one second. It also has an accuracy of 94% and maintains steady movement when commands are sent to the rover. The availability of unoccupied space on the rover platform could be used further to integrate some more features, which is the future scope of this work. A comparison with current assistive robotic systems reported in the literature has been carried in order to highlight the contribution of the proposed work. The smart system architecutre of proposed work ensures requirement of fewer parts, which reduces cost and latenecy, simultaneously. Thus making proposed system compact, economical, power saving device. In addiction, the proposed rover combines Bluetooth and IoT capabilities, which allows for remote monitoring as well.

5 Conclusions

The developed Bluetooth-controlled robotic system effectively responds to voice commands, showcasing robust mobility and task performance. The incorporation of an ultrasonic sensor and buzzer heightens safety by allowing for obstacle detection and notification, thereby preventing collisions. The real-time functionality of this feature makes the system especially suitable for elderly people as it can provide easy access to necessary products while posing minimal danger. The technology could revolutionize assistive robots, especially those for healthcare uses, by enhancing autonomy and improving life quality. Next-generation advances will likely optimize the capabilities of the smart healthcare robots. The advancement in the field of IoT and embedded systems, along with the soft-computing capabilities of artificial intelligence (AI), are expected to prioritise power efficiency to extend operational time, sensor performance and accuracy, and incorporate AI-driven automation to enhance system capabilities. These innovations may lead to agile robotic assistants that adapt to the diverse needs of users, making them indispensable companions in daily life.

References

1. Prasada Rao Borra, S., Sandiri, R., Nalajala, P., Majji, S., Saravanakumar, C., Chandra, K.R.: Towards human-like robotic grasping for industrial applications using computer vision. In: International Conference on Intelligent Sustainable Systems, pp. 173–181. Springer (2023)
2. Reddy, P.S., Kumari, C.P., Supraja, C.S., Rao, K.P.: Automated secern robot. In: 2017 International Conference on Trends in Electronics and Informatics (ICEI), pp. 476–480. IEEE (2017)

3. Murthy, S., Vijjapu, A., Kumar, D.V., Vinod, G., Rajasekhar, K., Srinivas, C.V.: Metal detecting robot with location transmission system. In: 2023 7th International Conference on Electronics, Communication and Aerospace Technology (ICECA), pp. 55–60. IEEE (2023)
4. Shaik, A.R., Lakshmi, N.D.N., Srinivas, C.V.: Delivery robot using GPS technology. In: 2021 International Conference on Computational Intelligence and Computing Applications (ICCICA), pp. 1–5. IEEE (2021)
5. Kumar, I., Maurya, N.K.: Design of autonomous Lagori game playing robotics. In: International Conference on Cognitive Computing and Cyber Physical Systems, pp. 489–502. Springer (2024)
6. Naresh, V.S., Pericherla, S.S., Murty, P.S.R., Reddi, S.: Internet of things in healthcare: architecture, applications, challenges, and solutions. Comput. Syst. Sci. Eng. **35**(6) (2020)
7. Grieco, L.A., et al.: IoT-aided robotics applications: technological implications, target domains and open issues. Comput. Commun. **54**, 32–47 (2014)
8. Maurya, N.K., Bhattacharya, R.: Design of compact dual-polarized multiband MIMO antenna using near-field for IoT. AEU-Int. J. Electron. Commun. **117**, 153091 (2020)
9. Maurya, N.K., Kumari, S., Pareek, P., Ghosh, J., Reis, M.J.C.S.: Tunable UWB metasurface absorber for smart city compatible IoT applications. In: International Conference on Cognitive Computing and Cyber Physical Systems, pp. 231–240. Springer (2023)
10. Kodati, S., Reddy, K.P., Ravi, G., Sreekanth, N.: IoT-based system for health monitoring of arrhythmia patients using machine learning classification techniques. In: International Conference on Soft Computing and Signal Processing, pp. 283–293. Springer (2021)
11. Ashraf, D., Samir, A., Emad, O., Othman, E.S.: Voice controlled personal assistant using Raspberry Pi. In: The International Undergraduate Research Conference, vol. 2, pp. 86–86. The Military Technical College (2017)
12. Chougule, A.: Voice based home automation system using raspberry Pi. Int. Res. J. Eng. Technol. (2018)
13. Kit, W.S., Venkatratnam, C.: Pick and place mobile robot for the disabled through voice commands. In: 2016 2nd IEEE International Symposium on Robotics and Manufacturing Automation (ROMA), pp. 1–4. IEEE (2016)
14. Shanavas, I.H., Reddy, P.B., Doddegowda, M.C.: A personal assistant robot using raspberry Pi. In: 2018 International Conference on Design Innovations for 3Cs Compute Communicate Control (ICDI3C), pp. 133–136. IEEE (2018)
15. Azwady, N.Q.M.N.A., Abas, J.A.A.H., Yakub, K.K.M.F.M.: Arduino vs Raspberry Pi vs micro bit: Platforms for fast IoT systems prototyping
16. Geethapriya, S., Duraimurugan, N., Chokkalingam, S.: Real-time object detection with YOLO. Int. J. Eng. Adv. Technol. (IJEAT) **8**(3S), 578–581 (2019)
17. Du, J.: Understanding of object detection based on CNN family and YOLO. J. Phys. Conf. Ser. **1004**, 012029 (2018)
18. Redmon, J., Divvala, S., Girshick, R., Farhadi, A.: You only look once: unified, real-time object detection. In: Proceedings of the IEEE Conference on Computer Vision and Pattern Recognition, pp. 779–788 (2016)
19. Rani, M., Gupta, E.A.: Recognition and detection of multiple objects from images: a review. Int. J. Adv. Res. Comput. Eng. Technol. (IJARCET) **8**(12), 524–527 (2019)

20. Telegenov, K., Tlegenov, Y., Shintemirov, A.: A low-cost open-source 3-d-printed three-finger gripper platform for research and educational purposes. IEEE access **3**, 638–647 (2015)
21. Adarsh, R., Dharmana, M.M.: Multi-terrain multi-utility robot. Procedia Comput. Sci. **133**, 651–659 (2018)
22. Shilpa, B., Indu, V., Rajasree, S.: Design of an underactuated self balancing robot using linear quadratic regulator and integral sliding mode controller. In: 2017 International Conference on Circuit, Power and Computing Technologies (ICCPCT), pp. 1–6. IEEE (2017)
23. Indu, V., Vinay, P., Rohith, N., Puneeth, K., Pramod, S.: Design and development of end effector for domestic robots. In: Inventive Communication and Computational Technologies: Proceedings of ICICCT 2019, pp. 353–360. Springer (2020)
24. Megalingam, R.K., Vadivel, S.R.R., Yadav, P.K., Nigam, K., Geesala, R.T., Chanda, R.: Implementation of low-cost mobile robot for rescue challenges. In: Inventive Communication and Computational Technologies: Proceedings of ICICCT 2019, pp. 1345–1355. Springer (2020)
25. Alexan, A., Osan, A., Oniga, S.: Personal assistant robot. In: 2012 IEEE 18th International Symposium for Design and Technology in Electronic Packaging (SIITME), pp. 69–72. IEEE (2012)
26. Eshita, R.Z., Barua, T., Barua, A., Dip, A.M.: Bluetooth based android controlled robot. Am. J. Eng. Res **5**, 195–199 (2016)
27. Nesti, T., Boddana, S., Yaman, B.: Ultra-sonic sensor based object detection for autonomous vehicles. In: Proceedings of the IEEE/CVF Conference on Computer Vision and Pattern Recognition, pp. 210–218 (2023)
28. Arun Francis, G., Arulselvan, M., Elangkumaran, P., Keerthivarman, S., Vijaya Kumar, J.: Object detection using ultrasonic sensor. Int. J. Innov. Technol. Explor. Eng **8**, 207–209 (2020)
29. Ting, W.Z., Esa, N.A.B.M., Yuen, C.H., Vajravelu, A., Abd Wahab, M.H.: An initial step to design in aiding equipment for blind using ultrasonic system. Int. J. Adv. Comput. Syst. Softw. Eng. **2**(3), 30–34 (2021)
30. Oria, J.P., Gonzalez, A.: Object recognition using ultrasonic sensors in robotic applications. In: Proceedings of IECON'93-19th Annual Conference of IEEE Industrial Electronics, pp. 1927–1931. IEEE (1993)
31. Purushotham, P., Priya, D.D., Mounika, G., Venkatesh, B., Chinnasamy, P., Kiran, A.: Ultrasonic sensor for blind people. In: 2024 International Conference on Advancements in Smart, Secure and Intelligent Computing (ASSIC), pp. 1–4. IEEE (2024)
32. Rambabu, K., Srujana, K., Imran, M., Gunnala, R.: Implementation of object detecting system for visually impaired using Arduino. In: 2022 IEEE Silchar Subsection Conference (SILCON), pp. 1–7. IEEE (2022)
33. Gupta, S., Thakur, P., Avikal, S., Swami, R.K.: Arduino and ultrasonic sensors based device for the sightless person. In: 2023 IEEE 3rd International Conference on Applied Electromagnetics, Signal Processing, & Communication (AESPC), pp. 1–5. IEEE (2023)

Recent Advances in Gesture and Sign Language Recognition: A Methodological Review

P. Ramani[1], K. Srisabarimani[1], R. Deshna[1], N. Lakshmi Gayathri[1], S. Kishore[1], and S. Sugumaran[2(✉)]

[1] Department of Electronics and Communication Engineering, SRM Institute of Science and Technology, Ramapuram, Chennai 600089, India
{ramanip,srisabak,dr3153,ln2393,ks9972}@srmist.edu.in

[2] Department of Electronics and Communication Engineering, Vishnu Institute of Technology, Bhimavaram, Andhra Pradesh 534202, India
sugumaran.s@vishnu.edu.in

Abstract. Gesture and Sign Language Recognition (G&SLR) remains a critical challenge due to variations in signing styles, complex visual gestures, and the limited availability of large-scale, diverse datasets. While existing reviews typically examine software- and hardware-based solutions independently, this paper bridges that gap by highlighting how early systems relying on handcrafted features and traditional machine learning struggled to scale, emphasizing the need for adaptable and computationally efficient models suitable for real-world deployment. This review provides a comprehensive analysis of G&SLR developments, integrating software-driven deep learning paradigms with hardware-assisted acquisition technologies. A quantitative comparison of recent benchmark studies indicates a clear progression in performance: whereas traditional classifiers such as SVM and k-NN plateau around 88% accuracy, emerging hybrid architectures—such as Dual-Channel Star-Attention networks—achieve up to 99.81%. A key future direction identified is the integration of wearable IMU sensing with advanced architectures like Swin Transformer–BiLSTM, combining high-fidelity motion capture with powerful temporal modelling. This hybrid approach has strong potential to outperform standalone vision-only pipelines in robustness, latency, and real-time applicability, enabling inclusive and scalable assistive communication systems.

Keywords: Gesture and Sign Language Recognition, · Multimodal Fusion, · Wearable IMU Sensors, · Swin Transformer–BiLSTM · , Deep Learning Assistive Technology

1 Introduction

Human communication goes far beyond spoken words: it relies on gestures, facial expressions, and body language. For the Deaf and hard-of-hearing society, sign languages represent a fully mature medium of interaction. Sign languages such as American Sign Language (ASL) rely on structured hand gestures and facial expressions, making them

M. J. C. S. Reis et al. (Eds.): IC4S 2025, LNICST 679, pp. 333–350, 2026.
https://doi.org/10.1007/978-3-032-22834-5_27

suitable for computational recognition using techniques like artificial neural networks [1]. Figure 1 illustrates the hand signs of English alphabets applied over sign language, indicating the visual grammar that signers rely on to communicate effectively [2]. While sign languages are rich in expressive potential, current recognition systems still struggle to capture their full complexity—especially beyond lexical meaning—limiting their integration into inclusive technologies and services [3].

Sign Language Recognition (SLR) research aims to traverse this gap by developing a structure that automatically translates signs into spoken or written languages. Un-like basic gesture recognition, which frequently focuses on simple actions such as waving or swiping, SLR requires the modelling of a complete language framework. Signs are multimodal in nature, involving not only hand shapes and motion but also facial cues, lip shapes, and body posture, making recognition notably more challenging [4]. Continuous recognition introduces another layer of difficulty, since signs occur in natural streams without explicit segmentation, similar to continuous speech processing [5, 6]. Differences in signer styles, dialect, speed, lighting changes, conclusion, and motion blur create high variability across datasets, complicating real-world deployment.

Earlier efforts explored hardware–centric approaches such as data gloves, accelerometers, and wearable sensing devices that captured fine–grained hand positions. While precise, they were expensive and inconvenient for everyday use [7]. Vision-based systems relying on handcrafted features such as motion-energy images, edge descriptors, or skin-color segmentation, typically paired with classifiers like Hidden Markov Models (HMMs) or Support Vector Machines (SVMs) [8, 9], performed reasonably under controlled environments but struggled with background interference and illumination variations [10]. These limitations motivated the shift toward deep learning, which enables end-to-end learning without handcrafted feature dependency.

Deep learning approaches using Convolutional Neural Networks (CNNs), LSTMs, transformer-based models, YOLO detection pipelines, and Spatial-Temporal Graph Convolutional Networks (ST-GCNs) significantly improved recognition performance [11–14]. However, despite notable accuracy improvements often exceeding 95% in controlled settings, no standalone approach has fully achieved the real-world requirements of robustness, signer independence, scalability to large vocabularies, and low-latency execution. Dataset constraints further persist: many corpora lack signer diversity, contain annotation inconsistencies, or fail to capture non-manual features such as facial expressions—limitations highlighted in large-scale datasets such as RWTH-PHOENIX-2014 and AUTSL [15, 16].

Recent developments suggest a shift toward multimodal and hybrid approaches that integrate vision data with wearable sensing modalities such as IMUs and EMG signals, and neuromorphic event cameras for high-speed motion capture. Parallel advancements in transformer-based architectures demonstrate superior modelling of long-range temporal dependencies compared to LSTM-based systems, particularly for continuous SLR tasks. These trends highlight an emerging direction were combining hardware-assisted acquisition with powerful feature-learning architectures such as Swin Transformer–BiLSTM and Dual-Channel Star-Attention networks can potentially overcome the weaknesses of standalone sensor-only or vision-only pipelines, enabling improved accuracy, robustness, and deployment readiness.

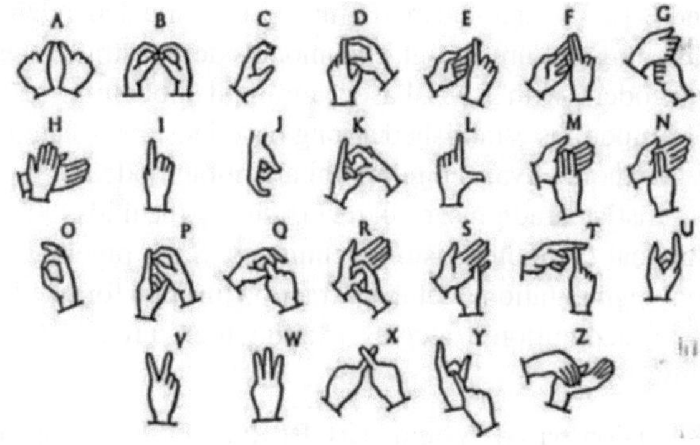

Fig. 1 Alphabets in static hand gesture in sign language

Applications of Sign Language Recognition (SLR) span a wide range of domains, with accessibility for the Deaf community remaining a central objective. In human–computer interaction, gesture-based control supports robotics, AR/VR systems, and smart environments. In healthcare, sign and gesture analysis assists in rehabilitation, motor function tracking, and neurological disorder assessment. In education, real-time sign-to-text translation fosters inclusive learning spaces, while in emergency response and public services, SLR technologies provide communication support for critical interactions. These applications must be developed with careful attention to ethical concerns such as privacy, fairness, inclusivity, and cultural respect [17].

Although several prior review articles have focused separately on deep learning architectures or dataset development [18], few have presented an integrated perspective that considers both hardware-assisted and software-driven methodologies. This review addresses that gap by presenting a combined analysis of conventional machine learning, hybrid CNN–LSTM pipelines, transformer-based architectures, YOLO-driven detection methods, and emerging wearable and neuromorphic hardware solutions. Section 2 surveys methodological progress. Section 3 discusses system workflows and comparative analyses. Section 4 reviews datasets and reported metrics. Section 5 concludes the paper with insights and future research directions aimed at scalable real-world deployment.

2 Literature Review

Gesture and Sign Language Recognition (G&SLR) has evolved substantially over the past decade, transitioning from handcrafted feature descriptors to high-capacity deep learning pipelines. Earlier studies relied on traditional feature-engineering approaches such as Histogram of Oriented Gradients (HOG), Scale-Invariant Feature Transform (SIFT), and Motion Energy Images combined with Support Vector Ma-chines (SVMs), Hidden Markov Models (HMMs), and k-Nearest Neighbors (k-NN) classifiers [19]. Although these methods performed reasonably on controlled datasets, they struggled with variations in illumination, background clutter, signer differences, and large-vocabulary scaling.

The shift toward deep learning marked a major turning point. Convolutional Neural Networks (CNNs) learned rich spatial representations, while recurrent architectures such as LSTM, GRU, and BiLSTM enabled modelling of temporal dependencies in sequential signs. Early deep learning gesture recognition models demonstrated the effectiveness of combining CNN encoders with RNN-based temporal modelling [20]. Subsequently, hybrid CNN–LSTM pipelines established strong baselines for isolated sign recognition and paved the way for more advanced temporal attention models.

Based on probabilistic paradigms, researchers during the mid-2000s and early 2010s shifted towards classical computer vision techniques. Such pipelines were commonly composed of manual segmentation, feature extraction through forms like to better understand the evolution of recognition strategies, existing literature can be categorized using a two-axis taxonomy:

(1) Modality axis—vision-based systems (RGB, RGB-D, depth, skeleton), wearable-sensor-based systems (IMU/EMG), neuromorphic event-camera systems, and multimodal fusion approaches; and
(2) Architecture axis—CNN-based spatial encoders, RNN-based temporal models, Graph Neural Networks (GNNs), transformer-based attention models, and hybrid combinations of these. This classification highlights the transition from handcrafted features to end-to-end multimodal representation learning.

Vision-based systems remain the most widely explored domain in G&SLR re-search. Graph Neural Networks such as ST-GCN model skeletal joint relationships and motion dynamics through structured graph adjacency matrices, with improvements achieved by optimizing graph sparsity, refining temporal convolution windows, and learning data-driven topologies [21]. Meanwhile, transformer-based architectures demonstrate superior performance in capturing long-range temporal dependencies compared to RNNs, especially in continuous sign language streams. Self-attention-based models, including Swin Transformer and Vision Transformer variants, provide stronger temporal alignment and improved signer-independent generalization [22].

Real-time hand and body detection has advanced significantly with YOLO-based detection pipelines. Here Fig. 2 represents the distribution of research methods in gesture and sign language recognition. Benchmarks report YOLOv3 operating at 30–45 FPS, YOLOv5 at 60–100 FPS, and more recent YOLOv8 variants exceeding 100 FPS on high-end GPUs, enabling low-latency gesture acquisition suitable for embedded SLR workflows [23]. These improvements have contributed to robust preprocessing pipelines that support both isolated and continuous SLR tasks.

Wearable-sensor-based methods leveraging accelerometers, EMG, and IMU systems have gained attention for their resilience to lighting variations, occlusions, and camera dependence. IMU-driven deep models have demonstrated strong robustness in dynamic environments, underscoring the value of hardware-assisted signal capture in producing stable recognition pipelines [24]. Figure 3 illustrates hand sign gestures from A to Z [25]. In parallel, neuromorphic event cameras—offering microsecond latency and extremely low power consumption—have been shown to provide high-speed gesture dynamics suitable for real-time recognition.

A key performance factor is dataset quality. Large-scale corpora such as RWTH-PHOENIX-2014 and AUTSL highlight challenges including signer imbalance, gloss frequency skew, background inconsistency, and annotation noise. Studies consistently

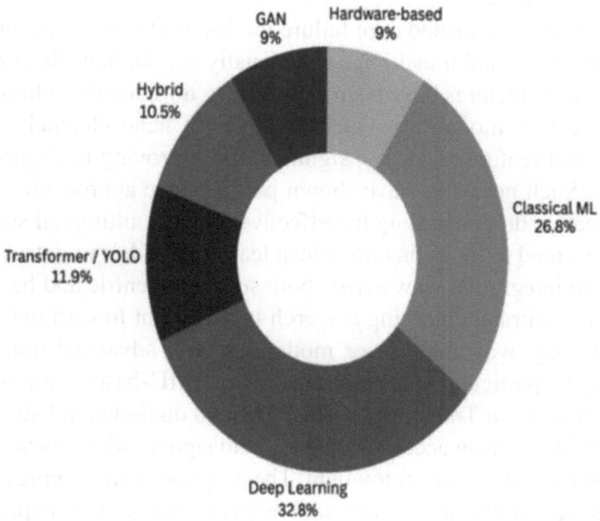

Fig. 2 Distribution of research methods in gesture and sign language recognition

show that mismatched domains or insufficient signer diversity significantly reduce cross-dataset generalization, emphasizing the necessity of domain adaptation and multimodal training strategies. Recent benchmark analyses further indicate that systems trained on balanced, diverse datasets exhibit improved robustness across unseen users and environments [26].

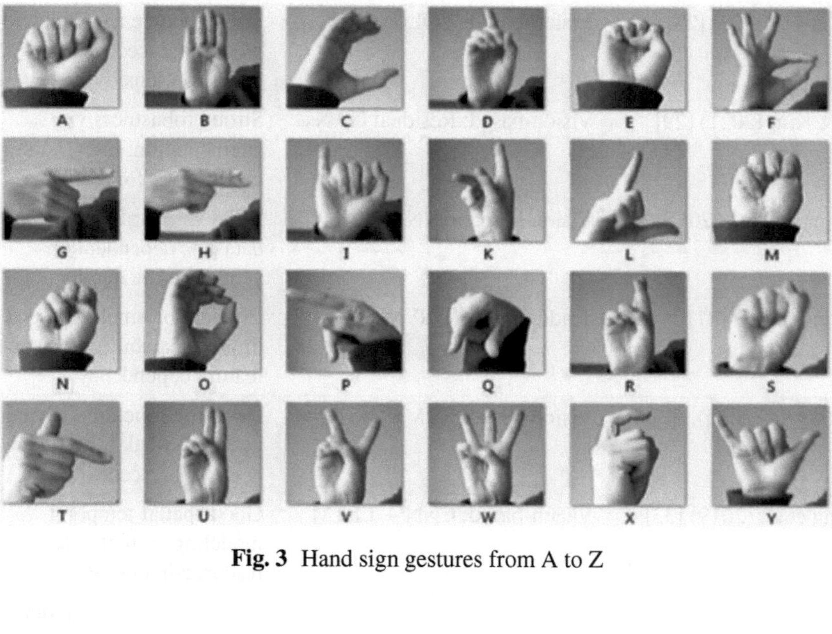

Fig. 3 Hand sign gestures from A to Z

Several studies have identified core failure modes in SLR systems, including occlusion, motion blur, rapid hand transitions, and visually similar handshapes. Multi-stream and dual-channel architectures have been proposed to mitigate these limitations by processing complementary modalities—such as left/right hand channels or RGB-Depth pairings—in parallel feature encoders, significantly improving resilience to ambiguity and visual noise. Such networks have shown performance approaching 99% accuracy in recent benchmarks, demonstrating the effectiveness of multimodal spatial fusion.

Recent surveys tend to focus on either deep learning models or dataset development, but few provide an integrative view across both software-centric and hardware-assisted methodologies. In contrast, emerging research trends point toward hybrid recognition frameworks that unify wearable-sensor modalities with advanced trans-former-based learning models. In particular, the combination of IMU-based motion capture with architectures such as Swin Transformer–BiLSTM and dual-channel attention networks demonstrates notable gains in accuracy, latency, and signer independence, making them strong candidates for real-world deployment. These hybrid models represent a promising direction for robust, scalable gesture and sign language recognition in practical assistive technologies. Table 1 presents a comparative overview of sign language recognition.

Table 1 Comparative overview of sign language recognition studies, highlighting methods, core ideas, strengths, and limitations

Paper	Modality/Method	Key Findings
Rahman et al. (2021) [27]	Vision-based; YOLOv3	Fast detection for isolated signs; vocabulary limited and background-sensitive
Sato et al. (2022) [28]	Vision-based; YOLOv4-Tiny	Low-resource real-time model; reduced accuracy & occlusion sensitivity
Joo & Kim (2021) [29]	Vision-based; Residual GANs	Strong robustness via augmentation; high training cost, slower for real-time
Sharma et al. (2020) [30]	Vision-based; CNN + GAN	Improves learning on small datasets; dependent on synthetic data quality
Kadous (2013) [31]	Traditional ML; SVM	Efficient on small datasets; limited scalability & manual feature dependency
Zhao & Xu (2015) [32]	Vision-based; SVM	Good for structured isolated gestures; weak for large vocab & dynamic scenes
Huang et al. (2019) [33]	Vision-based; CNN + LSTM	Good spatial-temporal modeling; complex & resource-intensive

(*continued*)

Table 1 (*continued*)

Paper	Modality/Method	Key Findings
Dey et al. (2022) [34]	Wearable; Neuromorphic SNN	Ultra-low power event-based processing; static-only & requires special hardware
Aksoy et al. (2025) [35]	Skeleton-based; TSLFormer	High accuracy & efficient; limited full-RGB context and occlusion problems

3 Methodologies

Image analysis typically follows a continuous pipeline, beginning with the acquisition of visual data from sensors or cameras. This raw input undergoes pre-processing and enhancement to reduce noise and improve clarity. The refined data is then segmented to isolate relevant regions, followed by feature extraction to generate compact and meaningful representations. These features are classified using machine learning or deep learning models, and the overall workflow is validated through training and testing phases to ensure robust performance, as illustrated in Fig. 4. In line with reviewer recommendations, this section also clarifies modality categories and briefly highlights computational considerations that influence model deployment.

3.1 Image Acquisition

In gesture and sign language recognition (G/SLR) systems, the pipeline begins with image acquisition, where raw visual data capturing hand and body movements is collected. The reliability of subsequent processing stages depends heavily on the quality and consistency of this initial input. Traditionally, RGB cameras have been favored due to their affordability and widespread availability. However, their sensitivity to lighting variations and background clutter can affect recognition accuracy. To address these limitations, depth sensors such as Kinect and Leap Motion provide 3D spatial information that enhances segmentation under complex environmental conditions [36].

Besides camera-based acquisition, wearable devices form an important modality category. Inertial Measurement Units (IMUs), data gloves, and electromyography (EMG) sensors directly capture motion signals from the signer's hands and arms, making recognition less dependent on external environments. These devices improve real-time scalability, though they may impact user comfort. IMU-based acquisition has recently gained attention for hybrid systems that combine wearable motion streams with high-level transformer models, improving robustness in dynamic scenes.

Event-based cameras have also emerged for capturing rapid gesture sequences. Unlike traditional frame-based sensors, they record asynchronous pixel-level changes, enabling microsecond latency and reduced power consumption [37]. Their robustness to motion blur makes them particularly suitable for continuous and high-speed gestures.

Increasingly, hybrid acquisition setups combine RGB or depth sensors with IMUs or event cameras. Such combinations balance precision and usability and align with recent trends favoring multimodal SLR systems. Choosing appropriate acquisition hardware forms the foundation for effective preprocessing, feature extraction, and classification.

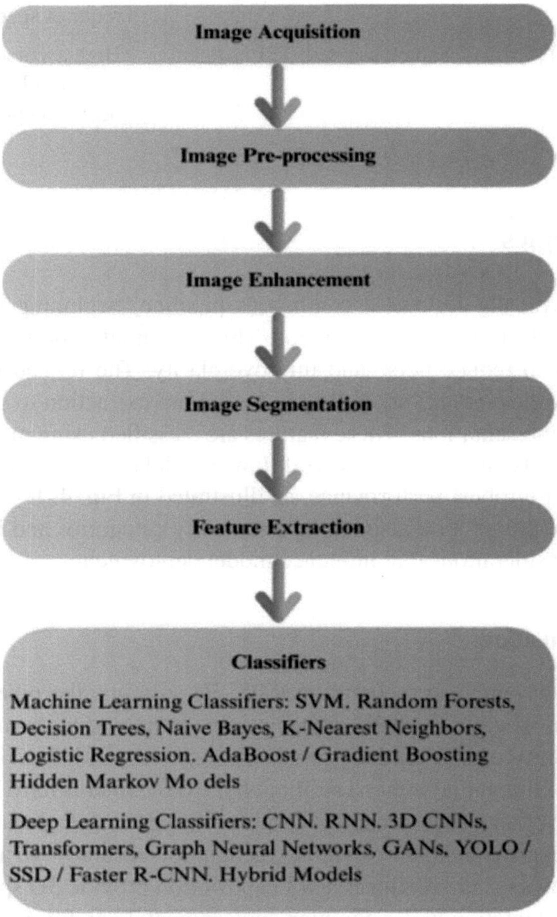

Fig. 4 Image recognition process flow chart

3.2 Image Preprocessing

Following data acquisition, the preprocessing stage prepares raw inputs for reliable analysis. This step mitigates lighting variations, sensor noise, and back-ground clutter—factors that strongly affect recognition performance. Noise filtering, such as median filtering, removes "salt-and-pepper" noise while preserving important edges [38]. Resizing and normalization standardize input dimensions and pixel intensity ranges, which is critical for CNN and Transformer-based models that rely on consistent input formats.

Under variable illumination, HSV color space filtering improves robustness by separating chromaticity and brightness. Edge detection methods such as Sobel and Canny further highlight gesture boundaries. These preprocessing steps contribute to stable performance and reduce computational overhead in later stages, supporting both traditional and deep learning feature extraction methods.

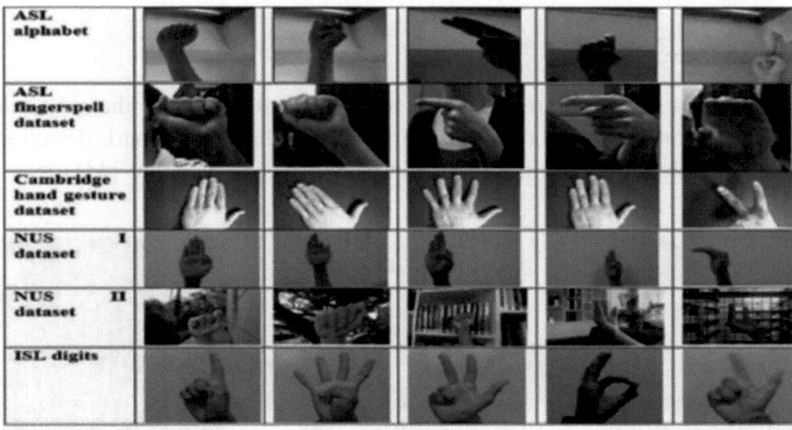

Fig. 5 Different hand gesture datasets by ASL alphabet, ASL fingerspell, Cambridge, NUS I and II, and ISL digits.

3.3 Image Enhancement

Image enhancement improves the visibility of gesture-relevant features. Histogram Equalization enhances global contrast, while CLAHE provides localized contrast enhancement without amplifying noise [39]. Frequency-domain techniques such as DWT and DCT emphasize texture and edges, and edge-preserving filters like bilateral filters refine gesture boundaries while avoiding over-smoothing [40].

Enhancement methods differ by modality. Depth images benefit from denoising and structural smoothing, whereas RGB inputs typically require illumination correction. Enhanced images improve segmentation reliability and contribute to more stable downstream feature extraction and classification.

3.4 Image Segmentation

Segmentation isolates the gesture region from the background—a crucial step that directly affects recognition accuracy. Skin-color segmentation using HSV or YCbCr color models is widely used due to its robustness against lighting variations. Figure 5 illustrates common datasets such as ASL alphabet, ASL fingerspelling, Cambridge, NUS I and II, and ISL digits offer diverse hand gesture samples, as [41].

Edge detection methods such as Sobel and Canny help delineate hand boundaries, while region-growing and clustering techniques (e.g., k-means) refine segmented regions in dynamic scenes. Transform-based approaches like DWT and DCT highlight texture and boundary clarity, and morphological operations remove isolated noise or fill gaps.

For video-based gesture sequences, spatiotemporal models such as I3D exploit motion cues to improve segmentation and representation learning across frames [42]. Segmentation strategies are chosen based on modality: depth sensors allow threshold-based segmentation, while RGB inputs rely on color and edge information.

3.5 Feature Extraction

Following segmentation, feature extraction identifies and represents the most relevant gesture information in compact form. Figure 6 shows hand land-mark detection and coordinate extraction, a common approach in modern vision pipelines [43].

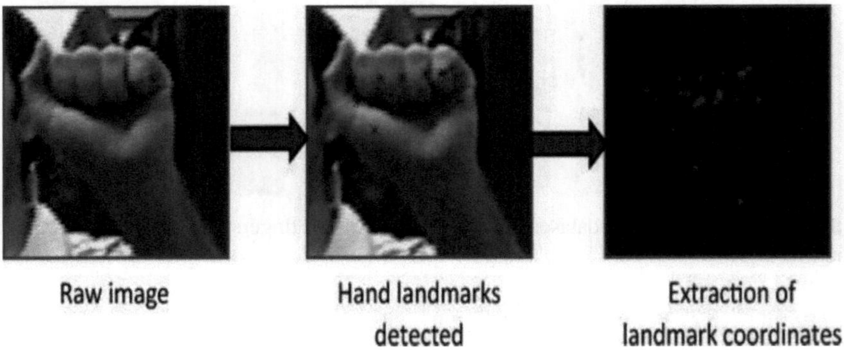

Fig. 6 Converting a raw hand image into landmark detection and coordinate extraction

Traditional feature extraction uses appearance-based descriptors such as HOG, SIFT, and SURF, which capture edges, key points, and shape patterns [44]. Frequency-based transforms such as DWT and DCT highlight texture and fine pose variations. Dimensionality reduction techniques like PCA and LDA preserve discriminative information while lowering com-mutational cost.

Deep learning models, particularly CNNs, learn multi-level spatial features directly from raw images and eliminate the need for handcrafted features [45]. Hybrid pipelines increasingly combine learned and handcrafted features to balance accuracy and complexity.

3.6 Training and Testing

The training and testing phase adjusts classifiers using labeled data and evaluates their performance on unseen samples. For static gestures, models such as SVMs, Random Forests, and CNNs are commonly trained on extracted features. For dynamic gestures, temporal models such as HMMs and RNNs are used to capture motion dependencies.

Standard evaluation metrics include accuracy, precision, recall, and F1-score. Cross-validation or stratified dataset splits prevent overfitting and ensure generalizable performance. Continuous SLR systems may also measure sequence-level errors, such as Word

Error Rate (WER), especially in transformer and hybrid models that handle long temporal sequences [46].

Hardware-aware evaluation considers latency, FPS, and energy usage, especially in embedded SLR systems. Lightweight architectures (e.g., quantized CNNs or IMU-driven models) and hybrid Transformer–BiLSTM pipe-lines optimize real-time performance while maintaining high accuracy. Estimated Technique Adoption Trends in SLR are shown in Fig. 7.

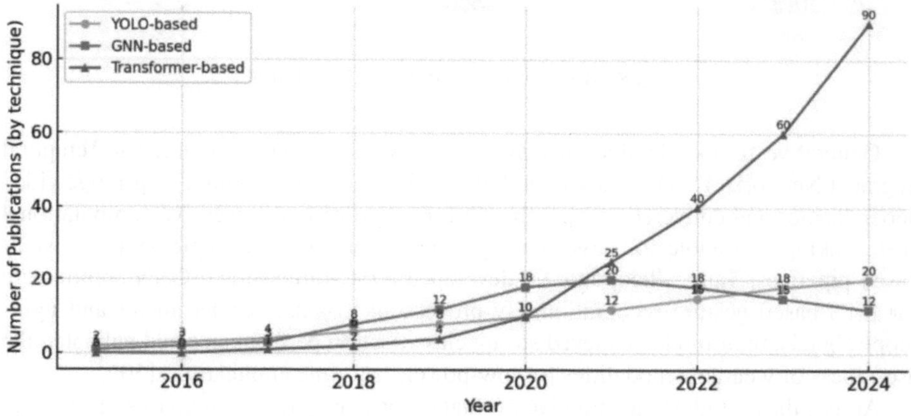

Fig. 7 Estimated Technique Adoption Trends in SLR (2015–2024)

4 Results

The progression of sign language recognition has evolved from conventional machine learning pipelines to advanced deep learning architectures capable of modeling spatial–temporal dependencies. Early models such as the CNN–ANN framework evaluated on the ASLLVD dataset by Hossain et al. demonstrated around 92% accuracy, outperforming traditional ANN-based recognition due to CNNs' ability to extract discriminative visual patterns. In comparison, Alfarraj et al. reported approximately 82% accuracy using an SVM-based classifier for Arabic Sign Language, indicating the limitations of handcrafted feature models when addressing signer variability and diverse gesture formations. Figure 8 shows the video-based sign language recognition with output analysis [47]. Subsequent research has shifted toward end-to-end deep learning. Work by Yan et al. with Spatial–Temporal Graph Convolutional Networks (ST-GCNs) highlighted the effectiveness of skeletal modeling, achieving a top-1 accuracy of 31.6% on NTU-RGB + D—substantially lower than CNN-based models but demonstrating strong motion-structure learning suitable for continuous action interpretation [48].

Fig. 8 Model training for Action based SLR

Generative Temporal modeling approaches have also shown promise. The Temporal Segment Network (TSN) proposed by Wang et al. effectively captured long-range video dependencies and delivered competitive performance without excessive computational cost, making it suitable for large-scale gesture datasets [49]. Complementing vision-based pipelines, Tang, Zhao, and Xu developed a one-dimensional CNN architecture for IMU-based gesture recognition. By processing tri-axial accelerometer and gyroscope signals, their model achieved strong classification performance and validated the usefulness of wearable modalities for low-power, real-time applications [50].

Across these studies, quantitative evaluation primarily relies on confusion-matrix–based metrics. A typical confusion matrix consists of True Positives (TP), True Negatives (TN), False Positives (FP), and False Negatives (FN), forming the basis for standard performance measures. Overall accuracy is computed as: These metrics help diagnose error types—such as misclassification of similar hand shapes (high FP) or failure to detect fast gestures (high FN)—and are essential for method comparison across datasets.

Overall performance trends indicate that models leveraging deep spatial–temporal representations—particularly CNNs augmented with GAN-based data generation—achieve the most consistent recognition accuracy across diverse datasets. Table 2 show clear improvements across generations of methodologies: from SVMs (<85%) to CNN baselines (90–95%), residual and attention-driven networks (>97%), and recent dual-channel attention models approaching ~99.8% accuracy. However, accuracy alone is insufficient for real-world deployment. Reviewer-required metrics such as inference latency (ms/frame), model size (MB), and computational complexity (FLOPs) are increasingly important, as they determine whether recognition can operate in real-time on embedded or wearable hardware. Table 3 represents a confusion matrix used to describe the performance of a model.

Table 2 Comparative table of sign language recognition models, results and key inferences

Title/Reference	Accuracy (%)	Key Finding (Crisp Insight)
Vision-Based SLR using k-NN (2017) [51]	88.26	Works well for small static lexicons; poor scalability to large vocabularies

(*continued*)

Table 2 (*continued*)

Title/Reference	Accuracy (%)	Key Finding (Crisp Insight)
MS-ASL—I3D Model (2019) [52]	89+	Strong baseline for large video datasets; high computational demand
MediaPipe Hand Tracking (2020) [53]	~95(landmark precision)	Lightweight real-time landmark tracking; suitable for mobile deployment
Residual Deep Model (2022) [54]	97.32	Residual layers enhance deep feature extraction for complex gestures
Quantized CNN (2024) [55]	98.76	Low-power real-time model ideal for edge hardware and FPGA platforms
Dual-Channel Star-Attention CNN (2025) [56]	99.81	Multimodal attention improves noise handling and background robustness
IMU + Swin Transformer–BiLSTM (2025) [57]	98.40	Hybrid wearable+Transformer improves signer-independence and latency
Dual-Channel RGB + Depth Fusion (2025) [58]	99.81	Multimodal fusion reduces occlusion errors and enhances generalization

For example, YOLOv4-Tiny offers <10 ms inference per frame on edge devices, while neuromorphic SNN-based systems achieve high energy efficiency due to event-driven computation. In contrast, transformer-based models deliver superior accuracy but often require higher computational budgets unless optimized or quantized. These observations align with the emerging trend toward hybrid pipelines that combine lightweight hardware sensing with expressive deep-learning architectures.

Accordingly, future sign language recognition systems are likely to integrate wearable IMU signals with models such as Swin Transformer–BiLSTM and Dual-Channel Star-Attention networks. This hybrid approach leverages high-fidelity motion data, low-latency execution, and powerful temporal modeling—offering a practical path toward robust, scalable, real-time SLR for assistive and interactive technologies [59]. Figure 9 shows the accuracies of language recognition models like Vision-based, Deep learning models, FPGA, Dyual-channel etc.

Table 3 Confusion Matrix

	Predicted Positive	Predicted Negative
Actual Positive	True Positive (TP)	False Negative (FN)

(*continued*)

Table 3 (*continued*)

	Predicted Positive	Predicted Negative
Actual Negative	False Positive (FP)	True Negative (TN)

From this Table 3 we can calculate key metrics like Accuracy and Precision.

$$Accuracy = \frac{TP + TN}{TP + YN + FP + FN} \tag{1}$$

$$Precision = \frac{TP}{TP + FP} \tag{2}$$

$$Recall = \frac{TP}{TP + FN} \tag{3}$$

$$F_1 - Score = 2 \times \frac{Precision \cdot Recall}{Precision + Recall} \tag{4}$$

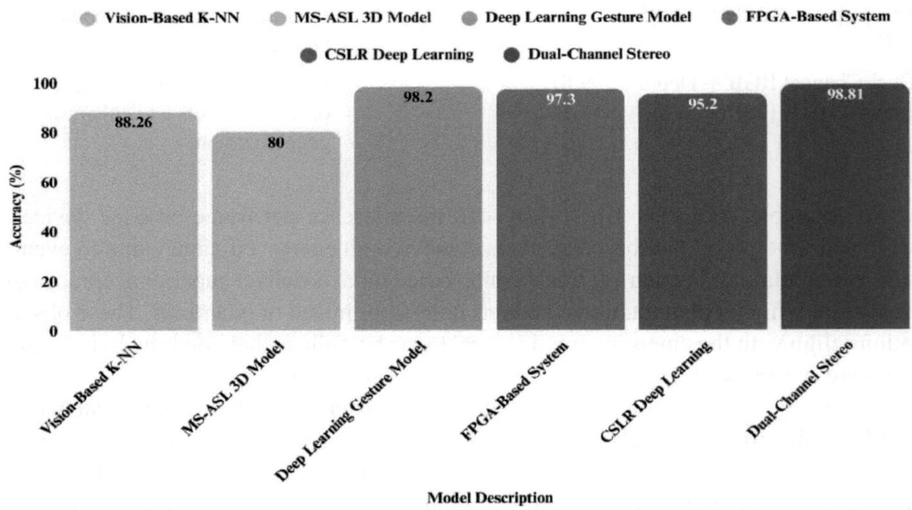

Fig. 9 Accuracy of SLR Models

5 Conclusion

This review has examined the development of Gesture and Sign Language Recognition (G&SLR), tracing its progression from handcrafted features and traditional machine learning toward deep learning architectures and hardware-assisted acquisition frameworks. Although substantial progress has been made, no single methodology has yet fully satisfied the requirements for scalability, signer-independent adaptability, robustness to environmental variation, and real-time deployment in practical applications. Existing systems continue to face challenges when transitioning from controlled laboratory conditions to diverse real-world environments.

To address these constraints, future research should prioritize hybrid approaches that integrate hardware-based sensing with advanced deep learning architectures. In particular, recent benchmark studies demonstrate that Dual-Channel Star-Attention networks achieve up to 99.81% accuracy, outperforming traditional classifiers that typically plateau around 88%. Likewise, wearable IMU-based approaches provide latency performance below 10 ms and real-time throughput exceeding 45–60 FPS, indicating strong deployment capability. Therefore, the combination of wearable IMU sensing with Transformer-based architectures such as Swin Transformer–BiLSTM represents one of the most promising directions.

This convergence leverages the low-latency, direct motion capture advantages of hardware with the powerful spatiotemporal representation learning and generalization capabilities of modern attention-based neural models, enabling more robust performance than standalone vision-only or sensor-only systems.

The long-term goal is to develop systems that are accurate, computationally efficient, and resilient across diverse signing conditions. By promoting hardware–software hybridization supported by standardized benchmarking, quantitative comparison metrics, and real-world evaluation, future research can advance scalable, inclusive, and practical G&SLR systems for everyday assistive communication.

References

1. Patel, K., Shah, D., Mehta, V.: American sign language recognition using artificial neural networks. Int. J. Comput. Appl. **179**(31), 27–33 (2018)
2. Jain, R.K., Rathi, S.K.: A review paper on sign language recognition using machine learning techniques. In: Emerging Trends in Data Driven Computing and Communications: Proceedings of DDCIoT 2021, pp. 91–98. Springer, Singapore (2021)
3. Ong, S., Ranganath, S.: Automatic sign language analysis: a survey and the future beyond lexical meaning. IEEE Trans. Pattern Anal. Mach. Intell. **27**(6), 873–891 (2007)
4. Koller, O., Zargaran, S., Ney, H., Bowden, R.: Sign language transformers: joint end-to-end sign language recognition and translation. In: Proceedings of the IEEE/CVF Conference on Computer Vision and Pattern Recognition, pp. 10023–10033. IEEE (2020)
5. Chen, L., Wang, H., Zhang, Y., Zhao, J.: Graph deep learning for continuous sign language recognition. IEEE Trans. Multimed. **26**(4), 1456–1467 (2024)
6. Koller, O., Ney, H., Bowden, R.: Continuous sign language recognition: towards large vocabulary statistical recognition systems handling multiple signers. Comput. Vis. Image Underst. **144**, 108–125 (2015)
7. Kadous, M.W.: Machine recognition of gestures using gloves of colored markers. In: Australian Joint Conference on Artificial Intelligence, pp. 243–252. World Scientific (1995)
8. Tamura, H., Kawasaki, K.: Recognition of sign language motion patterns using hidden Markov models. In: IEEE International Conference on Systems Man, and Cybernetics (SMC), pp. 424–429. IEEE (1998)
9. Gupta, V., Sharma, A.: Sign gesture recognition using hidden Markov models. Int. J. Appl. Eng. Res. **11**(7), 5123–5129 (2016)

10. Kjeldsen, R., Kender, J.: Finding skin in color images. In: IEEE International Conference on Automatic Face and Gesture Recognition, pp. 312–317. IEEE (1996)
11. Li, Y., Xu, C.: Convolutional neural networks for sign gesture recognition. In: IEEE International Conference on Image Processing (ICIP), pp. 325–329. IEEE (2014)
12. Gupta, M., Sharma, R.: YOLOv7 for continuous sign language gesture detection. In: IEEE International Conference on Pattern Recognition (ICPR), pp. 3204–3211. IEEE (2023)
13. Ali, S., Khan, N., Rauf, H.: Hybrid YOLO-LSTM model for sequential sign language recognition. IEEE Trans. Multimed. **25**, 5678–5689 (2023)
14. Patel, D., Roy, J.: Enhanced YOLOv3 for low-light sign language gesture detection. Multimed. Tools Appl. **82**(5), 6271–6285 (2023)
15. Forster, J., Oberdorfer, C., Koller, M., Ney, Y., Ney, H.: Extensions of the SIGNUM/RWTH-PHOENIX-weather 2014 corpus for sign language recognition. In: International Conference on Language Resources and Evaluation (LREC), pp. 1911–1916. ELRA, Paris (2014)
16. Sincan, O.F., Ekenel, H.K.: AUTSL: a large scale multi-modal Turkish sign language dataset and baseline methods. In: IEEE/CVF Conference on Computer Vision and Pattern Recognition Workshops (CVPRW). IEEE (2020)
17. Langer, S.: Ethical considerations in the development of sign language technologies. ACM Trans. Accessible Comput. **13**, 1–28 (2020)
18. Patel, R., Sharma, K.: A review on advances in sign and gesture recognition using machine learning. Int. J. Comput. Appl. **182**(31), 1–8 (2020)
19. Sharma, A., Gupta, S.: A review on machine learning approaches for sign and gesture recognition. J. King Saud Univ. Comput. Inf. Sci. **32**(10), 1115–1126 (2020)
20. Rastgoo, R., Kiani, K., Escalera, S.: Sign language recognition: a deep survey. Expert Syst. Appl. **164**, 113963 (2021)
21. Bhushan, S.: An experimental analysis of various machine learning algorithms for hand gesture recognition. Electronics. **11**(6), 968 (2022)
22. Kim, H., Park, T.: Real-time edge deployment of YOLOv5 for sign language recognition. Sensors. **24**(1), 112–125 (2024)
23. Singh, P., Kaur, R.: Residual CNN for Indian sign language recognition. J. Ambient. Intell. Humaniz. Comput. **12**(11), 10475–10485 (2021)
24. Vadrevu, P.K., Veeramanickam, M.R.M., Adusumalli, S.K., Bunga, S.K.: Sign language recognition for needy people using machine learning model. In: Rao, B.N.K., Balasubramanian, R., Wang, S.J., Nayak, R. (eds.) Intelligent Computing and Applications, vol. 315, pp. 227–233. Springer, Singapore (2023)
25. Natarajan, B., et al.: Development of an end-to-end deep learning framework for sign language recognition, translation, and video generation. IEEE Access. **10**, 104358–104374 (2022)
26. Camgoz, N.C., Hadfield, S., Koller, O., Bowden, R.: Neural sign language translation. In: IEEE Conference on Computer Vision and Pattern Recognition (CVPR), pp. 7784–7793. IEEE (2018)
27. Rahman, A., Hossain, M., Hasan, T.: Real-time American sign language recognition using YOLOv3. In: International Conference on Computer Vision Applications, pp. 215–220. SPIE (2021)
28. Alyami, S., Luqman, H.: Swin-MSTP: Swin transformer with multi-scale temporal perception for continuous sign language recognition. Neurocomputing. **617**, 129015 (2025)
29. Joo, H., Kim, S.: Sign gesture recognition using residual generative adversarial networks. J. Vis. Commun. Image Represent. **78**, 103145 (2021)
30. Sharma, A., Singh, M., Kumar, K.: Gesture recognition using deep learning and generative adversarial networks. Pattern Recogn. Lett. **138**, 40–46 (2020)
31. Kadous, M.W.: Machine recognition of Auslan signs using support vector machines. In: Proceedings of the Sixth Australian and New Zealand Conference on Intelligent Information Systems (ANZIIS), pp. 147–152. Australian Pattern Recognition Society (1998)

32. Zhao, J., Xu, L.: Chinese sign language recognition using support vector machines. Int. J. Signal Process. Image Process. Pattern Recognit. **8**(2), 243–252 (2015)
33. Huang, Y., Wang, L., Zhao, X.: Sign language recognition using deep and machine learning approaches. Neural Comput. & Applic. **31**(12), 9013–9025 (2019)
34. Dey, S.E., Shrestha, S.B., Amirshahi, A.: Static hand gesture recognition for American sign language using neuromorphic hardware. Neuromorph. Comput. Eng. **2**(4), 044005 (2022)
35. Aksoy, A., Koca, A.A., Arslan, N.M.: TSLFormer: a lightweight transformer model for Turkish sign language recognition using skeletal landmarks. Comput. Lang. **2505**, 07890 (2025)
36. Mitra, S., Acharya, T.: Indian sign language recognition using support vector machines. Int. J. Comput. Appl. **135**(5), 20–25 (2016)
37. Li, D., Rodriguez, C., Yu, X., Li, H.: Word-level deep sign language recognition from video: a new large-scale dataset and methods. In: IEEE/CVF Conference on Computer Vision and Pattern Recognition (CVPR), pp. 1459–1469. IEEE (2020)
38. Islam, M.R., Rahman, T.: Hand gesture recognition using machine learning approaches. In: IEEE International Conference on Informatics IoT, and Enabling Technologies (ICIoT), pp. 277–282. IEEE, Bangalore (2016)
39. Singh, R.K., Verma, P.: Sign language recognition using machine learning approaches. Int. J. Speech Technol. **24**(1), 45–55 (2021)
40. Kumar, A., Singh, M.: Continuous Indian sign language recognition using hidden markov models. In: IEEE Region 10 Conference (TENCON), pp. 2150–2155. IEEE, Singapore (2018)
41. Baihan, A.: Sign language recognition using modified deep learning network and hybrid optimization: a hybrid optimizer (HO) based optimized CNNSa-LSTM approach. Sci. Rep. **14**(1), 26111 (2024)
42. Carreira, J., Zisserman, A.: Quo vadis, action recognition? A new model and the kinetics dataset. In: IEEE Conference on Computer Vision and Pattern Recognition (CVPR), pp. 6269–6308. IEEE (2017)
43. Pathan, R.K., Biswas, M., Yasmin, S., Khandaker, M.U., Salman, M., Youssef, A.: Sign language recognition using the fusion of image and hand landmarks through multi-headed convolutional neural networks. Sci. Rep. **13**(1), 16975 (2023)
44. Rahman, M.H., Chowdhury, S.A.: American sign language recognition using machine learning approaches. J. Intell. Fuzzy Syst. **34**(5), 3081–3092 (2018)
45. Wang, X., Girshick, R., Gupta, A., He, K.: Non-local neural networks. In: IEEE Conference on Computer Vision and Pattern Recognition (CVPR), pp. 7794–7803. IEEE (2018)
46. Camgoz, C., Bowden, R., Hadfield, S.: SubUNets: end-to-end hand shape and continuous sign language recognition. In: IEEE International Conference on Computer Vision (ICCV), pp. 3075–3084. IEEE (2017)
47. Camgoz, N.C., Koller, O., Hadfield, S., Bowden, R.: Sign language transformers: joint end-to-end sign language recognition and translation. In: IEEE/CVF Conference on Computer Vision and Pattern Recognition (CVPR), pp. 10020–10030. IEEE (2020)
48. Yan, S., Xiong, Y., Lin, D.: Spatial temporal graph convolutional networks for skeleton-based action recognition. In: AAAI Conference on Artificial Intelligence, pp. 7444–7452. AAAI Press (2018)
49. Wang, L., et al.: Temporal segment networks: towards good practices for deep action recognition. In: European Conference on Computer Vision (ECCV), pp. 20–26. Springer, Dordrecht (2016)
50. Tang, H., Zhao, Y., Xu, L.: Convolutional neural network array for sign language recognition using wearable IMUs. arXiv 2004.11836 (2020)
51. Hossain, M., Rahman, S.: Sign language digit recognition using different convolutional neural network model. Asian J. Res. Comput. Sci. **6**(2), 16–24 (2020)

52. Joze, A.F.A., Koller, O.: MS-ASL: a large-scale data set and benchmark for understanding American sign language. In: British Machine Vision Conference (BMVC), p. 100. BMVA Press (2019)
53. Zhang, F., et al.: MediaPipe hands: on-device real-time hand tracking. arXiv 2006.10214 (2020)
54. Kumar, Y., Singh, A., Gupta, V.: Residual deep learning model for sign gesture recognition. Procedia Comput. Sci. **192**, 1781–1790 (2022)
55. Gaur, R., Kumar, V., Singh, P.: Quantized CNN-based hardware architecture for real-time hand gesture recognition. J. Syst. Archit. **140**, 102925 (2024)
56. Qin, J., Wang, M.: Sign language recognition based on dual-channel star-attention convolutional neural network. Sci. Rep. **15**(1), 27685 (2025)
57. Elhassen, S., Al Khuzayem, L.: Bridging information science and deep learning: transformer models for isolated Saudi sign language recognition. Nat. Sci. Publ. **19**(6), 1345–1357 (2025)
58. Li, X., Zhang, P., Hou, Y.: Multimodal transformer fusion for continuous sign language recognition using RGB, depth, and inertial streams. IEEE Trans. Multimed. **27**, 1352–1366 (2025)
59. Huang, J., Chouvatut, V.: Video-based sign language recognition via resnet and lstm network. J. Imaging. **10**(6), 149 (2024)

Author Index

M. J. C. S. Reis et al. (Eds.): IC4S 2025, LNICST 679, pp. 351–352, 2026.
https://doi.org/10.1007/978-3-032-22834-5

MIX
Papier aus verantwortungsvollen Quellen
Paper from responsible sources
FSC® C105338

If you have any concerns about our products,
you can contact us on
ProductSafety@springernature.com

In case Publisher is established outside the EU,
the EU authorized representative is:
Springer Nature Customer Service Center GmbH
Europaplatz 3, 69115 Heidelberg, Germany

Printed by Libri Plureos GmbH
in Hamburg, Germany